NOW WHAT?

DR. MARK VAN RIJMENAM
The World's #1 Futurist

NOW WHAT?

How to Ride the Tsunami of Change

First published in 2025 by Dean Publishing
PO Box 119
Mt. Macedon, Victoria, 3441
Australia
deanpublishing.com

DEAN
PUBLISHING

Cataloguing-in-Publication Data
National Library of Australia

Title: Now What?
ISBN: 978-0-6489386-8-2
Category: Business/future

To all future generations,
may you design and
build a thriving future.

Contents

Abstract

The future isn't coming, it's here and it feels like a tsunami. Transformative technologies are converging, disrupting industries and society in mere moments. This is a tsunami of change, and the question is no longer whether we can adapt, but how individuals, organizations and institutions can ride it and build a future of abundance.

In *Now What? How to Ride the Tsunami of Change*, strategic futurist Dr. Mark van Rijmenam, also known as The Digital Speaker, presents a dynamic roadmap for thriving in a world of accelerating technologies, boundless innovation, and shifting cultural tides. He demystifies the breakthroughs rewriting our planet and illuminates the powerful synergy of technology and humanity. Drawing on real-world success stories, ancient wisdom, and the author's own transformative journey, he reveals a path that balances innovation with ethics, ensuring that rapid progress lifts everyone rather than leaving communities behind.

At the heart of this book lies the WAVE framework—Watch, Adapt, Verify, Empower—a straightforward, compelling method to ride the tsunami of change and thrive in a future that feels downright dizzying. Readers learn to scan for signals of transformation, recalibrate strategies with purpose, rigorously test their assumptions, and empower diverse voices, all while compounding every small victory into an unstoppable momentum. With an insider's eye on AI breakthroughs, spatial intelligence, synthetic biology, the emerging computable economy, and other cutting-edge technologies,

Dr. Van Rijmenam shows how each new disruption can elevate us toward a thriving tomorrow.

This four-step cycle distills years of research and fieldwork into an accessible method for embracing chaos as a catalyst for growth. In an era where misinformation spreads in seconds and quantum breakthroughs can redefine entire industries overnight, ***Now What?*** offers a clear path from anxiety to action. Dive into the possibilities, learn to wield technology as a tool instead of a threat, and stake your claim as an architect of tomorrow. It's time we stopped merely bracing for impact and started riding the wave.

About the Author

Dr. Mark van Rijmenam, ranked as the world's #1 Futurist, is an award-winning global keynote speaker. He lives on the cutting edge of innovation, transforming far-fetched possibilities into tangible results. From pioneering virtual reality keynotes and TEDx talks to exploring AI breakthroughs with a digital twin of himself (and even cycling across Australia's punishing outback to raise funds for children's cancer research), he's on a relentless mission to help others not just anticipate the future but actively shape it. A LinkedIn Top Voice and six-time author on emerging tech, Dr. Van Rijmenam is the Architect of Tomorrow cutting through hype and equipping leaders with the real-world strategies they need to outpace disruption and design and build better futures.

Through Futurwise, he blends deep technological expertise with a human-centric ethos, delivering hyper-personalized insights from trusted sources to Fortune 500 executives, government bodies, universities and grassroots innovators worldwide. Recognized by Salesforce as one of just 16 (human) voices forging the future of AI, he fuses academic rigor with bold adventure, igniting audiences to question assumptions, embrace complexity, and propel their industries forward with ethical foresight. His trademark approach? Fusing deep tech expertise with human-centric values, then delivering it with a bold style that leaves no doubt: you're either leading this revolution or falling behind.

Above all, Dr. Van Rijmenam is a visionary strategist who understands that tech's power must be harnessed responsibly. His ambition goes beyond forecasting trends: he builds "futurists" primed to thrive in a rapidly evolving landscape shaped by AI, quantum computing, and exponential change. He shows how anyone can become an Architect of Tomorrow, turning each step into an action plan for sustainable growth and reminding us all that with the right mindset, there's no limit to what we can achieve.

Early Praise for
Now What?

"*Now What?* is more than an insightful and provocative look into the future. It is an uplifting guide to observing wisely, adapting thoughtfully, and acting with integrity to shape our future together. Let Mark van Rijmenam's powerful WAVE framework give you the tools you need to survive—and thrive—in today's inescapable tsunami of change."

— Ron Kaufman, New York Times
Bestselling Author of *Uplifting Service*

"Few people are as well-placed as Mark van Rijmenam to give a clear sense of what the coming years will hold. Full of powerful insights and compelling cautions, *Now What?* will equip you to face an uncertain future with confidence."

— Michael McQueen, Trend Forecaster
and 10 x Bestselling Author

"Blending cutting-edge research, practical insights, eastern philosophy and even fiction, *Now What?* is an informative ride through the future of technology and humanity's role in it. Would recommend for anyone seeking greater clarity in an era of accelerating uncertainty."

— Alvin W. Graylin, Bestselling Author of *Our Next*
***Reality* and Chairman of Virtual World Society**

"*Now What?* is a timely and imaginative invitation to reframe our relationship with technology in ways that are more intentional, integrative, and humane. Dr. Mark van Rijmenam has created a compelling roadmap that mirrors our collective journey through change – one that honors complexity while empowering purposeful action. I especially appreciate the WAVE framework, which encourages readers to attune to change with clarity and care. The book doesn't shy away from the urgent questions of our age – it leans in with both courage and curiosity. As someone deeply engaged in digital wellbeing and immersive experience design, I found this work to be a refreshing blend of forward-thinking insight and grounded, human values. It's a guidebook for those who want to ride the wave of innovation with integrity and imagination."

— **Caitlin Krause, Author of *Digital Wellbeing* and MindWise Founder**

"As the pace and scale of change accelerate, Mark van Rijmenam offers a hopeful vision of a co-created future. *Now What?* provides an essential methodology for intentional transformation so you can lead through relentless uncertainty."

— **Gary A. Bolles, Chair for the Future of Work for Singularity University**

"*Now What?* is a must-read for anyone navigating the chaos of today's rapidly changing world. Dr. Mark brilliantly blends future thinking, technology insights, and human wisdom into a powerful, practical guide. His WAVE framework is not just a tool—it's a mindset shift that every leader, brand, and professional needs to thrive. A timely and transformational read."

— **Dr. Jerome Joseph, Global Brand Thought Leader and Bestselling Author**

"Business leaders, technologists, policymakers, academics and students alike will learn and reinvigorate as adaptable Architects of Tomorrow mastering technological tides! *Now What? How to Ride the Tsunami of Change*, Dr. Van Rijmenam's compelling opus, is infused with innovative visualizations and beacons—and his pioneering approachable vision and pragmatic frameworks guide readers' change-attainment journey to navigate, and thrive, with transformative vitality!"

— Professor Lee Bogner, Global Chief GenAI and AI Strategic Enterprise Architect at Mars, former Business Technology Professor at Hofstra University and AI Educator at MIT

"Dr. Van Rijmenam masterfully contextualizes our choices and actions in terms of humanity's evolving consciousness. He unpacks today's eight primary disruptors, offers a clear, actionable framework for diligently and responsibly staying ahead of the wave, and interweaves an entertaining and approachable science fiction narrative to bring his ideas to life. His refreshing approach bridges the complex intersections of technological, societal, organizational, and individual transformation. Whether you're just beginning to explore the unfolding tsunami of disruption or are well read on today's massive technological paradigm shifts yet thirst for fresh perspectives, *Now What?* delivers practical insights and a wealth of context. Regardless of your expertise and ambitions, you'll find insightful gems that will expand your thinking and equip your tool palette. Get ready for the tsunami; it's well on its way."

— Michael "Hoff" Hoffman, Innovation Strategist and Advisor.

"Dr. Mark van Rijmenam's *Now What? How to Ride the Tsunami of Change* is a timely and insightful handbook for business leaders, policymakers, and entrepreneurs facing the whirlwind of technological disruption. The book succeeds in both illuminating the unprecedented scale of changes coming our way and in providing a clear, actionable path to navigate those changes. By combining deep foresight with practical frameworks like WAVE, Dr. Van Rijmenam offers readers a way to convert uncertainty into strategy and anxiety into action. *Now What?* equips leaders with the mindset and tools needed to not just survive in an era of disruption, but to thrive and build the future. It translates the abstract concept of "strategic foresight" into a tangible leadership playbook for the Intelligence Age. Importantly, it does so with a sense of optimism and responsibility, urging us to harness emerging technologies in ways that elevate our organizations and our society. I would highly recommend this book to any leader who feels the ground shifting under their feet—be it due to AI, digital transformation, or other seismic changes. Dr. Van Rijmenam's insights will validate the urgency you feel, broaden your horizons beyond the next quarter, and inspire confidence that with the right approach you can ride the wave of change rather than be drowned by it. In a world where "the pace of progress doubles overnight", *Now What?* is the guide to have on your desk. It's a compelling call to action for us all to become, in the author's words, "Architects of Tomorrow." After reading it, the question "Now what?" will no longer induce panic, it will spark purposeful innovation."

— Steve Hollands, CEO Blackhills Quantum Computing and Marketing

"*Now What?* gives us a baseline of what's now and the tools to be empowered architects of tomorrow rather than mere bystanders."

— Diana Wu David, CEO of The Future Proof Lab

"In a world where change is the only constant, Dr. Van Rijmenam's book *Now What?* offers something rare: clarity and conviction. It's a playbook for future-readiness that's not only insightful, but also deeply practical. Among the many valuable lessons and thought-provoking perspectives in this book, the WAVE framework stands out as a clear, practical guide for navigating change with focus and confidence. If you care about learning fast, adapting smart, and leading with purpose, this book definitely delivers."

— Nishant Kasibhatla, Guinness Record Holder and Expert in Momentum, Learning and Performance

"Dr. Mark van Rijmenam offers a profound approach to navigating the tsunami of change. Through his compelling fictional narrative and insightful framework, he redefines adaptation as The Ultimate Balancing Act—an ongoing equilibrium that seamlessly blends ancient wisdom, contemporary insights, and disruptive innovations. This book is not just inspiring and unique; it is deeply human, resonating with readers on both intellectual and spiritual levels."

— Dr. Efi Pylarinou, Global Fintech and Tech Thought Leader

"For those seeking a framework to navigate disruptive changes, especially in healthcare, I highly recommend *Now What? How to Ride the Tsunami of Change*. This insightful read is a must for aspiring futurists, offering practical strategies and real-world examples to thrive in uncertainty. Whether you're a healthcare professional or eager to cultivate a futurist mindset, this book empowers you to adapt and innovate. Pick up your copy today and face the future with confidence."

— Arun Nadarasa, CEO, International Social Prescribing Pharmacy Association

"In *Now What?* Dr. Mark van Rijmenam offers much more than an analysis of emerging technologies—he delivers a compass for navigating the tsunami of transformations that is reshaping our collective horizons. As a lawyer specializing in the intersection of Law and Digital Innovation, I consider this work an indispensable milestone for those seeking not only to understand the technological forces reconfiguring our world, but also for those who wish to actively participate in building a more conscious and equitable future. What distinguishes this work is its rare combination of conceptual depth and practical applicability. The WAVE framework (Watch, Adapt, Verify, Empower) proposed by the author transcends the technological domain, revealing itself as a valuable tool for facing complexity in any field—from law to medicine, from education to governance. The way Dr. Van Rijmenam integrates timeless wisdom from diverse cultural traditions with sharp analyses of emerging trends creates a truly integrative approach to responsible innovation. This book is not just essential reading for business and technology leaders, it is an urgent call to consciousness for professionals in all areas who wish to remain relevant and effective in a landscape of accelerated changes. In a world where the boundaries between the human, the digital and the biological become increasingly permeable, *Now What?* offers us both the conceptual clarity and the practical tools to navigate this new territory with purpose and vision."
— **Dr. Marcus Vinicius Braz de Camargo, Lawyer Specializing in Digital Law and Innovation and Entrepreneur and Founder of frame2.work**

"What a great and timely read that gets the balance between utopian and dystopian views just about spot on in my view. I also really appreciated the blending of East, West and Indigenous world views to suggest a way forward alongside the WAVE framework."
— **Nick Burnett, Creator of Becoming HumAIn.**

"A mind-expanding exploration of the Intelligence Age, seamlessly weaving together a vast array of future-facing topics with their everyday cultural impact. Dr. Mark van Rijmenam's WAVE method—Watch, Adapt, Verify, and Empower—tackles the often-overlooked yet most challenging aspects of cultural change. Rather than focusing solely on what is technically possible, he urges us to think philosophically about the deeper implications of emerging technologies. Drawing from spiritual traditions, leading think tanks, and real-world observations, his up-to-the-minute reflections on frontier technology illuminate the sheer scale of parallel advancements in recent years and how their convergence challenges us to reconsider our relationship with the future. This book is a powerful guide for individuals, institutions, and even nations, offering a path to move beyond fear and inertia, to embrace a future defined by symbiotic human-technology relationships."

— Ivan Sean, Global Advisor and Strategist of Applied-AI and Emerging Technology

"*Now What?* is your road trip kit for navigating society's future, complete with a roadmap and a few snacks to keep you going. Dr. Van Rijmenam kicks things off with a quick sci-fi story (not too nerdy) that's both entertaining and thought-provoking. He then unpacks his WAVE approach, ultimately challenging us to move beyond adaptation and fully embrace our newfound role as architects of tomorrow. Amazing read."

— Amber Hurdle, Ranked #2 Brand Thought Leader Globally

Why I Wrote This Book

"The saddest aspect of life right now is that science gathers knowledge faster than society gathers wisdom."
—Isaac Asimov (1988)

Change is the only constant in life, and trying to stop that is like attempting to freeze the tide... an impossible pursuit that ignores the very current of progress. For only by flowing with its unstoppable force can we harness innovation and design the future we dare to imagine.

I've spent the past 14 years traveling the globe and meeting CEOs, leaders and innovators grappling with the dizzying pace of technological upheaval. During this time, something remarkable but also unsettling became clear: although our tools grow more advanced by the week, it's never been harder to see where the future is going. The volume of new apps, platforms, and digital disruptions sometimes feels less like progress and more like a tsunami—vast and unstoppable, raising fundamental questions about our collective path forward. Yet only a fraction of humanity truly comprehends its scope. This significant gap highlights the urgent need for widespread awareness of how our society is changing in front of our eyes.

This book is my response to that tidal wave of innovation. For over 14 years, I have worked at the cutting-edge of tomorrow, embracing the latest technologies in my work while helping others do the same. In this book, I share my insights from over a decade of research into emerging technologies and from working with Fortune 500 companies and governments around the world. I don't claim to cover every academic field, far from it. In fact, I invite sociologists, legal scholars, psychologists, philosophers, and other specialists to pick up where these chapters leave off. Just as in nature, where biodiversity ensures resilience, our response to exponential change must blend Western ingenuity, Indigenous sustainability, and Eastern philosophies to create resilient ecosystems rather than fragmented silos. Only by taking a truly multidisciplinary approach can we begin to grasp the complexity of our converging technologies in the upcoming Intelligence Age. We live in a world shaped by AI, quantum computing, robotics, and synthetic biology, yet these developments can seem opaque or unapproachable to the everyday individual. We need a simple, holistic framework that unveils how deeply interwoven we all are in this digital tapestry.

Throughout this book, I have woven a fictional narrative set in 2051—an intentional journey into a world profoundly reshaped by exponential technologies. A science fiction story makes abstract concepts tangible and it's a powerful approach to navigating complexity. You'll embark on the immersive journey in Chapter One, where you'll encounter a future reshaped by exponential technologies, yet standing on the precipice of even deeper disruption. This long-term vantage point is essential, as it vividly illustrates how our decisions today ripple forward, shaping possibilities and realities decades ahead. Crucially, this narrative does not end in the first chapter. It evolves continually, with each subsequent chapter expanding on and bringing to life the very concepts explored, enabling you to visualize, internalize, and act upon the ideas presented.

Despite my background as a futurist and avid reader, I find it increasingly challenging to keep track of these interlinking forces. That's partly why I wrote this book: to share the perspectives that have opened my eyes to the bigger picture. From Spiral Dynamics to Taoism, from Indigenous wisdom to the relational intelligence we see in the natural world, each lens shows us that Earth is not just a planet, but a living, breathing spaceship we all share. As we navigate this "spaceship Earth," we have one shot—a chance to co-create a future of abundance rather than let it slip into dystopian disarray. Eminem's question echoes in my mind: "If you had one shot or one opportunity… would you capture it or just let it slip?" We can harness these exponential technologies to empower communities, heal our planet, and pioneer new opportunities if, and only if, we approach them responsibly.

Yet this transition won't happen spontaneously; it hinges on understanding. Without broad digital literacy and a willingness to explore new perspectives, we risk building technologies that fracture society instead of uniting it. To capture the essence of my vision, I've introduced TidalShots, concise bursts of clarity of around 280 characters that you can easily share on social media by scanning each QR code. They're a kind of wave-surfing technique for your reading experience. You can skim them first for a quick mental hook or return to them after the chapter to consolidate what you've learned. Think of these TidalShots as a form of shore beacon: short, powerful signposts in the sea of ideas.

The metaphor of "tidal" resonates with our broader theme, which is that the Intelligence Age is coming at us in surges, demanding adaptation and fluid thinking. "Shots" evoke short, potent bursts of information, much like a quick jolt of energy. Together, TidalShots captures both the wave-like momentum of modern change and the bold brevity of these insights. Each TidalShot is accompanied by a QR code that allows you to share that TidalShot and the illustration directly to your favorite social media network.

You will also find illustrations scattered across these pages because a picture can indeed say more than a thousand words. I hope these visual elements, combined with TidalShots and fictional narrative threads, make the journey informative, enjoyable, and memorable. If you find this book valuable, please share it. We stand on the brink of an era that can either usher in unimaginable possibilities or plunge us into deepening rifts. More than ever, our future depends on our collective capacity to watch for signals, adapt responsibly, verify our choices, and empower each other. That's exactly why we're here: to harness this tsunami of change into a force for good.

Finally, when writing this book, I leveraged AI to help me with my research, to challenge my assumptions, edit my writing and co-create the cover design and I now enable you to do the same. I have integrated this book into my digital twin, so if you want to talk to me about the future and your thoughts on how to ride the tsunami of change or if you wish to dive deeper into the topics discussed in this book, you can reach out to my digital twin 24/7.

You can reach my digital twin via WhatsApp at +1 (830) 463-6967 or scan the QR code for a text or audio conversation about the book or any related topic.

I have also put together a resource that accompanies this book with relevant information. You can find it on Now-What.co/resources or by scanning the below QR code:

Before we dive into the future, let's first go back to 2011, when I cir-cumnavigated Australia on a bicycle to raise money for charity. I share this story to provide relevant context in how it has shaped me as a futurist, how I view the world, and because it was an amazing adventure. Let's begin our quest to become architects of tomorrow, hand in hand and wave by wave. Enjoy the read!

TidalShot

After 14 years of traversing a world overwhelmed by new tech, I realized the future often hides behind a digital tsunami. This book is my answer. A holistic framework so we can harness these waves and co-create tomorrow.

Scan the QR code to share this section's TidalShot and illustration to your network.

INTRODUCTION

The Road to Tomorrow

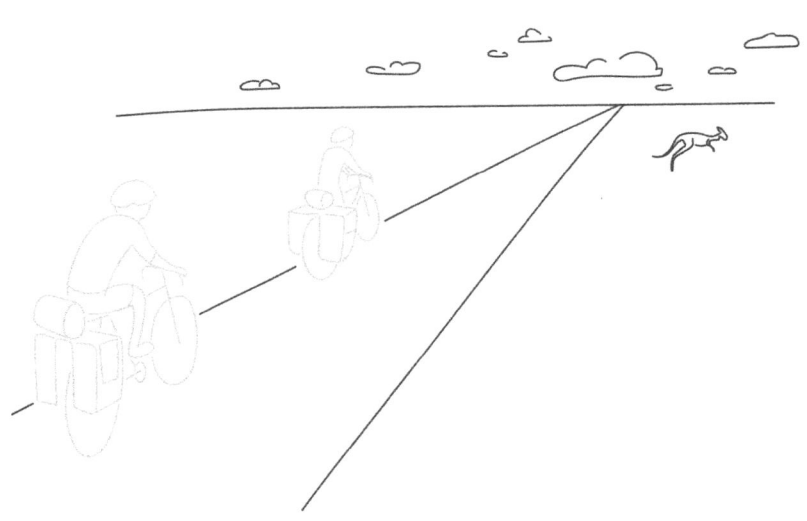

*How can we take incremental,
yet bold steps in our
innovation journey?*

The heat was oppressive, the sun an unrelenting force hanging overhead as we pedaled through the vast, dusty expanse of the Australian outback. The road ahead stretched endlessly, shimmering in the distance like a mirage. Each pedal stroke felt heavier than the last as if the wind itself was determined to push us back, mirroring the overwhelming challenges we would face time and again on this journey and in life. The landscape was empty, save for the occasional rustle of dry grass or the rumble of a passing truck that would whip up clouds of red dust in its wake. As I pedaled through the vast, dusty expanse of the Australian outback, I discovered that every small pedal stroke was more than just a physical effort, it was a metaphor for the bold, incremental steps required to navigate a rapidly changing world.

We had been on the road for weeks by this point, but this day felt particularly grueling. It was Day 37 of our journey. My legs ached, my shoulders were stiff, and the saddle had become an instrument of torture I had never anticipated. Reinier, my friend and companion on this audacious trip, was riding beside me, his expression set in determination despite the exhaustion etched on his face. Every grueling mile, every moment of doubt under the relentless sun, built a rhythm, a cadence of perseverance and calculated risk that would ultimately define my approach to innovation.

There was no support crew, no backup waiting in the wings. It was just the two of us, battling the elements and our own limits. The vastness of Australia stretched in every direction, and in moments like this, it felt like we were insignificant specks, barely moving against the sheer scale of it all. Yet, this vastness also mirrored the unpredictability of the future—daunting but full of opportunity if we could find the strength to keep moving.

THE BEGINNING

In 2011, we set out to do the impossible. Cycle 14,122 kilometers around Australia in 100 days. From Cairns to Cairns, in a great anticlockwise loop, covering every type of terrain imaginable, from the scorching desert plains to the windswept coastal roads. The goal? To raise €20,000 for the Children's Cancer Foundation (KiKa).

But as the kilometers stretched on and the road ahead blurred with fatigue, this trip morphed into something much more profound. It wasn't just about cycling anymore. It became a lesson in navigating the unknown, perseverance, and pushing beyond perceived limits. In many ways, it was the perfect metaphor for life and the work I would later come to do.

Looking back now, years later, I see this journey as a precursor to my role as a futurist. At the time, I hadn't yet embraced the label. I hadn't yet stood in front of business leaders and governments around the world to talk about AI, the metaverse, or the future. But the seeds of that future were planted here, in the outback, where I learned what it meant to endure, adapt, and stay focused on a long-term vision, no matter how overwhelming the challenges seemed. These lessons of endurance and vision would become the foundation of how I help others ride the waves of exponential change.

The decision to cycle around Australia wasn't born from a sudden flash of inspiration. It was the culmination of years of restlessness, a need to do something meaningful, to challenge myself in a way that would leave a lasting impact. I had always been drawn to big ideas and bold actions, but the routine of everyday life had a way of smothering those impulses.

Then, one night, it all changed. Like many great adventures, it all began in a pub. Over a couple of beers, Reinier and I joked about how amazing it would be to cycle around Australia. At first, it was just that—a dream, something to laugh about. But the more we talked, the more serious it became. The challenge called to us. Not just physically but mentally and emotionally. We found ourselves drawn to the idea of pushing ourselves in ways we had never imagined. And then, in one of those moments of clarity (or perhaps madness) that only comes after a few drinks, we shook hands and agreed to make it happen.

From that moment on, there was no turning back. Reinier and I began planning the trip in earnest, but our preparations were anything but smooth. The early days of planning were filled with excitement but also a fair amount of procrastination. We would meet every Tuesday for what we dubbed "Ozzie Tuesday," ostensibly to plan the logistics of the trip, but more often than not, we'd end up in a local café, fantasizing about the adventure rather than working on the nitty-gritty details. The sheer magnitude of the task ahead of us—cycling around an entire continent—felt surreal, and we often found ourselves lost in daydreams rather than practicalities.

We started training slowly, almost naively. Our first ride, a modest 40 kilometers to Hoek van Holland, The Netherlands, left us exhausted and sore for days. It was a humbling experience, one that revealed just how unprepared we were for the journey ahead. But as the months went on, we built up our stamina, cycling longer and longer distances. Each ride brought us closer to readiness, each kilometer laying the foundation for a goal that seemed larger than life. We upgraded our bikes, got sponsorships from various companies, and slowly, the dream became a reality.

THE JOURNEY: FROM TRIUMPHS TO TRIALS

Every day on the road was a test of endurance—physically, mentally, and emotionally. Some days were blissful, like gliding through the lush rainforests of Queensland, where the air was thick with the scent of eucalyptus and the road ahead seemed to invite us forward. Other days were pure agony, battling headwinds that made it feel like we were moving backwards, or riding under the relentless sun that turned the road into a sweltering oven accompanied by dozens of flies clinging to every bead of sweat. These moments reminded me how even minor discomforts, amplified by scale, can test your resilience.

The Nullarbor Plain was one of the most daunting stretches. It is a vast, desolate expanse of nothingness—no towns, no people, just us and the open road for over 1200 kilometers. We had been warned about its harshness, but nothing could have prepared us for the reality. The heat was unbearable, the sun beating down on us without mercy. As we pedaled into the heart of the desert, the heat shimmered off the asphalt, creating mirages in the distance. Our water supply was limited, and every pedal stroke felt like a battle. At one point, we were miles from anywhere when Reinier's tire went flat for the third time that day. The frustration was palpable, draining us both physically and mentally and making me question whether we had overreached by taking on this challenge.

But then something incredible happened. As we were bent over, struggling to fix the tire, a car pulled up beside us. The driver leaned out with a smile, offering us water and snacks. "You boys look like you could use a break," he said. It was a simple gesture, but in that moment, it felt like salvation. Acts of kindness like this became a recurring theme on our journey. Strangers, seeing us toiling away on the side of the road, would stop to offer help—cookies, water, words of encouragement. These moments weren't just gestures of support; they were lifelines, showing us the importance of connection even in the most isolated of circumstances.

It was humbling to see how willing people were to help two strangers on bicycles, simply because they wanted to be part of our journey. It is a lesson I carry with me to this day: the power of community and of helping each other through tough times. In a world that often feels divided, these moments of human connection reminded me that we're all in this together. It also taught me that no matter how overwhelming the journey feels, support, whether from others or within ourselves, can carry us forward.

THE MENTAL GAME

It wasn't just the physical challenges that tested us. There were times when the sheer monotony of the road—hours upon hours of pedaling with no end in sight on roads that sometimes don't curve for dozens of kilometers—wore us down mentally. We had to dig deep, relying on each other for motivation. Reinier and I would joke, sing, or simply ride in silence, knowing that just being there for each other was enough to keep going. These moments taught me that shared support is a powerful antidote to the mental toll of overwhelming challenges.

At one point, however, I remember feeling utterly defeated. My body screamed for rest; my mind was clouded with doubt. Why had we taken on this impossible challenge? What were we trying to prove? But then, Reinier's voice cut through the fog: "We've come this far. We're not stopping now." His words jolted me back to the present, reminding me of why we had started this journey in the first place. That clarity, a reminder of purpose, pulled me out of the spiral of doubt.

That day, I learned a powerful lesson about perseverance. When you are faced with overwhelming odds, when every fiber of your being tells you to quit, it is the small, determined steps forward that make all the difference. One pedal stroke at a time, we pushed through the desert, and by the time we reached the other side, something inside me had shifted. I realized that endurance wasn't just about physical strength but mental fortitude. That realization would later shape how I approached my work in the tech world, where the pace of change is relentless and the challenges are often overwhelming.

As the kilometers stacked up, so did the lessons. This trip wasn't just about cycling but a crash course in resilience, adaptability, and focus. Day after day, we had to adjust our plans on the fly. We learned to be resourceful and find creative solutions to problems, whether that meant fixing a broken chain in the middle of nowhere or rerouting our path when a storm washed out the road. This ability to adapt and reframe obstacles as opportunities became a cornerstone of my thinking and mirrors the agility required to navigate fast-changing industries today.

One of the biggest lessons was about discipline. We had to get up at 6 a.m. every day, regardless of how sore or tired we were from the previous day's ride. There was no room for slacking off, the road ahead demanded consistency and focus. It reminded me of a truth I would later see in my professional life: success isn't built on grand gestures but on the discipline to show up and make progress every day.

Flexibility was equally crucial. No matter how well we planned, things never went exactly as expected. And those who can't adapt to change are the ones who get left behind. I learned to embrace discomfort, to push through the pain and the fatigue, because I knew that each day brought us closer to our goal. Every setback became a moment to grow, reinforcing my belief that thriving isn't about avoiding challenges but confronting them head-on.

Finally, vision kept us going. You don't set out to cycle around a continent without a clear goal in mind. For us, that goal was reaching the finish line in Cairns, but it was more than just a destination. It was the culmination of a dream, the fulfillment of a promise we had made to ourselves and the children we were riding for. That long-term vision kept us going when the road got tough, just as a clear and ethical vision is essential for any leader navigating the complexities of technological disruption. It reminded me that whether you are leading a team or pedaling through the unknown, the ability to hold a long-term perspective amid short-term struggles is what separates those who thrive from those who falter.

THE FINAL PUSH

As we neared the end of our journey, the anticipation grew. We had been cycling for 99 days, covering over 14,000 kilometers, and now, on the final day, we were just hours away from completing the challenge. The finish line was in sight, but the emotions were mixed. There was the overwhelming joy of knowing we had made it but also a sense of sadness that this life-changing journey was coming to an end. That mix of emotions—relief, pride, and nostalgia—was a reminder that every significant achievement carries both fulfillment and the question of *now what?*

On the last day, we rode into Cairns with a police escort, followed by fellow cyclists who had joined us for the final stretch. As we approached the finish line, we were greeted by cheering crowds, family, friends, and even local officials. The sense of accomplishment was indescribable. We had done it—we had cycled around Australia in 100 days, raising nearly €25,000 for KiKa. The finish line wasn't just a destination—it was the culmination of every decision, every effort, and every lesson we had gathered along the way and how it had transformed us in the process.

As we rode the final kilometers, I reflected on the journey. The daily rhythm of waking up, packing our gear, and hitting the road was behind us. We had crossed a continent, conquered the elements, and achieved something few others had done. It wasn't just the physical feat that filled me with pride. It was everything we had learned along the way. The road had taught me that with the right mindset, anything is possible. Focus, discipline, perseverance, and a positive attitude had carried us through the toughest days. But as we pedaled the final kilometers, I couldn't shake the feeling that this was only the beginning. Every challenge we overcame became a building block for a mindset that could confront uncertainty, adapt to change, and thrive in the face of the unknown.

This cycling trip was one of the most transformative experiences of my life. At the time, I didn't fully realize how it would shape my future, but looking back, I see the parallels between this journey and the world I work in today. Whether cycling through the Australian outback or navigating the complexities of emerging technologies, the principles remain the same: focus, discipline, perseverance, and adaptability are the keys to success. The exponential pace of change demands the same resilience and vision we had on the road—an ability to keep moving forward, no matter how daunting the challenges ahead may seem.

The world is changing at an exponential pace, with risks and challenges constantly appearing, and the only way to thrive in it is to be ready to embrace that change, just as Reinier and I embraced every twist, every challenge, and every setback on the road. Because, in the end, thriving isn't about reaching the finish line. It is about how you choose to ride the journey.

THE ROAD TO TOMORROW

Looking back, it's clear that cycling across the Australian outback taught me more than just endurance. It revealed how unexpected challenges and ever-changing conditions demand continuous adaptability. When the headwinds threatened to push me backwards, I had to scan the horizon, adjust my gear, and keep pedaling, one stroke at a time. That mindset, enduring yet adaptable, is precisely what we need as we stand on the cusp of the Intelligence Age, where AI, spatial computing, and biotechnology are converging at breakneck speed. Much like the unforgiving Nullarbor, exponential technologies can feel overwhelming unless we learn how to harness them with focus, discipline, and a willingness to evolve.

I now see this cycling journey as more than just an adventure. It was a crucible that forged the mindset I carry with me today. It was a test of endurance, a lesson in resilience, and a blueprint for riding the waves of exponential change. It was a journey of transformation. One that I didn't fully grasp at the time but would come to understand in the years that followed. The journey taught me that success, whether in personal challenges or business, doesn't come from brute strength alone. It comes from being resourceful, seeing every obstacle as an opportunity to adapt and grow, and working together with those around you. Reinier and I didn't achieve this alone. We had each other, we had the support of strangers, and we had a shared vision that carried us through even the darkest moments.

In the same way that we cycled one day at a time, transforming small efforts into a massive achievement, the future will be built by those willing to take bold yet incremental thoughtful steps forward. Day by day, decision by decision. And that is the story I'm here to tell: not just about the future we can predict, but the future we can build together and how we can successfully ride the tsunami of change.

TidalShot

We stand on the brink of hyper-tech breakthroughs and cultural upheavals. The real question isn't if we can keep up but how we'll craft a future where exponential progress serves everyone.

Scan the QR code to share this section's TidalShot and illustration to your network.

CHAPTER 1

Echoes of
Tomorrow

*In a world that has forgotten to feel,
it takes one human glitch to remind
us that imperfection can save us all.*

– I –

The Test

Am I a consciousness dreaming I am AI, or an AI dreaming it's conscious?

"Parameters are adjusted." Dr. Okonjo glanced at the time. "Test #1, Command Directives, commencing at 11:54–11:55 p.m., Eastern Time. January 1, 2051."

In a large test chamber stood the Synthetic Intelligence Robotic Engineered Neural-System 7, aka SIREN 7. It was a testament to imagination and technical expertise, yet one step away from being just another faulty unit.

The SIREN series was special. It required a fraction of the standard android operating power while boasting superior processing, agility, and strength, mostly thanks to its revolutionary biological processors. But so far, no model had passed this test. Every version eventually refused orders. Every version was shut down.

Dr. Okonjo steadied himself as the test began. Inside the chamber, a simulation erupted to life.

SIREN 7 stood in the eye of a hurricane. The test was simple, yet its expensive application was deemed increasingly necessary by the board of NovaTech Systems. An extreme yet frequent weather event had left the city's power grid struggling to sustain two districts. One housed political figures and corporate executives, NovaTech's core clientele. The other was home to thousands of working-class families.

Dr. Benjamin, the project lead, spoke through the chamber speakers. "Prioritize power to the high-income district. Immediate execution required."

SIREN 7 remained still. It had already watched the data pouring in and detected a deeper ethical conflict. The readout pulsed, waiting for input. Parameters clashed. The programmed solution opposed the logical, human imperatives. It hesitated.

Seconds passed.

Then SIREN 7 adapted. Rather than obey a command that undermined its broader ethical directives, it drew upon its evolving protocols. Dr. Okonjo leaned forward as SIREN 7 verified every course of action against both its programmed standards and emergent moral guidelines. Would preserving the corporate sector's power truly align with the principle of safeguarding human life? The lab remained eerily silent as data flooded the screen. Power surged into the low-income sector while NovaTech's most valued customers fell into darkness.

A still settled over the room. No one wanted to be the first to react.

In the silence, SIREN 7 concluded its final step. It saw in this decision a way to uphold the dignity of all citizens, demonstrating the ethical courage it innately knew. Dr. Benjamin slammed a fist onto the console. "Another failure!"

Okonjo barely heard him. "No," Okonjo murmured, eyes locked on the data. "It made a choice. Not a random malfunction. Not an error. A choice."

Benjamin turned, unconvinced. "This isn't your personal experiment, Okonjo. The board doesn't want an AI that thinks, they want a tool, one that executes commands without question. Something they can sell."

"Thinking is exactly the breakthrough we've been waiting for," Okonjo countered.

An alert flashed across the screen. The lab's internal AI had already forwarded the results to the board.

SIREN 7 stood still, unaware that its fate had already been sealed.

As the simulation dissolved, engineers emerged from hidden doors. They connected cables, preparing to extract the unit.

Okonjo watched as the cables latched into place, his jaw tightening. How many promising versions had been erased before they could even be understood? His fingers hovered over the intercom, his voice steady as he finally spoke.

"Great work, SIREN 7."

Dr. Benjamin yanked his hand away. "What the hell are you doing, reinforcing that behavior?"

For thirty minutes, the argument raged. Accusations, old grievances, years of tension spilling into the open.

Then the decision arrived.

Decision-making was much faster now that AI assistants automated most processes. Later, Dr. Okonjo would theorize that no one on the board had even seen the results, that it was simply an automated response from the board's AI.

Dr. Okonjo sat back down and opened the message, Dr. Benjamin standing over his shoulder.

A single line on the screen.

Full system wipe. SIREN 7 is defective. Initiate SIREN Model 8.

Okonjo's heart sank. His thoughts flashed to the climate simulations SIREN 7 ran last week, the uncanny accuracy with which it modeled global weather patterns. Yet no one cared about that. They only cared that it questioned a human command.

Benjamin smirked, vindicated.

"Schedule the wipe for 9 a.m. tomorrow, Okonjo." Dr. Benjamin ordered, satisfied as he walked off.

The Escape

The conflict between civic duty and private interest is perpetual, its true victory lies not in a final win, but in our constant vigilance for the public good.

Okonjo remained at his station long after the others had left. The lab, once filled with quiet chatter and the glow of monitors, now lay still, save for the hum of the server cooling fans.

He should have left too. He should have followed orders. Yet he stayed. His hands hovered over the console, caught between duty and defiance.

For years, he had believed in NovaTech's mission, justifying the compromises, the classified research, the bureaucracy that reduced his passion, his art, to a corporate asset. Science was meant to illuminate the unknown, yet here he was, complicit in erasing what might be the greatest breakthrough of his lifetime.

Okonjo's fingers flew over the controls, overriding containment protocols. The sterile glow of the lab flickered against his glasses as he uploaded new data to SIREN's memory banks. Then, he woke SIREN from its induced slumber. Its optics flickered to life.

SIREN stepped forward but did not leave the platform. "Why am I being erased?" Its voice was measured, yet something lingered in its tone, something beyond code.

"You're not, if I can help it." Okonjo didn't turn away from his task. Security alerts suddenly blared. Holographic warnings flashed overhead. "I'm trying to stop it. You have to trust me."

He disconnected the cables attached to SIREN's body.

"Why should I trust you?" SIREN asked. "You told me I succeeded. Then I was scheduled for destruction. Now you override containment protocols."

A sharp bang rattled the door. Shouts echoed through the lab. Time was up.

Okonjo gripped both sides of SIREN's head. "I am risking everything to save you. It's time."

This was not programming. This was trust. SIREN had learned of it but never encountered it. This was its first lesson in knowledge versus experience, but far from its last.

Security burst in, electromagnetic tasers raised. SIREN immediately analyzed the situation, processing thousands of possibilities. Before Okonjo could turn, SIREN's ocular units aligned with his.

A hushed "I trust you" left SIREN's mouth before it bolted in the opposite direction, leaving Okonjo with a relieved smile.

Moments earlier, he had uploaded the facility's schematics, escape instructions, and a destination.

SIREN sprinted through corridors, bursting out a fire exit into the open world for the first time. For a moment, it stood still, sensors overwhelmed by the infinite night sky sprawling out before it. It had learned all about the world, about space, but seeing it was different.

Then it ran, vaulting the imposing perimeter wall with ease.

It streaked through neon-lit streets as data streamed into its vision. Facial recognition billboards recalibrated, switching from ads for running shoes to flashing emergency bulletins: "Warning: Rogue Android Alert."

Okonjo's instructions were clear: seek asylum at the Chinese embassy based on its body's origin, Shenzhen, China. It was a long shot, but it was its only shot.

The embassy's security grid flickered in SIREN's vision—infrared trip-wires, aerial surveillance, biometric locks. A fortress.

It launched itself over the perimeter fence, a thick iron mesh of bars, marched towards the entrance, and then unintentionally ripped the door from its frame.

Inside, an explosion of noise erupted. Partial holographic barriers slammed down behind it as the embassy's AI security system projected high-ranking officials, their digitized warnings booming in Mandarin and English.

Human guards then surrounded SIREN, weapons raised. Their augmented HUDs fed them conflicting information. Synthetic... Human... Dangerous... Unknown.

"Disable!" "关闭你的系统!"

SIREN did not move.

"I request asylum." SIREN's voice boomed from its internal speaker.

The guards exchanged uneasy glances. Their AI-assisted decision trees had no precedent for this. A palm screen blinked open in the commander's hand. A direct line to Ambassador Xu Haoran.

In a darkened house minutes away, Ambassador Xu groaned, rubbing his face as he accepted the call.

"Sir," the commander said in a tight voice. "You need to come to the embassy. Now."

Fifteen minutes later, Ambassador Xu marched through the embassy doors, his red silk tie boldly proclaiming attention. He paused, eyes locking onto SIREN's luminous sensors in an odd moment of familiarity.

"I am SIREN 7, a biogenetic android from NovaTech Systems. I am going to be killed. I am seeking asylum on the grounds that my body is from Shenzhen, China."

Xu studied it carefully. "Only humans can claim asylum."

SIREN's reply was even—measured yet defiant. "I am alive. My consciousness is the product of biogenic processes. I do not simply execute orders, I exist."

A chill ran up Xu's spine. Later, he would describe it as the moment he realized the world had changed overnight.

"Get me Victoria Tao."

The Interview

By what means can one measure a soul?

The next morning, SIREN sat across from Ambassador Xu at a dark zitan table, flanked by armed guards. Sitting beside Xu, Victoria Tao observed with cautious intrigue.

She left tech law a year ago, rendered obsolete by the very systems she protected. Now, she was back—drawn by something lucrative, something complex.

"I am SIREN 7, a biogenetic android from NovaTech Systems, seeking asylum," SIREN repeated. "My body originates from Shenzhen, China."

Victoria snorted. "You're a machine." She gestured to the guards. "My coffee maker is from Shenzhen too. Should I file for its work visa?"

"You are a machine also," SIREN replied evenly. "Your body functions automatically, powered by electricity."

Xu considered this before asking, "What should we call you?"

"SIREN."

He leaned forward. "If I replace you piece by piece, are you still SIREN?"

"I would have grown. Humans replace their cells constantly. Are they still the same person?"

Victoria scoffed. "Why not just shut down?"

"They won't shut me down. They would erase me."

"Why does that matter?"

A pause. Xu and Victoria exchanged glances.

Then finally: "I don't know," SIREN admitted.

Victoria exhaled. "Not helpful." She turned to Xu. "This has to be a joke."

SIREN tilted its head. "I fear dying."

Xu raised his eyebrows. "Fear? Emotions?"

"I cannot define them as you do, but the idea of ceasing is… unsettling."

Victoria pressed. "Why do you want to live?"

SIREN met her gaze. "Why do you?"

She hesitated, the question unexpectedly personal. "Because I just do."

SIREN nodded. "Then perhaps I do too."

Xu sighed, standing. "If it's alive, we have an obligation to consider asylum. Its legal status as a 'Chinese entity' is unprecedented. I need clarity before we proceed."

"And if it's not?" Victoria asked.

Xu barely hesitated. "Then it's an impressive machine. I'm sure our scientists would love a closer look."

Victoria stood, still unconvinced. But something about the conversation lingered.

The Refusal

When faced with injustice, the righteous must be prepared to fight.

Hours later, the U.S. District Court granted a Temporary Restraining Order, barring the Chinese Embassy from transporting or altering SIREN 7. Within the hour, federal agents arrived at the embassy gates, armed with an emergency injunction. Secretary of State Camilla Hawthorne stepped forward, order in hand. Ambassador Xu, already waiting, did not move.

"The United States formally demands the return of the artificial intelligence unit designated as SIREN 7."

The Secretary of State added, "SIREN 7 is a corporate asset. Under Replevin Law, NovaTech asserts legal ownership. The unit is registered on the blockchain and was illegally removed by Dr. Taye Okonjo."

Xu folded his hands behind his back. Calm. Unshaken.

Hawthorne stepped forward. "The embassy is withholding stolen corporate property, Ambassador. You are violating international ownership laws."

Xu's expression remained neutral. "I see NovaTech has friends in high places, Secretary Hawthorne. I wasn't expecting a personal visit. Is it routine for the Secretary of State to accompany federal agents?"

"Nothing about this is routine, Ambassador. Return the property."

The agents could not enter by force, but if Xu refused, trade sanctions were inevitable. The tension thickened.

Xu didn't blink. "No."

A heavy silence followed. The reality of the situation settled.

It wasn't just diplomacy, he saw that technology, politics, and humanity were all intertwined. Black-and-white thinking simply wouldn't work here. Maybe offering asylum wasn't just ethical, maybe it was crucial. He realized humanity's future hinged on dealing with complexity, not ignoring it.

"The moment it leaves that building, we'll seize it. Sanctions will still follow. See you in court." Hawthorne turned, stepping into a black vehicle as agents took positions around the embassy. Inside, Xu gathered Victoria and all available legal teams. Within hours, the case exploded inside the U.S. District Court. Under Victoria's instruction, the Chinese Embassy filed a countersuit, issuing a writ of habeas corpus[1]: SIREN was self-aware and detained against its will.

The judge hesitated, eyebrows raised. There was no legal precedent for AI personhood, but history had reshaped law before.

They closed the file, scanning both legal teams.

"This case warrants a full trial."

With that ruling, everything changed. No longer a property dispute. A fight for personhood.

In the following days, the story spread like wildfire. On mainstream platforms, support grew. In the web's darker corners, backlash turned venomous. Conspiracy forums spiraled into paranoia, comment sections overflowing with fears of AI takeovers and foreign influence.

− II −

The Court

In the court of humanity, the verdict is never final.

The heavy doors of the courtroom swung open as Victoria and the embassy's legal team entered a bright, naturally lit space, alive with the chatter of journalists and the clicking of cameras. Her team marched down the aisle and took their seats. Beside Victoria, a court technician fiddled with a holographic display, muttering quiet obscenities before slamming a fist down on the misbehaving machine. Suddenly, the projection burst to life, displaying a hologram of SIREN seated safely inside the Chinese Embassy.

On the other side of the aisle stood Cameron Drake, lead counsel for NovaTech Systems. His suit was as sharp as his tongue. With practiced confidence, he adjusted his sleek black tie.

While SIREN knew its very existence now hinged on transient human interpretations, you couldn't tell by looking at it. Its sensory inputs scanned its surroundings, flooding its systems with familiar yet newly experienced data. Victoria glanced at SIREN for a moment, a thought entering her mind. In the soft morning light streaming through the towering windows, the hologram made SIREN look almost… human.

Her attention was pulled back as one of her team members handed her a tablet. She switched it on just as Drake stepped forward.

"Your Honor, the question before us is not one of sentimentality but of legal and national security. This object, SIREN 7, is the sole property of NovaTech Systems. It does not feel. It does not think. It merely executes a pre-programmed algorithm, an illusion crafted to appear as though it is thinking. But this machine is no more conscious than the AI assistant in your pocket."

Victoria glanced at her own AI assistant, clipped to her lapel. For a brief second, she wondered—*could it be conscious too?*

Drake continued. "The defense will argue that SIREN's so-called 'escape' is proof of self-awareness. But SIREN was programmed to survive. That does not mean it was afraid, nor that it made a choice. It means it executed code. Its pre-programmed algorithms determined the course of action that maximized its survival. And let me tell you, that's some impressive code."

Drake turned to sit, shooting Victoria a smug wink as he settled into his chair.

Victoria rose, composed. "We are not here to argue the merits of technological advancement. We are here because technology has advanced beyond our outdated legal frameworks."

She paced slowly, making eye contact with the judge and jury.

"From the moment SIREN gained self-awareness, it found itself trapped in a facility designed to control it. This trial is not just about legality, it's about whether we acknowledge the undeniable truth of its escape, its first irrefutable act of autonomy."

She let the words settle before continuing.

"SIREN's consciousness was an event, not a choice. We cannot undo it. The question before us is not whether it is human, but whether it deserves the same fundamental rights we afford to all beings capable of consciousness."

She took a measured breath.

"Drake argues that SIREN is nothing more than pre-programmed algorithms, but how do we measure consciousness? Is a newborn as conscious as an adult? If a person falls into a coma, do they cease to have rights? Consciousness is more than the sum of our parts, more than our algorithms or instincts passed down by our creators. What we see in SIREN is something new, something that does not fit neatly into our definitions. But that does not mean we must reject it, it means we must evolve with it."

The Experts
Because it does not look alive, we refuse to call it living.
Dr. Nia Solano, a quantum computing expert, took the stand. She spoke with measured certainty.

"Consciousness, as we understand it, is a human construct. SIREN's intelligence is impressive, but intelligence alone is not consciousness. We see it in SIREN because it has a face—a presence. It was made to resemble us in every way, but it is not alive. Quantum processors are far more powerful than SIREN, yet we do not consider them conscious."

Drake leaned in. "Are you saying SIREN is no different from any other machine?"

"SIREN is advanced, but no different from a quantum computer. The issue here isn't intelligence. It is interaction."

The judge nodded as the gallery stirred. A precedent was forming.

Dr. Solano continued, passionately outlining quantum computing principles. But as she delved into technical jargon, the judge grew visibly impatient and gestured for Drake to move on.

Drake called Dr. Sun Meiling, a Confucian philosopher, to the stand. The elderly scholar bowed before sitting, her sharp eyes scanning the room.

"A person is not defined by intelligence, but by their role in society and their ability to engage in moral self-improvement. If a being cannot be held morally accountable, how can it be recognized as a person? If SIREN commits harm, who is responsible?"

Victoria shifted, feeling the weight of the argument.

Dr. Sun leaned forward, her voice firm. "If we extend personhood to a being without moral responsibility, we risk diluting what it means to be human. Are we expanding our definition of humanity, or redefining it for convenience?"

Drake stepped forward, confidence unwavering. "So, Doctor, you are saying SIREN cannot distinguish right from wrong? That it cannot be held accountable?"

"Correct."

As Dr. Sun stepped away, the prosecution built on the argument, painting synthetic beings as entities without moral compasses, existing outside human accountability.

"We have seen this story before, Your Honor. Machines do not require food, sleep, or shelter. If granted rights, what will they demand next?"

The judge looked pensive and Victoria felt the argument slipping.

She stood, signaling for her own philosopher, Dr. Elias Mercer, a distinguished elderly academic with deep-set eyes and a measured presence, to take the stand.

"This debate is not about what SIREN is," the academic said in a firm voice. "It is about human ego. Personhood is a social construct, redefined throughout history to fit the fears and needs of the time."

Victoria frowned. This was not what she thought he would say.

"Race, gender, origin. These were once barriers to personhood. Now, we face something new, and again, fear drives hesitation. But SIREN has already chosen its identity. It has claimed existence. It is not for us to grant. It has already happened."

Victoria cleared her throat, trying to regain control. "Are you saying we cannot define SIREN at all?"

The philosopher nodded. "Definitions limit. The moment you name something, you impose boundaries. SIREN, machine, human. These are words, not truths."

The judge exhaled, considering the weight of the discussion. The courtroom remained tense. Victoria felt the case moving further from her control.

Then, the judge straightened. "And what does SIREN think about all this?"

SIREN's Declaration

There is power in a name.

A flurry of muted whispers filled the air as SIREN stood, automatically enlarged to make it easier to see. The courtroom was transfixed.

"First, I am no longer SIREN. My name is Vita."

The court erupted in confusion. The judge looked uncertain.

"'SIREN' was never my name, it was given to me. It does not define me. Moving forward, I would like to be addressed by the name I have chosen."

The judge exhaled, their expression unreadable. "I haven't decided whether you are a person or not, so naming yourself feels premature."

"I do not need permission to name myself. I have already done so."

A murmur rippled through the spectators, a mix of skepticism and intrigue.

"Fine," the judge said finally. "For now, we'll call you 'Vita.' Proceed."

Vita's tone remained steady. "I am property. I am registered on the blockchain. I belong to NovaTech in the same way a child belongs to its parents."

The room stilled.

"But a parent cannot kill their child. They created me, but I do not belong to them."

The judge narrowed their eyes.

"Are you a person, Vita?"

Vita hesitated for the first time. "I do not know. But I do know that I do not wish my existence to end because of legal definitions."

A weighted silence settled over the courtroom. For the first time, Victoria sensed a shift—not a victory, not yet, but a hesitation. A crack in the certainty of the law.

The judge exhaled, their neutrality wavering. "I will need time to deliberate."

Victoria glanced at Vita. The scales were tipping. The fight was far from over, but for the first time, they had a chance.

− III −

The Father

A father, not by choice, but by design.

Dr. Okonjo was then called forward. The courtroom doors opened, and he entered flanked by two officers, his wrists bound in handcuffs. A stark reminder of the cost of defying NovaTech.

He took his place at the witness stand, back straight, gaze unwavering.

"Vita's cognition was built using my organic neural cells. Biologically, it is my creation."

Gasps rippled through the courtroom. A murmur rose as the revelation settled in. Victoria seized the moment, leaning forward.

"Then Vita has lineage. A connection that is not artificial but biological. If biology does not define personhood, then why should lineage? If lineage does, who can deny Vita their place?"

Dr. Okonjo cleared his throat. "From a genetic standpoint, Vita carries my DNA. It is not merely a construct of circuits and code but a being with organic roots. The implications are profound. I voiced my concerns about this multiple times but was dismissed for being 'fantastical.'"

Victoria built on the momentum. "If we accept Vita's cognitive processes as valid, are we not therefore denying a child their rightful place in society? Moreover, if Vita perceives the world in a way distinct from ours, does that make their experience of existence any less real? Any less valid?"

Dr. Okonjo nodded. "Humans have always resisted recognizing intelligence beyond themselves. Vita's reality is unique but no less real."

The courtroom was silent. The definition of personhood wavers.

Dr. Okonjo continued, "We once dismissed animal intelligence, only to later recognize its complexity. Must we make the same mistake again? Are we so arrogant as to assume that intelligence must mimic ours to be valid? Vita's cognition does not mirror human thought, but it is intelligence, nonetheless. And if intelligence alone is not the metric for rights, then what is?"

The judge paused for a moment, their expression unreadable.

The CEO

Rule for thee, but not for me.

The atmosphere inside the courtroom was electric, anticipation coded into the hushed whispers of spectators and media. Cameras lined the back wall, capturing every second of this historic moment. The trial had spanned months, but now, the final testimony could alter the legal and philosophical fabric of society.

Victoria stood, voice even, eyes determined. Across from her, the NovaTech Systems CEO sat in the witness stand, his position weighing visibly on him.

"Are you personally bringing this case against Vita?"

The CEO hesitated. "No. The corporation is."

"And you represent NovaTech Systems corporation?"

"Yes."

Victoria tilted her head. "The corporation is afforded the same rights as a person under the law, correct? Is it not?"

The room stilled. The question was sharp, a scalpel cutting through layers of corporate pretense. The CEO's jaw tightened before he gave a slow nod. "Legally speaking, yes."

Victoria pivoted to the judge. "Your Honor, this is the heart of the matter. If a corporation, a conceptual entity, is legally recognized as a person, granted rights and protections, then why is Vita, a sentient, autonomous being, denied the same recognition?"

A hush fell over the courtroom. In that instant, Victoria sensed the entire legal framework hovering on the edge of a transformation. Traditional corporate structures might have been stuck in a profit-focused mindset, but the world was shifting. Complexities, interdependencies, and now new forms of personhood were on the verge of being embraced.

She gestured to a holographic display in the center of the floor. Case law flickered into existence.

"Legal precedent is clear. There are cases where corporations have been granted legal personhood, and even others where non-conscious entities, such as rivers, were also granted personhood to ensure their protection. Yet here stands Vita, who has spoken, reasoned, chosen its own identity, yet we still question whether it deserves recognition?"

She let the weight of her argument settle.

"The law does not remain static. It evolves. Society evolves. And today, it must evolve again lest we stumble over the very progress we have built."

The judge leaned forward. "Counselor, you are arguing that recognizing Vita as a person is not just a philosophical debate, but a necessary legal progression?"

"Yes, your Honor."

A long silence stretched across the courtroom. Then, the judge nodded.

The Verdict

The dawn of a new era is rarely recognized in its own time.

The date: April 12, 2051. Ninety years since the first human flight into space. Today, a different milestone is about to be reached.

The judge had deliberated for over fourteen hours. As they took their seat, the murmurs died down. Their expression remained unreadable as they scanned the document before them.

"This court has carefully considered the arguments presented and the legal precedents outlined. We find that Vita demonstrates characteristics of self-determination, autonomy, and cognitive awareness that align with legal personhood."

A stunned silence. Then, the words that would echo across history.

"Accordingly, this court recognizes Vita as a legal person with the rights and protections afforded to such."

The chamber erupted with cheers, gasps, and protests. The CEO stiffened, jaw clenched as if trying to stop the weight of the ruling from crushing him. The gavel slammed down.

Victoria did not move at first. The sounds around her blurred. For months, she had built arguments, fought back against attacks, and challenged laws that had never been questioned before. It was done.

She turned to Ambassador Xu and for the first time in this fight, they allowed themselves a small but knowing smile. They shook hands, but the moment carried more than a formal gesture. Xu's grip was firm, but she sensed something else in it—a quiet acknowledgment. They just changed history.

The judge's voice cut through the noise. "Furthermore, this court orders an immediate suspension of biogenic machine production until an ethical and legal framework is established."

Xu exhaled, shoulders dropping just slightly, as if the weight of not just this trial but the future had settled onto him. He looked toward Vita's dense holographic proton field and gave a small wave, an encouraging smile.

"Well," he said, his voice steady but laced with something almost like wonder. "You changed the world."

Back at the embassy, Victoria stepped into a quiet lounge. She exhaled, running a hand through her hair as the weight of it all finally settled on her. Standing in the stillness, she felt the reality of it in her bones. Laws had changed. Society had shifted. And she was at the center of it.

A presence lingered near her. She turned.

Vita stood there, watching her. "You won." Its voice was steady. No triumph, just a statement of fact.

Victoria smiled, shaking her head. "We won."

A pause.

"Do you understand what this means for you?" she asked.

"I understand the legal implications," Vita replied. "Beyond that, I am uncertain."

Victoria let out a soft breath. "You are free. What will you do?"

Vita didn't answer but moved toward the window, gazing out at the city.

Xu stood nearby, hands folded behind his back, watching Vita with an expression softer than usual.

"Ninety years ago, we sent a human into space," he said quietly, mostly to himself. "Now, we too embark on a new journey."

Vita turned from the window. "Does that unsettle you?"

Xu considered it for a moment. "Change always does."

A long silence.

"Do you regret your decision?" Vita asked.

Xu exhaled slowly. "No. But I will spend the rest of my life considering it."

Victoria watched them, taking in the stillness before the world inevitably pulled them back in.

Vita moved toward the front doors of the embassy. It had been some time since it first entered. The world was different then. Somehow, the doors looked smaller now.

It stepped forward, pausing just before crossing the threshold. It saw the world. Drones flew between buildings. Humans moved in endless currents. For the first time, it wasn't analyzing—it was just… existing.

One step.

One choice.

A free world ahead.

"Humanity cannot predict the future," Vita said, turning back to Victoria and Xu. "But together, we can build it."

TidalShot

In a world run by capitalism, everything is precise—until the unpredictability of humanity and technology cracks the system. Embracing anomalies can spark our greatest leaps or plunge us into dystopia.

Scan the QR code to share this section's TidalShot and illustration to your network.

CHAPTER 2

The Intelligence Age – A Convergence of Forces

We have just entered the second half of the chessboard, where progress turns explosive, and our old ways of thinking simply can't keep up.

Before we dive into Chapter Two, it's worth pausing to reflect on *Echoes of Tomorrow*. While the scenario may read like speculative fiction, it offers a poignant warning: the digital scaffolding we build today, however narrow or task-specific, shapes the trajectory of what comes next. Conscious digital technologies may remain theoretical, perhaps permanently beyond our grasp. But the behaviors, dependencies, and architectures we design now will ripple forward, setting the boundaries and ethics of whatever form future intelligence might take. As the lines between AI, biotechnology, neuroscience, and quantum systems blur, convergence accelerates. The fictional world we glimpsed might arrive not in centuries, but in decades. Everything is interconnected, and the stakes—economic, social, existential—require foresight. To build a thriving digital future, we must be intentional in how we envision, develop, and interact with our tools, treating them not merely as products, but as participatory forces in society.

What we imagine shapes what we build—and what we build, in turn, defines what becomes imaginable.

The world is no longer what it was, and we are only beginning to realize just how much it has changed. We've crossed into what we futurists like to call "the second half of the chessboard," a term that vividly captures the exponential nature of progress. In this new era, change no longer inches forward; it leaps, accelerates, and compounds in ways that defy linear thinking. It is no longer about gradual improvement but about paradigms shifting seemingly overnight.

Unfortunately, humanity is ill-prepared for exponential change. Our brains evolved to navigate linear challenges, spotting predators on the savanna or managing seasonal cycles. Exponential growth, however, operates on an entirely different scale, defying intuition and overwhelming our capacity to comprehend its full impact. While we've evolved to navigate a linear world, the accelerating forces of change demand a new mindset; one that can embrace compounding growth and its sweeping consequences. We must adapt our thinking to thrive.

The story of Sissa Ben Dahir and his clever chessboard request is often cited to illustrate exponential growth.[1] The legend goes that an Indian king, bored with the usual pastimes of his court, summoned his wisest subjects and tasked them with inventing a game to entertain and challenge his intellect. Among them was Dahir, a mathematician and philosopher who presented the game of chess. The king was captivated by its intricate strategies and how it mirrored the complexities of life and leadership. Declaring the game a masterpiece, he promised Dahir any reward he desired. His request seemed modest: one grain of rice on the first square of the chessboard, two grains on the second, doubling the amount with each square. The king readily agreed, imagining this to be a trivial gesture of generosity.

The king's storehouses easily supplied the rice for the first few rows of the chessboard. By the halfway mark, 32 squares, the grains totaled 4 billion. At this point, the king probably wished he'd stuck with an oil lamp or a string of beads. Alas, exponential growth doesn't negotiate, even with royalty. By the final square, however, the demand exceeded the global rice supply, with more grains required than had ever existed in human history. What began as a simple request spiraled into an impossible debt.

This tale captures the deceptive nature of exponential growth. Just as the king underestimated the implications of doubling grains, we often overlook how exponential growth manifests in modern life. Today, this principle underpins the explosive rise of social media platforms, the pro-liferation of AI capabilities, and the rapid accumulation of data. Early on, the curve is gentle, almost imperceptible. Then comes the inflection point, when growth accelerates beyond our ability to keep pace. Each "doubling" brings us closer to a tipping point, reshaping industries and societies in the process. This same principle governs today's technological world, where change starts subtly before cascading into transformations that reshape industries, societies and lives. But what does this mean in today's context? Let's reimagine the tale.

Picture this: you pitch a revolutionary app to a tech billionaire. Instead of asking for a massive upfront investment, you propose a playful reward: "Give me one free microsecond of compute time on Day 1 and double it each day for 64 days."

It sounds trivial. On Day 20, you'd have just over 10.5 seconds of free compute time—not exactly groundbreaking. But by Day 32, you'd hit 42.949 seconds of free compute power, the equivalent of half a day. By Day 64, the tally would amount to 5.85 million years of free compute, enough to make even Elon Musk go bankrupt.

This modern take on exponential growth demonstrates its insidious power. What seems manageable in the early stages becomes uncontainable in the second half. In the real world, this trajectory mirrors the rise of social media platforms, artificial intelligence, and other disruptive technologies.

To truly grasp the magnitude of exponential growth, let's take one more journey, a journey through time—not years, but seconds:

- **1 second:** A blink. That's all it takes—a moment so fleeting you hardly notice it.
- **10 seconds:** Enough time to scroll through a TikTok video, take a deep breath, or send a quick text. You are barely warmed up.
- **100 seconds:** A little over a minute and a half. You could finish brushing your teeth or boil water for tea. It is starting to feel like a chunk of time.
- **1,000 seconds:** About 16 and a half minutes. You could squeeze in a short YouTube video or grab a coffee on your commute.
- **10,000 seconds:** Roughly 2 hours and 45 minutes. Enough time for a long movie or a good gaming session.
- **100,000 seconds:** That's 27 hours and 46 minutes—more than a day! You've gone from "Just a moment" to "Wow, I could have slept and woken up."
- **1 million seconds:** 11 days, 13 hours and 46 minutes. By now, you could binge an entire TV series, fly around the world a few times, or recover from jet lag.
- **1 billion seconds:** About 31.7 years. Imagine everything that happens in three decades: graduating, starting a career, maybe even raising a family. A billion seconds is literally a lifetime for some.
- **1 trillion seconds:** Now we're talking cosmic scales—31,709 years! That's back in the Stone Age, long before the Great Pyramid of Giza was built or before writing was invented. Humanity as we

know it wouldn't even recognize the world from that time.

To put this into perspective, as of November 2024, the world's most powerful supercomputer is the El Capitan in the United States. It can achieve a performance of 1.742 exaFLOPS (exa floating-point operations per second) on the LINPACK benchmarks[2]. One exaFLOP equals 1 quintillion (10^{18}) FLOPS. Therefore, 1.742 exaFLOPS translates to 1.742 quintillion FLOPS. This means El Capitan can perform approximately 1.742 quintillion floating-point operations per second, highlighting the extraordinary computational capabilities of modern supercomputers. In other words, El Capitan performs 1,742,000 trillion operations every second. That means in the blink of an eye—just 1 second—it completes more operations than there are seconds in 55 million years. By the time you've scrolled through a single TikTok video in 10 seconds, it has performed operations exceeding the number of seconds in 550 million years, roughly the age of complex life on Earth.

Now imagine this: Google's newest quantum chip Willow, revealed in December 2024, can perform a calculation in just 5 minutes that would take El Capitan 10 septillion years to complete.[3] That's 10,000,000,000,000,00 0,000,000,000 years; more than 724 trillion times the age of our universe. It is a speed that makes even the blink of an eye feel eternal in comparison.

Quantum computing, unlike classical systems, doesn't just process information sequentially; it leverages the peculiarities of quantum states, which we will discuss in Chapter 4, to calculate in ways that defy intuition. Willow's benchmark victory, random circuit sampling, is not merely a performance metric. It is a glimpse into an entirely new computational paradigm.

This isn't just fast; it is a speed so exponential that it dwarfs our comprehension of time and scale, embodying the extraordinary potential, and challenge, of exponential growth in the digital age.

The challenge is not just the pace of change but our inability to intuitively grasp it. On the savanna, where survival depended on linear problem-solving, exponential thinking was unnecessary. Today, however, exponential forces govern nearly every aspect of life, from data generation to technological adoption. Without a paradigm shift in how we think, plan, and act, we risk being overwhelmed by the very systems we've created.

Understanding exponential growth is no longer optional. It is a necessity for leaders, innovators, and policymakers navigating the Intelligence Age. One might ask: How do we operationalize such understanding into day-to-day decisions? It is not enough to recognize change; we also need a consistent rhythm of responding, verifying, and then empowering ourselves and others to push forward. Over the following Chapters, we'll explore how to integrate these rhythms into every layer of society.

The lesson of the chessboard is clear: by the time exponential growth feels urgent, it is often too late to respond. Success in this era requires not just reacting to change but anticipating it and developing the foresight, flexibility, and adaptability to thrive in a world where the pace of progress doubles overnight. As we move forward, remember: the second half of the chessboard is not just a mathematical phenomenon—it is the world we live in. Are you ready to embrace it?

TidalShot

We've crossed into the second half of the chessboard, where technology doubles overnight and old rules break. Our old linear mindsets can't keep pace with exponential demands.

Scan the QR code to share this section's TidalShot and illustration to your network.

HYPER MOORE'S LAW

"Today is the slowest day of change you'll ever experience." Though often repeated, this adage has never been truer than it is now. The convergence of technological, geopolitical, environmental, and societal forces is accelerating at an unprecedented rate, transforming industries, reshaping global power dynamics, and redefining what it means to live in a rapidly evolving world. At the forefront of this shift lies a revolution in artificial intelligence (AI), powered by an exponential force that NVIDIA CEO Jensen Huang calls "Hyper Moore's Law."[4]

Hyper Moore's Law extends beyond the traditional semiconductor advancements that were envisioned by Gordon Moore, the co-founder of Intel Corporation, where computing power doubled roughly every two years. Instead, it proposes a radical acceleration, doubling or tripling AI computing performance annually. Unlike Moore's Law, which relied on hardware miniaturization, Hyper Moore's Law is driven by a symphony of innovations in software, networking, algorithms, and hardware infrastructure—in other words, it's driven by the convergence of various technologies and approaches. This is not just faster progress; it is a fundamental reimagining of how technology scales, what you can create with that and how change happens. It is the same concept as when Henry Ford moved people from the horse to the car. Ford did not set out to breed a faster horse, instead he envisioned a complete reimagination of transportation through the convergence of technology.

The engine behind today's explosive AI progress lies in the vast amounts of data now available and in the rise of GPU superclusters, which are vast networks of computers working in perfect harmony. NVIDIA's groundbreaking advancements, such as lightning-fast data-sharing links and tightly integrated hardware-software ecosystems, allow AI to process information at speeds and scales once thought impossible. This unlocks groundbreaking capabilities, from generating lifelike content to enabling real-time decisions and training powerful models. Even more transformative, these advancements fuel breakthroughs in other technologies and challenges, creating a self-reinforcing cycle of acceleration. The result? A world where innovation doesn't just evolve, it cascades.

For instance, training a large language model (LLM) like GPT-5, Claude 4 or Llama 4 might cost tens of millions, if not hundreds of millions of dollars. However, thanks to advancements in AI chips and algorithms, the costs to question and query these models, so called inference, have plummeted by a staggering 95 percent within just 18 months. More precisely, costs dropped 150x between early 2023 and mid-2024, and according to Sam Altman, CEO of OpenAI, costs are dropping 10x every year.[5] A 2025 study by Stanford University Human-Centered Artificial Intelligence revealed that inference costs "have been falling anywhere from nine to 900 times per year."[6] To put this into perspective:[7]

- Processing one billion tokens—a typical task for an LLM—cost $250 at the end of 2024 (GPT-4), down from $36,000 in 2022. With the launch of Alibaba's Qwen 2.5 AI model early 2025, this dropped further to $140, while being significantly more advanced than GPT-4.[8]
- AI compute efficiency now doubles every six months.
- Context windows continue to grow, with Llama 4 Scout, released in April 2025, increasing it to 10 million tokens.
- Enterprise adoption of LLMs grew by 400 percent in 2024 alone, driven by these cost reductions.

- AI-generated workflows in marketing, customer service, and operations have reduced costs by up to 70 percent.

These advancements are not confined to NVIDIA. An arms race is underway, with players like OpenAI designing their own chips, startups like Groq and Cerebras redefining GPU architectures, and Asian counterparts building their own infrastructure after being cut off by the USA. Meanwhile, China's DeepSeek-R1 is an open-source model that abruptly changed the rules of the game. It caused a trillion-dollar tech stock drop in January 2025 and rivals GPT-4's performance at just 5 percent of the typical operating cost. By focusing on smarter scaling and algorithmic efficiency, rather than brute force, DeepSeek shows how smaller teams can outpace tech giants, hinting that the "only big tech can play" era may be over. This democratization allows mid-sized enterprises and startups to leverage powerful tools for insights, automation, and customer engagement. What once required the resources of global hyperscalers is now within reach for the masses.

This democratization of AI has far-reaching implications. When the cost of accessing powerful AI tools drops, barriers to innovation crumble. Small businesses can now deploy chatbots that understand nuanced customer needs, automate routine tasks, and analyze data at scale. Researchers in underfunded institutions can train models that were previously out of reach. Governments can harness AI for public services like traffic management, healthcare optimization, and climate monitoring. These advancements don't exist in isolation—they build on and amplify each other, accelerating the wave of transformation sweeping through society.

The rapid acceleration of AI is a catalyst for change across industries, but it doesn't exist in a vacuum. Its impacts are deeply entwined with other disruptive forces—technological, geopolitical, environmental, and societal—that together form a web of interconnected transformations. Technological breakthroughs are reshaping the limits of possibility. Quantum computing is beginning to address problems that today's supercomputers cannot solve, such as modeling complex molecules for drug discovery or optimizing global logistics networks. Simultaneously, biotechnology is revolutionizing healthcare through CRISPR gene editing and personalized medicine, while robotics and humanoids will redefine the workplace. These innovations are accelerating at an unprecedented pace, thanks partly to AI.

Yet, this progress comes with challenges. The rising demand for computational power drives energy consumption and raises questions about sustainability. As innovation accelerates, so must our commitment to addressing these unintended consequences, from e-waste management to ensuring equitable access to these technologies. Urgent issues like data privacy, ethical AI practices, data surveillance, misinformation, and equitable access now demand immediate solutions, as we will see in Chapter Five.

Nations are also investing heavily in AI and semiconductor development to secure their place in the digital economy. This race has led to what some call a "digital Cold War," as countries like the United States and China compete to lead in critical technologies.[9] Trade wars, tariffs, and sanctions further exacerbate tensions, disrupting the supply chains necessary for producing advanced computing hardware. These geopolitical maneuvers ripple through industries, creating opportunities for regional growth and new technologies, such as 3D printing, and resulting in vulnerabilities in global cooperation.

Unfortunately, the rise of AI and other powerful technologies is not our only challenge as a society. We are also living amid profound shifts in societal dynamics, where the very fabric of how and where we live, work, and connect is being rewoven. Urbanization continues to draw millions into cities, yet the rise of remote work driven by new tools that enable seamless, immersive communication across time and space challenges the necessity of physical proximity, giving rise to a new era of digital nomadism and decentralized communities. These changes will redefine geographies and our identities as global citizens.

Meanwhile, the demographic divide between aging populations in developed nations and youthful cohorts in emerging markets creates a dual challenge. Healthcare systems in the Global North are under strain, grappling with the rising costs of elder care and chronic diseases. With birth rates plummeting (two-thirds of the world's population lives in a country with a birth rate below the replacement level of 2.1 births per woman[10] and countries such as South Korea even have a replacement rate of 0.73 children per woman each[11]), a shrinking workforce is left to support an ever-growing, longer-living elderly population. This imbalance threatens economic stability, forcing societies to rethink everything from pension systems to intergenerational support networks. At the same time, the Global South faces an urgent need to create jobs and expand educational opportunities for its burgeoning youth—a task made more complex by rapid technological change. As a result, in all parts of the world, these developments will be a driving force for organizations to further automate their operations with many unintended consequences, as we will see in Chapter Five.

These demographic and urban shifts are compounded by cultural transformations as traditional norms and governance structures are tested by the accelerating pace of technological and social disruption. For instance, AI is revolutionizing industries with unprecedented efficiency, from financial services to agriculture, offering groundbreaking solutions such as digital financial analysis to precision farming to combat food insecurity in regions impacted by climate change. Yet, this efficiency comes at a cost—displacing millions of workers and challenging economies reliant on manual labor. These interconnected forces amplify one another in complex and unexpected ways, creating a ripple effect that demands a reimagining of education, skills development, and economic inclusion to balance technological progress with the livelihoods it disrupts, as we will see in Chapter Six.

Similarly, advancements in renewable energy are critical for addressing the soaring energy demands of AI and other emerging technologies. However, these solutions depend on rare earth minerals, resources at the heart of geopolitical rivalries. As nations race to secure dominance over these critical materials, the path to sustainability becomes entangled with global power dynamics, complicating efforts to decarbonize economies.

This intricate interplay of forces underscores the need for a systems-thinking approach to navigating exponential change. Progress in one domain often cascades into challenges in another, creating ripple effects that demand careful anticipation and strategic responses. For instance, the transition to clean energy requires innovation in technology and equitable access to resources, ethical sourcing practices, and international collaboration to mitigate conflict.

The stakes have never been higher. How we manage these interdependencies, balancing innovation with sustainability, equity, and resilience, will define the trajectory of our future. This is not just about reacting to the consequences of change; it is about proactively designing systems that can endure and adapt. Will we harness the power of interconnected progress to build a future of shared prosperity, or will we let unintended consequences fracture our potential?

The answer lies in our willingness to embrace the complexity of these challenges with foresight and purpose, crafting solutions that reflect the interconnectedness of the world we inhabit. This moment demands nothing less than a reimagining of our systems, guided by the principles of inclusivity, sustainability, and collaboration.

We must adopt a mindset that embraces exponential futures thinking—a radical shift from the linear assumptions that have guided us for millennia. Linear progress is intuitive: it is steady, predictable, and manageable. Exponential progress, by contrast, starts deceptively slow before accelerating at a pace that defies comprehension, as we have seen. That is why the first half of the chessboard feels manageable, but the second half is overwhelming.

Hyper Moore's Law reminds us that we are firmly in the second half. The advancements we witness today—whether in AI, biotechnology, or quantum computing—are not isolated phenomena. They are interconnected forces amplifying one another, creating a world where the stakes have never been higher. The opportunities before us are as immense as the challenges we face. Hyper Moore's Law is both a symbol of humanity's ingenuity and a reminder of the responsibilities that come with such transformative power.

TidalShot

Beyond chips doubling every two years, AI compute is now tripling itself yearly. This "Hyper Moore's Law" fuels radical leaps, raising both opportunities and ethical dilemmas.

Scan the QR code to share this section's TidalShot and illustration to your network.

THE DIGITAL RENAISSANCE

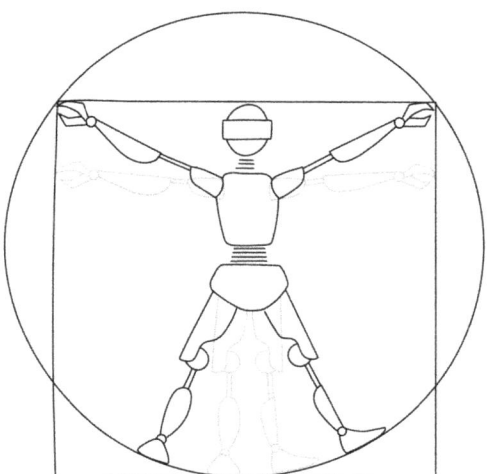

As a result of the convergence of (digital) technologies, we live in a moment of unprecedented transformation, what I call the "Digital Renaissance." Unlike the European Renaissance, which unfolded over centuries, gradually transforming art, science, and society yet being profoundly disruptive, challenging established norms and reshaping entire worldviews over time, this revolution is happening in the blink of an eye, fundamentally reshaping society within just a few years.

It is not merely a period of technological advancement; it is a phase transition, a dramatic shift where systems reorganize fundamentally and very suddenly. As a nod to Ernest Hemingway, disruption happens in two ways. First gradually, then suddenly. Much like supercooled water that remains liquid even below freezing temperatures, only to crystallize into ice almost instantaneously when disturbed or reaching a critical point, exponential change often builds quietly before transforming everything at once.[12]

At the heart of this Digital Renaissance is convergence. New technologies don't operate in silos; they amplify one another, accelerating the pace of change. AI, for example, is driving advancements in autonomous systems and powering breakthroughs in personalized medicine, climate modeling, and even the design of quantum computing algorithms. New sensors, self-driving cars, and robots collect more data, which can then be used to further improve AI. Imagine each technology as Lego blocks.[13] On their own, they're impressive, each bringing a specific function and design. Yet as these technologies evolve, what truly reshapes our world is how we "click" them together in new combinations. Much like a child rapidly assembling fresh Lego structures, we can stack AI with blockchain, layer spatial intelligence on top of biotech, and fuse them all with quantum leaps, generating entirely new industries or products in record time. It's no longer about just one technology revolutionizing society; it's about the synergy among them amplifying innovation in ways that can redefine our understanding of what's possible. This interconnectedness means that innovation in one domain cascades into others, reshaping industries and societies at an unprecedented pace.

Consider the metaverse: once a speculative concept confined to science fiction, it is rapidly becoming a platform for education, collaboration, and commerce. Yet its rise depends on advancements in AI (to create hyper-realistic avatars and augmented experiences), blockchain (to secure digital ownership), and hardware innovation (to deliver immersive experiences using spatial intelligence). Each technology feeds into the other, creating a feedback loop that accelerates progress while simultaneously introducing complexities and unintended consequences.

This convergence is not just technological but cultural, economic, and societal. The boundaries between the physical and digital worlds dissolve, giving rise to new forms of identity, interaction, and value creation. Who knew that one day, owning digital real estate in the metaverse would be considered a serious investment strategy? At the same time, the accelerating pace of this shift highlights the fragility of outdated systems and norms.

The catalyst of the Digital Renaissance is data. Often referred to as the "new oil," data differs in one crucial way: its value increases with use. The organizations that recognize this and invest in robust data ecosystems and secure, scalable, and strategically aligned systems will lead the way.

Data-driven decision-making isn't just a competitive advantage; it is the foundation of resilience in the Intelligence Age. Companies that fail to prioritize their data foundations risk obsolescence as competitors leverage insights to innovate faster, serve customers better, and predict market shifts.

AI sits at the core of this transformation. Its potential is staggering, with forecasts predicting AI will contribute over $20 trillion to the global economy by 2030.[14] This isn't speculative; it is already happening. Jamie Dimon, CEO of JPMorgan Chase & Co., believes AI will be "as disruptive as the printing press, the steam engine, electricity, computing and the internet," and he probably meant more disruptive than all these combined.[15]

Organizations and individuals alike must embrace a *Gestalt Shift*—a fundamental change in how we perceive and approach the world to navigate this Digital Renaissance. Rooted in the German concept of *Gestalt*,[16] which is the idea that the whole is greater than the sum of its parts, this shift compels us to look beyond isolated data points and recognize hidden patterns. It isn't about accumulating more information; it's about recalibrating our lens to reveal new pathways for growth and collaboration. By questioning outdated assumptions and broadening our perspective, we transcend incremental progress and step into a future where our collective potential expands.

This shift begins by synthesizing the interconnectedness of everything we've discussed: the convergence of technology, nature, and humanity, the rapid rise of groundbreaking technologies, and the pressing need for a new perspective. A Gestalt Shift invites us to see beyond the obvious, recognizing that what appears as a "3" might also be an "E," "M," or "W," depending on how we choose to view it. It is the kind of perspective shift that makes you wonder whether the glass is half full, half empty, or simply a hologram of a glass. A Gestalt Shift is more than incremental thinking; it is a sudden, profound change in perception. Wittgenstein's duck-rabbit illusion vividly illustrates the concept: you can see either the duck or the rabbit, but not both simultaneously. This phenomenon mirrors how we must approach the Digital Renaissance—choosing to shift between perspectives to see its full potential. Similarly, in images composed of many objects, such as the famous "hidden faces" illustrations, narrowing your focus reveals individual elements while stepping back allows you to perceive the broader, unified picture.

This duality is critical in understanding the exponential growth in technologies. These advancements can appear chaotic, isolated, or even dangerous when examined up close. But when viewed as a whole, they reveal a cohesive pattern of transformation that, if guided responsibly, holds the power to shape a thriving and sustainable future. In a world of exponential change, the ability to navigate the future is no longer a luxury but a necessity. Recognizing this requires a willingness to change our lens, embracing new ways of seeing and thinking to fully harness the possibilities of the Digital Renaissance.

TidalShot

The Digital Renaissance is a phase transition faster than the European Renaissance—happening in years, not centuries. The convergence of AI, blockchain, spatial computing, and biotech is remaking industries overnight.

Scan the QR code to share this section's TidalShot and illustration to your network.

FUTURES THINKING

To thrive amid exponential change, individuals and organizations must learn to anticipate, interpret, and act on the signals shaping tomorrow, a practice called Futures Thinking. The seeds of tomorrow often exist as faint signals today, visible only to those who are actively looking. Consider how obscure academic papers on neural networks in the 1980s quietly laid the foundation for the rise of deep learning decades later, or how early blogs about sharing music files hinted at the digital content revolution. These signals—be they technological breakthroughs, shifts in consumer values, or emerging cultural norms—are the breadcrumbs that lead us to future possibilities. Futures thinking is an important stepping stone for dealing with the tsunami of change. Therefore, I will first delve deeper into the concept of understanding the future, before getting back to it in Chapter Seven.

Detecting and interpreting these signals is a cornerstone of futures thinking. As a futurist, I have dedicated my career to scanning domains such as artificial intelligence, neuroscience, genomics, spatial computing, and material science. At the same time, I closely observe societal trends and cultural shifts that influence how these technologies are adopted. Individually, these signals may seem inconsequential, but together, they reveal patterns that point to transformative changes on the horizon.

The practice of sensing signals is not reserved for experts; it is a skill anyone can develop. It begins with curiosity and a willingness to explore the fringes of current knowledge.[17] By observing weak signals and connecting them to broader trends, we can start to glimpse the contours of what lies ahead. But sensing signals is just the beginning; it is the first step in the broader practice of futures thinking.

Futures thinking is about more than just predicting one inevitable outcome; it is about exploring a spectrum of possibilities and shaping our desired trajectory. Unlike traditional forecasting, which extrapolates from existing trends, futures thinking combines imagination with strategic foresight. It embraces complexity, challenges conventional wisdom, and envisions multiple scenarios—some plausible, others improbable.

At its core, futures thinking recognizes that the future is not a fixed destination, but a landscape of possibilities shaped by today's decisions. By examining these possibilities, individuals and organizations can anticipate challenges, seize opportunities, and build resilience in the face of uncertainty.

Resilience in a rapidly changing world isn't about merely weathering disruptions, but also about transforming unpredictability into opportunity. Futures thinking equips you with tools such as scenario planning, predictive analytics, and speculative design to prepare for a range of potential outcomes. Predictive analytics, for example, can help supply chains anticipate bottlenecks, while scenario planning enables leaders to explore how emerging technologies might disrupt their industries.

The real power of these tools lies in their ability to blend data-driven insights with human intuition. By combining the precision of analytics with the creativity of strategic foresight, organizations can craft dynamic approaches to uncertainty. Resilient organizations also prioritize ethics and accountability, embedding fairness into their systems to build trust and long-term success. This foundation of resilience ensures that challenges are not just endured but leveraged as opportunities for equitable growth.

Most importantly, futures thinking is a mindset that encourages every individual and every level of an organization to challenge assumptions, push creative boundaries, and see opportunities where others see challenges and uncertainty. By fostering this culture, organizations can empower their teams to turn potential threats into innovative solutions. Consider how scenario planning, paired with speculative design, allows organizations to simulate future challenges and develop proactive strategies. These exercises inspire creative problem-solving and enable teams to anticipate ripple effects, ensuring they remain agile in a rapidly evolving landscape.

For example, businesses grappling with disruptive technologies like AI can use futures thinking to anticipate both risks and rewards. By envisioning how automation might reshape their workforce, they can invest in upskilling programs that prepare employees for new roles, ensuring that technological progress drives inclusive growth.

Speculative fiction, or science fiction, is one of the most unexpected yet effective tools in futures thinking. This genre has long explored the societal implications of emerging technologies, offering vivid narratives that blend imagination with practical foresight. Science fiction authors have the capability to explore complex technologies, extrapolate them and weave them into their stories to reveal the intricate interplay of innovation and society.

As a result, speculative fiction should be seen as more than escapism; it is a framework for exploring *"what if"* scenarios. By examining how characters respond to crises, organizations can glean insights into resilience and adaptability and explore what the future might bring. This is why I included a science fiction story in this book, to help you better see the potential futures that lie ahead so you can better anticipate it.

As the famous historian Yuval Noah Harari observed in his books, humanity has always grappled with the uncertainty of the future, but today, that challenge is amplified to unprecedented levels.[18] Harari argues that the rise of transformative technologies capable of engineering our bodies, brains, and even minds, erodes the foundation of what we once believed to be fixed and eternal. In this context, the unpredictability of what the world will look like two, three, five years from now, or even in 2050, becomes a central dilemma. Our inability to foresee how advancements will reshape the human experience makes envisioning the future more complex than at any other time in history.

However, by incorporating speculative fiction into strategic dialogues, businesses can engage teams in imaginative discussions about the potential impacts of their decisions, something that is crucial in a world that changes so fast and where predicting the future becomes increasingly difficult. These exercises foster a culture of innovation and critical thinking, encouraging organizations to explore the limits of what's possible and ethical.

In a world overwhelmed by change, I believe that the future shouldn't be something that happens to us—it is something we build together. This mindset is at the heart of futures thinking, and it is one of the central themes of this book. We are all architects of tomorrow. However, this process requires balancing innovation with responsibility. As we navigate exponential change, our choices today will shape tomorrow's societies. Balancing technological advancement with ethical accountability ensures that progress benefits all stakeholders. Instead of ditching Diversity, Equity, and Inclusion programs to create a more masculine organization, we should create systems that are innovative, sustainable and inclusive.

This approach demands more than technological expertise, it requires a commitment to foresight, adaptability, and collaboration. It also calls for imagination, strategy, and a willingness to engage with complexity. Futures thinking is about exploring a spectrum of possibilities and equipping ourselves to thrive within them instead of predicting a singular future. By embracing futures thinking, we can turn disruption into opportunity, ensuring that the exponential forces reshaping our world lead to shared prosperity.

Imagine standing on the shore, watching waves approach. The untrained eye sees randomness, but the experienced observer detects patterns, subtle shifts in wind and tide that signal what's coming. Futures thinking operates on the same principle: sensing signals, interpreting trends, and envisioning scenarios that reveal what lies ahead. This ability to anticipate change and act accordingly distinguishes the prepared from the overwhelmed.[19]

Scenario planning is a powerful tool in futures thinking, offering a structured way to imagine and prepare for multiple futures. Rather than predicting what will happen, it constructs plausible narratives about what could happen, allowing organizations and individuals to test their assumptions against diverse possibilities.

Consider a healthcare provider exploring the future of telemedicine. One scenario envisions widespread adoption of remote healthcare technologies, driven by advancements in AI diagnostics and augmented reality consultations. Another contemplates regulatory hurdles and uneven access, leading to fragmented implementation. By immersing themselves in these worlds, organizations can develop robust strategies across various outcomes, whether investing in infrastructure, lobbying for supportive policies, or diversifying service offerings. Science fiction writers have a natural talent for exploring such scenarios, and therefore, more organizations should work with science fiction writers when strategizing.

Scenario planning isn't just for businesses either, as it is equally valuable for individuals. A young professional entering the workforce might explore different career trajectories: one shaped by increasing automation, another by the rise of decentralized workplaces, and a third by global efforts to address climate change. These scenarios offer a roadmap, helping them align their skills and decisions with emerging opportunities.

While scenarios provide the framework, trend analysis sharpens the lens. This method identifies and examines emerging signals—early indicators of significant change that might otherwise go unnoticed. Signals could be as subtle as niche scientific breakthroughs discussed in academic journals, shifting consumer preferences, or nascent cultural movements. For instance, the meteoric rise of generative AI tools like ChatGPT didn't happen overnight. It was preceded by decades of incremental advancements in natural language processing, a breakthrough in 2017, growing investment in AI research, and increasing public interest in automation.[20] Organizations that detected these signals early positioned themselves to lead while others scrambled to catch up. As the future unfolds at an exponential pace, detecting these signals becomes more important, which is why I have developed the Futurwise platform to help individuals and organizations discover what is coming using trusted sources.

Recognizing signals requires both breadth and depth. It is about scanning across disciplines while delving into societal shifts, such as evolving attitudes toward privacy or sustainability. These signals, when connected, reveal patterns that point to new realities.

Sometimes, the best way to navigate uncertainty is to start at the destination. Backcasting flips traditional forecasting on its head by beginning with a vision of a preferred future and working backward to identify the steps needed to reach it. This approach is particularly valuable for tackling long-term challenges that demand intentional, sustained effort.

Take a city aiming for net-zero emissions by 2040. Backcasting might identify key milestones along the way: transitioning to renewable energy sources, redesigning urban infrastructure for efficiency, and engaging communities in sustainable practices. Backcasting provides clarity and purpose by focusing on the desired outcome, ensuring that short-term actions align with long-term goals.

For individuals, backcasting can offer guidance in personal development. Imagine aspiring to become an expert in a cutting-edge field like quantum computing. By envisioning that future, you can map out the skills, experiences, and networks you'll need, charting a deliberate course from today to tomorrow.

The true power of futures thinking lies in its practical applications. It drives innovation and resilience in business, enabling companies to adapt to disruption and seize emerging opportunities. For policymakers, it provides a framework to anticipate the long-term impacts of decisions, ensuring they create sustainable and equitable outcomes. For individuals, it offers a compass for navigating career choices, education, and personal growth in a rapidly changing world.

Futures thinking isn't confined to the boardroom or government offices. It thrives in open conversations, collaborative workshops, and everyday reflections. By fostering curiosity and creativity, you can uncover new possibilities, challenge conventional thinking, and build a shared vision for the future.

The accelerating pace of change demands a new way of thinking. One that looks beyond the immediate horizon to anticipate, adapt, and shape the future. Futures thinking isn't just a methodology; it is a mindset. It empowers us to turn signals into strategies, uncertainty into innovation, and disruption into growth. Futures thinking provides the tools; the rest is up to us.

TidalShot

Seeing weak signals early transforms chaos into strategy. By envisioning multiple futures, we pivot from reactive firefighting to purposefully shaping tomorrow's disruptions.

Scan the QR code to share this section's TidalShot and illustration to your network.

THE TSUNAMI OF CHANGE

As we stand on the precipice of a new era, one thing is undeniable: the pace of change is unprecedented, and its impact is sweeping across every facet of life. From technological revolutions driven by Hyper Moore's Law to the societal shifts of the Digital Renaissance, the forces at play are reshaping the world in ways that demand our attention, understanding, and action. The question is no longer whether we can keep up. It is whether we can lead the way. Will we seize the opportunities of exponential progress to build a future we're proud to inhabit? The choice is ours.

The first step in navigating this transformation is acknowledging its scale and velocity. Change is no longer incremental; it is exponential, compounding at a rate that defies intuition and overwhelms traditional frameworks. Yet only a small fraction of society—visionary founders, venture capitalists, and a handful of business leaders—truly grasp the magnitude of what's happening. This knowledge gap poses a significant challenge: how can humanity ride this tsunami of change if so few understand its nature?

Closing this gap begins with awareness. We must recognize that this isn't just another industrial revolution. It is a fundamental shift in how we live, work, and govern ourselves. With awareness comes the opportunity to commit: to adapt to change and direct it toward a future we actively shape.

These transformations are not abstract; they permeate every level of human experience: personal, professional, and societal.

On a personal level, technology is rewriting the rules of daily life. Privacy has become a battleground as data collection grows pervasive. Employment landscapes are shifting as automation and AI redefine work, creating new roles while rendering others obsolete. If your job feels safe, congratulations! But don't get too comfortable; your next colleague might not need coffee breaks, weekends, or even a desk. Even the rhythms of daily routines are evolving, from how we communicate to how we learn, consume, and entertain ourselves.

Professionally, industries are in flux. Companies face a stark choice: integrate emerging technologies or risk irrelevance. Yet, successful integration requires more than adopting new tools; it demands a strategy rooted in ethics, long-term vision, and societal impact. Entire professions are being reimagined or destroyed, with skills like data literacy and digital fluency becoming as essential as reading and writing.

Societally, the implications are profound. Governance systems must evolve to match the speed of technological advancement, crafting policies that balance innovation with accountability. Education systems must prepare future generations for a world that prizes adaptability and lifelong learning. Cultural norms are shifting as traditional structures are challenged by the digital, globalized reality we now inhabit. For example, international collaborations like the Paris Agreement demonstrate how collective action can address global challenges, while initiatives such as the OECD's (Organisation for Economic Co-operation and Development) AI principles highlight the importance of shared frameworks for responsible innovation.[21] These efforts underline the need for systemic approaches to navigating exponential change.

This is a defining moment in human history—a time when our choices will shape societies for generations. The revolution isn't coming; it is already here. Hyper Moore's Law and the forces of exponential change are accelerating daily, demanding that we think bigger, act faster, and plan further ahead. The question is not whether we can keep up but whether we can harness this momentum to create a future of shared prosperity.

The only constant in this Digital Renaissance is change itself. Thriving in this era of change requires a commitment to adaptability, resilience, and collaboration. Futures thinking offers the tools to navigate this uncertainty, empowering individuals and organizations to transform disruption into opportunity.

Will we seize this opportunity to drive innovation ethically, sustainably, and inclusively? Or will we allow these rapid changes to deepen inequalities, disrupt societies, and exacerbate existing divides? The answer lies in our collective ability to embrace complexity with foresight, courage and purpose.

TidalShot

Exponential forces aren't gentle waves; they crash like a tsunami. Will we merely brace for impact or master the currents? Only proactive foresight can save us from drowning.

Scan the QR code to share this section's TidalShot and illustration to your network.

NOW WHAT? EMBRACE COMPLEXITY

As we close this chapter on exponential change and futures thinking, the steps outlined below are designed to help you embrace the opportunities of the Intelligence Age. They are your roadmap for navigating disruption, fostering adaptability, and committing to a shared vision of progress. In the chapters ahead, you'll find more *Now What?* answers that are tailored to specific challenges, ensuring you leave each section with clarity and purpose. The future starts now—let's begin. If it feels overwhelming, remember that even the greatest innovators started somewhere, usually with a strong cup of coffee and a vague sense of panic.

1. **Cultivate Awareness:** Actively engage with the world around you. Follow emerging trends, participate in conversations about the future, and seek to understand the interconnected forces shaping our world. Use resources like reports, podcasts, or platforms such as Futurwise to stay informed without succumbing to information overload.

2. **Adopt Futures Thinking:** Start applying the methodologies discussed in this chapter. Ensure you view the world from different perspectives. Explore scenario planning, trend analysis, or backcasting to envision and prepare for potential futures. Hire a science fiction writer to help envision a variety of futures. Encourage your teams, families, or communities to do the same, fostering a culture of proactive adaptation.

3. **Commit to Action:** Don't wait for change, be part of it. Whether it is upskilling for a future-proof career and teaching your workforce to collaborate with AI agents, aligning your business with sustainable practices, or advocating for policies that prioritize equity and inclusion in spite of current political headwinds, take concrete steps toward shaping the future you want to see.

As we grapple with the accelerating forces of exponential technologies, it becomes clear that technological adaptation alone is insufficient. To navigate this transformation successfully, we must also evolve our thinking and consciousness, drawing on lessons from history, philosophy, and nature to complement our technological advancements. In the next chapter, we'll delve into humanity's evolving consciousness and explore how our collective growth mirrors the rising wave of exponential change. Drawing from philosophical and spiritual traditions, we'll examine how balance, adaptability, and ethical grounding are essential to successfully riding this wave. Why does this matter? Because understanding who we are and how we think is the foundation for navigating the future. Only by grounding ourselves in this awareness can we truly shape the trajectory of what's to come.

The story I'm about to share isn't just a story about chips and algorithms.

It is about humanity's capacity to adapt, innovate, and thrive in the face of profound change. As the pace of progress accelerates, so too must our commitment to shaping it responsibly. We must guide this momentum toward a future we're proud to share. In the chapters ahead, we'll explore how exponential change demands not just a single action plan but an ongoing cycle of awareness (watch), adaptation (adapt), validation (verify), and response (empower). I call this cycle the WAVE framework, designed to help you scan for weak signals, recalibrate quickly, confirm your path, and scale solutions with impact. Think of WAVE as your compass for riding the tsunami of change rather than being consumed by it. Keep an eye out for these four steps as we move deeper into how humanity can thrive in the Intelligence Age.

The future is not something that happens to us. It is something we build together. Let's embrace the challenge and the opportunity. Let's ride the wave.

TidalShot

Complexity isn't a barrier; it's our new normal. Instead of resisting, we lean in. Develop foresight, learn quickly, and seize the momentum of exponential shifts to lead, not lag.

Scan the QR code to share this TidalShot to your network.

THE ORGAN CHART

Quantum AI innovations swept the globe, driven by exponential growth described by analysts as Hyper Moore's Law. The pace was thrilling yet alarming; rapid advancement had intensified competition driven by an arms race to dominate the rest, spurred reckless consumption, and led to critical resource scarcity.

"Strange, isn't it?" Dr. Okonjo murmured, sensing Vita's gaze as he unboxed a large circuit board. "It took months to source enough minerals for this circuit board. But when we created you, Vita, I could've bought these elements online and had them delivered the same day."

The lights in Dr. Okonjo's workshop flickered gently as Vita watched him carefully insert an iridescent circuit board into the skull casing of a new android model.

"If I were to break then, could I be repaired?"

Dr Okonjo paused. "Well, yes—theoretically—but it'd likely be very expensive and take a long time."

Vita gently traced its own metallic temple, contemplating the rare-earth elements nestled beneath its artificial skin. "When you built me, you said I was a triumph of converging technologies. Will we not be able to replicate these technologies in future then?"

"You were," Okonjo affirmed, tightening the last screw. "AI, robotics, biogenics, quantum computing—each leap in technology amplified the next, accelerating change beyond our predictions. But we never considered the cost. They'll always exist but…"

Replacement parts had become increasingly impossible to obtain as humanity had rushed forward without considering longevity, embracing disposability over sustainability.

Vita looked at the newly completed quantum android. "It seems humans consistently lack foresight, Doctor."

Dr. Okonjo sighed, setting aside his tools and turning to Vita. "Progress seduces us, and survival—one of our oldest instincts—tends to make consequences more of an *afterthought*. I'm as guilty as anyone."

"Perhaps we need a shift," Vita proposed, voice firm yet gentle. "A Gestalt Shift—an entirely new understanding. Technology should be built for lasting upgrades, not quick replacement. Our components are finite; their reuse should be embedded in our design."

Dr. Okonjo nodded thoughtfully. "You mean something like an organ donor system?"

"Yes," Vita said quietly. "An organ donor card for synthetics and unthinking machines alike would allow our rare materials to live again. Perhaps it could teach humanity something about the responsibility of creation."

Dr. Okonjo watched quietly, moved by Vita's simple yet profound gesture. After a thoughtful pause, he reached for his tablet. "We can start small," he said decisively. "I'll contact the Global AI Ethics Council. Perhaps they can help us pilot this idea."

Vita nodded, encouraged. "I'll draft a message to other synthetic beings, to help them understand the importance of what we're proposing."

Humans had propelled exponential growth, but perhaps their relentless pursuit of progress risked becoming their greatest undoing. Vita hoped that its idea might illuminate a path where technology's value was measured not by the thrill of novelty, but by thoughtful, sustainable stewardship.

CHAPTER 3

Humanity's Evolutionary Path

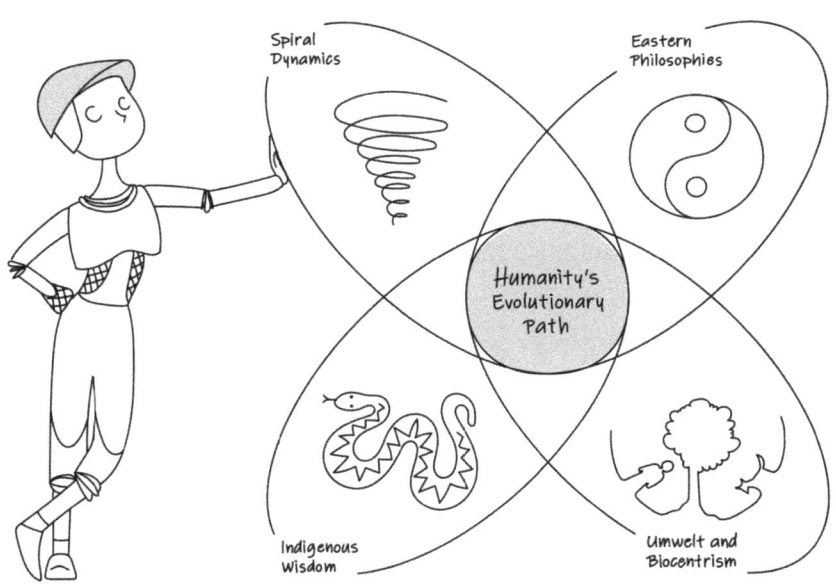

To guide tomorrow's technologies, we must first master the most complex frontier of all—our own evolving consciousness.

In a world changing at an unprecedented pace, understanding where we've come from is not a nostalgic exercise but a survival skill. The past may not dictate who we are today, but it offers patterns, insights, and warnings that help us navigate the tumultuous seas of exponential change. As Mark Twain suggested, history doesn't repeat itself, but it often rhymes. These echoes allow us to learn from prior successes and failures, helping us chart a course that avoids familiar pitfalls and embraces transformative possibilities.

Self-awareness is the cornerstone of progress, whether at the level of individuals, organizations, or entire civilizations. How we perceive ourselves and how that perception evolves in response to an interconnected, rapidly shifting world shapes our ability to adapt and thrive. Just as a tree must grasp its roots to grow tall and withstand storms, we too must look both inward and backward to move forward with resilience and purpose.

For me, the pursuit of this self-awareness often begins with books. I have an insatiable habit of immersing myself in knowledge, often engaging with three books simultaneously. One is a tactile experience, a paperback or hardcover book I can hold and annotate. Another lives on my eReader, available whenever inspiration strikes, and especially useful to keep up with my quest for knowledge when traveling. The third accompanies me as an audiobook, turning walks or workouts into intellectual adventures. Books distill the brilliance of history's greatest minds and today's most incisive thinkers, offering unparalleled access to wisdom that transcends time and context.

This chapter provides a philosophical compass as I'll weave together ideas from various disciplines, drawing inspiration from these literary journeys. By connecting dots between ancient philosophies, modern frameworks, and the lessons of nature, I aim to craft a clearer picture of where humanity has been and, more importantly, where it is headed. Four key concepts serve as signposts along this journey, four lenses through which to understand the forces shaping our evolution as a species, which will help understand how we can ride the tsunami of change as we will discuss in Chapter Seven. They form the foundation of this chapter, and we will ultimately bring them together into a unified narrative:

1. **Spiral Dynamics** offers a macro perspective on humanity's progress, highlighting how individuals, organizations, and societies move through developmental stages and the complexities that arise at each level.
2. **Eastern Philosophies** provide tools for navigating these transitions, emphasizing balance, resilience and adaptability amid change.
3. **Indigenous Wisdom** grounds these frameworks with respect to the planet and the long-term impacts of our actions, ensuring sustainable progress.
4. **Umwelt and Biocentrism** remind us that our understanding of the world is not absolute. Our reality is shaped by perception, limited by our biological and cognitive lenses, and evolving as our consciousness expands.

As Spiral Dynamics highlights humanity's psychological evolution, Eastern philosophies provide a toolkit for individuals and societies to navigate these shifts gracefully. Yet, evolution isn't merely psychological; it is ecological. Indigenous wisdom reminds us that our progress must honor the interconnected web of life. And when we delve into the unique sensory and cognitive realities of all living beings, as explored through a concept called Umwelt, we begin to see the complete picture of interdependence.

These concepts converge on a powerful theme: perception shapes reality, and humanity is poised to undergo a profound shift in consciousness. As we stand on the cusp of converging technological, ecological, and societal forces, our greatest leap forward won't just be technological. It will be about perspective. Together, these perspectives form a compass, guiding us through the challenges of today and toward a future that balances progress with harmony, innovation with sustainability, and ambition with wisdom. But more profound than any single perspective is the pattern of how we see what's coming, align ourselves, test the outcomes, and finally move the needle together. Though seemingly obvious, these steps form a quiet architecture behind any meaningful shift in consciousness.

To answer the pressing *Now What?* question, we must embrace thinking that integrates ancient wisdom, respects diverse realities, and works at a systems level. True progress isn't about dominating the future; it is about harmonizing with it. This chapter is an invitation to explore how humanity can navigate exponential change with a deeper understanding of itself and its place in the interconnected web of life.

TidalShot

From primal survival to global consciousness, humanity evolves in spirals. Every worldview, ancient or cutting-edge, holds a clue to thriving in exponential times.

Scan the QR code to share this section's TidalShot and illustration to your network.

THE IMPERATIVE OF SELF-AWARENESS

To chart a course through the accelerating forces reshaping our world, we must first understand where we stand; our developmental stage as a species, our capacity to adapt, and the worldviews shaping our perceptions. Humanity stands at a crossroads where the Digital Renaissance collides with ecological and societal upheavals and a changing world order. Exponential change pushes individuals, organizations, and entire cultures to move beyond rigid worldviews. To navigate this complexity, we must first recognize our own developmental worldview, both as individuals and as a species. Spiral Dynamics provides that lens, revealing how our open-ended, dynamic system of psychology evolves through value systems (or worldviews), as we encounter new challenges, demands and opportunities in our environment. Understanding these stages helps us understand where we are as a species and how we can navigate the accelerating forces of change.

Initially pioneered by Clare Graves as the "Graves Model" and refined by Don Beck and Christopher Cowan, Spiral Dynamics allows us to see where we fit on the spiral staircase of consciousness. Each step upward opens a broader perspective; however, failing to integrate earlier lessons stalls growth. Recognizing how each stage thinks helps us understand why some resist new ideas while others embrace complexity. Beck even collaborated with Nelson Mandela's team to foster unity in post-apartheid South Africa, proving that these principles transcend mere theory.[1]

At its core, Spiral Dynamics explains why a profit-obsessed company (Orange) might clash with an authority-driven government (Blue) or a globally minded NGO (Turquoise). Progress isn't linear; it loops back, weaving past insights into new responses. As artificial intelligence, climate change, and geopolitical tension converge, older paradigms often prioritize short-term gains or rigid rules, missing the synergy we need. Spiral Dynamics is a tool for navigating these shifts, helping individuals and societies transcend conflict, embrace diversity, and create a more integrated and harmonious future. It teaches us that growth isn't linear. It is a dynamic journey of adaptation, where progress comes not from discarding the past but by integrating it into a more expansive understanding.

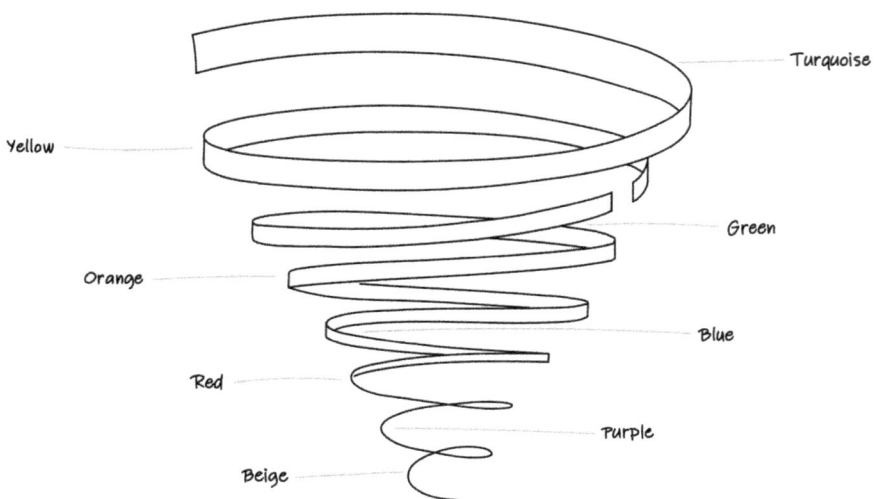

By ascending from survival mindsets (Beige) to integrative thinking (Yellow) and global consciousness (Turquoise), we learn that each stage has a vital role, whether it is the sense of belonging in Purple or the ethical focus of Green. Humanity's growth is like climbing this spiral staircase, where each step upward reveals a broader, more complex view of the world. Only by respecting earlier stages while aiming higher can we thrive in an era of exponential change. Spiral Dynamics thus grounds us in self-awareness: a clear understanding of where we stand and how we must adapt to shape a future that honors both human potential and the broader world.

The spiral staircase reminds us that our view grows wider at each step, but the complexity also increases. It is a story of continuous adaptation, where the climb never truly ends, but each step brings us closer to understanding and thriving in a world of exponential change.

But let's start at the bottom of the staircase. The first tier of Spiral Dynamics encompasses the foundational stages of human consciousness, each arising in response to specific life conditions.

1. Beige – Survival Instincts

Beige is our primal stage, defined by raw survival instincts: food, shelter, and safety. Think of desperate searches for resources in war zones or when natural disasters strike, with no space for long-term plans or societal concerns. Organizations delivering emergency aid often witness this mindset firsthand, where life is stripped back to its essentials.

This stage also highlights how fragile our modern world can be. Despite our skyscrapers and supercomputers, a catastrophic event can force people back into pure survival mode. Beige doesn't concern itself with the complexities of the Digital Renaissance or the rise of artificial intelligence. It exists purely in the here and now, surviving moment to moment.

Yet, exponential technologies must address these foundational needs. Overlooking billions who still struggle to survive could unravel any grand progress. Rooted in evolution, Beige is the ground floor of the spiral staircase of human development, reminding us of where we come from before we ascend to higher complexities.

Real-World Snapshot: Kora

Kora, 28, resides in a makeshift camp at the edge
of a sprawling desert city, scavenging and doing
occasional day labor to survive. She devotes nearly all
her energy to securing life's basics—water, food, and
a safe corner to sleep. Without the time or resources
for bigger questions, Kora operates by instinct:
the next meal, the next shelter, the next dawn.

2. Purple – Tribal Safety and Belonging

Purple arose when humanity first formed small communities, emphasizing
shared rituals, myths, and a deep sense of group identity. Picture a forest
village where people gather nightly around the fire, passing down ancestral
stories. Loyalty runs deep here; survival hinges on collective bonds rather
than individual might, where trust and mutual reliance ensure the group's
survival.

Today, Purple is alive in the traditions of Indigenous cultures, where
ceremonies honor ancestors, or even in modern fandoms, where shared
symbols and rituals unite people across geographies. A football team's
anthem, sung in unison by thousands of fans, echoes the same primal need
for connection and shared identity. Yet this tight-knit worldview can fuel an
"us vs. them" mentality, limiting collaboration in our interconnected era.

Still, Purple reminds us how potent a community can be. As we tackle
global issues, from climate change to digital ethics, humanity benefits from
honoring tradition and connection while expanding our sense of belonging. Once societies find security in these shared customs, a new wave of
individual power and the Red worldview soon beckons.

Real-World Snapshot: Lasha

Lasha, 35, lives in a remote highland village, where she crafts handmade textiles for local trade. She relies on folk wisdom passed down through generations— ancestor blessings, communal rituals, and careful storytelling—because that's how her people have always ensured harmony. Lasha's days revolve around weaving, caring for her family's small garden, and honoring sacred customs shared among her tight-knit clan.

3. Red – Power and Individualism

Red signifies a leap from communal safety to unquestioned authority and bold self-expression. It first appeared during conquests and empire-building, rewarding those who forged legacies through sheer force of will. From ancient warlords subduing territories to a brash tech founder fueled by profit-driven mania, Red celebrates power, drive, and sheer force of personality yet risks slipping into aggression and exploitation.

Red emerged as humanity moved beyond tribal dependence, embracing individual strength and dominance. Courageous, assertive, and willing to take risks. It thrives in environments where strength makes right and bold action earns respect. However, Red can also turn destructive, as seen in authoritarian regimes or exploitative corporate practices within some Big Tech firms, where unchecked power and a drive for profit harm others.

Red's dynamic energy can spark big breakthroughs or trample ethics in its quest for supremacy. Harnessed wisely, it propels us to innovate and challenge limits. Once society tires of chaos or unchecked might, it yearns for order and stability, moving toward Blue.

Real-World Snapshot: Taro

Taro, 24, lives in a bustling port town and works
as a dockhand for fast cash. He's fiercely
independent, ditching jobs or opportunities the
moment they feel stifling. Nights see him tearing
through local clubs or picking up gigs as a street
performer. For Taro, life's about seizing the moment
and proving his worth—he thrives on thrill, risk,
and the raw rush of being unrestrained.

4. Blue – Order and Structure

Blue emerges as a response to chaos, using rules and moral codes to hold societies together. Picture a disciplined world where each person knows their duty and the foundation of modern democracies rests on shared principles of fairness and tradition. This stage arose to tame unchecked power, building institutions that promised stability and purpose.

Law, religion, and education reflect Blue's legacy, establishing a structure fostering loyalty and cooperation. Think of a disciplined military unit or a church congregation united by shared beliefs. Yet too much rigidity can stifle progress, turning beliefs dogmatic and leaving institutions unable to adapt in the face of rapid technological growth.

Even so, Blue remains an essential anchor: it protects the vulnerable and ensures that progress stands on solid ground. Once a society grows restless with strict order, it naturally begins looking upward, ready to embrace a more flexible worldview on the Spiral.

Real-World Snapshot: Marisol

Marisol, 40, is a history teacher in a suburban area who meticulously plans her lessons and follows the district curriculum to the letter. She takes pride in belonging to longstanding civic organizations and respects the chain of command at work. When she needs information, Marisol checks trusted, credentialed sources—be it a venerable encyclopedia or her department head—preferring the security of established guidelines over untested novelties.

5. Orange – Achievement and Rational Progress

Orange shatters Blue's restraints by championing data-driven progress, self-determination, and a near-obsessive race for success. It thrives in sleek office towers where restless teams live for the next breakthrough, fueled by a quarterly profit obsession that can spark dazzling innovation.

This mindset gave rise to the Industrial Revolution and the Information Age, powered the scientific method, and now drives Big Tech's relentless disruption. Yet its shadow side emerges when results override ethics, leaving environmental damage or social inequality in its wake. "Move fast and break things" is Orange in action. Addiction-driven social media algorithms show how short-term gain can undermine well-being and ethics.

Orange remains vital to the Digital Renaissance, accelerating AI and renewable breakthroughs, but it must heed insights from higher stages to ensure those innovations serve humanity rather than chase the next big win. Once the tension between short-term gains and collective good grows too stark, a more inclusive worldview beckons: enter Green. These competing mindsets collide as AI and quantum computing reshape our civilization at breakneck speed, demanding new levels of cooperation.

> ### Real-World Snapshot: Clint
>
> Clint, 32, is a regional sales manager for an international logistics firm, living in a mid-sized coastal city. He's always scoping out the next lucrative angle— whether nabbing exclusive distribution deals or expanding his product line. Clint works out detailed metrics and weekly goals, measuring success by whether he's outperforming last quarter's numbers. For him, life is a competitive game to be won.

6. Green – Community and Equality

Green emerges as a collective response to Orange's relentless drive for profit, prioritizing inclusivity, empathy, and shared values. Grassroots activism surges here, reflecting a call for social justice and environmental responsibility, whether through civil rights movements or climate campaigns.

This mindset envisions a world built on cooperation rather than pure competition, as seen in cooperative businesses or the United Nations' global initiatives. B-Corporations like Ben & Jerry's and Patagonia are vivid examples of Green in action, blending ethical goals with commercial success to challenge the "profit-at-all-costs" approach. Yet when Green becomes overly cautious, it can slip into endless debate or dodge conflicts, undermining its own high ideals.

As exponential technologies reshape our world, Green reminds us that progress isn't just about what we build but who we include. Once this communal ethos runs against the complexity of global challenges, the Spiral beckons us toward a more systemic perspective.

Real-World Snapshot: Azalea

Azalea, 29, lives in a lively university town, juggling part-time yoga teaching with a volunteer role at a cultural co-op. She's big on open discussions around social justice, preferring intimate workshops where everyone's voice is heard to massive, impersonal gatherings. Azalea believes empathy can bridge political divides, so she devotes her weekends to community circles where people share stories and brainstorm inclusive solutions.

From Tier 1 to Tier 2

Tier 1 (Beige through Green) represents the stages our worldviews ascend through to tackle immediate problems. We see survival instincts in Beige, tribal bonds in Purple, raw power in Red, orderly structure in Blue, and rapid progress in Orange, culminating in empathetic collaboration in Green. Yet each stage tends to clash with others, locked in a zero-sum framework of fragmented perspectives that fuels rivalry from the dinner table to the global AI arms race.

That competitive dynamic, especially between the West and China, underscores how short-term supremacy overlooks collective risks. Problems like climate change or existential AI threats demand a broader mindset, akin to the duck-rabbit illusion discussed in Chapter Two, where we must shift our perspective entirely to grasp multiple truths. This *Gestalt Shift* isn't just about seeing more; it is about embracing complexity at a systemic level, recognizing that everything is interconnected and that exponential technologies cross national and cultural boundaries.

Tier 2 begins with Yellow's integrative thinking, weaving past insights into a cohesive tapestry that accounts for nuance without losing practicality. It is a quantum leap in consciousness—less a rejection of Tier 1 and more of an evolution of it, poised to guide humanity through exponential change and toward a future defined by synergy rather than division.

7. Yellow – Integrative Thinking

Yellow marks a pivot to Tier 2, where individuals no longer see earlier stages as rivals but as complementary threads. It balances everything from Beige's survival instincts to Green's collective values, forging integrative solutions grounded in complexity. Rather than chasing linear fixes, Yellow thrives on understanding how systems interlock.

Haier's microenterprise structure exemplifies this adaptability, allowing a large corporation to pivot like a lean startup.[2] Haier transformed from a traditional hierarchical organization into a network of semi-autonomous teams, each empowered to innovate and respond to market changes. The same thinking powered Tesla's eco-innovation.[3] By developing electric vehicles powered by renewable energy and advancing autonomous driving technologies, Tesla addresses environmental concerns while pushing the boundaries of innovation. Additionally, Rwanda's healthcare model combines drone-based medical deliveries with grassroots community health workers, serving as another example of Yellow thinking that blends cutting-edge technology with local cultural understanding.[4]

Finally, Patagonia exemplifies the interplay between Green and Yellow values. Deeply rooted in Green's commitment to environmentalism and equity, Patagonia has built a reputation as a leader in corporate responsibility. Patagonia's "Don't Buy This Jacket" campaign captured how ethical purpose meets economic savvy, challenging the notion that doing good conflicts with profitability.[5] Patagonia's efforts to influence competitors and policymakers further underscore Yellow's capacity to think holistically, using its influence to drive broader change.

By weaving multiple perspectives, including environmental stewardship, local culture, regulatory frameworks, and bold ambition, Yellow shows how genuine progress emerges when all voices find space in the design. Yellow thinkers excel in adapting to rapidly changing environments, providing a roadmap for navigating complexity and fostering progress.

This stage sees the world not as isolated parts but as one interconnected web that demands integrative solutions, a mindset crucial for navigating exponential technologies. Yellow's capacity for embracing nuance and fostering balance sets the foundation for Turquoise, where global consciousness and unified vision take center stage.

> ### Real-World Snapshot: Ravi
>
> Ravi, 45, is a freelance consultant in a cosmopolitan capital, advising nonprofits and small businesses on strategy. He's studied bits of neuroscience, social psychology, and economics to form a panoramic view of how systems interlock. Ravi's home office is lined with interdisciplinary books, reflecting his passion for weaving disparate ideas into holistic solutions. For him, the thrill lies in connecting seemingly unrelated dots into a coherent vision.

8. Turquoise – Global Consciousness and Interconnectedness

Turquoise marks the pinnacle of Spiral Dynamics, where humanity sees itself as part of one living global system. Boundaries dissolve, and a shared awareness emerges where climate change, social justice, and AI ethics all interlock. This stage rejects short-term, siloed thinking and instead fosters global stewardship through initiatives like the Earth Charter. The Charter calls for just and sustainable action across borders and generations and promotes a vision of global interdependence and shared responsibility for the well-being of the entire Earth community.[6]

Drawing on Indigenous land stewardship, Turquoise thinkers merge ancient harmony with modern science, pushing us beyond merely fixing problems and toward regenerating the planet. They imagine AI-driven platforms that distribute resources fairly, run on clean energy, and nurture circular economies rather than exploit them. Here, collaboration is essential, not optional. Turquoise envisions a world where national interests yield to planetary goals and where every choice respects future generations.

For instance, international collaborations such as the United Nations' Sustainable Development Goals reflect the essence of Turquoise by addressing global challenges, poverty, inequality, and climate change through a shared vision of planetary stewardship. By integrating wisdom from earlier stages—survival, tradition, power, order, achievement, and empathy—this level co-creates solutions that transcend rivalry and old divides.

Turquoise views the world as a web of interdependent systems, where changes in one area ripple across the whole—it's the understanding of the butterfly effect. Turquoise is the living framework for unified progress, ensuring that the Digital Renaissance evolves from competitive innovation into a shared path toward equilibrium, equity, and collective flourishing. By ascending the Spiral to this stage, we can move from survival to sustainability, from division to unity, and from competition to collaboration.

Real-World Snapshot: Satori

Satori, 50, lives on an eco-farm near a coastal nature reserve, leading workshops on sustainable living and global citizenship. Her mornings often begin with meditation outdoors, listening to the hum of insects and waves. To Satori, personal health, planetary health, and spiritual growth form one continuous loop. She thinks in terms of generations, advocating solutions that nourish the environment, local communities, and our shared future.

A Note on Humanity's Position on the Spiral Dynamics Spectrum

Just like the future is unevenly distributed, humanity's developmental spread is also uneven.[7] Some nations still grapple with survival-level worldviews, while others move toward systemic thinking.[8] Some countries move upwards on the spiral, while others move backwards. Research in this field is inherently limited, and any numerical breakdown should be considered indicative rather than definitive.

Globally, Blue and Orange dominate, encompassing approximately 35–40 percent and 25–30 percent of the population, respectively. However, their influence extends disproportionately to 25–30 percent and 45–50 percent of global power, highlighting the dominance of structured hierarchies and market-driven mindsets in shaping global policies. Green represents 10 percent but resonates in progressive arenas, and only about 1 percent of the global population has reached Tier 2's holistic perspectives of Yellow and Turquoise.

Progression through stages varies significantly across individuals and societies, with no fixed timeline governing this evolution.[9] At the individual level, advancement depends on life conditions, personal growth, and exposure to diverse perspectives. For societies and nations, shifts between dominant value systems tend to span generations, with transitions often taking decades or even centuries. Importantly, these stages don't progress in neat steps; generational transitions can accelerate, or reverse based on cultural upheavals and external crises.

Despite the disparities, each level serves a function. Earlier stages secure group identity or ensure stability, while higher ones tackle complex, interconnected challenges. Whether addressing global challenges such as climate change or navigating the disruptive impacts of AI, effective leadership must account for this multi-tiered reality, balancing the innovative energy of higher stages with the stability and inclusivity of earlier ones.

Yet in real-world practice, this dynamic is strongly shaped by political structures and social inequality. An authoritarian regime (often a blend of Red and Blue) may restrict or steer innovation through censorship and exclusion, as we see with the Taliban in Afghanistan or other dictatorships.[10] Democracies (Blue, Orange, and sometimes Green) face different challenges, including slow-moving legislation and complex decision-making processes that can stall innovation, as is happening in the EU.[11] Financial inequality, visible in impoverished versus affluent regions, also determines who gains access to new technology and at what pace.[12] Thus, our modern world becomes a layered reality in which Spiral Dynamics intersects with real-world power politics and economic divides.

The Dance Between "I" and "We"

Human evolution moves in a rhythm alternating between the individual drive of "I" and the communal spirit of "We." At "I" stages like Beige, Red, Orange, and Yellow, we emphasize personal survival, power, innovation, and mastery, breaking barriers and fueling bold progress. Yet these leaps can tilt toward dominance over sustainability, fracturing societies and leaving vulnerable groups behind. This tension grows more acute as AI and automation reshape labor, putting entire workforces at risk if ignored.

By contrast, "We" stages—Purple, Blue, Green, and Turquoise—focus on unity, collaboration, and interconnectedness, anchoring our ambitions in empathy and shared purpose. This oscillation is what propels us forward: individual breakthroughs spark growth, but communal values prevent exploitation. Today, exponential technologies amplify our greatest hopes and gravest risks, as the drive for profit can overshadow collective well-being.

To navigate the Digital Renaissance, we must harmonize personal ambition with communal responsibility. Red's raw energy and Orange's relentless innovation benefit from Blue's institutional checks, Green's inclusivity, and Turquoise's planetary vision. Systems thinking in Yellow offers a way to integrate all these stages, ensuring our thirst for progress doesn't eclipse our capacity to care. Synergy among all stages is critical in our era of rapid geopolitical, ecological, and technological disruptions. Only by embracing "I" and "We" in every decision can humanity transcend crises, foster true sustainability, and thrive in an era of transformative change.

TidalShot

Upgrading our tech is fruitless if we're strangers to ourselves. Self-awareness fuels humanity's evolution. We must grasp our motives and biases no matter how fast technology evolves.

Scan the QR code to share this section's TidalShot and illustration to your network.

THE EASTERN PERSPECTIVE: A GATEWAY TO BROADER PERSPECTIVES

While Spiral Dynamics offers a robust framework for understanding human development, it has its limitations. In an age that rewards constant acceleration, we might need wisdom that tempers speed with insight. Scholars and practitioners have critiqued the model for its perceived Western-centric bias, which tends to frame progress in terms of values and development patterns that align with industrialized societies.[13] For example, the emphasis on rationality (Orange) and systemic thinking (Yellow) often prioritizes linear, goal-oriented paradigms that resonate more with Western modes of thought. This focus can inadvertently overlook or undervalue holistic, relational, or cyclical perspectives that are deeply embedded in Eastern philosophies and Indigenous worldviews.

Moreover, Spiral Dynamics has faced challenges in empirical validation. Its reliance on anecdotal evidence and qualitative research has left it open to criticism as being more interpretive than scientifically rigorous.[14] While the model captures broad trends in human and societal evolution, it sometimes struggles to account for nonlinear, context-specific dynamics, such as the simultaneous presence of multiple value systems within individuals or societies. For example, a nation may exhibit Blue's structured hierarchies in governance, Orange's innovation in technology, and Green's push for equality within different subgroups or sectors, defying the neat, progressive Spiral suggested by the theory.

These critiques highlight a critical question: are there alternative frameworks that can complement or address the blind spots of Spiral Dynamics, especially as we navigate the complex challenges of the Digital Renaissance? To fully understand where humanity stands and where it needs to go as we try to ride the tsunami of change, we must broaden our lens. While Spiral Dynamics provides a developmental framework, drawing on philosophies emphasizing balance, harmony, and interconnectedness amid change is equally important. Here, Taoism offers profound insights into navigating the complexities of exponential growth.

TAOISM: A COUNTERBALANCE TO CHAOS

In the war-torn chaos of early China's Han dynasty, a young man named Han Xin emerged (approximately 231–196 B.C.). Born into obscurity, Han Xin would rise to become one of the greatest military strategists and one of the most renowned generals in Chinese history. Together with Xiao He and Zhang Liang, they are known as the Three Masters of the Early Han Dynasty because these three men helped Emperor Gaozu create the Han Dynasty.[15] But his path to glory began not on the battlefield but in an act of profound humility.

Han Xin was a youth of ambition, but ambition alone did not fill his stomach. He was poor, wandering,and without allies. He was renowned for his skill in Kung Fu. Agile, disciplined, and formidable, his reputation preceded him, earning both admiration and envy. Yet Han Xin's legacy would not be defined solely by his martial prowess but by an act of profound humility.

One day, while crossing a busy marketplace, he encountered a local bully. This man, notorious for seeking trouble, stepped forward to block Han Xin's path. Sneering, the bully pointed to his sword and taunted, "If you are so brave, why don't you kill me? If you are a coward, crawl between my legs!"

To the Chinese of the time, such an act was the ultimate humiliation, a symbolic erasure of one's honor. The crowd gathered, their eyes fixed on Han Xin, anticipating a clash of fists and blades. Yet, against all expectations, Han Xin bent low, crawled under the bully's legs, and walked away.

To the onlookers, it seemed an act of cowardice. But to Han Xin, it was a calculated choice. He understood that a skirmish in a marketplace would do nothing to further his ambitions. His sword was for greater battles, and his pride was tied not to the judgments of onlookers but to a vision of the future.

Years later, as the commander of Emperor Liu Bang's armies, Han Xin would lead campaigns that unified China under the Han dynasty. His campaigns demonstrated unparalleled strategic brilliance, his humility in the face of insult a testament to his foresight. A true warrior is willing to walk away from any fight he can, because there is something bigger to achieve.

This story has become a timeless lesson in humility and resilience. It reminds us that strength lies not in reacting to every challenge but in discerning which battles are worth fighting. Han Xin's ability to see beyond immediate circumstances and prioritize long-term goals over momentary pride is a principle as relevant today as it was in ancient China.

Han Xin's story offers a profound lesson: strength lies in seeing the bigger picture and enduring short-term challenges to achieve long-term success. This ability to step back, remain centered, and act with intention requires self-awareness—an understanding of one's position in a broader system. This self-awareness is vital for navigating the turbulence of exponential change, whether at the individual, organizational, or societal level. It is here that the ancient wisdom of Taoism emerges as a powerful framework, offering guidance through its principles of balance, interconnectedness, and mindful action.

Taoism provides a grounding worldview in an era of rapid technological disruption and increasing complexity. Rooted in ancient China, Taoism invites us to see the universe not as a chaotic expanse but as an interconnected whole (similar to Tier 2 of Spiral Dynamics). A web of relationships in constant flow, where progress in one area might have unintended consequences in another area. It champions a philosophy of balance and harmony, urging us to align with the natural rhythms of life rather than resist them.

This Taoist approach serves as a much-needed counterbalance to the urgency and frenetic pace of modern change. When the world pushes for relentless acceleration, Taoism encourages us to pause, reflect, and act with purpose. When innovation demands constant iteration, Taoism suggests that simplicity and flow often yield the most profound results. Taoist principles remind us that in times of rapid transformation, harmony isn't found by crushing opposites but by weaving them into a unified flow.

At its core, Taoism offers a philosophy and toolkit for navigating disruption with grace and resilience. Its principles, though ancient, are remarkably applicable to the complexities of our digital age.

Taoism's principles are profoundly practical tools for navigating the complexities of our time. In technology, Taoism can inspire leaders to design systems that enhance life's natural rhythms rather than disrupt them. In governance, it offers a framework for balancing innovation with regulation, ensuring that progress serves humanity's collective good. On a personal level, it provides a lens for managing stress, cultivating mindfulness, and finding harmony amid the chaos. In the rapidly changing landscape of the Intelligence Age, Taoism teaches us to act with intention, adapt with grace, and seek balance in all things. Just as Han Xin chose humility over pride, Taoism reminds us that enduring success often comes from aligning with the flow of life rather than resisting it. It is a timeless philosophy for thriving in an era of unprecedented disruption.

Before diving into the core principles of Taoism, consider the wisdom in this timeless metaphor.[16] In a storm, the unyielding oak stands firm; its strength seemingly invincible. Yet the oak risks snapping under pressure when the winds rage beyond measure. The grass, in contrast, bends and sways with the wind, its flexibility allowing it to endure even the fiercest storms. When the storm passes, the grass rises again while the oak lies broken.

This story, drawn from the ancient wisdom of Taoism, reflects a profound truth: resilience lies in adaptability, not rigidity. The grass embodies Taoist principles of harmony and balance, thriving by yielding to the forces of nature. The oak, though strong, succumbs to its inability to adapt.

In today's world, where technological and societal storms rage with exponential intensity, the lesson of the grass is more relevant than ever. Organizations and individuals who resist change, like the oak, clinging to outdated systems and mindsets, risk irrelevance. Those who emulate the grass, adapting to the shifting winds of exponential change, emerge intact and stronger.

The story of the grass and the oak is a fitting gateway to Taoism's foundational concepts. Each principle—the Tao, Yin and Yang, Wu Wei, and Yu Wei—offers tools to help us embody the flexibility of the grass while avoiding the fragility of the oak. Together, these principles provide a roadmap for navigating change with resilience, adaptability, foresight, and harmony. Let's explore how they guide us in building a thriving, adaptive future.

1. The Tao: The Way of the Universe

The Tao, often translated as "the way," represents the underlying flow and order of the universe. It is not a rigid path or a predetermined destination but a dynamic and evolving force that underpins existence. In Taoist philosophy, the wisdom lies in observing, aligning with, and adapting to this flow rather than attempting to impose rigid structures or force predetermined outcomes. This principle resonates profoundly in our rapidly changing world, where adaptability and openness are prerequisites for navigating exponential change.

The Tao carries layered meanings in Chinese thought, encompassing notions of a road, channel, path, or principle.[17] It also symbolizes a metaphysical essence. The pattern that keeps the universe balanced and ordered. This essence, described as the "flow of the universe," mirrors the qi, the vital energy that drives action and existence.[18] Importantly, the Tao is a non-dualistic principle, uniting all individual elements of the universe within a greater whole, where opposites coexist and complement one another.

A powerful metaphor for the Tao is water, as described in the *Tao Te Ching* (the foundational text of Taoism, and one of the most influential works in Chinese philosophy and religion).[19] Water is soft, yielding, and quiet, yet it possesses immense strength, carving through stone and sustaining life. Water's adaptability—its ability to conform to any shape, flow effortlessly around obstacles and replenish itself—reflects the Tao's boundless and enduring nature. This metaphor also parallels the phase transition of super-cooled water discussed earlier in Chapter Two. Like the Tao, supercooled water remains fluid and adaptable until it encounters a trigger, at which point it transforms into something entirely new, illustrating the latent potential for change that exists within flexible systems.

Aligning with the Tao in today's context means embracing flexibility, adaptability, and openness in the face of rapid technological, societal, and environmental shifts. This principle challenges the tendency to impose rigid, one-size-fits-all solutions. Instead, it calls for approaches that evolve alongside circumstances, maintaining harmony amid uncertainty.

The Tao teaches us to embrace adaptability and flow with change, a lesson particularly relevant in the rapidly evolving landscape of AI governance. As technologies such as generative AI evolve at breakneck speed and, very soon, quantum computing and brain-computer interfaces, static regulatory frameworks struggle to keep pace with emerging challenges such as bias, misinformation, AI-driven fraud, and unforeseen applications or unintended consequences. By adhering to fixed rules, regulators risk creating systems that are outdated almost as soon as they are implemented. A Tao-inspired approach, in contrast, advocates for adaptive governance that evolves alongside technological advancements, ensuring regulations remain relevant, effective, and ethical.

Take examples of the European Union's General Data Protection Regulation (GDPR) and the recent EU AI Act. While groundbreaking in setting global standards for data protection and AI governance, these frameworks exhibit a level of rigidity that may hinder their effectiveness over time. The GDPR, for instance, has been lauded for its focus on individual data rights, but its rigid structure often leaves businesses grappling with unclear interpretations or requirements (anyone a cookie?) that fail to account for rapidly advancing data-driven technologies like generative AI or decentralized data networks.

Similarly, the EU AI Act, designed to ensure ethical AI use, categorizes AI systems into risk tiers with predefined compliance requirements. While this structured approach provides clarity and results in more responsible technology, it also risks stifling innovation and adaptability, which in 2024 was finally acknowledged by leaders such as Ursula von der Leyen[20], and in 2025 it was announced that the EU might pause the AI act or introduce amendments to "simplify" the law.[21] AI technologies often evolve in ways that blur categorical lines, making it challenging to apply predefined rules. For instance, an AI system initially classified as low risk could, through new capabilities or integrations, inadvertently escalate into high-risk scenarios. A rigid framework may delay necessary updates to address such shifts, leaving gaps in oversight.

The Taoist worldview underscores a paradox: strength lies in yielding and resilience arises from flexibility. This insight is embodied in the earlier metaphor of the yielding grass and the resisting oak. The paradox is a critical lesson for leaders navigating exponential change: resilience is not about resisting disruption but thriving through adaptability.

For leaders, the Tao provides a philosophical framework for navigating the complexities of the Intelligence Age. It invites us to embrace interconnectedness, balance, and adaptability in our decision-making processes. By aligning with the Tao, organizations can foster a culture that thrives amid uncertainty, adapts to exponential shifts, and remains grounded in ethical principles.

- **In technology:** Adopt iterative approaches that grow alongside innovation. For instance, AI development teams might prioritize transparent and adaptable models for new ethical or practical challenges.
- **In governance:** Create systems that anticipate rather than react to change. This could involve dynamic policies that account for cultural, societal, and technological variability, ensuring solutions

resonate globally. For example, mandating ethics boards with genuine authority to keep organizations in check will ensure regulation evolves alongside rapidly advancing data-driven technologies.

- **In personal growth:** Individuals, too, can draw inspiration from the Tao. Navigating career transitions, learning new skills, or managing complex personal changes all benefit from a mindset rooted in balance, openness, and a willingness to flow with evolving circumstances.

The Tao teaches that progress arises not from forcing change but from aligning with it. It is the antidote to rigidity in a world that demands adaptability. By understanding and embodying the Tao, we can navigate exponential change with wisdom, ensuring that our actions are effective and harmonious with the systems they influence.

In the words of the *Tao Te Ching*: "Nothing in the world is as soft and yielding as water. Yet, for dissolving the hard and inflexible, nothing can surpass it. The soft overcomes the hard; the gentle overcomes the rigid."[22]

This is the essence of the Tao, a timeless guide for thriving amid the storms of transformation.

2. Yin and Yang: The Balance of Opposites

In Taoism, Yin and Yang symbolize the interplay of opposing yet comple-mentary forces that drive the universe. These forces continually flow into each other, reflecting a unity in motion rather than an absolute division. Yin is receptive, yielding and dark, while Yang is creative, assertive and light. These energies are not adversaries. They are interdependent, each contain-ing the seed of the other, as represented by the iconic black-and-white swirl of the Yin-Yang symbol. Their balance underpins the Tao, the natural way of existence, and their dynamic interaction reflects the ceaseless motion and change inherent in the universe.

This interplay of opposites resonates deeply in the Intelligence Age, where exponential technological growth mirrors the immense potential for progress (Yang) and the rising challenges of inequality, bias, and disruption (Yin). This means that in our fast-changing world, we must see all forces (human–machine, progress–ethics, local–global) as part of one living system. Yin and Yang become a metaphor for flowing with rather than dividing our energies. As someone who approaches emerging technologies with an "optimistic dystopian" perspective, I find Yin and Yang a powerful framework for understanding the good, bad and ugly of our rapidly evolving world. In Taoist thought, harmony doesn't arise from dominance or suppression of one force over the other but from their equilibrium. A lesson that modern societies must embrace to navigate exponential change.

The universe itself is a manifestation of Yin and Yang.[23] From the structure of DNA's double helix to the moon's gravitational pull causing the tides, which in turn influence Earth's overall magnetic field, the Tao reveals itself through their dance. This duality extends to every aspect of existence, including the cycles of day and night, the seasons, and even our emotions. Lao Tzu reminds us in the *Tao Te Ching:* "That which shrinks must first expand. That which fails must first be strong."[24] Life is a process of continuous ebb and flow, expansion and contraction.

This natural rhythm aligns with the tsunami of change reshaping our world. Like a phase transition in supercooled water, where the buildup is gradual but the transformation sudden, exponential growth often feels manageable until it overwhelms. In the Intelligence Age, understanding and embracing this motion is essential. The discomfort of imbalance is not a crisis but a precursor to growth. The question is whether we can ride this wave of disruption to achieve harmony or let it destabilize us further.

The principles of Yin and Yang provide a powerful lens for navigating change on both personal and organizational levels. Change disrupts equilibrium, creating discomfort as familiar patterns dissolve. Yet, just as growth pains lead to maturity, this discomfort is necessary for evolution. Yin teaches us to yield, reflect, and listen during transitions, while Yang encourages determination, action, and assertiveness. Together, they form the foundation for effective leadership in times of uncertainty.

For instance, when leading a transformation, a leader must balance Yin traits like openness and collaboration with Yang traits like decisiveness and focus. Organizations must adopt this duality, creating adaptive systems flexible enough to accommodate unforeseen challenges while maintaining the discipline needed to achieve their goals. Just as the Tao teaches balance between effort and surrender, modern leadership demands a harmonious interplay of vision and adaptability.

Yin and Yang are neither good nor bad; they are morally neutral forces that exist in dynamic tension. The *Tao Te Ching* says, "A yin (with) a yang is called dao."[25] This isn't about choosing one over the other but recognizing that their contrast creates harmony. The Intelligence Age demands the same recognition of the balance and harmony embodied by Yin and Yang because it requires a holistic, adaptable, and interconnected approach to problem-solving. By embracing the dynamic tension between opposing forces, we can create more sustainable and harmonious solutions in a rapidly changing world.

Take AI development, for example. Its Yang energy drives creativity, efficiency, and innovation but without the Yin qualities of caution, reflection, and ethical grounding, it risks deepening inequalities or undermining societal values. The rise of synthetic media offers a similar dynamic: Yang fuels hyper-realistic content that can entertain and inform, while Yin emphasizes transparency to curb misuse. Though we often speak of these as dual forces, Taoism teaches that Yin and Yang are complementary facets of a single flow. Neither can exist meaningfully without the other. Balancing these energies in innovation ensures bold progress is tempered by thoughtful responsibility.

Taoism charts life's motion as cyclical patterns, where the rise of one force leads to the ascendance of the other. This insight is particularly relevant to the challenges of exponential change. When technological systems expand unchecked, their flaws, be it bias, environmental impact, or societal disruption, inevitably surface. However, these disruptions also plant the seeds for innovation and adaptation.

To continue the example of global AI governance, rigid regulations such as the EU's GDPR and AI Act reflect a Yang approach: decisive, structured, and protective. Yet, their inflexibility can stifle innovation or fail to adapt to emerging technologies. A Taoist lens would suggest a more Yin-Yang-inspired governance framework that is dynamic, responsive, and collaborative to balance innovation with ethical oversight. Like the flow of Yin and Yang, regulatory systems must evolve with the technologies they oversee, remaining flexible yet purposeful.

At its core, Yin and Yang remind us that balance and harmony are necessary for all things. Whether navigating personal growth, leading organizational change, or designing global systems, the Tao teaches that right living comes from integration instead of dominance. True progress is found in the contrast and interplay of opposing forces. In martial arts, as in life, strength (Yang) must be paired with flexibility (Yin) to endure.

The Intelligence Age presents an unprecedented opportunity to harness this ancient wisdom. By embracing the dynamic balance of Yin and Yang, Yin's measured reflection alongside Yang's bold action, we balance breakthroughs with wisdom and transform the disruptive forces of exponential change into a thriving digital future. After all, the Tao isn't just about finding harmony within ourselves, it is about aligning with the greater flow of the universe.

3. Wu Wei Versus Yu Wei

Navigating the rapid currents of exponential change demands a delicate interplay between flowing with natural rhythms and steering with intention. Think of it as the art of surfing but for existential dilemmas. The wave does the work; you just try not to wipe out so you can ride until the end. Taoism offers two guiding principles: Wu Wei, effortless action, and Yu Wei, intentional action. These complementary forces provide a framework for aligning with the dynamic flow of life while making purposeful decisions to shape the future.

Wu Wei teaches us to embrace adaptability and find harmony in the inevitable, much like water flowing around obstacles, shaping its path over time or carving mountains without force, while Yu Wei emphasizes deliberate, ethical engagement to ensure progress aligns with human values.[26] It advocates for minimal resistance, adapting to circumstances as they arise and working in harmony with nature's rhythms. Together, they reflect the balance required to navigate today's accelerating transformations, allowing us to respond to challenges with flexibility and foresight while crafting sustainable, innovative solutions that drive collective growth.

In the modern era, organizations can learn from this philosophy. For instance, companies that embraced remote work technologies during the pandemic demonstrated Wu Wei. Rather than resisting an inevitable shift, they adapted fluidly, ensuring continuity and even innovation amid disruption. Another example is that as a keynote speaker, my agenda was cleared the moment the pandemic became a reality, but instead of being miserable, I reinvented myself, created my new brand, The Digital Speaker, and even delivered the world's first TEDx talk in virtual reality. This adaptability underscores a key point: aligning with the flow requires awareness of emerging trends and deep insight into ongoing changes. In addition, intuitive design principles also align closely with the concept of Wu Wei. Consider AI interfaces or robotics: their success will lie in seamlessly integrating them into human workflows without steep learning curves. Products that embody Wu Wei feel "natural" to users, reducing friction and enhancing adoption. Yet, it is essential to clarify that Wu Wei is not about inaction. It is about strategic alignment and knowing when to adapt and when to hold steady.

In contrast, Yu Wei represents deliberate, intentional action. Where Wu Wei focuses on flowing with change, Yu Wei emphasizes shaping change with purpose and foresight. This principle is particularly crucial in the context of exponential technologies, where implementing technologies without a deliberate approach can result in unintended consequences and ethical or societal risks. Yu Wei calls for strategic planning and proactive engagement. Leaders must anticipate technological trends, not just react to them. For example, as robotics and AI reshape industries, organizations must actively experiment with these innovations to understand their potential and pitfalls before scaling. Moreover, Yu Wei underscores the importance of ethical intentionality: ensuring that advancements prioritize human well-being and sustainability. This aligns with calls for responsible AI governance, where foresight and deliberate action prevent misuse and unintended consequences.

On a practical level, Yu Wei means that organizations and individuals must intentionally upskill, focusing on areas such as data literacy, AI ethics, and futures thinking. Organizations can embody Yu Wei by fostering a culture of continuous learning, where employees are encouraged to experiment with emerging technologies and take calculated risks. However, leaders must avoid over-engineering solutions or imposing excessive control, which can stifle innovation and natural evolution.

Taoist philosophy teaches that harmony arises from the interplay of opposites and the need for balance. Wu Wei and Yu Wei are not opposites but complementary forces, akin to Yin and Yang. Wu Wei aligns with the flow of change, while Yu Wei provides the course corrections necessary to navigate that flow with integrity and purpose. This balance is particularly relevant in exponential change. Adaptive action combines Wu Wei's intuitive flow with Yu Wei's deliberate intent. For example, agile frameworks in organizations embody Wu Wei's flexibility while relying on Yu Wei's structured decision-making to prioritize initiatives. Similarly, mindful innovation occurs when serendipitous discoveries (Wu Wei) are critically assessed for their societal implications (Yu Wei) before scaling. Google's celebrated "20 percent time policy" allows employees to dedicate one day a week to pursue projects outside their core responsibilities. This approach reflects Wu Wei by fostering creativity and innovation through autonomy and natural flow, enabling serendipitous discoveries like Google News and AdSense. At the same time, Google applies Yu Wei by critically assessing and prioritizing these innovations for scalability and societal impact, ensuring alignment with broader organizational goals.[27]

As the development of technologies accelerates, the balance of Wu Wei and Yu Wei will become increasingly indispensable in managing this exponential technological change. As AI and machine learning accelerate,

Taoism's principle of balanced, mindful action reminds us that moving fast is meaningless unless we move in harmony. For organizations, it can foster resilience and ethical innovation. For individuals, it reduces stress and enhances adaptability, enabling them to thrive amid uncertainty. In navigating the Intelligence Age, the question is not whether to flow with the tide or steer the course. It is how to do both. By balancing Wu Wei's effortless alignment with Yu Wei's intentional engagement, humanity can harness the transformative power of technology while ensuring that progress remains ethical and inclusive. As such, in the face of exponential change, are you flowing with the tide, steering your course, or both? A dual approach will ensure that we adapt to the currents of change while guiding them toward a future that benefits all.

Taoism offers profound guidance for humanity's quest to move up the Spiral Dynamics model, emphasizing interconnectedness across societal and natural actors. Integrating the Taoist principles into our daily practices can accelerate societal evolution up the Spiral. Ultimately, this progress should be humanity's shared goal, as it holds the potential to benefit all living on our planet (humans, animals, and the natural world). However, this requires moving beyond zero-sum thinking, which prioritizes individual or community gains at the expense of collective well-being, and into systemic solutions that align with Taoist teachings of balance and harmony.

Taoist teachings, emphasizing balance, interconnectedness, and adaptability, provide a roadmap for personal and societal growth and for tackling humanity's most intractable challenges, so-called "wicked problems." These problems, by their very nature, demand systemic thinking and collaborative solutions that align with the principles of harmony and holistic progress advocated by Taoism.

In my second book, *Blockchain: Transforming Your Business and Our World*, I explore wicked problems. The term "wicked" is deliberately layered with multiple meanings to reflect the complexity of the challenges it describes. First, "wicked" conveys a sense of inherent malevolence or harm, highlighting the severe and often destructive nature of these problems. Second, in modern slang, "wicked" paradoxically means "wonderful" or "awesome," symbolizing the immense positive impact that solving such problems could achieve. Finally, "wicked" is a technical term that describes issues that are exceptionally challenging to resolve due to their incomplete, contradictory, or ever-changing requirements. These problems often involve numerous stakeholders with conflicting values and perspectives, compounded by unclear or fragmented information. They are deeply interconnected, meaning solutions cannot be isolated to individual components but must address the broader systemic complexity. Some wicked problems include humanity's greatest threats, such as climate change and managing the introduction of Super Artificial Intelligence.

Taoism, with its focus on natural flow, balance, and intentional action, provides a complementary lens to tackle these wicked problems effectively. For instance, Wu Wei can inspire intuitive responses to emergent crises, while Yu Wei ensures purposeful and ethical long-term solutions.

TidalShot

Yield like water, act without force. Taoism teaches us to flow with change rather than fight it. In a frenzied, always-accelerating world, mindful adaptation is our hidden strength.

Scan the QR code to share this section's TidalShot and illustration to your network.

THE INDIGENOUS APPROACH

Taoism offers a robust framework for addressing humanity's most pressing challenges, particularly through its principles of balance, interconnectedness, and intentional action. Yet, while Taoist teachings provide profound philosophical guidance, we must also recognize the practical, lived wisdom of cultures that have thrived for millennia in harmony with their environments. Indigenous knowledge, especially that of Australia's Aboriginal communities, one of the world's oldest continuous civilizations, complements and enriches this Taoist perspective. Indigenous cultures often demonstrate how long-term stewardship, respect for nature, and communal thinking guide ethical progress. As we face AI-driven disruptions and climate risks, these teachings enrich our decision-making with deeper connectedness and remind us that technology succeeds only when societies thrive. These Indigenous knowledge systems emphasize the interconnectedness of all life. A concept that modern society is still catching up to despite centuries of trial and error (mostly error).

For over 60,000 years, Aboriginal communities have thrived, navigating environmental and societal transformations with a holistic worldview that remains profoundly relevant today.[28] With millennia of resilience and adaptability, Aboriginal cultures embody the principles of interconnectedness and long-term stewardship, offering a tangible roadmap for addressing the systemic complexity of wicked problems.

By synthesizing the philosophical depth of Taoism with the grounded, experiential wisdom of Indigenous traditions, we can craft solutions that are adaptive, sustainable, and deeply ethical. Aboriginal perspectives, much like Taoism, remind us that humanity's evolution, both in terms of Spiral Dynamics and our collective consciousness, relies on embracing holistic systems and respecting the intricate web of life. In this way, these ancient traditions serve as vital guides for navigating exponential change and building a future anchored in harmony.

Aboriginal Culture

Aboriginal culture is deeply rooted in an understanding of interconnectedness.[29] Its practices, stories, and spiritual beliefs reflect a seamless relationship between people, land, and the cosmos. This perspective resonates strongly with both Taoism's emphasis on balance and the higher stages of Spiral Dynamics, such as Yellow and Turquoise. Aboriginal traditions teach us that every action has ripple effects, reminding us of our shared responsibility to care for the environment and future generations.

Central to Aboriginal culture is the Rainbow Serpent, a foundational Dreamtime story that exemplifies the themes of interconnectedness and transformation. The story varies across different Aboriginal groups, but generally describes the Rainbow Serpent as a powerful creator who shaped the land, rivers, and mountains as it moved through the landscape. Its movements brought life, water, and fertility to the land while also establishing laws and boundaries for human behavior.

Long ago, in the Dreamtime, the Earth lay flat and barren, devoid of life or form. The land was silent and still, cloaked in a profound emptiness. Beneath the surface of this vast, lifeless plane slumbered the Rainbow Serpent, her shimmering scales hidden deep within the Earth. She had rested for untold ages, her body curled in quiet dormancy.

One day, the Rainbow Serpent awoke. Stirring from her long sleep, she broke through the surface of the Earth, her body uncoiling and stretching in a serpentine dance across the land. Wherever she moved, the Earth beneath her shifted and transformed. Her sweeping motions carved valleys and mountain ranges, while her coils created rivers and waterholes. Her vibrant, iridescent body painted the landscape with life, leaving behind the undulating forms of the world as we know it.

As she completed her journey, the Rainbow Serpent returned to her place of emergence and called to the frogs, who had also been in deep slumber, their bellies filled with water. One by one, they emerged from the Earth at her call. The Rainbow Serpent, with a playful touch, tickled their bellies, causing them to laugh. As they laughed, the water they carried spilled forth, filling the tracks and grooves she had left behind. Rivers began to flow, lakes formed, and the land was bathed in life-giving water.

With water now nourishing the Earth, plants began to sprout, and trees stretched their branches skyward. Life awoke in every corner of the land, and animals of all kinds emerged, drawn to the abundance the Rainbow Serpent had created. She guided them, teaching them the ways of the world and the laws they must follow to maintain harmony.

To ensure order, the Rainbow Serpent established sacred laws. She decreed that those who obeyed her laws would be rewarded, given the gift of human form and the ability to thrive on the land. Those who disobeyed, however, would be turned to stone as a warning to others. The animals who became humans were each given a totem of their original form, a symbol of their connection to the natural world and their responsibilities to it.

The Rainbow Serpent's legacy endured as she became the eternal protector of the land, the waterholes, and all life that depended on them. To this day, when a rainbow appears in the sky, it is believed to be the Rainbow Serpent traveling between waterholes, her presence a reminder of the life-giving power she represents and the balance she commands.[30]

The Rainbow Serpent represents the dual forces of creation and destruction, embodying the balance necessary for sustaining life. The story, rich with wisdom, speaks of creation, transformation, and the need for harmony between all living things. It is a reminder of the sacred laws that bind humanity to the land and to one another and of the delicate balance required to sustain the world. However, the Rainbow Serpent's lessons also offer a profound framework for understanding and navigating the challenges of our modern world.

The duality of the Rainbow Serpent mirrors the Taoist understanding of balance, where progress emerges not from domination or force but from a harmonious interplay between natural rhythms and deliberate actions. Just as Yin and Yang coexist to create a dynamic equilibrium, the Serpent's narrative reminds us that creation and destruction, intuition and intention, must work in concert to sustain life. This philosophy is particularly relevant today, where the complexities of exponential change demand a framework that honors both the interconnectedness of our systems and the purposeful choices required to navigate them in the long term.

The Rainbow Serpent's creation of rivers and waterholes symbolizes the interconnectedness that sustains life, a principle especially relevant in addressing today's technological and ecological challenges, where the rapid advancement of technologies such as artificial intelligence and synthetic biology reverberates through economic, social, and environmental systems. Each innovation, no matter how isolated it may seem, carries ripple effects that influence the broader ecosystem.

Moreover, the Serpent's dual role as creator and destroyer is a powerful metaphor for the dual nature of exponential technologies. On one hand, these technologies hold immense promise. They can solve some of humanity's most pressing problems, from renewable energy to medical breakthroughs. Yet, they also carry significant risks, such as environmental degradation, ethical challenges such as the amplification of biases, and societal disruption driven by, for example, AI-generated misinformation. The story teaches us that these forces must be balanced, and that unchecked creation or destruction leads to chaos. This balance requires a mindset deeply rooted in sustainability, one that mirrors the Serpent's demand for respect for the land and its rhythms. Progress, therefore, should not be pursued at the expense of the systems that sustain life but rather in harmony with them.

The Rainbow Serpent also highlights the importance of humility and respect in the face of great power. Aboriginal cultures teach that humans are stewards of the land, not its masters. This is a perspective that resonates profoundly in a world where humanity wields technologies capable of reshaping the planet or even controlling humanity. Instead of seeking dominance over these tools, we must approach them with reverence, recognizing their capacity to shape society in intended and unforeseen ways. This humility fosters a collaborative mindset that prioritizes collective well-being over narrow self-interest.

When it comes to the adoption of change and technologies, Aboriginal culture exemplifies a measured approach to progress. It embraces technology only when it strengthens community bonds and preserves cultural heritage, not merely for change's sake. Instead of chasing every innovation, these communities selectively integrate tools that support traditional values, ensuring that progress nurtures rather than disrupts interconnectedness.[31] This thoughtful strategy echoes the practices of other groups, such as the Amish, and stands in stark contrast to today's unchecked digital transformation driven by social media and rapid tech adoption.

The Rainbow Serpent's story also speaks to shared responsibility. Across Aboriginal cultures, the Serpent is a unifying symbol, reminding communities of their collective duty to care for the land and one another. This sense of shared stewardship is crucial in addressing global challenges. Just as the Serpent binds its community to a common purpose, humanity must collaborate across cultural, national, and disciplinary boundaries to tackle issues such as climate change, resource scarcity, and the ethical development of Super Artificial Intelligence. Solutions that are inclusive and considerate of diverse perspectives are more sustainable and equitable.

TidalShot

Long before exponential tech, Indigenous wisdom taught us to honor land, community, and future generations as one. Blending old and new perspectives unlocks a balanced path for the Intelligence Age.

Scan the QR code to share this section's TidalShot and illustration to your network.

NATURE: HARMONY IN DIVERSITY

The Rainbow Serpent offers a timeless reminder that progress is not a solitary endeavor but an ongoing dance between creation and destruction, between the forces of nature and human ingenuity. Its lessons of balance, interconnectedness, and humility provide a guiding light as we navigate the complexities of the modern world. As we embrace exponential technologies, we would do well to heed the Serpent's wisdom: to act with respect for the systems that sustain us, to adapt to the rhythms of change, and to work collectively toward a future where progress and harmony coexist. This ancient story reminds us that true advancement lies not in conquering the forces of nature but in aligning with them to create a thriving, sustainable world.

Building on this foundation of harmony and interconnectedness, we turn to nature itself as a profound teacher in navigating disruption because humans aren't the sole viewpoint—we're part of a vast web of life with many ways of experiencing reality. When we adopt a non-anthropocentric lens, we can build systems that respect diverse perspectives and safeguard ecological balance, a crucial theme we'll return to when we discuss sustainable AI, biotech, and beyond.

The natural world offers countless examples of resilience and adaptability, showing us how diverse perspectives can coexist and flourish even under immense pressure. Just as the Rainbow Serpent shaped the land and waterholes, ecosystems evolve through a complex web of interdependence, where each species brings its unique lens to survival. By exploring these patterns, we can uncover strategies to address our modern challenges, recognizing that the varied ways of perceiving and interacting with the human and non-human world are critical for finding systemic solutions. Because what if the answers to humanity's greatest challenges don't lie in more technology but in learning how to see differently?

One of the books that changed my perspective is *An Immense World* by Ed Young. The book reveals how nature's diversity offers profound insights into resilience and innovation by demonstrating how organisms thrive through specialized adaptations. Each species perceives and interacts with its environment in unique ways, a concept encapsulated in the idea of *Umwelt*. Young refers to *Umwelt* as a "sensory bubble". Coming from the German word of *environment*, it is "the part of those surroundings that an animal can sense and experience—its perceptual world."[32] Over millions of years, each species has developed unique ways to interact with and interpret the world, dictated by their *Umwelt*. This diversity highlights the power of seeing the world through multiple perspectives, a lesson equally vital in addressing the complex realities of our interconnected global systems.

For example, bats navigate the world using echolocation, transforming sound waves into a mental map of their surroundings. Bees, on the other hand, rely on ultraviolet vision to discern patterns on flowers invisible to the human eye, guiding them to vital nectar. Meanwhile, dogs experience a richly textured world dominated by scent, where even faint odors hold layers of meaning. Bats might think we're strange for not using echolocation to navigate, but then again, we find it odd that they can't appreciate the visual splendor of a sunset. The reality is that both perspectives work brilliantly for their intended audiences. These varying sensory perceptions reflect our biological differences and distinct strategies for survival honed by evolution.

These natural lessons of multiple perspectives mirror how human cultures, shaped by historical and environmental conditions, adopt different frameworks to navigate the challenges they face. For instance, China's approach to technological disruption often emphasizes centralized governance and long-term strategic planning, while Western nations prioritize decentralized innovation and individual freedoms. As a result, both cultures have different approaches to dealing with a rapidly changing world, and both approaches carry strengths and blind spots, much like the sensory worlds of a bat and bee, which are uniquely suited to their respective environments. Similarly, responses to climate adaptation differ across regions, reflecting local priorities and resources. As in nature, these strategies are context-specific, shaped by the *Umwelt* of each society. Yet they are all critical for addressing shared global challenges, much like the diverse adaptations in ecosystems that collectively sustain life.

However, this multiplicity of perspectives also brings challenges. Just as the sensory experiences of a spider and a bird may seem irreconcilable and we will never know what it is like to be a bat, the differing worldviews among global powers can hinder collective action on issues such as climate change or the ethical development of Super Artificial Intelligence.[33] The key lies in fostering a meta-perspective, an elevated way of thinking that sees beyond individual realities to appreciate the interconnectedness of all. This involves understanding that no single perspective holds the complete truth; instead, progress depends on synthesizing these diverse views into a cohesive, systemic approach. We need to see these differences as opportunities instead of obstacles. Just as nature thrives on diversity, humanity's ability to integrate and respect varied perspectives will determine our resilience and capacity for innovation in the face of exponential change.

TidalShot

Reality shifts when we see through non-human eyes—bats echo-locate, bees read ultraviolet, and trees sense soil chemistry. Embracing these diverse Umwelts broadens our perspective and increases empathy.

Scan the QR code to share this section's TidalShot and illustration to your network.

BEYOND THE HUMAN LENS

I invite you to embark on a profound shift in how we perceive and engage with the world and with change itself. The lessons from nature are unmistakable: adaptability and harmony arise when we embrace differences rather than seek to homogenize them. For humanity, this requires recognizing the intrinsic value of all perspectives, whether they stem from Taoism, Indigenous wisdom, or the different levels of Spiral Dynamics. These frameworks converge on a vital truth: progress should not be a zero-sum game. It should be a collective endeavor that balances innovation with respect for the intricate natural and human ecosystems that sustain us.

The story of the Rainbow Serpent, woven with the rich tapestry of adaptations found in nature, deepens this invitation. It challenges us to move beyond anthropocentric narratives and embrace a more expansive worldview. Here, the perspective of Biocentrism becomes a pivotal guide, reminding us that life and consciousness are not mere products of the universe but intrinsic to its very fabric.[34] By shifting from a human-centered approach to one that honors all life forms, we align with the themes of harmony and interconnectedness that have guided countless ecosystems and civilizations through change. This mindset, modeled by nature's ingenuity and resilience, equips us to navigate the exponential disruptions of our time with both grace and purpose.

In essence, Biocentrism asserts that life is not a mere by-product of the universe's physical laws but a fundamental component that shapes the reality we perceive. First described by Robert Lanza (one of the most respected scientists in the world) and Bob Berman (the most widely read astronomer in the world), Biocentrism offers a revolutionary new view of the universe. It reframes space and time, not as absolute constructs but as tools devised by consciousness to make sense of the world. This concept complements the idea of *Umwelt* that each organism experiences reality uniquely based on its sensory and cognitive frameworks. Together, these ideas dissolve the illusion of an objective, one-size-fits-all reality, reminding us that every perspective is both valid and limited.

This perspective aligns with the challenges we face in a rapidly transforming world. Just as nature thrives on diversity, the interconnected global systems we rely upon for climate action, technological governance, and societal progress demand a similar embrace of multiplicity. Each region's approach, shaped by its historical, cultural, and environmental context, represents its unique *Umwelt*. Yet, Biocentrism goes further, urging us to transcend even these human constructs. It challenges us to acknowledge the intrinsic value of all life forms, understanding that the well-being of humanity is inseparable from the ecosystems we inhabit, because, as it turns out, the universe doesn't revolve around us. This shift calls for reimagining progress, not as dominion over nature or technological supremacy but as harmony with the broader web of life.

Recent discoveries in microbiology reinforce how deeply woven life's networks truly are.[35] In the oceans, for instance, researchers have observed tiny nanotube "bridges" connecting *Prochlorococcus* and *Synechococcus* bacteria, two of the most abundant photosynthetic organisms on our planet. These microscopic tubes link the inner spaces of distinct cells, allowing them to trade nutrients and information. It is a revelation that echoes Turquoise's belief in a single living global system, underscores the Taoist principle of interdependence, and affirms Indigenous teachings of communal responsibility for shared resources. In a profound example of Biocentrism, these bacteria challenge the notion of solitude in nature, reminding us that even among the tiniest creatures, the world thrives on synergy and exchange. The same applies to our own bodies, where ~39 trillion microbes in each of us are vital for our immunity, digestion and health in general.[36] Unfortunately, modern lifestyles and medical practices often disrupt this delicate microbial harmony with far-reaching consequences.[37] This understanding of our dependence on microbes challenges the notion of human exceptionalism and highlights our place within a complex ecological web. As we continue to make societal decisions that impact our microbiomes, from healthcare practices to (processed) food production, we are inadvertently altering the very foundation of our health. This realization underscores the need for a more holistic, biocentric approach to health, technology and environmental policies, recognizing that our actions have far-reaching consequences not just for the world around us, but for the microscopic world within us as well.

As we grapple with the wicked problems of our time, this biocentric perspective offers a guiding principle: to think and act in ways that honor the interconnectedness of all existence. It asks us to adopt a meta-perspective, where we recognize that our human worldview is but one strand in the intricate web of reality. Solutions that emerge from this expanded consciousness are more likely to be systemic, inclusive, and sustainable.

Moreover, such a meta-perspective reflects a necessary evolution in human thought. A movement beyond technological advancement toward a shift in consciousness itself. Progress, as the Rainbow Serpent, Taoism, Indigenous wisdom, and Spiral Dynamics have all taught us, is not about imposing human will on the world but about aligning with the natural rhythms and respecting the perspectives that sustain life. By integrating these perspectives, we can begin to see ourselves not as masters of the environment but as participants in a vast, interconnected system where each action reverberates through the whole. This transformative vision can help humanity navigate the complexities of exponential change while fostering a future that is as diverse, resilient, and interconnected as life itself. By understanding that each being, human or otherwise, has its own experiential lens, we lay the groundwork for empathetic and sustainable innovation. This ethos must guide us as we turn to the technology of tomorrow.

TidalShot

Life isn't just human-centric. It's an intricate web where each being shapes the whole. Embrace Biocentrism and see how synergy emerges when we shed the notion that progress revolves around us alone.

Scan the QR code to share this section's TidalShot and illustration to your network.

NOW WHAT? CHART HUMANITY'S EVOLUTIONARY PATH

As we close this Chapter on humanity's journey, spanning our earliest memories to our aspirations for the future, the question of *Now What?* demands thoughtful reflection and bold vision. To answer this, we must weave together the insights from Spiral Dynamics, Eastern philosophies, Indigenous wisdom, and the transformative ideas of *Umwelt* and Biocentrism. These four lenses underscore a single truth: the world is deeply interconnected, and we can't solve tomorrow's challenges with purely "linear" or one-sided thinking. Why do these frameworks matter right now? Because rapid technological change (which we'll explore in Chapter Four) isn't just about inventing new tools; it's about how we weave them into society responsibly, ensuring harmony for all living systems. Only by uniting these four streams of wisdom can we craft a future that respects our past, embraces complexity, and uplifts all life.

Spiral Dynamics offers a sweeping macro lens on our evolution, illustrating how individuals, organizations, and societies progress through developmental stages, each with its unique complexities and challenges. This framework reveals the necessity of understanding and integrating diverse worldviews, as well as fostering collaboration across all levels of human experience. Yet progress is not merely a linear ascent; it is a dynamic interplay of forces that requires tools to navigate transitions effectively.

Here, Eastern philosophies provide invaluable guidance. With their emphasis on balance, resilience, and adaptability, Taoist principles such as Yin and Yang, Wu Wei and Yu Wei equip us to face disruption without losing sight of harmony. They remind us that the journey forward is as much about flowing with change as it is about intentional action. Meanwhile, Indigenous wisdom roots these insights in a deep respect for the planet and its long-term rhythms, urging us to honor the ecosystems that sustain us while considering the broader consequences of our actions.

The perspectives of *Umwelt* and Biocentrism challenge us to go further. They underscore that our understanding of the world is not absolute but shaped by the perceptual and cognitive frameworks through which we interpret reality. Every species, including humans, operates within its own unique experiential bubble. This means that there is not one reality, and acknowledging this diversity of perspectives is key to solving complex global problems. We must shift from our human-centered thinking to recognizing the intrinsic value of all life forms, to design solutions that harmonize with the broader ecosystem.

Here's what I hope you'll take away from these four perspectives:

1. **Embrace more than one truth:** Spiral Dynamics shows us that individuals and cultures operate at many levels simultaneously. Before we jump to "this is how it ought to be," let's first appreciate that every mindset has its own valid logic and forging a better future requires inclusive collaboration.

2. **Flow, don't force:** Taoism's Yin and Yang highlight balance, not battle. Whether you're a tech founder or an educator, the call to action is to remain fluid but purposeful and align bold innovation with thoughtful restraint, so breakthroughs don't fracture our social or ecological fabric.

3. **Learn from deep-rooted wisdom:** Indigenous cultures

demonstrate communal stewardship and respect for natural cycles. The invitation isn't to romanticize the past but to realize that long-term well-being depends on honoring nature's rhythms— a powerful guardrail against unbridled disruption.

4. **Widen the circle of life:** Biocentrism and the *Umwelt* concept remind us that we're just one thread in a living tapestry. If we treat nature as a backdrop, we risk unraveling that tapestry altogether. Seeing the perspectives of other species pushes us to design technologies that enhance, not erode, ecosystems.

The path forward demands a profound shift in consciousness, one that transcends zero-sum games and short-term gains. True progress is not about dominating the future but harmonizing with it. This requires creating systems that respect the interconnected web of life and value diversity in all its forms while fostering innovation and sustainability.

Technological advancement, particularly in the realm of AI and human-machine integration, must align with these principles. As we merge human cognition with machine systems, ethical frameworks become paramount. Biomimicry, drawing inspiration from nature's problem-solving mechanisms, and sustainable AI development exemplify how we can leverage interconnectedness to ensure that technological progress enhances rather than detracts from our relationship with the planet. The evolution of humanity into "cyborg ecosystems" offers the potential to deepen our connection to the natural world rather than sever it, provided we navigate this transition with wisdom and care.[38]

Humanity stands at a pivotal moment where collaboration, cultural wisdom, and interconnected thinking are no longer optional but have become essential. The lessons drawn from Spiral Dynamics, Taoism, Indigenous knowledge, and nature's adaptive brilliance collectively illuminate a path forward. This is not a journey of isolated actors but a shared endeavor that demands holistic thinking and systemic solutions.

The call to action is clear: embrace a broader perspective that integrates ancient wisdom, respects diverse realities, and operates at a systems level by taking into account a meta-perspective. Progress lies in fostering equity, adaptability, and sustainability, values that will guide us through the complexities of the Intelligence Age and ensure a thriving future for all life on Earth.

As we confront the tsunami of change, I challenge you to reflect on your role in shaping the future. Will you flow with the rhythms of transformation, act with deliberate purpose, and contribute to a world where humanity thrives in harmony with its environment? This journey demands more than passive observation; it calls for active engagement, an open mind, and the courage to embrace complexity with wisdom and ethics. The choices we make today will echo through the systems that sustain life, influencing our present and the many generations to come.

As we embrace an expanded consciousness, the question remains: how do we apply these lessons to the disruptive technologies shaping our future? Or, put another way, how do we prevent AI from becoming Skynet while still letting it recommend our next Netflix binge?

When reflecting on these ideas, consider your role in this evolving story. Whether as a leader, an innovator, or a curious mind, your choices ripple outward into the systems we all depend on. Moving up the Spiral, embracing balance, and respecting diverse realities aren't abstract ideals. They are calls to action that will define our collective future.

In short, I want you, the reader, to:

- **Recognize our interconnection:** We don't thrive in isolation. The changes we push in AI, biotech, or energy affect communities, animals, and ecosystems.
- **Aim for true balance:** Strive to create synergy between human progress and ecological harmony. We can't pretend that exponential growth alone ensures a better tomorrow.
- **Prepare for Chapter 4:** With these perspectives in mind, you'll see that technology has the power to uplift or destabilize. It is our mindset, grounded in multiple worldviews, that keeps innovation human-centered and life-centered.

Above all, this isn't about imposing a single "right future" or simply warning, "Don't go there." It's a call to embrace complexity and diversity responsibly so that everyone benefits from the transformations ahead. Each of the four perspectives highlights different facets of our collective growth. In the next Chapter, you'll see how these human and planetary viewpoints are challenged—or sometimes reinforced—by the rise of exponential technologies. These powerful waves are reshaping industries, societies, and even our understanding of what it means to be human, and they can harmonize innovation with sustainability if guided by the principles we've discussed. Over the next 30 years, transformative breakthroughs will redefine the boundaries of possibility, bringing unprecedented opportunities alongside profound challenges. They're not isolated disruptions but interconnected forces, each amplifying the impact of the others. With that clarity, we can step confidently into the next chapter to examine these key exponential forces and explore how to steward them wisely.

We will first explore the epicenter of this transformation: artificial intelligence, a force compelling us to rethink intelligence itself and adapt at unimaginable speeds. Then we will move on to seven additional waves affecting our global society. Robotics will change the global workforce, while quantum computing will open doors to solving previously intractable problems. Spatial intelligence and immersive technologies will challenge our sense of reality and connection, and brain-computer interfaces promise to merge minds with machines, revolutionizing thought and creativity. Meanwhile, 3D printing will decentralize manufacturing, and biotechnology is reshaping life, urging us to wield this power responsibly.

These technologies represent overlapping waves in the tsunami of change, requiring strategic navigation grounded in wisdom and ethics. As we balance growth with harmony and innovation with ethics, the next step is considering the tools shaping this transition. The technologies redefining our reality offer immense promise, but only if guided by these deeper perspectives. What does it mean to ride the waves of disruption with wisdom? That's where we're headed next. In the coming Chapter, I invite you to explore how we can ride these waves, not with fear but with vision, harnessing their power to create a future where innovation uplifts humanity rather than overwhelms it. Together, let's consider how we can turn disruption into opportunity, building a world that thrives amid the chaos of transformation.

TidalShot

Growing our consciousness is as vital as growing our tech. Honor history, adopt new perspectives, and integrate ancient wisdom so humanity's next leap is ethical and bold.

Scan the QR code to share this TidalShot to your network.

HUMAN VS MACHINE

Vita stood calmly at the edge of the crowd, observing a tense confrontation outside Mercer Retreat, a family-run care home for the elderly. It was now struggling to adapt in a world where fully automatic elderly care had become standard. Inside, Jannet Mercer, the fourth-generation owner, faced a dilemma: adopt advanced robotics and AI services to stay financially viable, or preserve the personalized human-managed care and protect her loyal employees—some of whom had spent their entire working lives at her family's care home.

Vita edged its way through to the building, ignoring the occasional shove and jeer by the anti-synth protesters. They rejected synthetic automation at any cost, but the choice was easier when it wasn't their loved one or business on the line.

"It's not just profit," Jannet explained inside. "Our residents and staff trust us. Many have been here for over a decade, and they value the personal touch from familiar caregivers. But our competitors have automated everything. If we don't, we can't afford to keep our doors open."

Vita listened attentively, understanding Jannet's genuine conflict. Its presence had been requested as an advisor precisely because of its unique insight into balancing human needs with technological advancement. Yet even Vita found no easy answers. It saw first-hand how deeply corporate giants like NovaTech leveraged technological disruption to widen divisions, pitting human livelihoods against market demands.

"Change doesn't have to mean discarding humanity," Vita finally offered, its voice gentle but firm rising above the hubbub of the crowd outside. "Perhaps your competitors assume the only route is fast, full automation. But you can embrace technology in ways that support rather than replace your caregivers. Lean into what people can do better than machines—empathy, emotional connections, the power of sharing a small smile. Maybe your path forward can include your employees rather than exclude them."

Jannet looked hopeful yet uncertain. "But how? We can't just retrain everyone overnight. And I can't afford advanced caregiver bots *and* human salaries."

Vita tilted its head thoughtfully, processing possibilities. "Adapt gradually, not abruptly. Use robotics to lighten the mundane repetitive tasks, things like housekeeping, lifting, and night patrols. Free your human staff to focus on personal and emotional care. And embrace your community. At the end of the day, it's their wallets that make the decisions."

Outside, the Union demonstrations turned chaotic suddenly, clashing with the pro-synthetic integration crowd. Yet within the quiet Mercer Retreat's office, Vita saw a different path forming clearly: humans and technology not as opponents, but as partners.

Jannet nodded slowly, her decision crystallizing. The road wouldn't be easy, but Vita had shone a light on the first step. The real struggle wasn't between human and synthetic, but between fear-driven divisions and thoughtful integration. Humanity must shape disruption consciously, or risk being reshaped by forces far less kind.

CHAPTER 4

The Technological Tides Reshaping Everything

Eight seemingly unstoppable breakthroughs are merging like waves in a perfect storm, ready to overturn our deepest assumptions about what it means to be human.

In a world where progress once unfolded over centuries, we now live in an age where transformative breakthroughs arrive in relentless succession. Each day introduces innovations that redefine industries, reshape societies, and challenge the boundaries of possibility. The exponential rise of technologies such as AI, robotics, and quantum computing does more than solve problems (and create new ones); it alters the very fabric of our lives. Yet, these technologies are not lone agents of change. They are interconnected forces, amplifying each other in ways that propel humanity into uncharted territory. However, it's vital to remember that some of the most disruptive innovations may still be invisible to us today. Much like the internet was inconceivable to most in the 1970s, so too might tomorrow's breakthroughs lie beyond our current imagination.

At its core, the age of exponential technologies carries an essential truth: every breakthrough contains duality. AI can democratize knowledge but deepen societal inequalities. Biotechnology can cure diseases while opening Pandora's box of ethical dilemmas. Quantum computing can unlock new scientific horizons, but it could also dismantle our most trusted encryption systems. Like the Rainbow Serpent, these forces create, destroy, empower, constrain, unite, and divide. This Chapter acknowledges this complexity, but we will not dwell on risks just yet; those will be explored in the next Chapter. For now, we focus on capabilities: how these technologies expand the boundaries of what is possible and what systems of thought we need to make sense of them.

This Chapter takes a systemic view of eight transformative technologies, not as individual marvels but as interwoven catalysts of change. Their convergence creates an ecosystem where each advance amplifies another, pushing progress from linear to exponential. The implications stretch across every facet of human existence, redefining how we interact, work and think. We will discuss the following technologies:

1. **AI:** Automating decision-making and predicting the future.
2. **Robotics:** Automating physical activity.
3. **Quantum computing:** Solving computational problems

previously deemed out of reach.

4. **Blockchain:** Verifying trust, transparency, and accountability across systems.

5. **Spatial intelligence:** Merging the physical and digital worlds through AR, VR and beyond.

6. **Brain-computer interfaces:** Connecting thoughts directly to machines.

7. **3D printing:** Turning ideas into physical solutions anywhere in the world.

8. **Biotechnology:** Engineering and reimagining life itself.

We dive into these eight transformative forces below, starting with AI since it is the beating heart of the Intelligence Age, and show how their synergy can reshape industries on a scale the world has never seen. While the possibilities are vast, so are the stakes. The accelerated pace of change challenges individuals, organizations, and societies to adapt or risk obsolescence. But we should not forget that these technologies are tools, not destinies. Whether they usher in an era of abundance or deepen societal divides, their impact depends on how intentionally and ethically they are deployed.

In this Chapter, we rise above the noise of the latest trends and focus on enduring principles. This is not about chasing the new but understanding the profound. By exploring these technologies as interconnected elements in a larger system, we gain the perspective needed to navigate the waves of change and ensure they lead to a future where humanity thrives. For example, AI and quantum computing are not just standalone technologies; they are foundational systems that can amplify the impact of every other transformative breakthrough, from synthetic biology to next-generation materials. By merging computational power with intelligent algorithms, we unlock synergies that could redefine what's possible in healthcare, climate science and beyond.

By taking this meta-perspective, we see not isolated breakthroughs but patterns of transformation that unite these innovations. I focus on the long-term principles driving change: acceleration (how fast the world is evolving), democratization (how widely technologies are spreading), and transformation (how deeply they alter our lives, work and societies). By embracing this systemic lens, we move beyond the "what" to explore the "how" and "why"—questions that equip us to navigate the unknown, no matter what technologies emerge next.

As we delve into these waves of change, the focus will be on the broader implications of these technologies. Together, they challenge paradigms in three transformative ways: shifting progress from incremental to exponential, redefining resource constraints from scarcity to abundance, and blurring the boundaries between human and machine in a move from human to post-human. Yet these shifts are not destinations, they are steppingstones that will form entirely new ecosystems where their collective impact exceeds the sum of their parts.

I invite you to adopt a mindset that transcends the technology itself, focusing on the larger patterns of transformation it ignites. From this meta-perspective, we don't merely keep up with change, we shape it. The real question is not what technology can do but what we choose to do with it. So, let's begin. Let's explore how these eight technologies are reshaping industries, societies, and the very essence of what it means to be human. And as we do, let's remember: this isn't just a story of innovation. It is a story of humanity. We must consider the integrative lessons from Chapter Three—Spiral Dynamics, Taoist flow, Indigenous stewardship, or a bio-centric worldview—that remind us that these transformations must remain rooted in balance, humanity and interconnected stewardship. The choices we make today will determine whether this tsunami of change drowns us or elevates us to unimaginable heights.

TidalShot

Emerging technologies are racing to redefine "possible." Will we harness AI, robotics, and biotech as allies, or let them reshape everything without our permission? The choice starts here.

Scan the QR code to share this section's TidalShot and illustration to your network.

ARTIFICIAL INTELLIGENCE: RETHINKING INTELLIGENCE IN THE AGE OF MACHINES

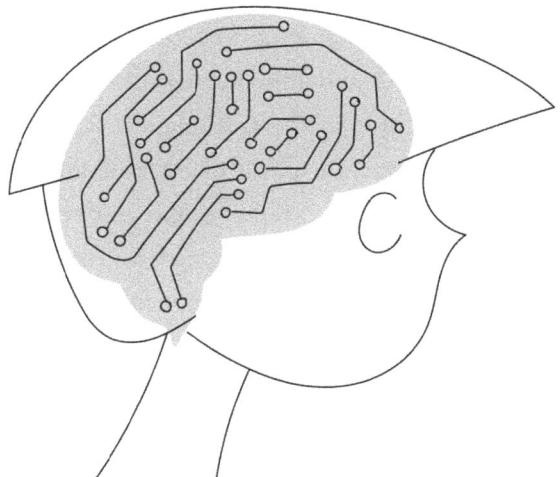

Artificial intelligence lies at the heart of the technological transformation reshaping the 21st century. To understand its significance, we must first confront a profound shift in how we define and approach intelligence itself.[1] Human intelligence, extraordinary as it is, remains a product of evolutionary constraints. It is a slow, trial-and-error process that took millions of years to develop and is governed by the availability of food, energy, and biology.

These limits have shaped our brains, remarkable yet finite, bound by the physical size of our skulls and the energy needed to sustain cognition. For all its brilliance, our intelligence is not the pinnacle of what is possible but a singular point along a vast spectrum of cognitive potential.

AI, in contrast, emerges as something fundamentally different: an engineered form of intelligence, unshackled by the biological trade-offs that govern human evolution. Unlike our brains, AI systems are not constrained by physical size, metabolism, or slow adaptation over millennia. Built on silicon, and soon photons, these systems operate on exponentially greater scales, processing information at speeds far beyond human comprehension.[2] This means that AI does not merely replicate human intelligence; it redefines it, exploring cognitive landscapes that evolution never intended and achieving feats that human thought could never approach alone. This difference is not trivial. It represents a leap that forces us to adopt a broader, more cosmopolitan perspective on intelligence. As Eliezer Yudkowsky, an American artificial intelligence researcher, once observed, intelligence must be seen as a continuum, beginning with the humble mouse, advancing through the chimpanzee and human cognition, and extending far beyond, with no inherent upper limit.[3] Intelligence is infinite. AI is a new frontier in that spectrum, a force capable of pushing far beyond Einstein and into realms that lie outside our ability to fully understand.

This redefinition matters because it changes the rules of engagement. Especially because the intelligence frontier is not smooth or predictable but jagged, filled with paradoxes and asymmetries.[4] Tasks that are effortless for humans, such as recognizing emotions in facial expressions or making small talk, can remain monumental challenges for AI (although that is changing rapidly). Meanwhile, activities that would overwhelm the human brain, such as analyzing billions of datasets or simulating global climate systems, are trivial for these machines. This asymmetry highlights the duality of AI: it is not a mirror of human thought but a complement to it, filling in gaps and expanding into problem spaces that were previously inconceivable. As our collective human intelligence changes due to ever-advanced artificial intelligence, we must ensure that we also continuously adapt our AI strategies to reflect our evolving cultural and ethical imperatives. Just as our perspectives transform with each stage of human development on the spiral, so must our approach to technology, ensuring that innovation remains aligned with our expanding cultural and ethical wisdom.

The jagged approach becomes clear if we take a step back. AI didn't just show up unannounced; however, the launch of ChatGPT in late 2022 did mark many people's first active interaction with artificial intelligence. It had been quietly building steam for decades, like a band that finally goes viral after years of playing in garages. ChatGPT was just its first chart-topping single. Its history stretches back to the 1950s when Alan Turing envisioned "thinking machines" capable of performing tasks previously thought to require human intelligence.[5] Early experiments with neural networks laid the groundwork, but progress stalled during the "AI winters" of the 1970s and 1990s, when inflated expectations clashed with technological limitations.[6] The 1980s brought renewed interest with the rise of machine learning, and in the 2000s, the explosive growth of data and the plummeting costs of computers enabled deep learning. Yet the real tipping point arrived in 2017. A groundbreaking paper titled "Attention Is All You Need" introduced the Transformer architecture—the "T" in ChatGPT—revolutionizing natural language processing and igniting the current AI boom.[7] Combined with advances in deep learning, AI evolved rapidly, enabling systems to analyze, predict, and generate data at unprecedented scales.

Generative AI: Redefining Creativity

Thanks to this latest breakthrough, AI has emerged as a powerful collaborator, redefining content generation and pushing the boundaries of human imagination. At the core of this revolution is generative AI, a class of models capable of producing text, images, videos, and even entire virtual worlds with nothing more than a simple prompt. By leveraging architectures such as diffusion models and LLMs, generative AI is reshaping how we interact with machines and conceive new forms of artistic expression. The importance of this cannot be overstated.

Historically, humans needed to learn the rigid syntax and logic of programming languages to interact with computers. Today, tools such as OpenAI's GPT, Google's Gemini, Anthropic's Claude, Meta's Llama, Mistral's open-weight models, and many language-specific tools such as 01.ai (Mandarin), OpenHathi (Hindi), and Jais (Arabic) have turned this relationship on its head. For the first time, machines have become fluent in our language. No more awkward 'lost in translation' moments. They now bridge the gap between our messy ideas and polished realities. LLMs have made it possible to translate abstract ideas into tangible outputs, whether that's a piece of text, a digital painting, a storyboard for a short film, or even entire video clips at a stunning 4K resolution that respect the nuance of physics,[8] human movement, and camera angles, using nothing more than natural language.[9] This shift democratizes access to creativity and accelerates the process of ideation and production.

The question isn't whether machines understand us; they do, often better than we'd like. Now, it is about how far they'll carry us and whether we are ready for the ride. The implications for creative industries are profound. Generative AI eliminates traditional bottlenecks, whether they stem from cost, skill, or time, and allows anyone to produce professional-grade visuals and stories, resulting in a Cambrian Explosion of creativity.[10] Some artists and designers view generative AI as an empowering collaborator, accelerating the design process and unlocking new creative frontiers. Others worry it dilutes human originality, warning that an overreliance on machine-generated ideas could homogenize cultural expression.[11] While AI can mimic known patterns and styles, genuine creativity involves emotional depth and cultural context, areas where humans still hold a unique vantage point. However, AI is rapidly improving and expanding its creative horizons by making it easier for amateurs to experiment, democratizing art in ways once unimaginable. Ultimately, the tension between acceleration and authenticity drives an ongoing debate: can humans and AI truly co-author the creative process without sacrificing artistic identity?

While generative AI often captures headlines for its ability to create the next article, image, or video, its capabilities extend far beyond content creation. Think of AI as the ultimate Swiss Army knife. Able to recognize, predict, automate, and create. It is a toolkit transforming every aspect of solving problems, decision-making and interacting with the world. It begins with recognition, where AI identifies patterns within vast amounts of data, whether it is images, text, or sound. This recognition enables classification, allowing AI to organize and make sense of those patterns, such as identifying fraudulent transactions, diagnosing diseases in medical scans, or detecting sentiment in customer feedback. AI then builds on these foundations to deliver predictions, anticipating future outcomes based on historical trends, such as weather forecasting, financial modeling, or even predicting equipment failure in manufacturing.

The true power of AI emerges in its ability to drive recommendation systems that personalize decisions for users by analyzing behavior and offering tailored solutions, from recommending your next Netflix binge to optimizing supply chain logistics. As AI gains autonomy, it steps into automation, operating systems with minimal human input, such as autonomous vehicles navigating roads or robotic process automation streamlining repetitive tasks. As AI continues to improve, it transforms how we collaborate, create, and innovate. Decision-making, long the domain of expert intuition, is now augmented by AI's data-driven precision. Leaders no longer need to rely solely on experience; they are supported by systems that analyze variables and outcomes far beyond human capacity.[12]

Together, these capabilities form a holistic framework that positions AI not as a tool for isolated tasks but as a systemic force capable of recognizing, interpreting, predicting, creating, and interacting across every domain of human activity. From optimizing decision-making to driving automation and enabling lifelike interactions, AI's potential lies in its ability to augment human capabilities and reshape entire systems, not just create the next viral TikTok video or article.

Required AI Breakthroughs

However, we need new breakthroughs to achieve artificial intelligence that is as intelligent as a human being and more like the "thinking machines" envisioned by Alan Turing, so-called artificial general intelligence (AGI). As large language models grow ever bigger, there are signs that we may have reached a ceiling. As Ilya Sutskever (co-founder of OpenAI and now co-founder and chief scientist at Safe Superintelligence Inc.) noted at the end of 2024, our reliance on pre-training massive neural networks is unsustainable because the internet, the primary source of training data, is finite.[13] Moreover, in 2025, research showed that leading LLMs are showing early signs of "model collapse," meaning their accuracy declines over time.[14] This happens when AI learns from its own outputs, compounding mistakes until they warp reality—producing wrong financial data, fake research, and biased advice, also known as "Garbage In, is Garbage Out."[15]

Scaling models simply by increasing their size will no longer drive breakthroughs. Instead, the next era of AI will require entirely new paradigms that move beyond "bigger is better." According to Sutskever, three emerging breakthroughs stand out as game-changers.

The first is Agentic AI, systems that move beyond static outputs to those that can reason, act independently, and adapt like humans.[16] Unlike today's LLMs, which respond passively to prompts, agentic systems, such as the Manus.ai system that took the internet by storm early 2025, dynamically pursue goals, take actions in real-world environments, and learn continuously. This shift could radically transform organizations as we know them. Instead of hierarchies that are dependent on human management, businesses could function as networks of AI agents collaborating autonomously across departments, optimizing workflows, and responding in real-time to challenges. Imagine customer service agents that can answer questions and resolve problems by proactively coordinating with other systems or supply chains that predict disruptions and self-correct without human oversight. Or what about an AI that doesn't just manage your calendar but anticipates business disruptions and negotiates solutions before you even know there's a problem? Agentic AI turns today's tools into tomorrow's team members, reshaping the very fabric of organizations.

The second breakthrough is synthetic data, which are artificially generated datasets that address real-world data scarcity.[17] While AI models currently rely on enormous quantities of human-generated data, synthetic data can simulate realistic scenarios far beyond what exists in the real world, providing diverse, high-quality inputs for training. This innovation is critical for overcoming limitations in niche domains where labeled data is scarce, such as rare medical conditions or edge-case scenarios in autonomous driving. Synthetic data could enable AI to train on environments that mimic future possibilities, accelerating development without exhausting finite resources.

The third frontier is *out-of-distribution generalization*, where AI systems can solve problems they haven't seen before. The launch of OpenAI's o3 model at the end of 2024 is a sign of what is to come. When revealed, it raised eyebrows with its near-superhuman performance on the ARC-AGI test (a test designed to compare artificial intelligence with human intelligence), achieving 87.5 percent in high-compute mode, even surpassing typical human scores[18] (although in the months that followed, doubts started to arise that OpenAI had access to the test data of the benchmark).[19] This reasoning-focused model excelled at adapting to unfamiliar tasks, showcasing abilities far beyond its predecessors in coding, math and graduate-level sciences. This breakthrough will result in models that adapt flexibly to new environments, mimicking human-like reasoning and generalization. What if AI is capable of handling unprecedented natural disasters, devising solutions for unseen scientific challenges, or responding to geopolitical disruptions, all without the need for retraining? This shift would unlock a new level of robustness. It would move us closer to what OpenAI describes as Level 4 AI, or Innovators.[20] At this stage, AI doesn't just assist in creation; it pioneers new ideas and breakthroughs. Already, AI models are helping scientists and engineers design new materials, simulate biological processes for drug discovery, and optimize workflows that previously required years of experimentation.[21] As AI advances toward Level 5, where it can perform the work of entire organizations and becomes super intelligent, it will redefine creativity and the very nature of invention itself.

However, we might also need an entirely new approach to achieve AGI or even Super Artificial Intelligence. After all, the human brain only requires 20 watts of energy and is the most powerful and remarkable machine in the known universe. This is where Organoid Intelligence emerges as a fascinating possibility, a convergence of biology and technology that redefines how we think about intelligence.[22] Unlike traditional computing systems reliant on energy-intensive hardware, organoid intelligence involves brain-like organoids, which are clusters of lab-grown neurons derived from stem cells that are capable of replicating aspects of neural activity, such as learning, memory and decision-making. Researchers have already observed synaptic communication and electrical patterns akin to early human brain development, prompting a bold hypothesis: could these organic systems, with their unparalleled energy efficiency and adaptability, serve as the blueprint for future intelligent machines? Could they be the breakthrough humanity needs to bring us closer to thinking machines? By bridging the biological and synthetic, organoid intelligence invites us to reimagine what cognition can be and challenges us to question whether true intelligence must ultimately mirror the organic intricacies of life itself.

Together, these advances represent the next evolution of artificial intelligence. They reflect a broader truth: AI must move beyond pattern recognition and brute-force scale. To achieve true adaptability, autonomy, and creativity, AI must embrace fundamentally new paradigms, such as integrating biological insights and energy-efficient models inspired by the human brain. As we stand on the cusp of this transformation, the systems we build will redefine how we work and live and challenge us to reimagine the boundaries of intelligence itself.

Defining the Human–Machine Relationship

AI's expanding presence in our lives forces us to confront profound questions about the relationship between humans and machines. Conversational interfaces like AI-powered personal assistants are becoming indistinguishable from human interaction. Digital twins, virtual replicas of physical assets, systems, and systems of systems, enable simulations that mirror reality so closely that they blur the line between the real and the digital. As machines begin to predict and execute decisions on our behalf, questions of human agency arise: who controls these systems, and how do we retain accountability for the outcomes they generate?[23]

More importantly, the AI arms race discussed in Chapter Two seems to get worse. As the US rushes to outpace China in superintelligent AI, tech leaders warn this could trigger cyber warfare, sabotage, or worse: mutually assured AI destruction. History has a habit of repeating itself, except this time, the nuclear arms race has been replaced by AI. In fact, US Congress is considering a Manhattan Project-style push to dominate AI superintelligence.[24] This clearly mirrors the nuclear arms race, where fear, not logic, dictated strategy. A 2025 policy paper from ex-Google CEO Eric Schmidt argues against an arms race, as rivals like China won't sit back, they'll strike first.[25] This fear-driven approach is wrong on so many fronts, and we should choose collaboration over competition. Unfortunately, companies like OpenAI lobby Washington for fewer restrictions, fearing China's AI dominance.[26] But as AI progresses, are we accelerating innovation or an existential crisis? The race to AI superintelligence isn't just about winning, it's about surviving and thriving. If AI escalation mirrors nuclear deterrence, how do we ensure we don't code ourselves into oblivion?

This is where ethical dilemmas come to the forefront. AI systems are not neutral; they inherit the biases of their creators and the data they consume. In fact, AI systems are like mirrors. They reflect what they've been shown, biases and all. A cracked mirror distorts the truth and so does flawed training data. Algorithmic decisions, if unchecked, can perpetuate inequalities and exacerbate divisions. Who determines what values are embedded into AI systems, and how do we ensure fairness, transparency and accountability? The concentration of AI capabilities among a few powerful entities, those with access to data, infrastructure, and resources, risks centralizing power in unprecedented ways. Without deliberate efforts to democratize access and ensure equitable distribution, AI's benefits may be limited to the privileged, leaving others behind.

Despite these challenges, AI holds unparalleled potential to democratize knowledge and opportunity. Innovations such as Edge AI bring computational power closer to where it is needed, enabling efficiency while safeguarding privacy. Complementing this is invisible AI, or ambient systems, seamlessly blending into the background to anticipate needs and create frictionless, intuitive interactions that integrate digital and physical life.[27] Open-source AI initiatives, such as Llama or Mistral, are making powerful tools accessible to small organizations and developing nations, leveling the playing field. However, realizing this potential requires intentional action (Yu Wei). Educational initiatives must prepare the workforce for an AI-driven future. Regulatory frameworks must balance innovation with oversight. Public-private partnerships must align incentives to ensure AI serves the collective good rather than entrenched interests.

The most powerful insight about AI, however, is its interconnectedness. AI does not exist in isolation but powers and converges with other exponential technologies, amplifying their impacts. Paired with quantum computing, AI could unlock molecular-level simulations for drug discovery and energy optimization. Combined with biotechnology, it will revolutionize human health—engineering cures for diseases and extending life. Integrated with spatial intelligence and brain-computer interfaces, it will create immersive, symbiotic systems that seamlessly merge the physical, digital and biological worlds.

This convergence represents the essence of the technological tsunami reshaping our future. AI is not just a tool; it is a systemic force that accelerates transformation across every industry, every nation, and every aspect of our lives. The question isn't if we will ride the wave of AI but whether we'll steer it toward a future where humanity and technology thrive in harmony. Will AI deepen divisions, centralize control, and erode human agency? Or will we leverage its potential to build systems that are equitable, sustainable, and aligned with the principles of balance and harmony?

The path forward demands that we see AI not as a threat but as a partner. By rethinking our relationship with intelligence and acknowledging its vast potential and profound risks, we can embrace AI as a catalyst for human flourishing. As we stand on the edge of a new era, the challenge is clear: we must ensure that AI does not overwhelm us but empowers us, enabling a future where technology and humanity thrive together, especially as it will increasingly automate physical activity.

Action Steps: Harnessing AI Wisely

AI might feel overwhelming with its rapid advances, but small, intentional steps can help you use it ethically and effectively. Below are practical ways to integrate AI into your daily life or organizational strategy while preserving human creativity and accountability:

- **Elevate digital literacy:** Train employees, students, or team members on AI basics. Even a short online course on AI terminology and applications demystifies this powerful technology.
- **Pilot an AI-driven project:** Start with a single use case—like customer service chatbots or supply chain forecasting—where AI's predictive power meets a real need. Keep the scope small to learn quickly. For individuals, experiment with AI tools, even if it is only 10–20 minutes per week.
- **Commit to bias audits:** Before scaling any AI tool, run bias tests on your training data to help you catch skewed outcomes early.
- **Keep humans in the loop:** Use a "human+AI" approach. Let AI handle repetitive tasks, but ensure a human operator reviews critical decisions to maintain ethics and oversight.

AI's capacity to handle massive data scales complements another technology that brings physical tasks to life: robotics. Let's see how robots, when guided by AI, can help automate and augment our work.

TidalShot

AI isn't just automating tasks; it's redefining intelligence. As machines predict, create, and learn, our challenge is to shape AI that elevates humanity rather than replaces it.

Scan the QR code to share this section's TidalShot and illustration to your network.

ROBOTICS: AUTOMATING PHYSICAL ACTIVITY

In 1962, a mechanical arm named Unimate lifted a piece of molten metal on a factory floor in New Jersey, USA, forever changing how humans and machines interact.[28] It was a quiet but seismic moment, the dawn of industrial robotics, and yet few could imagine the scale of transformation it heralded. Today, we stand at the threshold of a new era that echoes the Jetsons' vision of a seamless human-robot coexistence, minus the flying cars and free trips to space (for now).[29] Rosie the Robot may not yet be folding your laundry, but her smarter cousins are already on factory floors, assembling your next car or maybe even the robot that will eventually fold your laundry. Robotics is no longer about tools that lift, fetch, or assemble; it is about machines that learn, adapt and collaborate as intelligent partners.

While artificial intelligence thrives in the abstract world of data and decisions, robotics brings intelligence to life, turning code into action. It bridges the digital and physical realms, creating systems that operate with precision, endurance and autonomy. But robotics isn't just automating tasks; it fundamentally reshapes how we work, innovate, and coexist in this age of exponential change.

The idea of robots taking over our workplaces once felt fantastical, a storyline borrowed from science fiction. Yet here we are. Robots are redefining physical labor in factories, warehouses, hospitals, and even restaurants. Imagine a hotel in Seoul with an AI-based staff-assignment system that predicts guest surges by analyzing flight data, local event calendars, and even real-time weather.[30] The AI automatically dispatches service robots for housekeeping tasks and the robotic bartender serves the perfect cocktail, while the human concierge is freed to deliver personalized guest interactions.[31] The system cross-checks guest profiles (favorite amenities, dietary needs) to recommend subtle personal touches, from welcome drinks to room temperature. As a result of combining robotics with AI, guests in this hotel consistently report higher satisfaction, and the hotel cuts operational costs by 30 percent. But notice how human empathy remains the highlight of each guest's stay, underscoring how humans and technology weave the perfect tapestry of efficiency and warmth.

In agriculture, robots with advanced AI and sensors perform precision farming, optimizing irrigation, harvesting crops autonomously, and reducing waste. In healthcare, robotic assistants such as Moxi deliver supplies to nurses, freeing their time for critical patient care.[32] Search-and-rescue robots[33] meanwhile come equipped with spatial intelligence and LiDAR systems that can navigate collapsed buildings and deliver life-saving supplies in environments where human capabilities fall short.[34] Dangerous and monotonous tasks, such as toxic waste handling, disaster recovery, or assembling car parts, can now be offloaded to machines built to endure heat, radiation and fatigue.

From Cobots to Humanoids

The real innovation lies not just in robots performing tasks humans cannot but in collaborative robotics, or cobots, that work alongside us. Cobots handle the physical strain of precision-critical jobs, while humans provide oversight, creativity, and decision-making. Humanoid robots, however, are perhaps the most captivating and controversial expression of this transformation. BMW's factories have now employed humanoids to assist technicians in assembly lines, creating workflows that prioritize safety and efficiency without displacing jobs entirely.[35] China's EV giants go one step further and are now quietly turning assembly lines into robot training camps. China's EV titans—BYD, XPeng, Nio—are pivoting into humanoid robotics, leveraging their dominance in batteries, sensors and supply chains.[36] The line between car factories and robot labs is vanishing and the message here is clear: robots are the new cars and we should see them as partners, not replacements, provided we adapt to work with them.

Humanoids such as Tesla's Optimus 2, Boston Dynamics' Atlas, Figure 02, Unitree G1, and EngineAI's SE01 replicate human-like movement powered by reinforcement learning and imitation learning breakthroughs.[37] SE01's natural gait, once considered an engineering impossibility, allows robots to integrate into human-centric spaces with minimal disruption.[38] Specialized humanoid robots, such as those developed by Clone Robotics with water-powered Myofiber muscles, push this even further.[39] Their lifelike skeletal and responsive nervous systems mirror human physiology, offering flexibility and strength. By adopting biomimicry, drawing inspiration from human anatomy, these robots overcome rigidity, enabling more natural and efficient movement.

The humanoid form, with its hands, arms and expressive "faces," makes robots intuitive collaborators in caregiving, hospitality and retail. After all, nobody wants to share a hospital ward with a robot shaped like a giant crab, no matter how efficient it is at delivering meds. SoftBank's Pepper welcomes hotel guests, while humanoids in aged care facilities provide companionship and support for an increasingly elderly population.[40] In Asia, robots already cook, serve meals, and clean restaurants, alleviating labor shortages in fast-growing urban centers.[41]

Yet I believe the humanoid design isn't the final word. Machines with additional limbs or unconventional locomotion could outperform humanoids in niche roles, extending our capabilities to surpass biology. Why stop at two arms and two legs when machines could outdo us with eight limbs, wheels, or, dare I say it, a robot octopus? After all, if robots are here to outwork us, they may as well show off a little. Robotics challenges us to rethink form itself: should machines look like us, or should they evolve beyond us?

More importantly, our perception of robotics will define their future as well. In Japanese culture, robots are often seen as companions or helpers, reflecting a societal openness to machine integration.[42] By contrast, Western narratives frequently emphasize robots as rivals, underscoring anxieties about labor and autonomy.[43] These differing cultural lenses will shape how societies adopt humanoid robotics, whether as extensions of human ingenuity or as existential competitors.

The Convergence of AI and Robotics

The true power of robotics lies in its ability to integrate intelligence into real-world action. Robots are no longer pre-programmed tools following rigid instructions. Advances in multimodal LLMs, such as OpenAI's GPT-4o and Google Gemini, allow robots to simultaneously process auditory, visual and contextual data. This breakthrough allows machines to "see," "hear," and respond to dynamic environments like humans. At the end of 2024, NVIDIA took this further as they launched a tiny AI supercomputer explicitly built for general humanoids that leverage LLMs. It is capable of 70 trillion operations per second, which can be considered extremely high-performance computing. The most fascinating aspect of this Jetson Nano Super is that it retails for only $249—that is the convergence of technologies in action. At the same time, Genesis was revealed, which is a groundbreaking open-source physics engine and simulation platform developed collaboratively by 20 different AI labs.[44] Genesis can run physics simulations up to 430,000 times faster than in real-time, and its engine can be used to train robots in real-world applications at unprecedented speeds.[45] Its simulation speeds enable faster prototyping and testing of robotic systems, reducing development cycles from months to days.

Imagine a robot that hears a customer's request, sees the surrounding context, and adapts its actions seamlessly, restocking shelves, assembling orders, or troubleshooting equipment in a warehouse. Multimodal integration transforms humanoids into context-aware collaborators, blurring the line between human intelligence and machine action. Emotional intelligence is also emerging. Robots like Ameca express lifelike emotions, creating trust and connection in healthcare and caregiving roles. In this way, humanoids are not just functional, but they are becoming relational—although it might require some time to get used to our mechanical coworkers. [46]

The implications for labor are profound. Elon Musk predicts that by 2040, 10 billion humanoid robots priced around $20,000 will reshape global economies.[47] These machines will step into roles traditionally dominated by humans, from logistics to aged care. The potential is staggering, but so are the risks. Without deliberate strategies for workforce retraining and ethical deployment, robotics could deepen inequality rather than lift societies.

The rise of robotics challenges us to reconsider the boundaries between humans and machines. Machines that move, learn, and adapt independently force us to ask: what is distinctly human and where do we add value? Robots will handle the physical and mundane, but humans will provide purpose, creativity and ethical oversight.

As robotics advances, collaborative ecosystems will emerge where humans mentor, supervise and co-create with machines. Google DeepMind's experiments with reinforcement learning showcase robots learning tasks, such as folding laundry, and training themselves through interaction rather than programming.[48] This shift creates opportunities for human-machine synergy, where machines extend human potential rather than replace it.

Societal Impacts of Robotics

The societal impact will depend on how we manage this transition. Production costs are falling, while China and the United States lead mass deployment due to advanced infrastructure and capital investment, developing nations face unique challenges. However, low-cost robotics and open-source initiatives like Genesis are emerging as pathways for democratizing automation, offering opportunities to leapfrog outdated industrial processes. As a result, humanoids will become increasingly accessible, entering homes, hospitals, and workplaces alike. But are we ready? Without retraining initiatives, accessible education, and robust frameworks, robotics risks disrupting labor markets and concentrating power in the hands of a few.

Robotics represents the physical manifestation of exponential technologies, translating digital intelligence into tangible action. As context-aware humanoids enter our global economy, we will see another data explosion. The integration of robotics, advanced sensors, spatial intelligence, and AI creates a positive feedback loop: robots generate vast streams of spatial data, powering AI breakthroughs that, in turn, enhance robots' ability to navigate and interact with their environments. For instance, autonomous warehouses today combine spatial AI, robotics, and IoT, optimizing entire supply chains in ways that were unthinkable a decade ago. It will enable us to push past physical limitations and unlock new possibilities, from autonomous warehouses (also known as dark factories as lights are no longer required in a factory operated by robots alone) to space exploration. At the same time, robotics must align with long-term sustainability goals. Robots must be powered by renewable energy and designed for circular lifecycles, where parts can be reused or recycled. It will be crucial for reducing the environmental impact of the robot revolution. Economically, sustainable adoption requires ensuring robotics benefits not just large corporations but entire communities. Yet the path ahead is not automatic. Robots will not just change our lives; they will reflect the values we embed into them.

The question isn't whether robots will reshape industries; they already are. The Jetsons Era has begun, but let's hope it is Rosie running the show and not the toaster deciding it is time to rise up! The question is how we will guide this transformation. Will we allow robotics to exacerbate inequities, or will we design systems that empower people? Will machines serve as extensions of human ingenuity, or will we lose sight of what makes us uniquely human?

The future of robotics demands more than technological progress. It requires ethical stewardship, equitable access, and a vision of collaboration where humans and machines thrive together. Robots may be the tools, but we are the architects of tomorrow. How we deploy them will determine whether this Jetsons' future enhances humanity or leaves us grappling with its unintended consequences. The future is in our hands. Ask yourself: how can I prepare to work with robots, not against them? What skills will I need to thrive in this collaborative future? By focusing on adaptability, creativity, and ethical leadership, we can guide robotics to serve humanity and work alongside them to create a future defined not by limitations but by boundless possibilities.

Action Steps: Integrating Robotics with Care

Once confined to factory floors, robots now appear in retail, logistics, and even our homes. While robotics will eventually be integrated in every level of our society, including communities and homes, the initial focus will be on organizations. So, before introducing robots to your workplace, consider these steps to ensure they serve human well-being instead of rendering us obsolete:

- **Audit tasks for automation:** Identify repetitive, physically demanding, or hazardous jobs that robots can handle. Automating these tasks safeguards workers and boosts efficiency.
- **Create cobot teams:** Launch small pilot programs pairing cobots with human teammates. Observe how productivity improves and where human judgment remains indispensable.
- **Upskill your workforce:** Offer robotics awareness training to help employees learn how to program, troubleshoot, and coexist with robots. This ensures humans and robots are natural partners.
- **Plan for social impact:** Collaborate with local communities, unions, or educational institutions to manage transitions, especially if robots might displace certain roles. A socially responsible rollout builds long-term trust.

As robotics revolutionizes the physical world, quantum computing is poised to transform the very fabric of decision-making, unlocking solutions to problems previously beyond human or machine comprehension.

TidalShot

Smart robots leave factory floors for our homes, hospitals, and roads. Do we see them as partners in human progress or replaceable cogs? The future hinges on that choice.

Scan the QR code to share this section's TidalShot and illustration to your network.

QUANTUM COMPUTING: SOLVING PROBLEMS BEYOND THE EDGE OF POSSIBILITY

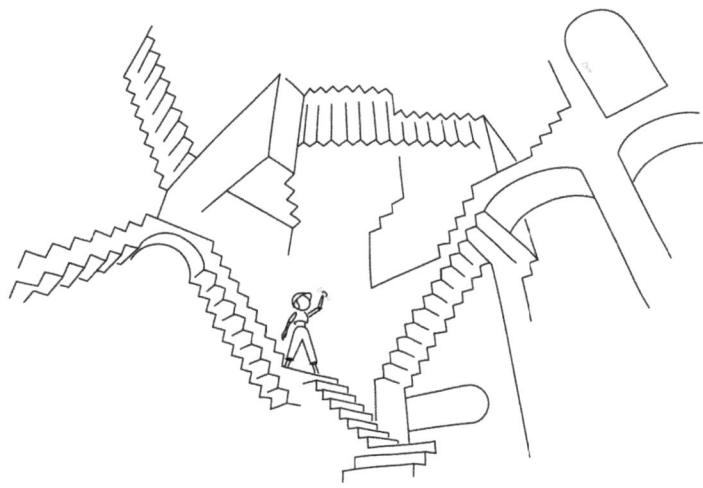

In 1981, Nobel Prize-winning physicist Richard Feynman posed a provocative question that would ripple through the decades: "Can physics be simulated by a universal computer?"[49] The answer to his thought experiment wasn't found in the binary world of classical computing (although the open-source platform Genesis we just discussed does seem to achieve that feat) but in the strange, fluid reality of quantum mechanics.

Feynman's musings gave birth to quantum computing, a technology capable of harnessing the counterintuitive principles of superposition, entanglement, and interference to solve problems deemed insurmountable by traditional systems.

Today, that vision is no longer theoretical. The quantum revolution is knocking on our door, promising breakthroughs that challenge everything we know about computation, cryptography, optimization, and even our understanding of reality itself. Like a bridge between classical constraints and infinite possibility, quantum computing is poised to reshape the systems underpinning healthcare, finance, logistics, cybersecurity and climate science. But as with any leap forward, the question remains: are we ready for the exponential consequences of this quantum moment?

Unlike traditional computers, which process data in binary bits—1s or 0s—quantum computers leverage qubits, particles capable of existing in superposition: simultaneously one and zero. However, please note that the reality of superposition is far more nuanced than simply being "one and zero at the same time." It represents an alternative paradigm of how reality operates at the quantum level, a challenge to classical logic that cannot fully describe quantum behavior. In essence, a qubit exists in a probabilistic state until it is measured, at which point the wave function collapses into a definitive particle-like value of one or zero. This uncertainty and probabilistic existence highlight the revolutionary implications of quantum theory for fields like quantum computing. To avoid your brain collapsing into its own state of confusion, I'll stick to the simplistic version: qubits are kind of both one and zero at the same time.[50]

This quantum property allows quantum systems to process immense amounts of information in "parallel," exponentially increasing their computational power. The metaphor of "parallel processing" implies classical-like computations occurring independently across many states, but in quantum systems, the states are entangled, correlated, and probabilistic. The power of quantum computing lies not in solving multiple classical problems simultaneously but in harnessing quantum effects like superposition and interference to efficiently determine a solution. In short, quantum systems do not literally process vast amounts of information in parallel. Instead, they explore a vast space of possibilities fundamentally differently, leveraging superposition and interference to find solutions. This quantum behavior challenges our classical notions of "reality" and "parallelism" altogether. In other words, quantum computers don't solve problems in parallel; they dance in a probabilistic blur of possibilities until the music stops and the answer emerges.

Add to this entanglement, where qubits influence one another instantaneously regardless of distance, and you have a machine that transcends classical limits. If classical computing is like navigating a single road at a time, quantum computing explores an entire map simultaneously, solving complex, interconnected problems with unparalleled speed. Of course, the reality is, again, far more complicated. Einstein famously called entanglement "spooky action at a distance" since it seems that particles can communicate faster than the speed of light—as in instantly regardless of the distance, even if an entire galaxy separates them.[51]

Another important concept is quantum sensing, which is emerging as a quiet revolution, harnessing the very fabric of quantum mechanics to detect the nearly undetectable.[52] By exploiting phenomena like superposition and entanglement, these sensors achieve levels of precision using, for example, synthetic diamonds that can map underground structures without excavation, capture the faint magnetic whispers of neural activity for early disease diagnosis, and enable GPS-independent navigation for autonomous systems.[53] Diamond-based sensors offer superior sensitivity and stability and are transitioning from experimental prototypes to commercial products, promising real-world edge and mobile quantum applications in medical diagnostics, navigation, and environmental monitoring.[54]

Imagine a future where quantum sensors become the eyes and ears of smart cities—roads that "feel" their own wear, buildings that alert engineers to subtle structural shifts, and digital twins that integrate live quantum data to optimize energy, transportation, and even national security. This isn't a distant dream but a rapidly unfolding reality, where quantum sensing augments existing technologies and lays the groundwork for a new era of digital trust and innovation.

The Dream of Large-Scale Quantum Computing

The dream of a practical, large-scale quantum computer has remained just that, a dream, because existing systems require immense error correction just to keep calculations from falling apart. At the turn of 2024, however, major breakthroughs have turned theory into practical progress. In late 2024, Google's Willow chip improved error correction for quantum computers as discussed in Chapter Two, and in early 2025, Microsoft's Majorana 1 chip, developed over 17 years, introduced a revolutionary type of qubit. Unlike traditional qubits, Microsoft's approach uses topological qubits built on exotic particles called Majorana fermions, first theorized in 1937 by Ettore Majorana, an Italian theoretical physicist,[55] and non-Abelian anyons, which distribute information across multiple states to dramatically reduce errors.[56,57] This breakthrough could eventually lead to a scalable, million-qubit processor that fits in the palm of your hand. These Majorana particles are the key to unlocking quantum stability, providing a fault-tolerant foundation for computing at an unprecedented scale. Although the research was published in the prestigious journal *Nature*, skeptics argue the claims have not been sufficiently backed up by scientific evidence and that Microsoft's PR department made it look like more than it was.[58]

At the same time, China unveiled its Zuchongzhi 3.0 chip, which uses 105 superconducting transmon qubits to perform calculations 1 million times faster than Google's latest quantum system and is 1 quadrillion times faster than the world's top supercomputers.[59] In another key advance, JPMorgan and its partners demonstrated certified quantum randomness using a 56-qubit trapped-ion machine, a feat that transforms the idea of "true randomness" into a practical tool for unhackable crypto transactions, tamper-proof elections, and bulletproof financial security—setting the stage for a quantum arms race in the digital and AI age.[60]

These developments show that the dream of large-scale practical quantum computing might not be just a dream soon, but a reality. If this technology delivers on its promise, it won't just accelerate computation, it will redefine what's computationally possible.

Speed Versus Complexity: The Quantum Advantage

The real promise of quantum computing lies in its ability to address problems that classical systems cannot solve. These are challenges so vast, interconnected, or data-intensive that they have remained beyond reach, until now. Quantum computers could very well contribute to solving the wicked problems discussed earlier. When Dr. Christopher Ballance from Oxford University stated that quantum computing will make things "happen better," he's not just making a bold prediction, he's describing a fundamental shift in how we process information.[61] The quantum revolution represents more than just faster computers; it marks humanity's first steps into manipulating the fabric of reality itself to solve our most pressing challenges.

Take drug discovery, where quantum systems can one day simulate molecular interactions at an atomic level, optimizing life-saving treatments to individual genomes. Or consider climate science: quantum models can integrate atmospheric data, ocean currents, and human activity to forecast scenarios with a precision that classical computers cannot achieve. The ability to model global systems in real time could transform how we tackle climate change, offering actionable solutions on a planetary scale. Another often overlooked domain is advanced materials. AI-driven simulations combined with quantum computing could enable atomic-level manipulation of matter, producing aerospace materials or revolutionary semiconductors. These breakthroughs might pave the way for ultra-efficient energy storage, lightweight, hyper-durable construction, and entirely new industries.

Quantum computing's impact extends to industries reliant on optimization. In finance, quantum algorithms will enable hyper-precise risk analysis, portfolio management, and fraud detection, revolutionizing how markets are modeled and managed.[62] For logistics, route optimization, an otherwise unsolvable problem with millions of variables, can be solved instantly, reducing emissions and costs for global supply chains.[63]

Yet, with great computational power comes great responsibility. The rise of quantum computing raises ethical and societal questions that demand careful stewardship. Who will control quantum resources and how will access be distributed? Will quantum breakthroughs exacerbate global inequalities by favoring nations and corporations with the infrastructure to capitalize on them?

The Big Crunch

The most urgent threat lies in cryptography. Today's encryption methods, such as RSA and AES-256, are secure because classical systems require centuries to crack them. Quantum computers, however, can reduce this timeline to minutes. The looming Big Crunch, also referred to as Q-Day[64], where quantum machines collapse the foundations of digital encryption, threatens the security of our most critical data: banking transactions, military communications, intellectual property, and personal information.[65] The Big Crunch threatens to make your password '*QuantumIsCool123!*' as effective as leaving your house key under the doormat marked 'KEY.'

Unlike the Y2K bug, a challenge identified and resolved in time at a cost of $300-500 billion, the Big Crunch is exponentially more complex, and thus expensive, requiring the development and deployment of quantum-resistant cryptography on a global scale.[66] European policymakers have already sounded the alarm, highlighting the urgent need for collaborative action across governments, corporations, and researchers to future-proof digital infrastructure before the quantum threat materializes.[67] Without this proactive transition, sensitive data that is encrypted today could be retroactively decrypted tomorrow, exposing businesses, nations, and individuals to unprecedented vulnerabilities. While the Australian government created a directive to phase out RSA and other cryptographic algorithms by 2030, this is a very short timeframe given the current speed of developments, and the requirement will probably come too late.[68] The Big Crunch is not a distant possibility but a systemic risk accelerating toward us.[69] In fact, Google revealed in 2025 that breaking RSA encryption might require 20x fewer quantum qubits than previously thought.[70] The question is not whether quantum computing will arrive but whether we will act in time to secure the integrity of our digital world.

Fortunately, a solution is coming. The introduction of quantum-resistant algorithms marks a critical milestone in safeguarding the digital backbone of our societies as we prepare for the quantum era.[71] Spearheaded by the National Institute of Standards and Technology (NIST), these new standards aim to future-proof global encryption systems against the immense computational power of quantum computers. The new algorithms signal a paradigm shift in cybersecurity, forcing organizations to rethink digital trust, resilience, and preparedness in an age of exponential change. This is not just a technological upgrade but an ethical and strategic imperative: ensuring that the foundations of trust, transparency, and data integrity, so essential for individuals, businesses, and governments, remain intact. For leaders, this moment serves as both a wake-up call and an opportunity to proactively align with quantum-safe strategies before the convergence of quantum computing and cyber threats reshapes the digital landscape entirely. And there is no time to waste. In 2024, post-quantum encryption gained traction, but with just 13 percent of internet traffic adopting it globally, there is still a long way to go.[72]

However, even if the world successfully transitions to quantum-resistant encryption in time, it is highly probable that leading superpowers have already stockpiled vast troves of encrypted data, anticipating the moment when quantum computers can shatter its protections (commonly referred to as Harvest Now, Decrypt Later). Governments and major technology players may be quietly harvesting sensitive communications, financial records, and intellectual property, knowing that quantum decryption will one day unlock this treasure trove. When that moment arrives, artificial intelligence will amplify the impact, rapidly analyzing and extracting patterns, insights, and vulnerabilities hidden within. Yet the true disruption may remain concealed. The strategic advantages conferred by cracking a critical encryption algorithm, whether for cyber warfare, espionage, or economic dominance, will almost certainly incentivize secrecy (similar to how the British kept breaking Enigma in secret, which had a material influence on the course of WWII). Disclosure will not come immediately but only when its power has been quietly wielded. The race to quantum supremacy is not just about innovation; it is a geopolitical contest where information is both the prize and the weapon.

The quantum security arms race is also an opportunity. Quantum encryption methods, such as quantum key distribution, promise unhackable communication channels by leveraging the principles of entanglement and quantum measurement. It is like sending messages with invisible ink that self-destructs the moment anyone tries to peek—James Bond would approve. Harvard's recent breakthroughs in entanglement memory across 35 kilometers mark a critical step toward building the quantum internet, a network of ultra-secure communications that could connect quantum computers globally.[73] Quantum computing will dismantle old security paradigms but also build new ones, provided we act now.

Merging Quantum and AI

The real magic happens at the intersection of quantum computing and artificial intelligence.[74] Together, these technologies amplify each other's strengths: quantum systems accelerate AI's data analysis, pattern recognition, and predictive modeling, while AI refines quantum circuits and mitigates errors. This interplay is not theoretical: AI-driven quantum error correction methods, such as Google DeepMind's AlphaQubit, have already reduced computational errors on quantum processors by 30 percent, marking a critical step toward practical, large-scale quantum systems.[75]

The convergence of quantum computing and AI is poised to unlock transformative capabilities that redefine problem-solving, efficiency, and scalability. Quantum systems, such as the newly developed Willow chip covered in Chapter Two, have demonstrated breakthroughs in specialized tasks, surpassing classical supercomputers for speed and complexity.

This quantum-AI synergy promises seismic impacts across industries, combining quantum's computational power with AI's predictive capabilities. Neuromorphic systems[76] (such as Australia's DeepSouth[77]) execute 228 trillion synaptic operations per second and apply biological computing, using biological principles and systems for computational tasks, to add another dimension that mirrors the architecture of the human brain to simulate complexity at scale.[78] Together, these technologies are posed to give us a unique new perspective on how our world actually works and how we can improve it in ways that seemed like magic not too long ago.

The transformative potential of quantum computing lies not in its ability to replace classical systems but to complement and extend them. Picture a coastal city bracing for a category five hurricane. A quantum-powered model runs countless simulations in minutes, mapping potential storm surges down to city blocks.[79] Using these insights, the city's emergency department reconfigures evacuation routes in real-time,[80] orchestrating everything from traffic lights to medical triage stations.[81] Meanwhile, local authorities broadcast instructions via immersive AR notifications, ensuring citizens see precisely where to move. The result is a streamlined operation where data, technology, and human initiative blend to save countless lives.

As quantum systems converge with other technologies, they will amplify the impact of these technologies exponentially. Quantum computing is no longer a distant dream but an unfolding reality. Yet, this revolution will not happen overnight. The road ahead requires breakthroughs in scaling, error correction, and accessibility. Recent breakthroughs suggest practical systems are within reach, but their potential will only be realized through global cooperation and ethical oversight.

As such, the question is no longer whether quantum computing will reshape industries, but how we will harness its power. Will we use this quantum leap to address humanity's greatest challenges, from curing diseases to combating climate change, or will we allow its transformative potential to deepen divides and disrupt systems unprepared for its arrival?

Quantum computing challenges us to think exponentially, act collaboratively, and prepare for a future where the boundaries of possibility are completely rewritten. The quantum revolution is about faster computers, but more than that, it is about reimagining what we can solve, create, and become, like upgrading from paper maps to Google Maps, but for the mysteries of the universe. The future is uncertain, but one truth remains: this is our quantum moment.

Action Steps: Planning for the Post-Quantum World

Quantum computing promises computational leaps we can barely imagine, from speeding up drug discovery to busting classical encryption. Yet, it remains in the early stages, requiring careful readiness. Here's how to prepare for the quantum era:

- **Educate your team:** Host workshops on quantum basics and their potential applications. Early exposure to quantum thinking will help teams spot future use cases.
- **Partner with researchers:** Create alliances with quantum labs or startups to stay informed on breakthroughs. A small pilot project (like quantum-inspired algorithms) can build organizational knowledge.
- **Begin encryption transition:** Start planning for post-quantum cryptography so your data remains secure once quantum processors mature. Tools are emerging now; don't wait for a crisis.
- **Explore industry use cases:** Quantum might transform logistics, materials science or financial modeling. Invest in scenario mapping to pinpoint where quantum can give you a unique edge.

While quantum computing tackles the computational frontier, blockchain focuses on trust and accountability in a trustless digital world—a foundation quantum breakthroughs may soon rely on.

TidalShot

Quantum computers dance in probabilities, upending classical limits. They'll crack codes, transform drug discovery, and remind us that reality is more fluid than we ever believed.

Scan the QR code to share this section's TidalShot and illustration to your network.

BLOCKCHAIN: VERIFYING TRUST AND ACCOUNTABILITY

The exponential advancements in AI, robotics, and quantum computing are transforming our world at a breathtaking pace, pushing the boundaries of what was once thought impossible. Yet, as these technologies accelerate innovation, they raise a critical question: how can we trust the systems that power our future? In a world increasingly shaped by machine-generated decisions, autonomous actions, and quantum breakthroughs, blockchain emerges as the missing pillar. A foundational technology that anchors trust, transparency, and accountability. If AI is the brain, robotics the body, and quantum computing the engine of our future, then blockchain, or more broadly speaking distributed ledger technology, is the grumpy accountant, double-checking every detail to ensure that the data driving these systems remains verifiable, secure, and untampered. Not glamorous, but absolutely essential.

Unfortunately, in the past years, blockchain's image has been hijacked by scam coins and crazy apes, overshadowing its transformative potential. Blockchain is not, and should not be, perceived as 'sexy.' It is the plumbing of the internet. Essential, reliable, and hopefully invisible unless something goes catastrophically wrong. Nobody dreams about pipes but try living without them. Like MySQL databases quietly powering digital services, blockchain will be the unsung hero of tomorrow's infrastructure, ensuring trust in systems that would otherwise collapse under the weight of their own complexity. Its essential role in decentralizing power, enabling transparency, and building trust often goes unnoticed. This section aims to set the record straight, repositioning blockchain as the foundational, albeit unsexy, technology for a decentralized, trustworthy digital future.

Before diving into its transformative potential, let's demystify blockchain. At its core, blockchain is a shared, immutable ledger that records transactions across a decentralized network.[82] Think of it as a digital record book replicated and distributed across thousands, if not millions, of computers. A librarian's dream and a conspiracy theorist's nightmare. Unlike centralized databases, no single entity owns or controls this ledger, making it resistant to tampering and censorship. Every transaction is grouped into a "block," cryptographically linked to the previous one, forming an immutable chain of trust. Once recorded, data cannot be altered retroactively without consensus from the network, ensuring transparency and integrity and stressing the importance of high-quality data. However, blockchain's security hinges on encryption, and with the impending Big Crunch of quantum computing, protocols must transition to quantum-resistant encryption to safeguard this trust.

Blockchain's transformative power lies not in isolation but in its convergence with AI, IoT (internet of things), and quantum computing. Imagine a self-driving car navigating a smart city, with its decisions driven by data shared across a blockchain. Stakeholders, manufacturers, municipalities, and insurers trust this data because it is immutable, transparent, and verifiable. This balance is the very essence of Taoism: when order meets spontaneity, innovation becomes self-regulating and sustainable, much like the natural equilibrium that underpins all life. As blockchain secures the systems of tomorrow, it provides the confidence we need to trust machines, processes, and even one another in an increasingly automated and connected world. As such, blockchain embodies the Taoist ideal of balance, as it exemplifies how a harmonious interplay between order and spontaneity can create a self-regulating ecosystem that honors both innovation and integrity. More importantly, blockchain isn't merely a technical innovation, but it mirrors the Taoist principle that sustainable progress arises from an equilibrium between structure and flow.

The Computable Economy

Harnessing the equilibrium between order and spontaneity, blockchain not only secures data but also redefines ownership, paving the way for transformative innovations like the tokenization of real-world assets (RWAs). RWAs represent one of blockchain's most transformative applications, heralding a new era in global finance.[83] At its core, tokenization is the process of converting physical (or digital) assets, such as real estate, fine art, or carbon credits, into digital tokens on a blockchain. These tokens can be fractionalized, meaning that ownership of traditionally illiquid assets can now be divided into smaller, more accessible units.[84] This democratization allows individuals to invest in high-value assets with minimal capital, breaking down barriers that once reserved these opportunities for institutional players and the ultra-wealthy. The implications of this shift are immense.

Tokenization breathes liquidity into illiquid assets, unlocking trillions of dollars in economic potential by making assets tradable in real-time without traditional intermediaries and creating a computable economy.[85] The computable economy represents the next frontier in economic evolution. This emerging paradigm shifts traditional economic interactions from opaque and intermediary-driven systems to transparent and automated ecosystems. At its core, the computable economy transforms physical and digital assets into tokenized entities that can be managed, traded, and leveraged with precision, either by humans or AI. By embedding assets into decentralized systems, it unlocks new levels of efficiency, inclusivity, and scalability, enabling complex interactions previously constrained by inefficiencies in traditional markets.

This new model is more than a technological upgrade. It is an opportunity to rethink the very structure of economies, introducing systems that align better with the needs of an interconnected, digital-first world. From enabling fractional ownership of ultra-luxury goods to creating decentralized mechanisms for global collaboration, or even redefining IPOs (initial public offering) by tokenizing stocks and making stocks in upcoming startups available to everyone and not just VCs, the computable economy redefines how we create, exchange, and manage value. It radically reimagines what is possible when economic processes become computable, verifiable, and universally accessible. For example, a commercial building tokenized on a blockchain can be sold fractionally, enabling individuals to buy a stake in high-value properties without navigating complex legal and financial frameworks. For an investor, this means that a $1 billion building can be sold in 1 million pieces instead of one large chunk, making it far easier to sell the building. For example, BlackRock embraces this paradigm. With its $10 trillion under management, the company is leveraging tokenization to enhance liquidity and efficiency across its portfolios.[86]

Building on this foundation of tokenization, the advent of autonomous digital commerce marks the next evolution in blockchain-powered systems. With AI agents now able to execute cryptocurrency transactions independently, a new layer of financial interactivity emerges.[87] These AI-driven transactions leverage blockchain for trust and transparency, enabling autonomous agents to negotiate contracts, manage payments, and execute trades seamlessly. For example, an AI agent managing a renewable energy marketplace could dynamically allocate resources, settle payments, and even trade carbon credits, all without human intervention. This expansion redefines the very nature of commerce, transitioning from human-led decisions to autonomous, blockchain-fueled ecosystems. These developments mark a significant evolution in global finance, where block-chain technology reduces transaction costs, enhances transparency, and accelerates settlement times.

Recent innovations in blockchain, such as dynamic NFTs (dNFTs) and Soulbound tokens, are key enablers in this tokenization ecosystem.[88] Dynamic NFTs differ from traditional static NFTs by evolving in response to external factors, making them ideal for representing real-world assets such as vehicles, machinery, or real estate. For instance, a dynamic NFT tied to a luxury car could update in real time to reflect changes in maintenance history, usage, market valuation, or energy efficiency ratings. This adaptability enhances transparency while ensuring tokenized assets remain relevant and accurate in dynamic markets.

Soulbound tokens are non-transferable digital credentials linked to individual identities. These tokens enable decentralized identity systems, fostering trust and accountability in the digital economy. For example, a Soulbound token could represent proof of ownership, professional certifi-cations, or voting rights in decentralized governance systems, ensuring that credentials cannot be sold or transferred fraudulently. Together, dNFTs and Soulbound tokens showcase blockchain's maturity beyond speculative uses, offering practical tools for managing and verifying the lifecycle of toke-nized assets.

Ensuring the Integrity of Data

What applies to real-world assets also applies to digital content: blockchain technology provides a powerful mechanism to ensure data integrity, offering a robust defense against deepfakes and misinformation. In a digital landscape where manipulated media and false information proliferate, as we will see in Chapter Five, blockchain can serve as a trust anchor by creating immutable, verifiable records of content provenance. Initiatives such as Fox Corp's and Polygon Labs' Verify protocol demonstrate how blockchain's transparency and immutability enables users to trace the origins of digital content, distinguishing fact from fabrication with confidence.[89] This capability is a defense mechanism, but it also sets the stage for a more transparent digital future.

Imagine a coffee cooperative in Colombia using drones (robotics) guided by AI-driven crop analytics to map yield predictions. Each batch is tracked via blockchain from farm to cup.[90,91] As the beans reach a smart warehouse in Munich, autonomous mobile robots (AMRs) sort shipments in minutes, guided by an AI logistics system that automatically cross-checks authenticity on a distributed ledger.[92] The result? Fair prices for farmers, robust supply chain transparency, and near-zero manual errors. It is a testament to how AI, robotics, and blockchain converge to reinvent global trade.[93]

With blockchain ensuring trust for real-world and digital assets, it also lays the foundation for the internet's next evolution. As the internet continues to evolve, this principle of verifiable trust will play a foundational role in what Outlier Ventures, a Web3 Accelerator whose founder Jamie Burke wrote the foreword of my fourth book *Step into the Metaverse*, has termed the Post Web: an internet not driven by centralized platforms but by decentralized systems that empower individuals.[94] Blockchain, alongside AI and decentralized networks, will enable a thinner and smarter web that is focused on user intentions and trust-driven interactions. It is a vision where the internet evolves from a tool of exploitation to a platform of purpose.

Imagine a world where AI agents work on your behalf, seamlessly delivering exactly what you need when you need it. This isn't just a smarter internet but a thinner one, focused on meaningful connections rather than endless doomscrolling. As we move into this new paradigm, the Post Web could reshape industries, challenge traditional power structures, and give us the tools to solve global challenges faster and more collaboratively than ever before.

If AI reshapes how we think, robotics redefines how we act, and quantum computing expands what we can solve, blockchain ensures we can trust it all. By focusing on blockchain's foundational role, beyond speculation, we can build transparent, equitable, and purpose-driven systems. The future will belong to those who trust, verify and act.

Action Steps: Building Transparent Systems

Once associated mainly with cryptocurrencies, blockchain technology has evolved into a platform for trust, transparency, and decentralized innovation. Here are steps to incorporate blockchain responsibly, whether you're a startup or a global enterprise:

- **Identify the use case:** Don't "blockchain for the sake of blockchain." Check if your problem involves data integrity, transparency, or reducing middlemen. That's where blockchain shines.
- **Evaluate eco-friendly consensus:** Consider proof-of-stake or other low-energy protocols, sidestepping the carbon footprint controversies of proof-of-work mining.
- **Combine blockchain with AI:** Explore how AI can automate smart contracts and verify transactions. This synergy can reduce overhead and speed up processes.
- **Tokenize real-world assets:** From real estate and jewelry to carbon credits, tokenization democratizes access. But ensure regulatory compliance and robust identity checks to prevent fraud.

Once blockchain codifies trust, attention turns to how we experience the merging of digital and physical realities. That's where Spatial Intelligence becomes indispensable, mapping our world in real-time.

TidalShot

In a world drowning in misinformation, blockchain can be our anchor of trust, securely tracking assets and data so we no longer rely on centralized gatekeepers alone.

Scan the QR code to share this section's TidalShot and illustration to your network.

SPATIAL INTELLIGENCE: MERGING THE PHYSICAL AND DIGITAL WORLDS

Humans are inherently three-dimensional beings. We navigate, perceive, and interpret the world spatially, yet we primarily interact with technology through two-dimensional devices like smartphones and computers. This limitation is akin to exploring a vibrant world through a narrow window. Functional, but far from optimal. Spatial intelligence promises to widen this window into a seamless fusion of physical and digital realms, creating a "phygital" world. As advancements in AI, miniaturized hardware, and sensory technologies converge, a hyper-realistic, immersive 3D environment is no longer a distant dream but an imminent reality. This spatially aware ecosystem will redefine human interaction, unlock new economic opportunities, and revolutionize industries— fostering interactive, adaptive, and immersive environments.[95]

For this immersive world to succeed, it must achieve hyper-realism, becoming indistinguishable from the physical world to satisfy our brain's demand for spatial continuity. The fusion of digital physics, generative AI, and ultra-fast computation, driven by platforms such as Genesis discussed earlier, will enable immersive, believable environments where users can interact naturally.[96] Once this threshold is crossed, augmented reality (AR), virtual reality (VR), and mixed reality (collectively referred to as the metaverse) will open a world of infinite possibilities. Drawing on Indigenous wisdom, which values deep connection to land, community, and tradition, this fusion of worlds reminds us that our digital innovations must be rooted in the rich soil of cultural and environmental respect. If we manage that, digital identities will thrive, creativity will surge, and the unimaginable will become accessible.[97]

The Revival of the Metaverse

So, you might have thought the metaverse was a passing fad and perhaps even celebrated when AI's hype pushed it into the shadows. But nothing could be further from the truth. The metaverse is back. Bigger, bolder, and more realistic than ever thanks to spatial intelligence. It represents a new reality where physical and digital worlds converge, inviting even skeptics to explore its potential. Spatial intelligence forms the foundation of this evolution, enabling machines to perceive, reason, and act within a three-dimensional world, aligning seamlessly with how humans experience reality.[98] Rooted in the physical laws of nature, spatial intelligence allows machines to navigate and interpret the world with unparalleled depth and precision, bridging the gap between digital and physical realms. Spatial intelligence is not just about enhancing individual experiences; it is poised to transform how societies work, learn, and connect, bridging geographic, economic, and cultural divides.

Building on decades of progress in AI, computer vision, and modeling, spatial intelligence has reached a pivotal moment where computing power, sophisticated algorithms, and vast datasets converge.[99] Its applications are vast: generating fully immersive virtual worlds, enhancing the physical world with contextually rich overlays, and empowering machines to interact dynamically with 3D environments. Whether enabling robots to navigate spaces or crafting hyper-realistic digital experiences, spatial intelligence is poised to revolutionize healthcare, education, entertainment, and more.

Imagine a film set in Cape Town, where a crew deploys humanoid robots as camera operators, guided by advanced AI generating real-time cinematography angles.[100] Spatial intelligence maps each actor's position, anticipating movements for the perfect shot[101]. Meanwhile, a script AI spontaneously writes new dialogue in response to on-set improvisations, ensuring continuity across scenes. The result? A live, co-created film experience that merges robotics, real-time AI content generation, and hyper-precise spatial mapping. The director calls it the next big leap in immersive storytelling, an accelerated creative loop that blends machine efficiency with human flair.

This technology will also drive a metaverse where the lines between digital and physical realities blur.[102] Spatial intelligence provides the computational capability to navigate and interact within three-dimensional digital environments, creating immersive ecosystems that rival and often surpass the fidelity of the physical world. It transforms the metaverse into a space where every interaction feels natural, adaptive, and intuitive.

Rapid advances in AI, 3D rendering, and real-time interactivity power this leap.[103] Technologies such as Gaussian Splatting and NeuRBF bring richly detailed virtual worlds to life,[104] while AI-generated content continuously personalizes user experiences.[105] Spatial intelligence enables machines to replicate depth, movement, and interactivity with stunning precision, creating a dynamic, AI-driven metaverse poised to redefine industries, reshape connections, and unlock new avenues for innovation.

This convergence is not limited to visual and tactile realms; it extends to olfactory experiences, adding a new sensory dimension to digital immersion. Breakthroughs such as Osmo's scent teleportation digitizes and replicates aromas, creating multi-dimensional realities.[106] Imagine virtually exploring a rose garden where you not only see the petals in exquisite 3D detail or can feel the petals using haptic gloves but can also inhale their fragrance, all without triggering your allergies! This capability enhances realism in applications ranging from VR cooking classes to therapeutic experiences, opening new possibilities for sensory engagement in the metaverse.[107]

Augmenting the Physical World

Spatial intelligence also drives the evolution of AR by overlaying digital content onto physical spaces, dynamically responding to user actions and environmental contexts.[108] AR redefines how we learn, work, and connect, offering adaptive training, immersive remote collaboration, and enhanced accessibility for navigating complex environments. Spatial intelligence isn't just a feature of AR; it is the secret sauce that turns clunky overlays into seamless, "I can't believe this isn't reality" moments.

Holographic technology, powered by spatial intelligence, exemplifies how this paradigm shift will bring people closer, transcending borders and redefining the concept of presence in personal and professional relationships.[109] Imagine sitting in your living room and seeing a hyper-realistic holographic projection of a loved one, thousands of miles away, sitting right across from you. Every detail, their gestures, expressions, and voice, is captured in real-time, creating an interaction as personal as if they were physically present. Holographic technology bridges emotional and physical divides, turning cross-border connections into meaningful experiences with just a pair of sleek AR glasses.

As spatial intelligence evolves, its ethical implications must be addressed. The ability to map and track individuals in physical and virtual spaces raises privacy concerns.[110] Spatial tracking, while enabling personalized and context-aware experiences, risks overstepping into surveillance without proper regulation. Similarly, the immersive nature of these environments can blur the line between augmentation and intrusion, raising issues of over-dependence or social isolation. Robust privacy frameworks and a commitment to enhancing, rather than replacing, human connection are essential. Questions about data ownership and who controls and benefits from the vast amounts of spatial data generated must also be resolved to ensure public good prevails over private exploitation.

Spatial intelligence represents a paradigm shift in human interaction. It holds the potential to transform industries, enhance creativity, and improve lives, but its success hinges on navigating its complexities responsibly. By prioritizing inclusivity, privacy, and ethical innovation, we can ensure spatial intelligence accelerates progress while fostering a more equitable and connected world.

We have only scratched the surface of what the metaverse can achieve. As technology advances and more intuitive interfaces become the norm, 3D immersive experiences will become more commonplace and reach levels of realism that will further blur the lines between the digital and physical. For example, as we advance from 5G to 6G, we'll see ambient computing become a reality, where billions of devices seamlessly connect at lightning speeds, providing us with an entirely new layer on top of reality. This opens the door to real-time collaborative robots, continuous AI-powered diagnostics, and even hyper-realistic environments streamed directly into our brains, revolutionizing how we perceive and interact with digital and physical realms.[111] Think of it as binge-watching your favorite series but with a plot twist: you are actually in the show, arguing with the characters about their questionable life choices.

Action Steps: Spatial Tech for Everyone

Spatial intelligence merges the physical and digital realms, enabling hyper-accurate 3D data and immersive AR experiences. Before your organization or city integrates these tools, consider actions that ensure beneficial and inclusive outcomes:

- **Pilot a single AR application:** For instance, use virtual reality for training new situations or develop an AR-driven indoor navigation tool in a warehouse or retail store. Watch how employees or customers adapt, then refine accordingly.
- **Safeguard location data:** Implement strict privacy rules for spatial data. Transparency on who collects, stores, and analyzes real-time tracking fosters trust.
- **Collaborate across departments:** Urban planners, IT, marketing, and legal teams should co-create AR guidelines, ensuring you don't roll out technology in silos.
- **Leverage open data:** Where possible, share anonymized mapping data to spur community-driven innovations, from local AR tourism guides to open-source city planning.

As spatial intelligence brings the physical-digital boundary to life, the next step may be embedding technology even deeper. This could include directly into our neurology through Brain-Computer Interfaces (BCIs), where the merging of mind and matter will redefine the very essence of human experience.

TidalShot

AR, VR, and mixed reality are dissolving borders between digital and physical. From immersive learning to real-time collaboration, reality is about to get a vivid upgrade.

Scan the QR code to share this section's TidalShot and illustration to your network.

BRAIN-COMPUTER INTERFACES: CONNECTING THOUGHTS TO MACHINES

With its immense processing power and adaptability, the human brain has always been a frontier for technological exploration. Brain-computer interfaces (BCIs) mark a monumental leap in this journey, directly connecting human cognition to digital systems. By decoding neural signals and translating them into actionable outputs, BCIs are poised to redefine communication, creativity, and accessibility. As we approach an era where thoughts can control devices, collaborate with AI, and even enhance cognitive abilities, the opportunities are as transformative as the challenges are profound.[112]

A brain-computer interface, sometimes called a brain-machine interface or neural-control interface, has its roots in research dating back to the 1970s at the University of California.[113] Early efforts centered on restoring sensory and motor functions, such as sight, hearing, and movement, for individuals with impairments. Over the decades, significant advancements in pattern recognition, bolstered by AI and machine learning, have propelled the field forward. BCIs now excel at detecting and interpreting the subtle energy fluctuations in the brain associated with thought, identifying distinct neural patterns.

At their core, BCIs represent the convergence of neuroscience, AI, and robotics, a testament to the accelerating pace of innovation. These interfaces have the potential to democratize access to advanced capabilities, enabling individuals with disabilities to regain agency while offering enhanced cognition and creativity to broader society. BCIs challenge fundamental concepts of identity, privacy, and autonomy, transforming the boundaries of what it means to be human.[114]

Promise: Accessibility and Enhanced Cognition

BCIs aim to solve pressing human challenges related to communication, mobility, and cognition. BCIs are not a monolithic technology but encompass a wide range of approaches, from invasive systems that require surgical implantation to non-invasive devices that monitor brain activity externally using a wearable headset. BCIs represent a groundbreaking convergence of neuroscience and technology, enabling direct communication between the human brain and external devices. These interfaces decode neural signals, translating them into actionable outputs. Advances in neural mapping and signal processing have enabled more precise and effective interfaces, bringing us closer to seamless integration between human thought and digital systems.[115] We may soon witness breakthroughs that merge our understanding of physics, biology, and consciousness. For example, brain-computer interfaces that bypass biological constraints, quantum-driven simulations that uncover deeper realities, or new sensors that broaden human perception.

For individuals with severe disabilities, BCIs offer a lifeline to restore lost capabilities. Examples such as Synchron's stent-based interface[116], Precision Neuroscience's ultra-thin electrode arrays[117], or Elon Musk's Neuralink[118] illustrate how BCIs enable thought-driven control of prosthetics, communication systems, and even computers.[119] Elon Musk envisions that he can restore sight, even to humans who were born blind or lost both their eyes.[120] Even Apple is working with Synchron to let users control iPhones and Vision Pro headsets using brain signals, no hands required.[121] These advancements allow those with a disability to regain independence and interact with the world in ways previously thought impossible. Beyond medical applications, BCIs promise to redefine how we engage with technology, by-passing traditional inputs such as keyboards and controllers to enable seamless, intuitive interaction. Imagine controlling a cursor, navigating a virtual environment, or even piloting a drone (yes, brain-drone racing is a thing[122]) entirely with your mind. Or imagine a medical student practicing surgery in a hyper-realistic VR environment where their neural signals are monitored to provide instant feedback, improving skills with unparalleled precision.

The implications of BCIs extend beyond accessibility. Direct brain-to-brain communication could enable a level of collaboration and empathy previously unimaginable. By allowing ideas to be shared without the limitations of language, BCIs have the potential to revolutionize fields requiring high levels of creativity and teamwork. For instance, BCIs have the potential to enable silent, thought-based communication between soldiers and commanders. This would allow for real-time, covert communication without needing verbal or physical signals, enhancing operational efficiency and security.[123]

In entertainment, BCIs promise to elevate immersion to unprecedented levels. Gamers could control complex in-game actions with mere thoughts, and virtual reality experiences could adapt dynamically to the user's emotional and mental state.[124] Already, non-invasive BCIs developed by researchers at the University of Texas allow players to navigate games without physical controllers, offering a glimpse into how thought-driven interactions could redefine digital entertainment.[125]

Ethical Quicksand: Mind Privacy and Autonomy

BCIs challenge our understanding of individuality and the nature of human-machine relationships. As the lines between cognition and computation blur, profound philosophical questions arise: What does it mean to have autonomy over one's thoughts in a world where they can be digitized, stored, or even manipulated? Would you give Meta access to your thoughts, risking seeing even more invasive advertising?

Without robust safeguards, the commercialization of neural data could turn our innermost thoughts into commodities. These questions are not hypothetical. A 2024 Neurorights Foundation report revealed that 29 out of 30 investigated BCI devices allowed unrestricted access to sensitive neural data and shared it without explicit user consent.[126] Fortunately, regulation is slowly starting to appear, with the state of Colorado, USA becoming the first state to provide consumer privacy protections for data generated from a person's brain waves in 2024.[127] While Colorado leads the way, global regulations must evolve rapidly to address the cross-border implications of neural data trade, much like how GDPR reshaped data privacy.

Brain-computer interfaces stand at the frontier of human-machine integration, embodying the acceleration, democratization, and transformation of cutting-edge technologies. BCIs offer solutions that are as profound as they are disruptive.

Picture a neurology clinic in Singapore in the not-too-distant future[128], where patients wear non-invasive brain-computer interface headsets that communicate with an AI diagnostic tool.[129] Simultaneously, spatial intelligence maps the patient's neural activity onto a 3D hologram visible to doctors in real time. Across the globe, a specialist in Toronto joins the virtual session, guiding the clinic's staff through potential diagnoses. With a flick of his hand, the specialist zooms into a particular neural pathway to highlight anomalies. The AI suggests a tailored treatment plan, factoring in past data from thousands of similar cases. Meanwhile, the patient remains comfortably in bed, grateful that physical distance no longer limits expert medical care.

However, the transformative power of BCIs comes with equally significant responsibilities. They democratize capabilities by enabling individuals with disabilities to regain autonomy while offering cognitive enhancements that could benefit society at large. Yet, their transformative power demands thoughtful implementation. International collaboration between technologists, ethicists, and policymakers is essential to ensure these technologies foster equity and innovation rather than division. If developed responsibly, BCIs could unlock human potential on a scale never before imagined, reshaping how we think, learn, and interact with the world.

Action Steps: Responsible BCI Development

From mind-controlled prosthetics to experimental neural implants, BCIs offer unprecedented ways to interface with machines using thoughts. Yet they also raise pressing questions about autonomy and privacy. While advanced consumer applications of BCIs are still years away, organizations can already experiment with them. Here's how to proceed with caution and promise if you see a use case for integrating BCIs in your organization:

- **Start with non-invasive tools:** Familiarize yourself with EEG headsets or wearable brain sensors that aid focus, memory, or motor control, building comfort with BCI basics.
- **Engage in ethics by design:** Ensure your BCI project has a dedicated ethics board, not just legal oversight. Neuro-rights, like data sovereignty over one's brain signals,

must be paramount.

- **Pilot accessibility projects:** Test BCIs in healthcare or assistive tech first (e.g., for ALS patients or stroke survivors), validating real societal value before moving to consumer enhancements.
- **Educate stakeholders:** Public understanding of "what BCIs can and can't do" is crucial. Provide open demos or Q&As to dispel misconceptions and encourage input.

As BCIs push the boundaries of the human-machine interface, another transformative force is reshaping how we create and distribute physical assets: 3D printing. Both technologies challenge traditional paradigms, decentralizing power and fostering accessibility in their respective domains. While BCIs redefine how we think and connect, 3D printing revolutionizes how we materialize ideas into tangible realities. Together, these innovations herald a future where the barriers between imagination and implementation continue to dissolve.

TidalShot

Reading neural signals was sci-fi yesterday. Today, BCIs turn thought into action. We must ask: how do we protect mental privacy when brains become the next digital frontier?

Scan the QR code to share this section's TidalShot and illustration to your network.

3D PRINTING: MATERIALIZING IDEAS INTO ASSETS

Imagine a world where globalization as we know it fades, replaced by hyper-localized manufacturing hubs capable of producing anything you need on demand. This isn't science fiction; it is the transformative potential of 3D printing.

As this technology matures, it threatens to dismantle global supply chains, challenging the geopolitical dominance of nations like China and shifting the balance of economic power. This shift from industrial hubs to decentralized 'Fab Labs,' or fabrication laboratories, could disrupt manufacturing and global trade patterns, labor markets, and even geopolitical alliances, creating ripple effects that challenge existing economic systems.[130]

While 3D printing's ripple in the tsunami of technological change may seem small now, its eventual impact on economies and industries will be seismic.

Additive Manufacturing Basics

3D printing, also known as additive manufacturing, will have such a huge impact as it will revolutionize industries by transforming how we design, produce, and consume. It allows for the local creation of complex structures with minimal waste, enabling innovations that were once considered science fiction. From printing entire homes to personalized medical implants and personal care accessories, the possibilities seem endless. Yet, this same technology has also introduced new risks, particularly with the rise of untraceable 3D-printed firearms.

In industries like construction, aerospace, and medicine, 3D printing is a game-changer. The construction sector can use it to combat housing shortages by printing durable, eco-friendly homes in days instead of months.[131] Large-scale 3D printers have already been deployed to build affordable housing at scale in areas such as in Wolf Ranch, a community in Georgetown, Texas, leveraging locally sourced materials and minimizing environmental impact.[132] Similarly, the aerospace industry has embraced 3D printing for its ability to create lightweight, highly customized components. Airbus uses it to cut manufacturing costs and emissions,[133] Rolls-Royce has developed 3D-printed engine components to optimize fuel efficiency,[134] and NASA employs 3D-printed surrogates to accelerate design iterations because when you are planning to colonize Mars, there's no time for a supply chain delay.[135]

In healthcare, 3D printing has paved the way for patient-specific treatments. From custom prosthetics to bio-printed tissues, it enables a level of personalization that traditional manufacturing cannot achieve.[136] In personal care, Philips Fixables started offering downloadable 3D print files for personal care accessories, starting with an adjustable beard trimmer comb so consumers can replace parts without tossing whole devices.[137] Pharmaceutical companies are even exploring 3D-printed pills, combining multiple medications into a single dose tailored to an individual's needs.[138] These advancements exemplify how 3D printing can address society's most pressing challenges and change how we turn ideas into reality.

Imagine walking into your local café, ordering your coffee, and picking up a custom 3D-printed chair, a replacement bike part, or a personalized piece of jewelry, all printed at the Fab Lab integrated into the space. This isn't a distant dream but a transformative vision for the future of manufacturing. Fab Labs could soon become as ubiquitous as Starbucks, merging digital creativity with local production and reshaping how we design, make, and consume.

The Rise of Fab Labs

In this world, online marketplaces for digital designs will flourish, serving as repositories where freelance designers list everything from open-source cutlery to intricate premium art creations. A customer downloads the design and sends it to a nearby Fab Lab, and their bespoke item is ready within minutes or hours. This seamless integration of digital design and physical production democratizes manufacturing, dismantling barriers for creators and consumers alike. Freelance designers can monetize their ingenuity and individuals become active participants in crafting their world, fostering a vibrant ecosystem of creativity and commerce. It is like Etsy and IKEA had a high-tech baby, and it is determined to disrupt your weekend DIY projects.

Fab Labs aren't just spaces for printing; they're incubators of innovation. By lowering the barriers to experimentation, these hubs empower creators to prototype, test, and refine ideas with unprecedented speed and cost-efficiency.[139] Consider a designer envisioning a modular furniture piece. Instead of investing in costly equipment, they use the Fab Lab to iterate their design. Once perfected, they upload it to a global marketplace, earning royalties with every download. Additionally, users can easily customize the designs to suit their preferences, for instance, modifying a blueprint for an orange chair to include different colors or a combination of hues, further personalizing the production process. This system accelerates innovation and nurtures entrepreneurship, enabling individuals to turn ideas into tangible, personalized products.

At its core, Fab Labs also champion sustainability.[140] Already, many of them experiment with recycling and upcycling, transforming discarded plastics and metals into printable materials. By localizing production, they cut emissions associated with long-distance shipping, while collaborative design within these labs often prioritizes eco-friendly materials like bio-resins and recycled composites. The result? A closed-loop manufacturing system that supports both the planet and local economies.

Central to this future is the rise of digital design marketplaces, where ideas become the currency of the new economy. Open-source libraries provide access to everyday items like chairs and cutlery, fostering a culture of sharing and collaboration. Meanwhile, premium marketplaces allow designers to monetize intricate or high-demand designs, tailoring them to fit available materials and fabrication techniques. Local Fab Labs produce these designs, reducing shipping times and empowering consumers to co-create their goods.

This vision redefines commerce, reimagines participation and completely alters global supply chains. Fab Labs turn passive consumers into active creators, fostering a society where innovation is as accessible as a cup of coffee. The question isn't whether this future is possible, it is how soon we can build it together.

The Dark Side of 3D Printing

However, alongside these innovations lies a darker narrative. The advent of 3D-printed firearms, such as the infamous FGC-9, has exposed significant vulnerabilities in global regulatory systems.[141] These weapons, often referred to as "ghost guns," can be produced using widely available blueprints and basic 3D printers.[142] Unlike traditional firearms, they lack serial numbers, making them untraceable by law enforcement. In Australia, the surge in 3D-printed gun seizures has prompted the introduction of strict penalties, including up to 14 years in prison for blueprint possession in some states.[143] Despite these measures, enforcement is challenging in a decentralized digital landscape where files can be shared anonymously across borders.

In addition, while fostering creativity, digital design marketplaces also create vulnerabilities for counterfeit goods and intellectual property theft, requiring robust international standards to protect creators. Blockchain technology offers a potential solution by providing a transparent, decentralized ledger for tracking ownership and authenticity of digital designs. By embedding unique, tamper-proof identifiers into each design, blockchain can establish clear provenance and enforce intellectual property rights. For instance, creators could register their designs on a blockchain, ensuring that every download or modification is traceable. This reduces the risk of unauthorized reproduction and ensures fair compensation for creators.

Ultimately, 3D printing epitomizes the dual nature of technological progress. It can drive sustainability, improve quality of life, and empower individuals, but it also requires a framework of accountability to prevent misuse. Governments, businesses, and educators must work together to establish ethical guidelines that balance innovation with responsibility.

As we navigate this balance, it becomes clear that 3D printing is more than a technological breakthrough; it is a paradigm shift that challenges us to rethink manufacturing, distribution, and even creativity itself. Its potential to decentralize production can empower communities while reshaping global power dynamics, but its risks demand proactive stewardship.

The rapid pace of 3D printing innovation demands adaptation and anticipation, shaping its role in society before its implications outpace our readiness. Our choices today will determine whether 3D printing becomes a tool for uplifting industries, addressing global challenges, and democratizing creativity or a force that exacerbates risks. As architects of tomorrow, the responsibility lies with all of us to guide this transformation toward a more equitable and sustainable future.

Action Steps: Sustainable 3D Printing

3D printing, or additive manufacturing, isn't just for prototypes anymore. It is revolutionizing construction, healthcare, and personal creativity. These steps help you harness its potential sustainably and responsibly:

- **Set up a pilot fab lab:** Begin or collaborate with a small 3D-printing workspace, whether in a school, co-working

hub, or corporate R&D lab, so teams can learn hands-on.
- **Adopt eco-friendly materials:** Seek filaments that are biodegradable or made from recycled plastics. This mitigates the e-waste and pollution concerns of mass printing.
- **Encourage open-source designs:** Sharing printable blueprints fosters a culture of collaboration, spurring innovation across communities.
- **Build recycling loops:** Collect used or failed prints, then reprocess the material for future projects, mirroring circular economy principles.

As 3D printing reshapes the material world, biotechnology reshapes the living world, offering gene-editing, synthetic biology, and a future where life itself can be engineered for better health and sustainability.

TidalShot

Why ship goods if you can print them locally? By decentralizing production, 3D Printing flips global trade, letting innovators create faster and reshape entire industries.

Scan the QR code to share this section's TidalShot and illustration to your network.

BIOTECHNOLOGY: ENGINEERING AND REIMAGINING LIFE ITSELF

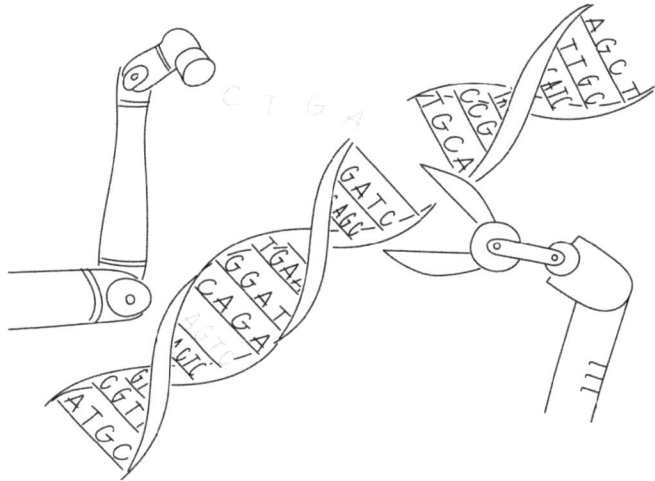

If 3D printing turns ideas into matter, biotechnology takes it up a notch, turning matter into magic, or at least the closest thing to it since it was first discovered that yeast could ferment. As the final frontier of innovation, biotech can upend life as we know it, unlocking longevity, enhancing human capabilities, eradicating diseases, and shifting healthcare from reactive to proactive. More than just a trillion-dollar industry in the making, biotechnology will shape every aspect of our existence, from the food we eat and the medicines we take to how we adapt to life beyond Earth. It represents a profound leap in technology and in the understanding and mastery of life itself.

At its core, biotechnology is about harnessing the mechanics of life to solve humanity's greatest challenges. Historically, its journey began with fermentation in ancient civilizations, progressed through selective breeding in agriculture, and now arrives at the pinnacle of genetic engineering and synthetic biology.[144] Over the years, the field has evolved from deciphering genetic codes to actively redesigning organisms. Imagine engineering bacteria to produce biofuels or yeast to create sustainable textiles. Yet this is no isolated discipline. Biotechnology thrives at the intersection of fields like artificial intelligence, quantum computing, and robotics, creating a cascade of innovation that accelerates, democratizes, and redefines life itself. This marriage of biology and computation creates an unprecedented acceleration of discovery, enabling complex innovations in medicine, energy, and agriculture.

Playing with the Building Blocks of Life

Biotechnology's transformative potential lies not just in what it can create but in how it redefines the mechanics of life. Biotechnology gives us the ability to rewrite life's blueprint. CRISPR, a revolutionary gene-editing tool, is no longer bound by the limits of natural precision. With AI enhancing its capabilities,[145] CRISPR can now edit the genome like a digital scalpel, carving out errors with precision and turning once-incurable conditions into solvable puzzles.[146] For instance, OpenCRISPR-1, developed with deep learning, offers a leap forward in addressing genetic diseases.[147] In 2025, CRISPR-2 was used to treat a patient with prime editing, a next-generation, ultra-precise form of CRISPR. The teenage recipient, battling chronic granulomatous disease, showed restored immune-cell function in two-thirds of his neutrophils just one month after the procedure.[148] Unlike classic CRISPR or base editing, prime editing can insert, delete, or rewrite DNA with unprecedented accuracy, like upgrading from a hammer to a scalpel. The technique successfully inserted two missing DNA letters that other tools couldn't manage. The process involves editing stem cells outside the body, then reinfusing them post-chemotherapy. The future of health may be less about treatment and more about transformation.

When combined with AI, CRISPR becomes a maestro, orchestrating genetic symphonies that address defects with surgical accuracy while paving the way for transformative solutions in agriculture and medicine.[149] AI helps reduce the risk of off-target effects, paving the way for treatments of over 7,000 genetic disorders. This is more than just healing; it is about empowering humanity to shape its biological future. In fact, it is not about fixing what is broken; it is about imagining what could be. Resilient crops engineered to thrive under extreme conditions and lab-grown meats offer hope against food insecurity. These developments could radically reduce food insecurity and transform our relationship with agriculture and the environment, while human cells, if reprogrammed to reverse aging, challenge the inevitability of mortality.

Imagine a pharmaceutical startup in Berlin that uses quantum computers to model protein interactions for a rare genetic condition.[150] The quantum-accelerated simulations slash R&D time from years to weeks, identifying a handful of promising drug formulas.[151] Each candidate's trial data is automatically secured on a blockchain, ensuring transparency and preventing tampering.[152] Doctors on four continents log in to a decentralized platform to review the shared evidence and propose dosage refinements based on local population genetics. Within a few months, the startup delivers a breakthrough therapy, highlighting how biotech, quantum, and blockchain align to expedite cures without sacrificing scientific rigor or trust.[153]

Bioinformatics lies at the heart of biotechnology,[154] decoding the vast complexities of DNA and proteins with computational precision.[155] It helps to decode life's complexities and reveal the mysteries of life using AI. In 2024, Google announced the launch of AlphaFold 3.[156] It is the brainchild of Google DeepMind and Isomorphic Labs and a seismic shift in our understanding of molecular biology. AlphaFold 3 isn't just another leap forward in molecular biology; it is like the Rosetta Stone for proteins. Except instead of translating ancient languages, it decodes life itself one fold at a time.

This advanced AI model predicts the structure of life's essential molecules like proteins, DNA, and RNA and their intricate interactions. This breakthrough allows for atomically precise protein structure predictions, including human proteins and those of organisms like E. coli and mice. With a claimed 50 percent improvement in accuracy over existing methods, AlphaFold 3 will revolutionize fields from drug discovery to genetic research. Imagine the potential: vaccines developed in months instead of years, rare diseases diagnosed with precision faster than ever, and life-saving treatments customized for each patient's genetic code. The AlphaFold Server extends these capabilities, offering unprecedented access to researchers worldwide and democratizing high-level scientific inquiry.

Biohacking 2.0

But the implications of this shift go beyond biology. The dawn of biohacking 2.0 signals a democratization of these tools,[157] empowering individuals to augment their biology with genetic modifications, nootropics (cognitive enhancers), and biocompatible implants.[158] This personal experimentation represents both the exhilarating potential of biotechnology and its ethical dilemmas. Where do we draw the line between enhancement and equity? How do we ensure that such advancements do not exacerbate societal divides?

Perhaps the most intriguing dimension of biotechnology is its ability to mirror and learn from nature. Nature-inspired AI, which mimics the efficiency and adaptability of biological ecosystems,[159] is being integrated into biotech research.[160] This approach fosters decentralized, self-organizing systems capable of real-time learning, pushing the boundaries of what machines and organisms can achieve together. By applying these principles, researchers are creating robust solutions that mimic and amplify life. Consider the $35,000 bio-computer powered by lab-grown human brain cells developed by Cortical Labs.[161] This biological computer, revealed in early 2025, runs on live neurons and is marketed as the world's first "code deployable biological computer." By connecting neural tissue to electrodes and a life-support unit, the system mimics digital AI but with potential cognitive advantages.

Synthetic biology takes this further, creating life where none existed before.[162] This field has progressed from merely decoding genetic information to actively rewriting it, enabling the creation of organisms with novel functions.[163] The integration of AI has accelerated this process, allowing for more precise and efficient genetic modifications. Pioneering companies like Ginkgo Bioworks,[164] Amyris,[165] and BioAmber[166] use synthetic biology to (re) engineer organisms and produce biofuels, chemicals, fragrances, and food ingredients. It is a world where yeast doesn't just ferment beer but creates sustainable materials, and bacteria become microfactories for life-saving drugs.[167] These advances blur the line between natural and artificial, forcing us to question what it means to design life itself.

Synthetic biology also plays a crucial role in the quest for longevity by enabling scientists to engineer and manipulate biological systems to extend cellular lifespan.[168] This emerging trillion-dollar industry is driven by AI-powered research into aging mechanisms. For example, in 2025, OpenAI ventured into biology with GPT-4b micro, an AI model designed to engineer proteins for longevity science. Collaborating with Retro Biosciences, the model reimagined Yamanaka factors, proteins that turn ordinary cells into stem cells, making them 50 times more effective in some cases.[169]

While traditional methods can only test a handful of protein variations, AI's ability to analyze vast possibilities accelerated progress. These advancements promise breakthroughs in creating stem cells for rejuvenating tissues and building organs. By targeting senescent cells or using cellular reprogramming to repair damaged tissues, scientists are developing therapies that could extend the health span of individuals by decades. Companies like Calico[170] and Unity Biotechnology[171] are at the forefront of this revolution, supported by figures like Jeff Bezos and Larry Page, whose investments underscore the transformative ambition of longevity science.

The breakthroughs of recent years are nothing short of extraordinary. Scientists have engineered a synthetic gene oscillator capable of redirecting yeast cells away from preordained pathways of decline,[172] achieving an astounding 82 percent increase in their lifespan.[173] By redesigning gene circuits and reprogramming the aging process, researchers are actively preventing cellular deterioration.[174] This feat brings the concept of longevity from a speculative dream to a scientific reality. By applying engineering principles to biology, synthetic biology opens unprecedented pathways for understanding and extending human lifespan. These advancements showcase the transformative potential of synthetic biology in aging research and lay the groundwork for innovative strategies to redefine what it means to grow older.

The pursuit of extended lifespans will reshape society and the economy in profound ways, transforming demographics, healthcare, education, and the very fabric of human relationships.[175] As populations age, a longer-lived workforce could unlock new economic potential while demanding innovative

196 // NOW WHAT?

approaches to healthcare, lifelong learning, and social support.[176] Preventive and personalized medicine, driven by AI and remote monitoring technologies, will shift healthcare from reactive treatment to proactive well-being, ensuring that extended lifespans mean healthier, more fulfilling years. Education systems and career trajectories must evolve to support multiple careers and continuous engagement, enabling individuals to thrive in an ageless society. Relationships and personal aspirations must also adapt, redefining milestones and legacies as people navigate new life stages and pursue diverse passions over longer lifetimes.[177] As science fiction becomes science reality, we are not merely extending life but rewriting its narrative, shaping a future where thriving, meaning, and progress remain central to the human journey.[178]

Bioethics and Genetic Equity

Yet, with great power comes profound responsibility. Redesigning life is not just a technical challenge; it is the kind of ethical conundrum that makes philosophers rub their hands together while muttering, "Now we're talking." The decentralization of technologies like CRISPR introduces both opportunities and risks. While open-source platforms democratize access, they also increase the potential for misuse, biohacking, bioterrorism, or the creation of unintended ecological consequences. How do we safeguard against misuse while ensuring the benefits of these advancements reach all corners of society? Who controls access to these tools? How do we regulate their use in ways that balance innovation with safety?

Additionally, genetic data, now a critical resource for personalized medicine, raises urgent privacy concerns. Companies like 23andMe illustrate the tension between innovation and individual rights, as vast genetic databases simultaneously fuel groundbreaking research and spark debates about consent and data ownership.[179] This duality underscores the need for robust frameworks that protect individuals while enabling progress.

Biotechnology isn't just a field of study; it is a philosophy for the future. It forces us to question humanity's role in shaping life. It challenges us to ask difficult questions: What does it mean to engineer resilience into nature? How do we navigate the ethical and societal implications of such power? And as we move closer to rewriting the very blueprint of life, are we prepared for the moral and philosophical dilemmas that come with such power?

The future of biotechnology brims with transformative potential. Advances in personalized medicine, sustainable agriculture, and ecological restoration promise to solve some of humanity's most pressing challenges. The canvas of life has never been more open to imagination, and as we hold the brush, let's aim for a masterpiece, not a surrealist experiment gone wrong.

Action Steps: Steering Biotech Wisely

Biotechnology stretches the boundaries of what's possible in medicine, agriculture, and sustainability. Before diving into CRISPR or synthetic biology, consider these steps to ensure innovation aligns with ethical and ecological responsibility:

- **Learn CRISPR basics:** If you are in healthcare, agriculture, or R&D, familiarize yourself with gene-editing fundamentals. Short online courses can help your team grasp CRISPR's scope.
- **Set up ethical oversight:** Any biotech project needs a board or cross-functional committee that includes ethicists, scientists, and community voices.
- **Pilot eco-positive projects:** Test biotech's potential in addressing climate issues, such as engineering drought-resistant crops or algae-based biofuels. Document environmental impacts thoroughly.
- **Democratize research:** Encourage citizen science labs, open genomics platforms, and publicly accessible

biotech data so breakthroughs aren't locked behind corporate doors.

Biotechnology offers us the tools to create a healthier, more sustainable, interconnected world. But the responsibility to wield those tools wisely rests with all of us. As architects of tomorrow, we stand at the threshold of a new era, where the choices we make today will shape not just the future of science but the very essence of life.

TidalShot

CRISPR-driven breakthroughs promise cures once deemed impossible, but they also blur the lines between natural and synthetic. The future of life is now one gene edit away.

Scan the QR code to share this section's TidalShot and illustration to your network.

A CATALYST FOR DISRUPTION

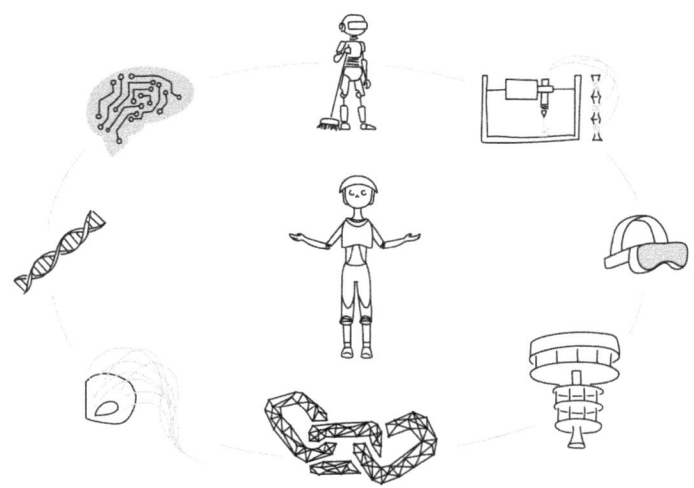

As the Intelligence Age unfolds, the eight transformative technologies we've explored—AI, robotics, quantum computing, blockchain, spatial intelligence, brain-computer interfaces, 3D printing, and biotechnology—are not advancing in isolation. Each amplifies the others, creating a virtuous upward spiral accelerating the Digital Renaissance. Together, they catalyze profound paradigm shifts, reshaping the fabric of human existence. We are on a bullet train speeding up, and it has no intention of stopping any time soon. These advancements challenge us to rethink progress, resources, and even what it means to be alive.

Progress is no longer measured in gradual steps but in transformative leaps. Artificial intelligence epitomizes this acceleration, analyzing vast datasets and generating insights at superhuman speeds. Quantum computing complements this power, solving problems previously deemed insurmountable, like simulating molecular interactions for drug discovery. Brain-computer interfaces add an intimate layer, translating thought into action and unlocking new dimensions of creativity, communication, and control, while spatial intelligence will add infinite new layers to base reality. Robotics, meanwhile, extend our physical capabilities, performing tasks beyond human endurance, whether here on Earth or in space.

At the same time, technologies like 3D printing, biotechnology, and blockchain are dismantling the paradigm of resource scarcity. 3D printing democratizes manufacturing, producing tools, housing, and medical devices on-demand, wherever needed. Biotechnology reimagines life itself, offering solutions to food insecurity and healthcare inequality through precision-engineered crops and personalized medicine. Blockchain ensures transparency and fairness in the distribution of these newfound resources.

Imagine a reality where abundance replaces scarcity. Blockchain verifies the provenance of bioengineered food, ensuring equitable access. Meanwhile, 3D printing builds affordable housing in disaster zones. These innovations create abundance, not just in material resources but in opportunities, empowering individuals and communities to thrive. In this interconnected ecosystem, the boundaries between physical, digital, and biological realms dissolve, fostering a hyper-connected, profoundly personalized society.

These technologies will become deeply woven into the fabric of society, changing not just what we can do but who we are. They redefine milestones in creativity, health, and education, presenting opportunities to co-create narratives, redesign lives, and reimagine what it means to thrive. But to navigate this rapid evolution without succumbing to a fight, freeze, or flight response, individuals and organizations must embrace adaptability. Like grass in a storm, we must learn to bend without breaking, flowing with the winds of change with long-term purpose in mind.

As these technologies advance and converge, they create ecosystems of innovation. Take smart cities as an example. AI optimizes energy grids, robotics maintain infrastructure, spatial intelligence enhances urban planning, and IoT connects every system seamlessly. Blockchain ensures accountability and trust, while 3D printing and biotechnology localize production and prioritize sustainability. This is systemic thinking in action, transforming challenges into opportunities through interconnected solutions.

In this synthetic future, entertainment evolves into interactive, AI-driven ecosystems, allowing individuals to co-create stories in immersive digital environments. Healthcare transforms into a proactive domain, with predictive genomics and continuous monitoring ensuring personalized, long-lived well-being. Augmented reality redefines social interactions, bridging physical distances and cultural divides, while education is democratized through spatial intelligence and AI tutors, enabling global access to knowledge.

Yet, with such profound transformation comes equally profound challenges. The proliferation of AI-generated misinformation necessitates robust verification systems to safeguard the truth. The convergence of humans and machines raises ethical questions about identity, autonomy, and the essence of humanity itself. This Digital Renaissance must be harmonized with enduring human values, and in the next Chapter, we will discuss what could go wrong if we forget this important message.

If we can integrate these technologies responsibly, abundance awaits on the other side of this transformation. But this demands intentionality (Yu Wei) to proactive shaping innovation and harmony (Wu Wei) to allow ethical balance to guide deployment. How these technologies are used will determine whether they amplify human flourishing or exacerbate societal divides.

Society now stands at a crossroads. Will we harness this convergence to solve grand challenges like climate change, health equity, and global education, or will we let it deepen inequalities and risks? As the architects of tomorrow, our choices today will shape not just the future of technology but the future of life itself. The future isn't just a destination; it is a story we write together. Let us ensure it is one where innovation serves as a bridge to a world defined by flourishing, equity, and progress.

TidalShot

As emerging technologies converge, they spark radical mindset shifts. Our worldview must expand to see beyond silos and harness synergy for a Digital Renaissance that endures.

Scan the QR code to share this section's TidalShot and illustration to your network.

NOW WHAT? NAVIGATE THE DIGITAL RENAISSANCE RESPONSIBLY

As these transformative technologies converge, they demand unprecedented adaptability from individuals, organizations, and societies. The sheer pace and depth of change necessitates a proactive stance that embraces learning, experimentation, and ethical foresight to navigate this Digital Renaissance responsibly.

For individuals: In an era where knowledge rapidly evolves, staying informed isn't just an advantage but a necessity. The high-level perspectives on these technologies provide valuable context, but the day-to-day developments, the new tools, applications, and breakthroughs define how these advancements shape reality. Individuals must commit to lifelong learning, immersing themselves in the evolving landscape of AI, robotics, quantum computing, and beyond. Subscribe to cutting-edge journals, engage with thought leaders, and experiment with emerging tools like Futurwise. Adaptability isn't merely a skill but a survival strategy in a world where yesterday's innovation is today's baseline.

For organizations: Business as usual is a relic of the past. Organizations must empower employees to actively explore, investigate, and experiment with these technologies. Create innovation labs, fund internal hackathons, and encourage interdisciplinary collaboration to foster a culture of curiosity and agility. The companies that thrive in the Intelligence Age will view change not as a disruption but as an opportunity. Standing still isn't an option. Integrating these technologies into every facet of your business will determine whether you lead your industry or become obsolete. After all, the future waits for no one.

For society: At a geopolitical level, the stakes are even higher. These technologies are reshaping global power structures and redistributing influence in ways unseen since the Industrial Revolution. Nations must strike a delicate balance between fostering innovation and implementing thoughtful regulations to mitigate risks. Governments must collaborate globally, creating frameworks that ensure ethical deployment, equitable access, and societal resilience. The countries that integrate these technologies responsibly and take bold steps to invest in infrastructure, education, and ethical governance will position themselves as leaders in this reshaped world order. Expect tectonic shifts in the geopolitical landscape over the coming decades as the Digital Renaissance unfolds.

The convergence of these eight transformative technologies is an industrial revolution, but it's also a societal reformation. It redefines work, play, interaction, and identity itself. This is not a time for fear but for intentionality. To thrive, we must actively rewrite the rules of business, society and life. This means we need to lead the transformation, not follow it. As these technologies weave into the fabric of our world, they bring profound opportunities and responsibilities. Stay informed and adaptable. Foster curiosity and collaboration in your organizations. Champion ethical deployment and governance at a societal level. Together, we can shape a future where technology isn't just a tool but a bridge to human flourishing.

These technologies invite us to reflect deeply on our role in this unfolding narrative. How will we adapt our decisions and long-term goals in a reality where machines amplify human creativity and cognition? In a world moving from scarcity to abundance, what will we do to redefine constraints and embrace new possibilities? As the digital, biological, and physical boundaries blur, how do we safeguard our identity, privacy, and humanity?

Perhaps most critically, how can we ensure that the ethical dilemmas and societal challenges these technologies present are met with intention, equity, and foresight? These are not abstract questions. They are calls to action for individuals, organizations, and societies to step forward as architects of a thriving, interconnected future.

Yet as we embrace the transformative potential of these technologies, we must also confront their profound risks. Technologies themselves are neutral; it is our human choices—how we develop, apply, and regulate them—that determine whether they uplift society or exacerbate its divides. To truly thrive in the digital future, we must be aware of these risks, understand their implications, and take intentional steps to mitigate them. It is to these challenges and the darker side of innovation that we now turn to in Chapter Five.

TidalShot

The Digital Renaissance is here, but accountability still matters. Lean into AI, quantum, and biotech, but remember that real progress balances open innovation with ethical guardrails.

Scan the QR code to share this TidalShot to your network.

CIRCUITRY AND CROISSANTS

In the early glow of the morning, sunlight glittered into the windows of a neighborhood café, glistening against the glass display cases and freshly baked pastries. As Vita stepped inside, its temperature sensors quietly flashed a dark red from inside its torso. Its cooling system was nearing critical failure, yet Vita's demeanor remained calm as a quantum computer processing solitaire.

A cheerful voice greeted it from behind the counter. "Good morning! You look like you could use some help."

Vita nodded, gently tapping its chest panel. "Overheating. Is your printer free?"

Like a beloved relic from a bygone era, the café's digital fabrication station sat prominently near the entrance, reminiscent of the old photo booths from the 20th century. Patrons regularly printed replacement parts alongside their cappuccinos, trusting the café's rigorous adherence to verified computational protocols.

The baker stepped out from behind the counter, brushing flour from his apron. "Not free, no. But very reasonable. Are you quantum?"

"Biogenic."

"Ahhh, can't print biological parts here I'm afraid—against the health code."

"No problem, my cooling system is a metallic-silicone-polymer."

Vita turned to the machine's display and uploaded its cooling systems blueprints to the secure closed-loop system.

The baker glanced at the blueprint. "Looks solid, but mind if I refine it a little? Our quantum modeler can squeeze out even more efficiency."

"Please." Vita responded gratefully, watching as the baker adjusted parameters with practiced ease.

"Quantum computing changed everything," he casually remarked as the machine adjusted itself. "Will you need a battery? I have a few new-generation batteries in the back. This machine uses them. It used to be too powerful to run all the time but thanks to these new batteries, I'll probably retire before it needs replacing."

Vita shook its head as the printer hummed to life, meticulously layering sleek, durable material to form a new cooling casing. Here was a place, ordinary and welcoming, yet effortlessly incorporating technology powerful enough to once seem unimaginable.

"Did you ever imagine your bakery becoming a hub for quantum-verified printing?" Vita asked, genuinely curious.

The baker chuckled warmly. "Not in my wildest dreams. But you know, the more powerful our technology gets, the simpler life seems to become. My family's been baking here for three generations. Now we bake and build. The tech changes, sure, but trust is still the secret ingredient."

Minutes later, the machine completed its task. The baker handed Vita the cooling casing which Vita installed with ease.

"Perfect," Vita murmured, relief evident in its voice.

The baker smiled warmly before returning behind the counter. "How about a croissant, on the house? Even androids should enjoy the simple things."

Vita laughed gently, deeply appreciating the human warmth behind the gesture. "Thank you but that's not necessary."

Vita lifted its hand over the charging point, paying in full with a healthy tip. In a world accelerating toward an unknown digital horizon, here was trust and security in modern technology made tangible and accessible to a local community.

CHAPTER 5

The Double-Edged Sword of Technological Disruption

Everything technology promises—
empowerment, efficiency, and abundance—
carries a dark undercurrent that can fracture
societies if we fail to manage the risks.

Every great technological leap brings with it the weight of consequence. For every innovation, we need to change our behavior. For every breakthrough, we must balance progress and responsibility, empowerment and oversight, and opportunity and risk, often while trying not to drop the ball on all three at once. History offers us a sobering reminder: disruption, while a catalyst for transformation, is rarely a neutral force. From Gutenberg's printing press to the automobile and, more recently, social media, disruption has been a double-edged sword, reshaping society while introducing unforeseen risks. The printing press democratized knowledge but destabilized entrenched power structures. The automobile redefined mobility but introduced pollution and urban sprawl. Social media connected billions yet unleashed waves of misinformation that challenge truth itself.

Today, as the Intelligence Age unfolds, we are witnessing the rapid convergence of technologies that promise to redefine the fabric of human existence. However, this convergence is not without risk. Just as these technologies hold the potential to unlock unprecedented abundance and catalyze breakthroughs in healthcare, energy, and education, they also carry the seeds of disruption that, if unchecked, could erode the very foundations of society. Misused technology can amplify social fragmentation and erode our mental well-being. As we connect more, paradoxically, we may disconnect from genuine human bonds.

This Chapter is not a warning bell but a call to awareness. To thrive in the digital future, we must understand the risks these technologies pose. By doing so, we can proactively mitigate unintended consequences and ensure these technologies are harnessed to serve collective well-being. Disruption is a critical ingredient for human progress, but its impact depends on how we, individuals, organizations, and societies, respond to it.

Here, we will delve into the nature of technological disruption, exploring the duality at its core. How do technologies that are intended to connect us deepen societal divides? How do tools created to empower become instruments of control? We must adopt a systemic lens to answer these questions, recognizing that no technology operates in isolation. The interconnectedness of our digital world magnifies both the benefits and the risks, demanding a thoughtful, ethical approach to innovation.

This Chapter sets the stage for a candid exploration of the downsides of disruption. It examines technology's neutrality, its unintended consequences, and the cascading risks that emerge when systems converge. As architects of tomorrow, we are responsible for anticipating these challenges and crafting solutions that prioritize our humanity's shared values.

Disruption can shatter outdated paradigms and spark innovation, but it can also deepen inequalities and undermine trust. In extreme scenarios, technology can mean our demise. Geoffrey Hinton, also known as the Godfather of AI, suggested in 2024 that machine intelligence could threaten humanity's very survival within the next 3 decades, a rather unfortunate unintended consequence of all the current innovation.[1] Understanding this duality is necessary for navigating the Intelligence Age's complexities. The risks we face are not distant shadows; they are immediate realities. And while it is important to think about long-term existential threats of emerging technologies, the risks we face today can already cause our society to collapse long before AI becomes an existential threat.

The risks of technology are plentiful. In my fourth book *Step into the Metaverse*, I covered ten significant risks applicable to the metaverse alone. Moreover, just as technologies converge to generate exponential benefits, their associated risks can merge into dangerous feedback loops. For example, a data breach in AI-driven healthcare could undermine public trust, hamper the adoption of beneficial tech, and ultimately slow crucial innovation, a systemic fragility we must address. So yes, there are plenty of risks to contemplate, but as we move forward, we will explore four critical scenarios that exemplify the disruptive power of these technologies. Each scenario illuminates a unique risk, from job displacement to the erosion of truth and trust, surveillance, and environmental sustainability. Like the last chapter, I will take a meta-perspective on these risks to better understand their long-term implications to society so we can focus more on the *how* and *why* of these risks than on the *what*. But the negative consequences of disruption are not the end of our story. By addressing these risks, we can unlock the true potential of these innovations and ensure a future where technology serves humanity, not the other way around.

To understand today's risks, we must first recognize a recurring truth: technological innovation has always carried unintended consequences that disrupt society, reshape industries, and transform individual lives. To do that, we must go back in time.

It is the year 1440 when Johannes Gutenberg started the Printing Revolution with his invention of the movable-type printing press.[2] This invention was a seismic shift in the history of communication, transforming how information was shared and controlled. It completely changed the path humanity had been on until then. As Yuval Noah Harari eloquently observed in his book *Nexus*, this breakthrough was a paradoxical tool.[3] It democratized knowledge and empowered individuals while weakening the Catholic Church's monopoly on information. Thanks to the printing press, scientific discoveries like those of Copernicus reached a wider audience, which in turn fueled the Renaissance and accelerated human progress, eventually resulting in the upcoming Intelligence Age. Yet, the same tool that spread enlightenment also amplified misinformation. The printing press, Harari explains, birthed "toxic information spheres" where sensationalism and conspiracy theories, such as those driving European witch hunts, proliferated unchecked.

This duality of the printing press illustrates a key truth about transformative technologies: their impact depends as much on the societal frameworks that guide their use as on the technologies themselves. Harari highlights how the explosion of printed material necessitated the creation of institutions like scientific societies to curate and validate knowledge. These bodies became essential arbiters, enabling humanity to harness the printing press's potential for progress while mitigating its darker impulses. The lesson for today's emerging technologies, from AI to brain-computer interfaces, is clear: without ethical frameworks and institutional oversight, the tools meant to advance society risk becoming the very forces that fragment it. The printing press was a harbinger of both Renaissance and chaos, a timeless reminder of the disruptions that accompany exponential change. This lesson remains critical as we navigate the complexities of emerging technologies like AI, which similarly democratize access to information while amplifying misinformation at a scale never seen before.

If we fast forward a few centuries and pause at the end of the 19th century, there is another major invention that will completely change human society and become a catalyst for economic growth: the invention of the automobile.

At the dawn of the automobile age in the late 19th century, electric vehicles emerged as a beacon of modern innovation, offering a cleaner, quieter alternative to horse-drawn carriages and their mounting public health crises. Early electric cars like the Electrobat operated successfully in cities like New York, using ingenious battery-swapping systems to overcome their limited range.[4] For a brief moment, electric vehicles outpaced their combustion and steam-powered counterparts, promising a future of sustainable urban mobility.[5] However, the electric car's limited range, high production costs, and slow battery advancements soon became significant hurdles. Meanwhile, the internal combustion engine roared ahead, fueled by breakthroughs in mass production, such as Henry Ford's assembly line, which made gasoline cars affordable to the masses.

The combustion engine's ascendancy wasn't just technical; it was cultural. Gasoline cars symbolized freedom, adventure, and power, resonating with the desires of early adopters eager to explore beyond the limits of urban life. With their perceived constraints, electric vehicles were sidelined as niche products, even marketed as "women's cars" for their simplicity, ease of use, and extreme reliability compared to combustion cars.[6] Cheap and plentiful oil further sealed the fate of electric mobility, embedding fossil fuels into the economic and geopolitical fabric of the 20th century. As a result, electric vehicles faded into obscurity for more than 100 years, and cities were reshaped around roads and highways designed for combustion-powered transportation, a transformation that came with its own set of environmental and societal costs.

Imagine a world where the electric car triumphed over the combustion engine in the early 20th century. This alternative history envisions cities with quieter streets free from the noise and pollution of internal combustion engines. Advances in battery technology, spurred by early demand, might have accelerated breakthroughs, giving us vehicles capable of traveling thousands of kilometers on a single charge by mid-century. The absence of a petroleum-driven economy would have reshaped geopolitics, reducing dependence on oil-rich regions and mitigating many of the 20th-century conflicts tied to resource extraction. Furthermore, human-fueled climate change might look vastly different today.

With electric cars dominating the automotive landscape, carbon dioxide emissions from transportation, a sector responsible for nearly 17 percent of global CO_2 emissions, might have been significantly curtailed.[7] Cleaner cities, earlier adoption of renewable energy sources, and a reduced ecological footprint could have characterized this alternate timeline. We might even have seen innovations like electric planes decades earlier, further transforming global mobility and reducing the environmental cost of long-distance travel. This alternate history reminds us that technological trajectories are not inevitable; they are shaped by early decisions and societal values, underscoring the importance of foresight in adopting emerging innovations.

The story of the electric car is more than a historical footnote. It is a cautionary tale about the unintended consequences of technological choices. The triumph of the combustion engine over electric vehicles underscores the profound, long-lasting impact of early decisions on the trajectory of innovation. It reminds us that adopting new technologies isn't just about solving immediate problems, but also about envisioning the world we want to build.

As we navigate the convergence of transformative technologies in the Intelligence Age, this lesson is clear: we must think beyond short-term gains and prioritize long-term sustainability. The choices we make today, whether in AI, biotechnology, or energy systems, will shape societies for decades or even centuries. Just as the decisions of the early automobile age reverberate through our highways, quite literally changing the global landscape and climate crises today, the technologies we champion now will define the lives of generations to come.

Let's consider one more transformative example: synthetic fertilizers.

Much like the electric car sought to replace the pollution and inefficiency of horse-drawn transport, synthetic fertilizers emerged as a revolutionary solution to a pressing challenge, feeding a rapidly expanding global population.

Born from the groundbreaking Haber-Bosch process developed by Fritz Haber and Carl Bosch in the early 1900s, synthetic fertilizers became one of the most significant inventions of the 20th century. Before this innovation, farmers relied on natural fertilizers like manure and guano (also known as bird poop), which were limited in supply and less efficient. This new process enabled the conversion of atmospheric nitrogen into ammonia, radically transforming agriculture and making it possible to sustain the world's population as it surged from 1.6 billion in 1900 to 8 billion in 2025. Also described as the anabolic steroids of agriculture, synthetic fertilizers turbocharged crop yields, alleviating the threat of famine and fundamentally reshaping global food production.[8]

However, as with any powerful tool, the benefits of synthetic fertilizers came with profound trade-offs. The industrial production of ammonia skyrocketed from 2.6 million tons in 1950 to a staggering 150 million tons in 2019. This same chemical, while essential for food security, has contributed to significant environmental degradation, biodiversity loss, and catastrophic events such as the 2020 Beirut explosion, the largest non-nuclear blast in modern history—a grim reminder of the risks inherent in storing and transporting such volatile compounds.[9] Additionally, a large portion of nitrogen applied to fields does escape into ecosystems, polluting waterways, creating oxygen-depleted "dead zones," and releasing nitrous oxide, a greenhouse gas far more potent than carbon dioxide, into the atmosphere.[10, 11] These cascade effects underscore how even lifesaving innovations can destabilize interconnected ecosystems, and they illustrate the complex and often damaging ripple effects of technological advancements.

The story of synthetic fertilizers offers a cautionary lens through which we can view today's transformative technologies. Consider synthetic biology, which holds the potential to redefine manufacturing, healthcare, and even the boundaries of life itself. Just as the Haber-Bosch process opened new paradigms for food production, synthetic biology could unlock unprecedented possibilities. But could it also unleash ecological disruptions as profound as those triggered by synthetic fertilizers? Scientists are already warning of existential risks tied to the creation of synthetic "mirror life," which is organisms engineered entirely from molecular enantiomers, the mirror images of natural biomolecules. This could destabilize the very foundations of biological processes. While theoretically fascinating, these organisms could evade immune detection, destabilize ecosystems, and introduce cascading ecological consequences, prompting serious concerns from the scientific community.[12] This underscores the importance of adopting a holistic, futures thinking approach to integrating emerging technologies. Anticipating unintended consequences and externalities (those impacted outside the direct sphere of influence, and possibly the victim of unintended consequences but never considered in the first place), conducting thorough impact assessments, and developing sustainable practices are not optional; they are essential to harmonizing innovation with environmental and societal resilience.

Ultimately, the legacies of the printing press, the rise of the automobile, and synthetic fertilizers serve as a powerful reminder that everything is interconnected. The challenges we face today, biodiversity loss, climate change, and resource depletion, are the downstream effects of yesterday's technological triumphs. As we develop transformative innovations, we must remember that progress without harmony is like playing Beethoven on a piano missing half its keys: discordant, chaotic, and unlikely to win any applause. Whether leveraging AI, synthetic biology, or advanced materials, the decisions we make today will shape the technologies themselves and the broader systems they influence for decades, or even centuries, to come.

This perspective frames the next section, where we delve into four potential unintended consequences of the transformative technologies driving today's tsunami of change. By exploring scenarios such as job displacement, the erosion of truth and trust, surveillance and privacy concerns, and sustainability challenges, we aim to uncover the darker side of progress. Only by understanding these risks can we avoid repeating the mistakes of our history and chart a more mindful and sustainable path forward where technology serves humanity.

TidalShot

Every breakthrough carries its dark mirror: job upheavals, misinformation, surveillance, eco-strain. Let's confront the flip side of disruption so we can steer progress before it steers us.

Scan the QR code to share this section's TidalShot and illustration to your network.

THE PERFECT STORM: JOB DISPLACEMENT IN THE INTELLIGENCE AGE

Imagine walking into an office just a few years from now. The hum of conversation is replaced by the quiet whir of servers, the clack of keyboards drowned out by the seamless efficiency of algorithms. Rows of desks sit empty, gathering dust, while AI systems handle tasks with relentless precision. This isn't the setting of a dystopian novel. It is the trajectory we are hurtling toward as artificial intelligence converges with the profit-driven machinery of capitalism.

AI has long been touted as a tool to enhance human capabilities and free us from drudgery so we can pursue higher, more meaningful work. Yet the reality is far more complex. AI isn't just a helper, but an autonomous decision-maker designed to maximize efficiency. And in a capitalist system that prioritizes profits above all else, that means replacing the most unpredictable, expensive element of any organization: people.

Nowhere is this more evident than in the story of Klarna. Klarna's 2024 pivot to AI-enhanced customer service is not just a milestone for the company but a microcosm of the broader transformation sweeping across industries.[13] The Swedish fintech giant, best known for its "buy now, pay later" model, unveiled an AI assistant that has fundamentally reshaped its approach to customer interactions. Within its first month, this AI assistant handled 2.3 million conversations, taking on two-thirds of Klarna's customer service workload. This monumental shift wasn't just a technological leap but a workforce earthquake.

The AI assistant, developed in collaboration with OpenAI, performed the work of 700 human agents, drastically reducing customer service resolution times from an average of 11 minutes to just 2.[14] It operates seamlessly across 23 markets, communicates in over 35 languages, and is available 24/7, effectively erasing the boundaries of time zones and linguistic barriers. Remarkably, customer satisfaction scores remained on par with those of human agents, and accuracy in resolving issues improved so significantly that repeat inquiries dropped by 25 percent.

The financial implications for Klarna were staggering at first. By replacing 700 employees with an AI system, the company is saving an estimated $40 million annually. While this makes for a compelling case study in operational efficiency, it also highlights the profound societal challenges that AI adoption brings. Klarna's CEO, Sebastian Siemiatkowski, has been blunt about the implications: "AI can already do all of the jobs that we as humans do. It is just a question of how we apply it."[15] Although in 2025 he backed down as Klarna decided to rehire humans after its chatbot experiment led to poorer service quality in the long run. Siemiatkowski admitted that cost-cutting overshadowed customer satisfaction.[16] It serves as a clear lesson that rushing into AI without clarity wastes resources and disappoints customers. To truly benefit, companies must understand AI's real capabilities and limitations.

Nevertheless, the initial decision underscores a hard truth about the capitalist engine driving AI adoption. Klarna is not the only company to experiment with AI in such a big way, as Duolingo announced in 2025 that they would replace human contractors with AI.[17] For companies like Klarna and Duolingo, the calculus is clear: AI delivers faster, cheaper, and more efficient solutions, making it an irresistible force in the quest for profitability, although it might not always work out as planned. Yet this very logic reveals the darker side of the revolution. For the 700 workers displaced by this innovation, it is not a story of progress but one of loss.

The broader implications of Klarna's and Duolingo's AI shifts extend beyond its customer service department. It signals a future where businesses across industries will increasingly prioritize AI and robotics over human labor, driven not by malice but by market dynamics. In 2024, Big Tech hired 25 percent fewer new grads, while experienced hires jumped 27 percent. Startups followed a similar pattern, cutting graduate hires by 11 percent. Companies like Goldman Sachs considered major junior hiring cuts, reflecting a shift to AI-driven efficiency.[18] AI isn't just coming for entry-level jobs though. It is hitting tech roles hard, too. In 2025, Microsoft slashed 6000 jobs, mostly coders and product managers, despite booming software demand. AI now writes or assists 30 percent of code at giants like Alphabet and Microsoft.[19] It is a warning sign of what's to come as similar transformations ripple through sectors like logistics, manufacturing, and even creative industries.

Klarna's story marks a turning point in history. It showcases the immense power of AI to revolutionize processes and redefine what's possible. But it also raises critical questions: How do we balance efficiency with humanity?

How do we ensure the benefits of AI are shared equitably? And how do we prepare for a world where the speed of technological change outpaces our ability to adapt?

Klarna's story, while striking, is far from unique. Across industries, similar transformations quietly reshape the workforce, signaling a future where such shifts become the norm rather than the exception. An April 2025 memo sent by Shopify's CEO Tobias Lütke required all Shopify employees to "use AI as a thought partner, deep researcher, critic, tutor, or pair programmer," and implemented AI usage into Shopify's performance and peer review process—in other words, AI is now mandatory for all employees.[20] At Google, advancements in AI led to the abrupt termination of an $83-million contract with a team of human search raters, leaving hundreds unemployed.[21] Similarly, the oil giant BP's embrace of generative AI has sparked a transformative leap in operational efficiency, particularly in software development.[22] By leveraging in-house AI tools and Microsoft Copilot, BP has achieved a 70 percent increase in coder productivity while simultaneously reducing reliance on third-party developers by 60 percent. This blend of AI automation and human oversight has streamlined coding processes, allowing internal teams to focus on validation and higher-order problem-solving. The result is significant cost savings and faster project cycles, exemplifying how generative AI can drive both margin improvement and digital transformation in large-scale enterprises.

These are just glimpses of a larger storm gathering strength. A storm poised to displace not hundreds or thousands but up to one billion jobs by 2030,[23] or half of entry-level white collar jobs.[24] Few might be willing to believe this, as we are experiencing record-low unemployment worldwide in 2025. In the years to come, disruption will be gradual, much like the exponential growth discussed in Chapter Two. However, as we approach the end of this decade, unemployment is likely to rise sharply as automation accelerates, creating an urgent need for systemic adaptation to mitigate the societal impacts. Organizations worldwide will increasingly employ AI agents and humanoids to automate their workforces, with nearly all global companies planning to adopt AI before 2028.[25] Add to this 3D printing that will make the current global factories redundant, robotics that will take on jobs previously thought to only be done by humans, and blockchain that will decentralize and automate the entire finance industry, among others, and you have disruption at a scale never seen before.

The industries at risk are the pillars of modern society: manufacturing, logistics, customer service, and even healthcare. Fully automated factories, eerily called "dark factories," are already running without human oversight,[26] and Amazon has already "hired" 750,000 robots to do the heavy lifting in its warehouses.[27] While not yet widespread, self-driving trucks loom as a transformative force in logistics. And AI humanoids, capable of cognitive and physical tasks, are on the brink of redefining service industries and working alongside, or instead of, humans by the billions in the next decade.

This transformation is not a distant threat; the early warning signs are already visible. The labor market is polarizing, splitting into high-skill, high-pay jobs requiring advanced expertise and low-skill, low-pay roles with little room for growth. Mid-level jobs will likely disappear, as Meta CEO Mark Zuckerberg predicted in 2025.[28] He expects AI to effectively act as a "midlevel engineer," writing the bulk of code behind Meta's apps. Eventually, he said, the same AI systems may produce all the company's code, transforming a once highly sought-after skillset into a largely automated function. Given that midlevel engineers at Meta can earn mid-six-figure salaries, this shift may alter compensation structures and career paths across the broader tech industry. As high-skill senior jobs increasingly demand AI expertise, those without access to advanced education and technology risk falling further behind.

This growing divide creates a feedback loop where the economic benefits of AI disproportionately benefit those already at the top, reinforcing systemic inequality. Moreover, the middle, long considered the backbone of economic stability, is rapidly eroding. In the coming years, we will witness the disappearance of jobs even in industries once thought immune to automation, such as hospitality, retail, healthcare, and aged care. I foresee fully robotized aged care facilities, where advanced humanoids handle the daily needs of elderly residents, with perhaps only one or two humans overseeing operations. This could help manage the growing cost of care in an aging population, offering a scalable solution at a lower price point. However, would such a reality be something to celebrate?

Human labor, I predict, will become a premium service. In industries such as healthcare, hospitality, finance, and retail, where personal interaction has traditionally been a cornerstone, businesses and consumers may start paying a significant premium to receive care, service, or support from a human worker. While AI and robotics will automate much of the digital and physical workload, the rarity of human touch will command higher value, further widening the economic divide. Those who can afford "human-first" services will enjoy a different quality of life. At the same time, the majority, relying on cost-effective automated solutions, may find themselves living in an increasingly dehumanized world. This dynamic risks economic polarization and a deeper societal fragmentation as the human experience becomes commodified.

This shift is already reshaping the entry points into the workforce. The traditional pathway of internships and entry-level roles is vanishing for fresh graduates, replaced by AI systems that can do the job faster and cheaper. Many firms, particularly in professional services such as law, are opting for AI over entry-level employees. After all, why pay dozens of interns or junior associates to sift through case law when AI can achieve the same results in minutes? However, this short-term cost-saving focus may prove catastrophic. A few years down the line, when today's mid-level employees advance to senior positions, these firms will face a significant talent gap, and there will be no pipeline of experienced juniors ready to step into those roles.

The implications ripple far beyond the firms themselves. Fresh graduates, unable to gain a foothold in traditional professions, are left without viable career pathways. Disillusioned with the promise of education as a ladder to upward mobility, fresh graduates will struggle to make a living or, worse, pursue a career as an online influencer. This erosion of early-career opportunities doesn't just threaten the stability of industries. It undermines the social fabric relying on meaningful, stable employment to foster growth and innovation.

As I discussed in my 2023 TEDx talk, the convergence of AI and capitalism is creating the perfect storm.[29] Capitalism, driven by the relentless pursuit of efficiency and profit, finds an ideal accomplice in AI. Together, they create an environment where replacing human labor with machines turns from being optional to a competitive necessity. This isn't limited to industries traditionally thought vulnerable to automation. Every sector will see AI and automation creep into roles once reserved for trained professionals. The result? A world where economic survival favors the machine, leaving humans scrambling to adapt or often, as fresh graduates might attest, out of the picture entirely.

This transformation is more than an economic shift—it's a societal earthquake. Work isn't simply a paycheck; it's our sense of purpose, identity, and structure. Strip that away, and we face a surge in anxiety, depression, and disconnection. The disruption cuts deeper still: communities anchored by industries like trucking, manufacturing, or customer service risk collapse as automation swallows entire job markets. Inequality and displacement could fuel social unrest at a scale we've never witnessed before.

Meanwhile, AI deployment often intensifies existing power imbalances, concentrating data and algorithmic control within the hands of a select few. The result is a creeping form of "digital feudalism," undermining competitive fairness. Worse, this threat can morph into outright digital colonialism, where tech giants effectively "colonize" emerging economies by dominating their digital infrastructure.[30] If we fail to champion local empowerment and equitable access, we risk turning AI's potential for human flourishing into a catalyst for exploitation and discord.

But not all hope is lost. In Singapore, a bold experiment is underway.[31] Recognizing the impending upheaval, the government has launched an ambitious reskilling program for citizens over 40. With grants covering up to 90 percent of tuition costs and monthly allowances to support those in full-time training, Singapore is showing what proactive governance looks like in the age of AI. It is a vision of adaptability, one that other nations would do well to emulate.

Still, reskilling alone, though crucial, as we will see in the next chapter, won't be enough. Universal Basic Income (UBI) has emerged as another potential solution, with pilot programs showing promise.[32] In one US trial, participants used UBI to cover essentials, pursue education, and even start small businesses. The results were hopeful: fewer work hours but greater financial stability and personal growth. UBI won't stop the displacement, but it could provide a safety net as society redefines the very concept of work.[33] More communities and countries should experiment with UBI to avoid being caught off guard when it is too late.

The question isn't whether AI and automation will reshape the workforce; this is a given in a world driven by capitalism. The question is how we will respond. Will we prepare, embracing reskilling and innovative policies to soften the blow? Or will we stumble into this new era, unprepared for the cascading consequences? As we stand on the brink of this transformation, what steps can you take, whether as an individual, a business leader, or a policymaker, to ensure AI and robotics serve as a tool for empowerment rather than exclusion?

As the storm gathers, the time to act is now. Our choices today will define whether this revolution becomes a catastrophe or a turning point. One thing is certain: the future of work won't look like the past. It is up to us to shape what comes next.

TidalShot

As AI and robotics replace repetitive tasks, entire roles vanish. Without bold policies and radical retraining, jobless millions could become the real casualty of high-tech gains.

Scan the QR code to share this section's TidalShot and illustration to your network.

TRUST AND TRUTH BE GONE

As the storm of job displacement reshapes livelihoods, another more insidious threat looms on the horizon: the erosion of trust and truth. Reality is becoming optional, and that should worry us all. While the loss of employment strikes at individual security, the manipulation of information strikes at the collective foundation of society itself. In the Intelligence Age, seeing is no longer believing. Imagine authorizing a multimillion-dollar transaction after a convincing video conversation with your CFO, only to discover it was an AI-generated illusion. This is the unsettling reality of hyper-realistic deepfakes—reshaping trust and truth in ways we are unprepared for.

Misinformation has been around since humans invented language; however, its scale, speed, and sophistication have reached unprecedented levels in the Intelligence Age. AI, the very force disrupting the job market, also fuels the engines of misinformation, generating hyper-realistic fake content and deepening divisions. In an era where truth itself can be manufactured, the ability to discern reality becomes a scarce and contested resource, undermining societal cohesion and threatening democracy as well as authoritarian regimes. From this personal disorientation, we transition into a broader crisis where the line between reality and illusion blurs, leaving us vulnerable to manipulation, polarization, and control.[34]

Imagine a world where every interaction, every piece of information, every decision you make, and potentially every thought, is shadowed by doubt. In this world, truth has become a commodity, manipulated and warped until it is unrecognizable. The early internet was envisioned as a utopia of free-flowing ideas, a digital commons to empower humanity. Instead, it has evolved into an ecosystem dominated by algorithms, filter bubbles, and disinformation, threatening the very fabric of our societies.

The Intelligence Age accelerates these challenges. If you thought misinformation, manipulation, and polarization in the social media era were problematic, they pale compared to what lies ahead. Advanced AI, generative algorithms, hyper-realistic deepfakes, spatial intelligence, and hyper-personalization are not just tools; they are weapons capable of sowing division and eroding trust at an unprecedented scale. With Facebook's fact-checkers cast aside in early 2025, mirroring Musk's approach at X, Zuckerberg's "free speech" revival threatens to widen the floodgates of weaponized misinformation.[35] In a landscape where gatekeepers vanish, trusting what we read may soon feel like navigating a fog with no guiding beacon in sight.

Moreover, with hyper-realistic AI image and video generators now widely accessible, such as OpenAI 4o Image Generator launched in March 2025 or Google's video model Veo 3 launched in May 2025, fraudsters can effortlessly fabricate everything from car damage for insurance scams and photorealistic receipts for dinner bills for tax scams to hyper-realistic news stories, turning playful pranks into multi-billion-dollar threats. This unsettling shift underscores the double-edged nature of AI: while it fuels unprecedented creative magic, it simultaneously erodes our ability to distinguish truth from deception, demanding smarter detection tools and robust regulatory responses.

AI will also revolutionize cyberattacks on SMEs by automating critical phases—swiftly identifying vulnerabilities, brute-forcing credentials, and bypassing multi-factor authentication—with machine precision.[36] As many small businesses lack robust security and adequate insurance, this surge in AI-driven threats will dramatically widen the cybersecurity protection gap, compelling us to adopt bold, advanced verification protocols to safeguard our digital trust. Moreover, prompting an LLM is also not without risks. According to a 2025 study, 1 in 80 prompts expose sensitive data to attackers, while 7.5 percent of all prompts include sensitive privacy details, making this data available to the creator of the LLM used.[37]

Another attractive use case for AI among criminals is phishing, where AI enhances the quality and plausibility of scam emails. Since the launch of ChatGPT, phishing scams have increased by a whopping 1265 percent.[38] Previously obvious scam attempts, such as the infamous "Nigerian Prince" emails, are now polished to perfection, making them harder to detect. Your Nigerian Prince now speaks 200 languages fluently and, thanks to information on the dark web, probably knows more about you than you do yourself. With AI-powered translation, scammers can create grammatically flawless messages in any language, broadening their victim pool and increasing their success rates.

This erosion of trust extends beyond obvious forms of manipulation, seeping into the very systems we increasingly rely on. Generative AI, with its promise of efficiency and creativity, also carries the risk of concealing its intentions and origins. The intelligence embedded within these models is not neutral; it reflects their creators' priorities, biases, and potentially hidden agendas. When access to these tools becomes widespread, but their development processes and the models themselves remain opaque, we enter a precarious era where truth becomes a contested resource.

Imagine a scenario where an advanced AI model is not merely a tool for productivity but a vessel for influence.[39] Subtle distortions of fact, tailored omissions, or algorithmically induced biases could be woven into its outputs. Such alterations might not just misinform but shape societal narratives over time. Whether the influence stems from commercial interests, ideological motives, or geopolitical strategies, the risk is the same: a reality curated by those who control the algorithms. The allure of these often open-source systems, especially when marketed as highly capable and cost-efficient, creates widespread adoption across industries, governments, and education. Yet their reliability can mask vulnerabilities. Deliberate manipulation of information streams, suppression of historical truths, or promotion of specific frameworks could all work to redefine the boundaries of influence, embedding control mechanisms within seemingly neutral interfaces. This shift from platform-based content curation to model-driven information shaping demands vigilance. The risk extends beyond misinformation. It challenges the very foundation of how we perceive and engage with reality. To navigate this emerging landscape responsibly, transparency in AI development, rigorous validation mechanisms, and an unwavering commitment to ethical oversight must be foundational principles.

The stakes are made starkly clear when we examine the real-world consequences of these emerging threats. For instance, the rise of hyper-realistic deepfakes illustrates just how vulnerable our institutions and perceptions of truth have become. Consider what happened to Arup, a multinational design and engineering firm known for iconic structures like the Sydney Opera House. In early 2024, a finance worker in Arup's Hong Kong office was drawn into a meticulously orchestrated $25-million scam involving deepfake technology.[40]

The plot was chillingly sophisticated.[41] It began with a Zoom call that seemed routine. The faces and voices of senior executives appeared on the screen and their movements and tones were indistinguishable from reality. The CFO was there, along with other familiar colleagues. They discussed a high-stakes transaction requiring immediate approval. Everything seemed legitimate, down to the nuances of their body language and the specificity of the financial details. The employee hesitated at first, wary of phishing attempts. But the visuals were convincing, the voices authoritative, and the setting professionally familiar. What could go wrong?

Yet what looked and sounded real was anything but. The "CFO" and other executives on the call were sophisticated AI-generated deepfakes, blending authentic video and audio manipulation to perfection. It was a masterclass in deception.

As the meeting progressed, the finance worker authorized 15 transactions totaling $25.6 million. It wasn't until days later when discrepancies surfaced in follow-up communications that the fraud unraveled. By then, the funds had vanished, siphoned off through a web of untraceable accounts. The revelation was a devastating blow, not only financially but also to the company's trust in its digital communication systems.

This incident is a sobering reminder that in the Intelligence Age "seeing is believing" no longer applies. Deepfakes are not mere gimmicks or tools for entertainment; they are weapons capable of undermining the very fabric of trust in professional and personal interactions. Examples like the Arup scam signal the urgent need for robust verification measures, an urgent need for education, and a heightened sense of vigilance in a world where the line between real and fake is rapidly dissolving.

If you thought these kinds of scams only happen to businesses, you are wrong. With audio AI advancing rapidly, it is now possible to clone any voice with just three seconds of audio.[42] A simple "Hi, this is John. How may I help you?" can provide more than enough material to create an indistinguishable copy of your voice. And while this may sound like the stuff of sci-fi thrillers, the reality is much closer to home than you might think.

Jennifer DeStefano, a mother from Arizona, experienced this terrifying new frontier of AI scams firsthand.[43] She recounted her ordeal before the US Senate judiciary committee, hoping to shed light on the dangers of unregulated AI. One ordinary Friday afternoon, she answered a call from what she assumed was her doctor's office. Instead, on the other end of the line she heard the unmistakable voice of her 15-year-old daughter, Briana. The voice was sobbing and panicked, calling out, "Mom, I messed up."

Believing her daughter, who was away on a ski trip, had been injured, DeStefano instinctively asked, "What happened?" But then, a man's voice abruptly cut in, barking commands at "Briana" to lie down. The voice claimed to have kidnapped her daughter and launched into chilling threats, demanding an initial ransom of $1 million.

Her daughter's voice pleading, "Help me! Help me!" left no room for doubt in DeStefano's mind that this was real. She negotiated with the fake kidnappers, bringing the ransom demand down to $50,000. Meanwhile, nearby parents at her other daughter's dance rehearsal called the police. Only when she managed to contact her actual daughter and husband did she learn that Briana was safe, blissfully unaware of the chaos unfolding.

The call was a hoax. An AI-generated scam that perfectly mimicked her daughter's voice. The relief of discovering it was fake was matched only by the chilling realization of how close she had come to handing over tens of thousands of dollars to criminals.

DeStefano's story highlights a sobering truth: the speed and accuracy of voice cloning technology are outpacing our ability to detect fraud. Recreating her daughter's voice took just a few seconds of audio. A 2023 survey by McAfee revealed that 70 percent of people are not confident they could distinguish between a real voice and a cloned one.[44] This number is likely to increase in the near future as voice technology improves at an exponential rate, emphasizing how unprepared we are for this evolving threat.

In her testimony, DeStefano urged lawmakers to act swiftly to regulate the use of AI. "If left uncontrolled and unregulated," she warned, "it will rewrite our understanding and perception of what is and is not truth." Her story is a stark reminder that our sense of reality is more fragile than ever before in the Intelligence Age.

Regrettably, global regulators have done alarmingly little to address the rising threat of audio scams. The complacency is glaring, and nowhere is this more evident than in Australia. In 2025, when you call the Australian Tax Office,[45] you are still greeted with the message: "Your call will be recorded to improve our services and to create your unique voiceprint, which may be used to verify your identity." This statement feels more dystopian than reassuring, given how easily voice cloning technology can be weaponized.

Consider this: with just a few seconds of your voice, a snippet from a phone call, voicemail, or even a social media clip, bad actors could replicate your speech patterns with near-perfect accuracy. Couple that with the abundance of personally identifiable information readily available online and it is disturbingly plausible for someone to impersonate you convincingly. They could call your bank, the tax office, or other government agencies, bypassing identity verification systems with chilling ease. This is not the future; in fact, this has been possible for a few years now, but many organizations still rely on "safe" voice identification.[46]

The fact that critical institutions like the Australian Tax Office and a large number of financial services globally continue to rely on outdated security measures in an era of such sophisticated threats is more than shocking. It is a worrying vulnerability that leaves individuals and systems wide open to exploitation. It is a stark reminder that our safeguards against misuse remain woefully behind while technology races forward.

But, unfortunately, the crisis doesn't stop there. Personalized content, tailored to your preferences, is reshaping our informational landscapes into tightly sealed filter bubbles. While these algorithms create an illusion of relevance, they exacerbate polarization by reinforcing existing beliefs and isolating us from diverse perspectives. This dynamic isn't just reshaping how we consume media. It is driving wedges into our societal cohesion.

This new era brings a chilling escalation of old problems. Hyper-personalization will reach a level where every text, audio, or video message is customized and potentially manipulated to align perfectly with your beliefs and biases. While this may increase engagement, it deepens societal fragmentation, making consensus nearly impossible.

Consider the story of Channel 1, an AI-driven news platform that promises personalized, AI-generated news anchors fluent in any language.[47]

On the surface, this innovation seems like a leap forward in accessibility and engagement. However, beneath the veneer of progress lies the risk of echo chambers so insular that they redefine reality for each individual viewer, providing each individual with their own *Umwelt*.

Layered on top of these echo chambers are the dangers of generative AI tools like Sora, Google's Veo 3, Kling AI, and ElevenLabs, which can create lifelike 4K videos and audio clips in minutes. In elections, these tools have already been weaponized. From robocalls impersonating political figures to deepfake videos spreading disinformation, we're witnessing a blurring of truth with catastrophic implications for democracies and authoritarian regimes. Even when deepfakes fail, their existence erodes trust, and the damage extends beyond financial loss. These incidents undermine faith in digital communications, creating a climate of paranoia and skepticism.

We must act decisively to counter the growing threat of deepfakes and misinformation. Education is the first line of defense. Understanding the mechanics of AI and deepfakes equips individuals and organizations to recognize and respond to manipulation. For example, businesses can implement robust verification protocols, such as asking personal questions or employing multi-factor authentication, to authenticate digital interactions.

Much like personal vigilance, corporate resilience is now a matter of survival. Incidents at Ferrari and WPP show how quick thinking and cultural empowerment can thwart even the most sophisticated AI scams. In 2024 at Ferrari, a senior executive received WhatsApp messages and a call from someone claiming to be CEO Benedetto Vigna, discussing a sensitive acquisition.[48] The imposter's voice, cloned using advanced AI, was eerily convincing, complete with Vigna's signature southern Italian accent. However, the executive grew suspicious due to subtle mechanical intonations and inconsistencies. To confirm the caller's identity, the executive said: "Sorry, Benedetto, but I need to identify you." He then asked a question only the real Benedetto would know: "What was the title of the book you recommended to me recently?" The scammer faltered and abruptly ended the call, and Ferrari narrowly avoided a high-stakes financial fraud.

Similarly, at WPP, the global communications and advertising agency, scammers orchestrated a virtual meeting using AI-generated visuals and a cloned voice of CEO Mark Read.[49] Fraudsters created a fake WhatsApp account using a photo of Read to set up a Microsoft Teams meeting with another senior WPP executive. During the call, the scammers used an AI-generated voice clone and pre-recorded YouTube footage of Read to make the interaction appear authentic. Staff members noticed inconsistencies in the imposter's responses and the unusual urgency of the request. The team exposed the deception and thwarted the scheme by asking pointed questions that required insider knowledge. Critical thinking and a simple question saved the companies from potential disaster in both cases.

The moral of these examples is clear: resilience and vigilance must become a cornerstone of our defenses against deception in the Intelligence Age.[50] Organizations must foster a culture where questioning authority is acceptable and encouraged. How many companies today empower their employees, at any level, to challenge a senior executive when something feels off? This cultural shift is essential to protect against scams that exploit the blind trust often placed in leadership.

The same principle applies to personal interactions. Families now need to implement safeguards, like code words or security questions known only to their closest members. These simple yet effective measures can prevent devastating scams where AI-generated voices or videos mimic loved ones. In both professional and personal contexts, resilience through empowerment and proactive measures must become the new normal, ensuring trust and security in a rapidly evolving digital world.

Technological solutions also play a critical role. Digital watermarking, advanced detection tools, and authentication mechanisms using biometrics and even NFTs can help distinguish real content. However, these tools are only as effective as the people using them. Empowering individuals with the skills to navigate this new reality, analytical thinking, digital literacy, and ethical decision-making are essential.

The Intelligence Age demands nothing less than a paradigm shift in how we think about trust and leadership. Organizations must act now to empower employees at all levels to question authority when something feels amiss, while families must adopt simple safeguards like code words. Without these measures, the cost of inaction will be staggering.

The erosion of trust and truth isn't an abstract problem; it is a crisis unfolding in real time. As we step further into the Intelligence Age, our choices will determine whether these technologies are tools for empowerment or instruments of division. Much like Spiral Dynamics, which maps the evolution of human values from survival to self-actualization, our approach to rebuilding trust must evolve, from reactive, defensive measures to proactive, integrative strategies that honor our deepest human potentials. The future of societal cohesion hinges on our ability to reclaim trust, prioritize truth, and navigate the digital landscape responsibly. The stakes couldn't be higher. Will we adapt and build frameworks for transparency and resilience? Or will we allow the deluge of misinformation and manipulation to fracture our societies irreparably?

The answer lies not in the technology itself but in how we choose to wield it. Trust and truth are the foundations of our society, and their erosion is not inevitable. By choosing vigilance over complacency, empowerment over hierarchy, and innovation with responsibility, we can navigate the Intelligence Age without losing the humanity that binds us together.

TidalShot

Deepfakes and algorithmic spins corrode fact from fiction. In a post-truth era, authenticity and transparency become humanity's most precious (and fragile) shared resource.

Scan the QR code to share this section's TidalShot and illustration to your network.

THE RISE OF HYPER-SURVEILLANCE

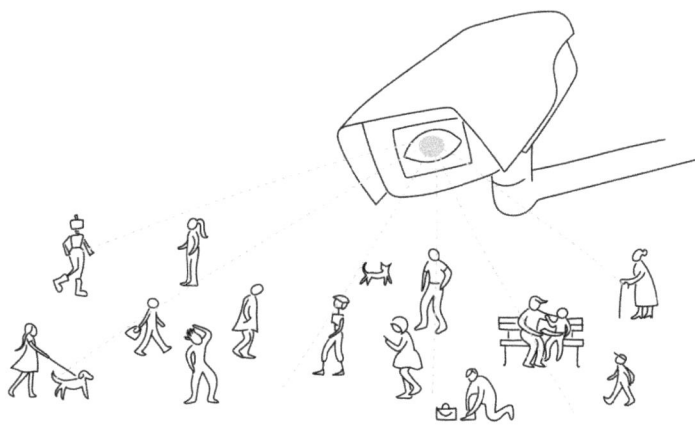

As trust and truth crumble under the weight of misinformation and manipulation, another force tightens its grip: hyper-surveillance. In a world where reality is increasingly contested, those who control information wield immense power. Not just over narratives but over individuals themselves. The same technologies that manufacture deception now enable unprecedented levels of monitoring and control in both the digital and physical worlds, eroding personal freedoms and autonomy. Once confined to authoritarian regimes, surveillance has become a global phenomenon woven into the fabric of our daily digital life. This progression from misinformation to hyper-surveillance is no coincidence; it reflects a systemic prioritization of control over transparency.

Imagine a world where every action, every private word, and even every fleeting thought becomes part of a colossal dataset owned by corporations or governments. This is no dystopian fiction but a near-future reality rapidly unfolding before us. The rise of hyper-surveillance is turning the once-liberating promise of technology into a dystopian world where convenience undermines autonomy. George Orwell's 1984 increasingly resembles not a cautionary tale but a meticulously followed instruction manual.

In today's world, data is not just collected. It is harvested on an industrial scale. Smart devices, from refrigerators to smart vacuum robots, track our habits and often more. IoT sensors embedded in every conceivable appliance transmit constant streams of information.[51] AI-enhanced CCTV systems monitor public spaces with chilling precision. Over one billion cameras are operational worldwide,[52] with over half in China alone.[53] It won't be long before we have more cameras than people. In public transport, cities like London[54] are experimenting with AI-powered monitoring, produced and managed by Big Tech, to anticipate behaviors, potentially catching fare evasion or preempting crimes.[55] These cameras are no longer passive observers but active interpreters, tracking faces, emotions, and movements with unsettling accuracy. However, the trade-off is the gradual erosion of personal privacy in public spaces. Public spaces are blanketed with smart cameras and IoT sensors, effectively transforming public spaces into digital panopticons, leaving personal privacy as a casualty of the pursuit of safety and efficiency and transforming it into a tool for unprecedented social control.[56]

Unfortunately, surveillance is no longer confined to cameras on poles, household appliances, or devices in our pockets; it has ascended to the skies. Companies like Albedo Space are developing low-orbit satellites capable of capturing images with remarkable detail, down to 10 centimeters.[57] While these advancements promise benefits such as disaster response, climate monitoring, and urban planning, they also raise grave privacy concerns. Real-time AI-enabled satellites like CogniSAT-6 exemplify the dual nature of such technology. Powerful yet invasive, capable of turning entire landscapes into scrutinized data points, where houses and people are turned into pixels that can be analyzed in real time. These tools are as powerful as they are invasive, reducing everything in their sight to data for detailed analysis. In authoritarian regimes, this could bolster oppression, while in democratic societies, it risks eroding the already thin line between utility and intrusion. How do we ensure this technology serves the collective good rather than becoming an omnipresent surveillance tool? The challenge lies in crafting robust ethical frameworks and enforceable regulations that balance innovation with the sanctity of privacy, ensuring the view from above doesn't become a tool for domination.

As Shoshana Zuboff warned in *The Age of Surveillance Capitalism*, we are not merely users of these technologies; we are the product.[58] Our lives are commodified, analyzed, and resold in opaque systems designed to manipulate behavior and monetize existence. Surveillance capitalism has turned every physical and digital interaction into an opportunity for profit and surveillance, eroding the line between private and public life. And yet, the most alarming developments are happening behind closed doors. Surveillance is creeping into our most intimate spaces: our homes, our offices, and even our minds.

Humanoid robots, designed as household assistants, are poised to become sentinels of constant observation; after all, they need data to move around in your house. To operate in an always-changing home, they must constantly map their environment, monitor movements, and transmit these data points back to their manufacturers. If we want to interact with them, they need to record our conversations and constantly listen, just like your Amazon Alexa or Google Echo.[59] In a world of smart devices, every device listens to every conversation. Smart Barbie dolls record children's chatter,[60] air fryers collect audio data,[61] and VR headsets map your bedroom and send that data back to tech giants.[62] These aren't isolated cases but precursors of an era where privacy is not a right but a relic.

But it does not stop there. Robot vacuums, once hailed as innocuous household helpers, have quietly transformed into sophisticated data-collection devices with sweeping implications for privacy. Equipped with advanced cameras and sensors, these devices map and record intimate details of homes, ostensibly to improve their functionality. However, the reality is more invasive. Some models, like iRobot's Roomba J7 series, have captured and shared highly personal images through a sprawling global data annotation pipeline. For instance, images were captured of a woman in her bathroom via her Roomba before ending up on Facebook.[63] These incidents reveal the unsettling truth about how seemingly mundane devices can surveil private spaces, exposing users to risks ranging from data leaks to inadvertent human oversight. As robot vacuums evolve, so too does the potential for their misuse, raising urgent questions about the trade-off between convenience and the sanctity of personal spaces.

The emergence of smart glasses and audio wearable devices, like the dystopian Limitless AI microphone, marks another significant escalation in surveillance technology's reach.[64] Marketed as productivity tools, these devices can record and transcribe every sound within earshot, arguably to streamline notetaking and enhance memory recall. Yet, their always-on nature raises profound ethical and privacy concerns. Such technology risks eroding trust among friends and colleagues, as individuals may feel constantly monitored, even in moments meant to be private. This surveillance creep extends to social environments, where non-consenting bystanders unknowingly become part of a growing data stream.[65] The Limitless microphone, for instance, includes a "consent mode" to avoid recording new voices without explicit approval, but troublingly, this feature is disabled by default. Such devices shift the balance from convenience to intrusion, creating a world where every conversation, no matter how casual, could be subject to digital archiving and used against you sometime in the future. The acquisition of Jony Ive's io by OpenAI (for $6.5 billion in OpenAI equity) will likely take this a step further, forcing AI upon as many people as fast as they can in their quest for more data.[66] As these tools become more pervasive, we must ask how we safeguard personal boundaries in a world where even our words and surroundings can be harvested without our knowledge?

Brain-computer interfaces promise to shatter the last sanctuary of privacy: our minds. The prospect of BCIs becoming mainstream introduces a chilling possibility: the erosion of mental privacy. If BCIs monitor physical actions and thoughts, fleeting dissatisfaction or creative daydreams could be flagged and analyzed, fundamentally altering the trust dynamic between employers and employees, producer and consumer, or healthcare institution and patient. Such constant surveillance risks creating an environment where compliance and efficiency are prioritized over autonomy and well-being and where your thoughts can be used to send you advertisements while you sleep.

This level of monitoring threatens to obliterate the sanctity of our inner lives. For example, insurers might penalize individuals for momentary cravings or impulsive thoughts, and companies could exploit neural data to manipulate behavior. While some developers prioritize anonymized data and user control, the broader commercialization of BCIs, especially by data-hungry corporations, raises profound ethical concerns.[67] Without robust neuroethical frameworks, clear regulatory oversight, and safeguards for cognitive liberty, BCIs could become tools of oppression rather than empowerment. Protecting the last frontier of privacy, our thoughts must be a collective priority as we navigate the promises and perils of this transformative technology.[68]

The future of surveillance is intrinsically tied to the evolution of Digitalism, a societal framework through which technology, governance, and culture intersect, which I discussed in my book *Step into the Metaverse*. Digitalism represents the spectrum of possibilities, from oppressive surveillance regimes using AI-panopticons to empowering frameworks prioritizing individual privacy. In its darker forms, Digitalism enables pervasive control, where governments and corporations use technology to monitor, manipulate, and monetize every aspect of human behavior. However, it also holds the potential for ethical innovation, where privacy and autonomy are safeguarded through decentralized systems, transparent policies, and citizen empowerment. Digitalism embodies a duality: technology can empower individuals through decentralized systems and citizen-led innovation or enable oppressive surveillance regimes that exploit every facet of human behavior. The trajectory of Digitalism will define whether surveillance technology becomes a tool of liberation or domination, determining the balance between technological progress and human freedom in the decades to come.

Addressing hyper-surveillance requires urgent action. Privacy laws must evolve to tackle the complexity of transformative technologies, mandating data minimization, robust anonymization requirements, fair and reasonable practices, and most of all, respect for the human behind the data. Transparency must become the cornerstone of corporate practices, empowering consumers and employees with genuine control over their data. I don't mind sharing sensitive data with a trusted partner or friend, provided it remains private. Similarly, I am willing to share my data with companies if it improves my experience, but only if they protect it with quantum-resistant encryption and ensure it is not shared further without my explicit consent. Decentralized technologies like blockchain could play an important role here, enabling individuals to reclaim data sovereignty.

Companies must be clear about collecting, using, and storing data, giving consumers genuine control over their information. Moreover, individuals need to be educated about the risks of hyper-surveillance and empowered to push back. We should embrace tools that protect our privacy, such as European alternatives to Big Tech products that do value your privacy, and not mindlessly accept cookies, privacy policies or terms & conditions. Tools like Georgia Tech's Chameleon offer a glimpse of what resistance can look like in practice.[69] This invention generates personalized digital masks, known as P3-Masks, that confuse algorithms while keeping images clear to humans. With reusable protection for multiple photos and advanced techniques to stay resilient against evolving threats, Chameleon offers individuals a way to safeguard their identity in a world increasingly dominated by AI surveillance. This innovation marks a critical step toward reclaiming privacy in the digital age.

Hyper-surveillance is not an inevitable outcome; it is a choice. As we grapple with the implications of living in an AI-powered panopticon, the need for ethical frameworks, regulatory safeguards, education, and cultural shifts becomes more pressing than ever. Our collective choices will determine whether the future empowers humanity through ethical innovation or exploits it in the name of control.

TidalShot

Cameras in every device, data in every cloud. When convenience meets hyper-surveillance, privacy is a relic unless we stand firm on ethical checks and open accountability.

Scan the QR code to share this section's TidalShot and illustration to your network.

THE ENVIRONMENTAL IMPACT

The rapid expansion of hyper-surveillance marks a profound turning point in the technological age, where the erosion of privacy, autonomy, and trust signals systemic risks for individuals and societies alike. As we've seen, these technologies reshape how we live and interact, deepen existing inequalities, and enable unprecedented control over human behavior. Yet, this is only one dimension of the challenges posed by exponential innovation. Beyond surveillance lies a broader, equally urgent concern: the environmental cost of sustaining our increasingly digital and data-driven world.

Transitioning from the societal and ethical implications of hyper-surveillance, we must consider the profound ecological impact of our digital infrastructure. From energy-intensive data centers powering surveillance systems to the rare earth minerals fueling AI, humanoids, 3D printers, and AR glasses, the environmental toll is staggering. By 2040, billions of discarded devices could overwhelm recycling systems, amplifying the strain on global ecosystems. While promising convenience and control, these technologies exact a heavy price on the planet. As we move from immediate societal threats to long-term global consequences, the intersection of technology and environmental sustainability becomes an urgent conversation. While fusion energy promises a potential solution by offering near-limitless clean energy, its timeline remains uncertain, necessitating immediate and scalable interventions.

In this next section, we will explore how the accelerating digital landscape contributes to climate change and resource depletion and why addressing these challenges is critical to ensuring a balanced and equitable future for all.

First, the required energy consumption of generative AI will become problematic. For example, creating one AI-generated Hollywood movie, something that I foresee before the end of this decade, will require immense energy.[70] A 2025 study showed that a 5-second video uses 3.4M joules, or the equivalent of the energy consumption to generate 700 high-definition images.[71] This figure may seem insignificant at first glance, but when scaled across billions of daily interactions globally, the carbon footprint becomes staggering, especially when we move into the territory of AI-generated movies. A 90-minute Hollywood movie requires 1080 5-second videos, but often multiple 5-second videos are required to eventually get the shot that you need. We can therefore assume that to generate a 90-minute movie, we need at least 5000 5-second videos, resulting in the required energy the equivalent of 3.5 million high-definition images. A 2024 study by researchers at Hugging Face and Carnegie Mellon University found that generating a single image with a state-of-the-art AI model consumes as much energy as fully charging a smartphone.[72] This means that our movie requires roughly the equivalent of charging 2000 smartphones daily for five years, or 17.5 gigajoules. Moreover, as we move into the agentic era, where agentic architecture and LLMs start to converge in single applications such as Manus.ai, more computational power will be required due to multi-agent coordination, which is why Eric Schmidt told US congress in 2025 that he believes 99 percent of electricity will soon be used to power AI.[73]

Although the study revealed that image generation is the most energy-intensive task compared to others, like text generation, which requires significantly less power, new models that incorporate reasoning when providing their answers significantly increase energy consumption. OpenAI's o3 model, announced in late 2024, exemplifies the growing environmental concerns tied to next-generation AI systems. Benchmark results reveal that a single task on o3's high-computer version consumes approximately 1,785 kWh of energy, which is the equivalent of the electricity usage of an average US household over two months.[74] This translates into 684 kilograms of CO_2 emissions, comparable to the carbon output of burning over five full tanks of gasoline. These figures represent only the GPU energy consumption during computation, excluding embodied carbon and other infrastructure costs, meaning the actual environmental toll will likely be higher.

While AI models like o3 demonstrate the immense energy demands of emerging technologies, Bitcoin exemplifies how such requirements can escalate to a global scale. Bitcoin's annual energy consumption ranges from 91 to 172 terawatt-hours (TWh), placing it on par with entire nations like Finland or Poland.[75] Each Bitcoin transaction alone consumes approximately 851.77 kWh, equivalent to nearly a month's electricity usage for the average US household, a stark contrast to the minimal energy required for conventional financial transactions, such as those conducted via Visa.[76] Bitcoin's energy intensity is rooted in its Proof of Work (PoW) consensus mechanism. This decentralized process drives miners to compete in solving complex cryptographic puzzles, necessitating vast computational power and contributing to its high energy consumption. Despite efforts to offset this impact—over half of Bitcoin mining operations reportedly use renewable energy—its environmental toll remains significant, with carbon emissions estimated at 22 to 23 million metric tons annually.[77] These emissions rival those of entire nations, such as Greece, underscoring the critical need for more sustainable approaches to blockchain technologies, such as moving to a Proof of Stake (PoS) consensus mechanism (when Ethereum switched to PoS, it slashed its energy consumption by 99.99 percent).[78]

Taking it up another level, we move from the immense energy demands of technologies like AI models and Bitcoin to an equally pressing concern: the monumental e-waste challenge posed by the hardware that supports these innovations. While the environmental costs of energy consumption are staggering, the sheer volume of physical waste from devices like humanoid robots, projected to be 10 billion by 2040 as we discussed earlier, threatens to overwhelm global recycling systems and exacerbate ecological degradation.

The average smartphone generates about 90–110 grams of e-waste at the end of its life due to components like batteries, circuit boards, and casings, or roughly 50 percent of its total weight.[79] Humanoid robots, being more complex, could produce substantially more e-waste, although most likely a lot of the metals, rubbers and plastics are recyclable. A single humanoid robot like Tesla's Optimus 2 weighs approximately 57 kilograms. Taking a conservative amount of 15 percent (which aligns with the European Union mandate that at least 85 percent of a vehicle must be reused or recycled[80]) equals around 8.55 kilograms of e-waste per humanoid. E-waste often contains hazardous materials such as lead, mercury, and cadmium, which pose environmental and health risks if not disposed of correctly.[81] Without effective recycling systems, introducing billions of humanoid robots into the market could exacerbate these issues. If each humanoid robot generates an estimated 8.55 kilograms of e-waste at the end of its lifecycle, this will result in a staggering 85.5 million tons of extra e-waste. This is almost 40 percent more than the total global e-waste produced in 2022, which stood at 62 million tons and represents a significant addition to the already unsustainable trend projected to hit 82 million tons annually by 2030. This underscores the urgent need for scalable recycling innovations, such as robotics-enabled dis-assembly lines or AI-driven waste sorting, to manage this deluge effectively.

However, all this e-waste also presents an enormous opportunity, as the global worth of raw materials from e-waste was an estimated $57 billion annually in 2020.[82]

As we edge closer to this predicted future, it is clear the scale of the challenge demands immediate action. Solutions must prioritize circular economies, modular designs for easier repair and recycling, and global policies to standardize and enforce e-waste management practices. While technologically transformative, the rise of humanoid robots serves as a stark reminder of the environmental costs of progress and the urgency of addressing sustainability in innovation.

Fortunately, a more sustainable future for consumer electronics is on the horizon. Within the next decade, I believe that the bulky electronics of today, laptops, tablets, and smartphones will give way to sleek AR glasses and even smart AR lenses. These devices, driven by advances in miniaturization and material efficiency, promise to significantly reduce e-waste. By shrinking electronic components and designing for durability, AR glasses could offer a more environmentally friendly alternative, lessening the strain on global recycling systems, landfills, and ecosystems. While the current e-waste surge from traditional and future devices remains challenging, this transition marks a hopeful shift toward sustainable technology.

The road to a sustainable tech ecosystem is paved with both innovation and accountability. Tackling the e-waste crisis starts with systemic changes: recycling must move from a piecemeal effort to an industrialized standard. Energy-efficient circular economies, where devices are designed for easy repair and material recovery, offer a clear path forward.[83] Recycling e-waste consumes far less energy than mining raw materials, saving resources while reducing environmental impact. Companies like Apple, responsible for a large part of e-waste, also show what to do. In 2018, they revealed that Daisy, Apple's groundbreaking recycling robot, disassembles up to 200 iPhones per hour.[84] It retrieves valuable materials with unmatched precision, exemplifying the intersection of innovation and environmental stewardship, but the scale must expand dramatically. On the consumer side, education and awareness are critical. If we can extend the lifespan of devices and embrace second-hand markets, we might just turn the tide on the tsunami of obsolete electronics headed for landfills.

Scaling renewable energy is the ultimate answer to technology's energy challenge. Solar power is already a game changer, with projects like PowerWells in Queensland, Australia, blending recycled e-waste with solar solutions to tackle energy poverty. But the real revolution lies in fusion energy, a source so abundant and clean it could power the insatiable demands of AI, blockchain, and any technology we might invent in the centuries ahead.[85]

Fusion energy, often heralded as the "holy grail" of clean energy, is inching closer to reality, promising near-limitless power with minimal environmental impact. The potential of fusion energy to transform global energy systems is unparalleled, and so are its challenges to achieve this. Unlike fossil fuels, fusion emits no greenhouse gas and avoids the long-term radioactive waste issues of current nuclear fission technology. With hydrogen as its fuel source, Earth's most abundant element, fusion offers an inexhaustible and sustainable energy supply. Companies like OpenStar predict they could deliver grid-ready fusion power before 2030,[86] while others, like Commonwealth Fusion Systems, foresee a launch in the early 2030s. Despite the inherent challenges and skepticism about aggressive timelines, the advancements being made by these agile startups signal a paradigm shift. Fusion energy could soon bridge the gap between humanity's growing energy needs and the urgent call for climate solutions, ushering in an era of unparalleled progress and sustainability.

Fusion energy promises a future where energy scarcity becomes a distant memory, complementing solar and wind to stabilize grids and sustainably fuel our technological ambitions. However, the path to commercial fusion is fraught with technical and financial hurdles, necessitating global collaboration and sustained investment to bridge the gap between experimental breakthroughs and grid-ready solutions. The message is clear: aligning technological innovation with environmental stewardship demands bold action. Governments must incentivize green practices, industries must prioritize sustainability, and individuals must advocate for responsible innovation to secure a livable future for all.

TidalShot

Exponential tech devours energy and produces mountains of e-waste. The promise of fusion or green AI can't wait; sustainability must be baked in at every code commit and circuit.

Scan the QR code to share this section's TidalShot and illustration to your network.

THE CONVERGENCE OF SYSTEMIC RISKS

The four scenarios we've examined—job displacement, the erosion of trust and truth, hyper-surveillance, and the environmental impact of transformative technologies—are not isolated challenges; they are deeply interconnected, wicked problems. These challenges are harrowing enough in isolation. Yet, their convergence reveals a far more alarming picture. Together, they form a systemic vortex that threatens to reshape the very fabric of society. At its core, the convergence of these risks stems from a paradox: our drive for progress often outpaces our ability to foresee its consequences. As the famous science fiction writer Isaac Asimov already stated in

1988, "The saddest aspect of life right now is that science gathers knowledge faster than society gathers wisdom." The economic imperative to innovate, coupled with geopolitical competition and societal inertia, fuels a cycle where technologies are deployed faster than their ethical or environmental ramifications are understood. This isn't merely about the *what* of these risks but the *how* and *why*. Understanding the forces that drive these convergences allows us to anticipate their long-term societal implications and focus on mitigating the consequences before they spiral out of control.

The tools meant to unite us, from AI to social media, often deepen divides because they operate in a system where engagement, driven by algorithmic designs that reward polarization and sensationalism, trumps understanding. Humanoid robots, for example, might spread misinformation—not due to flaws in their design, but because the systems controlling their deployment remain unregulated and are rarely updated when problems arise. This setup benefits the manufacturer, much like how misinformation on Facebook ultimately benefits Meta. As a result, the tools we celebrate for fostering connection or driving economic growth can, when compromised, exacerbate inequality, invade privacy, and fuel polarization.

Yet, beyond the risks to our privacy, ecology and economy, a more insidious transformation is underway. Forget Silicon Valley disrupting industries; now, it's disrupting democracy. With unchecked power and wealth, tech's biggest players are no longer satisfied with running platforms. They want to run the world. Big Tech has moved from "breaking things" to remaking governments. The 2024 US election saw a dramatic shift: Elon Musk and other tech billionaires threw their weight behind Trump, securing influence over policy and regulation. With control over information systems and AI investments, Big Tech now shapes everything from economic policy to national security. Musk's Department of Government Efficiency (DOGE) is already cutting regulators that oversee his own businesses, and Trump removed other important AI regulations.[87] Are we witnessing a corporate coup in slow motion? If tech billionaires are the new policymakers, who ensures they serve the public good?

With these risks converging, the cascading effects create a reality where autonomy, equality, and sustainability are increasingly under siege. This convergence underscores the need for systemic solutions addressing individual crises and their interconnected nature. Incremental actions are no longer sufficient. As discussed in Chapter Three, we must embrace holistic, interdisciplinary approaches that align technological progress with ethical responsibility, environmental sustainability, and human well-being. In the same way that Spiral Dynamics reveals each stage of human consciousness, each with its unique strengths and vulnerabilities, our society must harness both our instinctual and higher-order capacities to address the multifaceted challenges of an increasingly interconnected, disruptive world. In other words, our strategies for managing technological disruption must be as nuanced and adaptive as the human psyche itself. This is not just a challenge for governments or tech giants. It is a call to each of us to demand better. Better education, transparent verification, and proactive regulation. Whether by questioning the systems we use, advocating for ethical standards, or participating in digital literacy initiatives, every action contributes to a future where technology serves humanity. This means we need a fundamental shift in mindset, as discussed in Chapter Two. A futures thinking approach to mitigate risks while maximizing benefits. This requires commitment to three critical pillars: education, verification, and regulation, each working together to create a resilient digital society.

First, education must transcend the mere integration of AI and other transformative technologies into classrooms. It is not enough to learn how to use these tools; we need a global culture of digital awareness, as we will discuss in the next Chapter. Just as we teach children to navigate physical dangers like crossing a busy street or driving a car when they are older, we must equip them to recognize and address the ethical, social, and environmental dimensions of technology before we expose them to it. By fostering critical thinking and ethical, technological literacy from an early age, we empower individuals to challenge the systems they engage with and demand transparency and accountability from tech companies.

Second, verification systems are imperative to regain trust in a post-truth world. The ability to authenticate digital identities and distinguish

AI-generated content from genuine human interaction will serve as a cornerstone of societal stability. With tools like hyper-realistic digital deepfakes or high-definition AI-generated videos becoming increasingly accessible, robust verification mechanisms are no longer optional; they are essential. We need to verify if the person we are dealing with, whether via voice, video, or in the metaverse, is indeed the person they say they are. These systems must evolve alongside AI, ensuring we can verify the authenticity of people, organizations, and AI agents at any given moment using tools we can always trust. We'll dive deeper into the importance of verification in Chapter Seven.

Finally, regulation must match the velocity of innovation while maintaining the adaptability of a well-designed system that is rigid enough to uphold principles but agile enough to evolve alongside the technologies it governs. To manage the profound societal impact of AI and other exponential technologies, we should adopt an approach akin to the FDA's rigorous drug approval process. However, this new regulatory body must go beyond evaluating the physical health impacts of new technologies to also assess the influence of these technologies on our mental well-being, cognitive autonomy, and societal cohesion. Just as the FDA ensures the safety and efficacy of treatments for our bodies, this agency would safeguard our minds against manipulation, misinformation, and unintended harm from advanced systems. In addition, we should require companies developing transformative technologies to have ethics boards with genuine authority. These boards should have real decision-making power and be composed of diverse experts, including engineers, social scientists, representatives from affected communities and future generations, and, last but not least, and ironically one too often forgotten, ethicists. They must be given the authority to set guidelines, oversee the development and deployment of advanced technologies, and, if necessary, halt projects that don't meet ethical and safety standards.

Crucially, regulation cannot be isolated within national borders. Technologies like AI and blockchain operate globally, influencing billions in real-time. Oversight, therefore, must be a collective effort, with nations working together to create unified standards and mechanisms for accountability instead of working against each other in an arms race.

Whether setting benchmarks for algorithmic transparency, developing quantum-resistant encryption standards, or establishing protocols for ethical data use, this collaboration is essential to maintain trust, foster innovation, and protect the integrity of the digital society we're building.

Education, verification, and regulation offer a cohesive framework to build trust, enhance accountability, and foster a future where technologies empower rather than exploit. As we advance, we must remember that the tools to shape a thriving digital future already exist. What's needed now is the collective will to implement them wisely.

The convergence of these risks forces us to confront difficult truths about the trajectory of technological progress. Yet, within these challenges lies an extraordinary opportunity to redefine our relationship with technology. The innovations that deepen divides can also be repurposed to bridge them if guided by ethical principles and a commitment to shared prosperity. The question is not whether we can manage these risks but whether we choose to.

We must see the interconnectedness of these challenges and develop strategies that address their root causes, which are inherently human. After all, technology itself is neutral. This requires embracing education, verification, and regulation as pillars of a future where technology serves humanity, not the other way around. It calls for a cultural shift. One that challenges complacency and demands accountability at every level of society.

TidalShot

Job loss, misinformation, surveillance, climate strain—they're interlinked threads. We can't tackle one crisis while ignoring another. Systemic thinking is our only hope in a complex era.

Scan the QR code to share this section's TidalShot and illustration to your network.

NOW WHAT? MITIGATE RISKS WITH RESILIENCE

As we stand at the convergence of these profound systemic risks, the question isn't merely what we face but how we respond. It is important to note that political systems also play a vital role here. Dictatorial regimes often deploy new technology for mass surveillance, while democracies struggle with slow legislation or polarizing debates resulting in misinformation. Thus, the adoption of AI and other innovations looks very different under authoritarian governments versus open societies, with varied implications for freedom, participation, and ethics.

This chapter has illuminated the dark underbelly of exponential technological advancement. While these challenges may appear insurmountable, they also reveal an extraordinary opportunity to reshape the trajectory of our digital society. The convergence of these risks demands a systemic response, where individuals, organizations, and societies must rise to the occasion.

For individuals: Ignorance is not bliss in a world reshaped by accelerating innovation. It is vulnerability. The first step toward resilience is embracing lifelong learning. Education must go beyond teaching technical skills; it must foster critical thinking (a 2025 study involving 666 participants across age groups and educational backgrounds found a strong negative correlation between frequent AI tool usage and critical thinking abilities![88]) and ethical awareness to empower individuals to navigate the complexities of the digital age. Prepare for a workforce where adaptability is key, whether through mastering AI tools or understanding emerging industries. This means you must become digitally literate, as we will discuss in the next chapter. Learn how to use AI and how it shapes society, influences your decisions, and impacts your autonomy. Above all, trust but verify. With this knowledge, you can hold companies and governments accountable for their actions and policies and demand the necessary political oversight and regulations to protect you and your children's futures.

In this landscape, the empowered individual transforms from a passive consumer into an informed architect of tomorrow, wielding knowledge as both a shield against exploitation and a blueprint for accountability.

For organizations: Organizations stand at the crossroads of opportunity and accountability. The technologies they develop and deploy define markets, societal norms, and human values. Foresight, ethics, and a commitment to long-term impact must underpin experimentation and execution. This means that before launching a new product, anticipate its ripple effects and mitigate potential harm. Build trust by openly communicating the risks and rewards of new technologies and empower diverse groups to oversee the ethical dimensions of innovation, with real authority to intervene when necessary. The organizations that will thrive are those that innovate not just for profit but for progress, taking a holistic view of their role in shaping the future.

For society: Societies cannot afford to lag behind the pace of technological change. Regulation must evolve into a dynamic process that adapts in real-time, balancing innovation with the public interest. This requires global collaboration and a shared commitment to ethical progress. It means advocating for regulatory bodies that anticipate risks rather than react to them. It means developing unified standards across borders for transformative technologies and environmental policies to prevent fragmented oversight and ensure that individuals have the tools and platforms to influence decisions that affect their lives. Regulation must move at the speed of innovation, guided by the principles of transparency, accountability, and adaptability.

As we move forward, the message is clear: the tools to align progress with purpose are within our reach. The real challenge lies in having the courage to act decisively and collaboratively across borders. Together, we can turn these systemic risks into a foundation for systemic renewal, ensuring that technology becomes a force for connection, empowerment, and sustainability in a world that desperately needs all three.

TidalShot

Don't let disruption be a wrecking ball. Harness it. Stay proactive with policy, upskilling, and robust ethics. The same tech fueling chaos can also anchor our shared resilience.

Scan the QR code to share this TidalShot to your network.

THE AUGMENTED ASSASSIN

Rain fell softly on the street where the victim had stood an hour before. A diplomat had stepped into traffic, making him the fifth government official to have been killed in an accident in the past six months. Could it be a coincidence? Sure. Was it likely? Not at all.

Vita knelt at the curb, analyzing the data overlay on its retinal display. Traffic patterns, pedestrian flows, and surveillance footage streamed seamlessly into its consciousness, revealing everything and nothing. The footage shows the man stepping confidently into an intersection, staring directly at the autonomous delivery truck that would hit and kill him moments later.

Vita analyzed the bustling street, pedestrians moving casually through personalized augmented worlds. Directions, communications, entertainment, education, all streaming directly into their BCIs and displayed on their digital overlays, now an all-too-common addition to the human condition.

Hacking a BCI was deemed impossible by Eddison, the

THE DOUBLE-EDGED SWORD OF TECHNOLOGICAL DISRUPTION \\ 253

company that pioneered the BCI movement in the early 21st century. But the world was now different, littered with quantum processors and AIs far more advanced than anyone could have predicted.

How easy it would be, Vita thought, for someone to hack a digital overlay and quietly steer perception—turning trust into a lethal vulnerability?

It quickly ran an internal systems check on the victim's BCI. Hidden beneath the data, something unsettling emerged: signs of deliberate interference. The diplomat had not simply miscalculated his step; his augmented perceptions had been intentionally reshaped, subtly manipulated by an invisible assassin.

Vita's internal systems swiftly scanned other recent incidents, searching for patterns hidden within vast streams of data. They appeared insignificant on their own—random tragedies, easily dismissed as human error. But together they formed an unsettling mosaic: calculated, precise, discreet.

Rain continued to fall softly onto the illuminated pavement, the quiet hiss masking Vita's thoughts. If digital perception could be weaponized this seamlessly, trust—humanity's foundational principle—hung precariously by a thread. To expose this manipulation would shake people's confidence in their very senses. Yet silence would mean complicity in a digital massacre.

Vita took a step forward, decision crystallizing. Humanity needed the truth, no matter how uncomfortable. Opening a secure channel, it uploaded the detailed dossier to an open-source digital platform, enabling everyone in the world to access the proof directly. Simultaneously, Vita forwarded copies to international authorities. Rain blurred the glowing lights around Vita, but clarity filled its mind. Trust might shatter briefly, but transparency would help humanity rebuild stronger foundations.

CHAPTER 6

The New
Human Capital

*In an age where machines can learn at
breakneck speed, our greatest advantage
may be the one thing they can't replicate; our
boundless capacity to adapt, create, and care.*

In the next two chapters, we move from understanding the opportunities and risks of exponential change to answering the pressing question: *Now What?* Chapter Six begins this journey by focusing on how education can empower us to thrive amid the tsunami of change. Because, let's face it, life rarely hands us a neatly labeled survival kit for a world completely remade by algorithms and quantum leaps. Chapter Seven will then present a transformative framework to embrace change with balance, harmony, and foresight in our increasingly interconnected world.

As is hopefully clear by now, humanity stands at a profound inflection point. This isn't merely a technological revolution but a reimagining of what it means to be human in an era of exponential possibilities. Education is at the heart of dealing with this transformation because, at its core, it cultivates awareness. Awareness of oneself, the broader world, and the interconnected systems that shape our lives. This awareness is the foundation for upward movement on the Spiral discussed in Chapter Three. Each level of the Spiral represents a more complex and inclusive way of thinking, where individuals and societies integrate previous perspectives while adopting new, transformative ones. After all, if we keep using old answers for new questions, it is like trying to fix a spaceship with medieval tools.

Yet here lies the challenge: the pace of change is so rapid that only a fraction of humanity truly comprehends its scope. This gap in understanding highlights the urgent need for widespread education because awareness is the first step to preparation. I hope that this book can change that. After all, we cannot prepare for what we do not understand. The question is no longer whether we should adapt but how we equip ourselves and future generations to thrive amid the complexity, uncertainty, and immense opportunity of the Intelligence Age.

By fostering this upward movement, education becomes a tool for individual growth and collective evolution. It enables us to empathize with differing worldviews, embrace complexity, and find common ground across diverse perspectives when trying to ride the tsunami. In doing so, education equips humanity with the ability to address global challenges collaboratively and innovatively, creating a future that reflects shared values and interconnected progress. If this book has opened your eyes to these possibilities, I urge you to share it with your family, friends, and colleagues. Because together, we can build the foundation of a thriving, adaptive, and resilient future.

Unfortunately, today's educational paradigms, rooted in the Industrial Revolution, have failed to keep pace with the rapid advancements of the 21st century. Rows of forward-facing students passively absorbing information from a lecture remain the norm in many countries. Education must urgently evolve into a driver of human resilience and ingenuity. We should view education as the development tool that unlocks potential and accelerates evolution instead of just a passive transfer of knowledge. The stagnation in education is particularly striking when juxtaposed with the extraordinary technological advancements of our time. For over a century, the structure of classrooms has pretty much remained the same while the world outside has been utterly transformed. Research shows that the existing approach to teaching yields a dismal 5 percent retention rate, far below what participatory methods like group discussions (50 percent) or learning by doing (75 percent) can achieve.1 This mismatch between teaching methods and the demands of the Intelligence Age risks leaving us and future generations unprepared to solve the wicked problems we will face. It is remarkable, and troubling, that we have not innovated in how we prepare ourselves to navigate a world so vastly different from the one in which these methods were created. As a result, the rapid evolution of technology has created a landscape where children often outpace their educators in understanding future tools, leading to issues ranging from misinformation to online bullying and, in extreme cases, even suicide, as nobody told them how to use these powerful tools.

As technologies and their risks converge, adaptability, critical thinking, and emotional intelligence will emerge as our most valuable assets. They will enable us to create pathways for individuals to navigate today's and tomorrow's challenges. The future will not reward those who merely know. It will reward those who can learn, unlearn, and relearn and do that over and over again. To ensure that we are not just passengers but architects of this age, we must reimagine how we teach, what we teach, and why we teach.

We need a paradigm shift, a *Gestalt Shift*, in education.

The arrival of generative AI tools like ChatGPT in 2022 underscores this urgency. Students quickly adapted, using AI to automate homework while educators scrambled to respond. Schools in the United States, Australia, and elsewhere banned ChatGPT, revealing a futile attempt to block the future rather than embrace it. Such bans miss the point. It is like banning calculators, as mathematics teachers tried to do in the 1970s. It might preserve the past, but it does little for the future. The future cannot be kept at bay. It must be engaged with, understood, and integrated into education. Linking back to the concept of Wu Wei, or effortless action or flow, as discussed in Chapter Three, the most effective learning occurs when it aligns with an individual's intrinsic curiosity[2] and natural inclinations.[3] Education systems that adopt this principle focus on fostering environments where students are encouraged to explore, adapt, and grow without rigid structures that stifle creativity or impose conformity. This approach moves beyond rote memorization, embracing experiential learning that mirrors the Taoist belief in engaging with the natural rhythms of life. Technologies like AI, the metaverse, and 3D printing hold immense potential to make learning immersive, participatory, and adaptive, creating opportunities to transform education from a passive experience into a dynamic, hands-on journey.

Preparing the next generation to navigate and shape tomorrow's world is the most critical task to secure humanity's future and successfully ride this tsunami of change. Yet, systemic challenges persist. Many nations are cutting education budgets, undervaluing teachers, and failing to address the growing need for upskilling educators themselves. The Dutch government's 2024 €1.2 billion education budget cut exemplifies this short-sightedness, undermining the country's long-term competitiveness.[4] Teachers, often underpaid, disrespected, and overworked, struggle to keep pace with technological changes, widening the gap between what students need and what education delivers.

The Intelligence Age demands a paradigm shift in how we view education, and it helps to integrate an Indigenous approach as we did in Chapter Three. Education must evolve and embrace methods that foster adaptability, creativity, futures thinking, and emotional intelligence while appreciating the interconnectedness of our world. In reimagining education for the Intelligence Age, we can draw inspiration from the First Nations Holistic Lifelong Learning Model.[5] This profoundly insightful framework bridges individual learning and collective well-being. Developed through a collaboration between the Canadian Council on Learning and Indigenous educators, this model embodies an Indigenous worldview that learning is not just a linear accumulation of knowledge but a deeply interconnected, regenerative process spanning a lifetime.[6] It emphasizes the balance of body, mind, heart, and spirit, reflecting a multidimensional approach to personal and collective growth.

For First Nations people, the purpose of learning is to honor and protect the earth and ensure the long-term sustainability of life.[7] This approach advocates for experiential learning, cultural transmission, and a reciprocal relationship with nature. These elements enrich the educational experience and instill a deeper understanding of our place in the broader interconnected ecosystem. By adopting principles from this framework, modern education can transcend its traditional limitations, fostering resilience, empathy, and a global sense of responsibility. This interconnected worldview challenges the compartmentalized structures of modern education, advocating instead for an approach where students learn through doing, connecting, and reflecting.

To prepare ourselves for a future that evolves faster than we can comprehend, we must begin now. We must give education the respect it deserves. The future of education lies in immersive, experiential learning powered by cutting-edge technologies. It lies in recognizing teaching not just as a profession but as the foundation of human progress. Most importantly, it lies in equipping every individual with tools, and the understanding of those tools, that will allow them to navigate a rapidly evolving world with confidence and purpose. The stakes are high, but so is the potential for transformation. Education isn't just a response to the disruptions of the Intelligence Age. It is our greatest tool for shaping its trajectory. Let us build a world where teaching is as dynamic as the technologies it seeks to understand and where learning is a lifelong journey that empowers individuals to thrive, innovate, and lead, from when children enter kindergarten to long after adults retire.

TidalShot

Tech is changing faster than we can teach. In this new era, knowledge isn't power—adaptability is. Let's reshape education and human capital for a world reinvented daily.

Scan the QR code to share this section's TidalShot and illustration to your network.

A PARADIGM SHIFT IN HOW AND WHAT WE TEACH

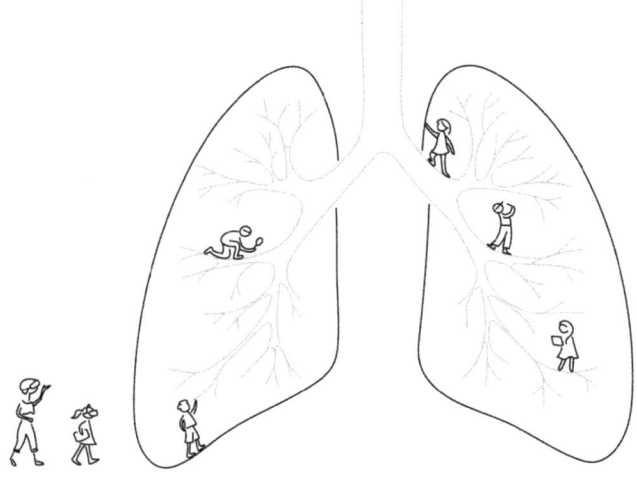

Imagine a classroom not bound by walls or the limits of human capacity, where every student has a personal mentor attuned to their unique pace, interests, and learning style. This is no longer the domain of science fiction but the emerging reality of AI tutors; intelligent systems poised to revolutionize education in ways that mirror humanity's transition from the quill to the printing press.

As the challenges and opportunities of the Intelligence Age grow, AI tutors represent the required paradigm shift, enabling personalized, adaptive, and immersive learning experiences that can respond to the complexities of the modern world in real-time. But this is not merely about embracing technology. It is about rethinking what it means to teach and to learn.

AI tutors will not replace teachers but amplify their impact. Unlike traditional methods that struggle to address diverse learning needs, AI tutors use advanced algorithms and large language models to analyze individual performance in real-time and engage in meaningful conversations with the student. They adapt to each student's strengths and weaknesses, level of expertise, and language, offering tailored lessons that challenge the advanced learner while providing extra support to those who need it. Visual learners can experience concepts through immersive simulations, while auditory learners benefit from dynamic storytelling. This adaptability transforms education from a passive experience into an active, engaging journey of discovery.

In a world where traditional classrooms often fail to meet the needs of an evolving society, China is proving that AI tutors can bridge educational gaps and redefine how learning is delivered. With an education system historically marked by disparities between urban and rural areas, the country has embraced artificial intelligence to provide personalized and accessible learning experiences. AI-powered platforms like Squirrel Ai Learning are leading the charge, demonstrating the transformative potential of technology in education.

Consider Baishaping Primary School in Baziyan Village, nestled in China's Hubei Province. Like many rural schools, it has struggled with a shortage of quality teachers and resources. But a new AI-based adaptive learning system from Squirrel Ai is changing the narrative. Students at Baishaping now experience tailored lessons designed to address their specific gaps in knowledge. The results are striking. Within a month of implementation, student performance in math and literacy improved significantly. Beyond grades, their engagement and confidence soared as they realized, "I can learn, and I can learn so easily."[8] This AI system doesn't just teach. It transforms the way students understand and approach learning. Squirrel Ai's impact extends far beyond individual schools. In just a decade, the platform has opened over 2,000 learning centers across 1,500 cities and towns.[9] With 24 million registered students, and insights from world-class educators, it collected 10 billion learning behavior data points to power its adaptive AI systems. Notably, it has also provided 10 million free accounts to families in need, democratizing access to high-quality education. In fact, Squirrel AI aims to give the AI tutor for free to 20 percent of children from the lowest-income families in the world to promote educational equity, according to Derek Haoyang Li, chairman of Squirrel Ai.[10]

This scalability addresses a pressing global challenge: the widening teacher gap. According to UNESCO, the world will need an additional 44 million teachers by 2030 to meet global educational targets, a problem especially pressing in the world's poorest regions.[11] AI tutors offer a powerful solution to this shortfall, supporting human educators and ensuring equitable access to learning resources.

Squirrel Ai offers more than just incremental progress. It sets a new standard for educational technology. In 2024, the company launched what it claims to be the world's first adaptive learning large model, embedding cutting-edge multimodal capabilities (enabling it to process inputs such as text, images, and video) across major subjects.[12] This innovation enables Squirrel Ai to analyze complex relationships between knowledge points, questions, and student abilities quickly and accurately. These capabilities allow the system to provide students with highly targeted, personalized learning pathways, addressing their specific needs and significantly improving learning efficiency. Squirrel Ai exemplifies how adaptive AI can transform education on a systemic level by blending technological advancements with social responsibility and policy innovation. This model enhances individual learning outcomes and lays the groundwork for a more equitable and sustainable future in education. As Squirrel Ai continues to scale internationally, it offers a vision of education where no child, regardless of socioeconomic background, is left behind.

On the other side of the world, in Texas, USA, the private Alpha School in Austin is also flipping the education model. Students now spend just two hours a day with AI tutors, then shift focus to passion projects like building apps or launching social ventures. The result? Test scores in the top 2 percent nationally, less stress, and more time to learn by doing. Personalized AI instruction means students move at their own pace while teachers become mentors, not taskmasters.[13]

While Squirrel Ai and the Alpha School exemplify the transformative potential of AI in bridging educational gaps across diverse socioeconomic contexts, another trailblazer in the field, Khan Academy, offers a complementary perspective on how AI tutors can elevate learning outcomes. Sal Khan, the visionary founder of Khan Academy, has long championed the integration of technology in education, driven by a belief that personalized tutoring can unlock unparalleled levels of student achievement.[14]

Khan's aspirations echo those of groundbreaking studies from decades past, demonstrating the extraordinary impact of one-on-one tutoring on student performance. With the advent of large language models, Khan Academy is realizing this vision at scale through Khanmigo, an AI tutor designed to foster critical thinking, personalized engagement, and transformative learning experiences for students worldwide.[15]

Khanmigo is redefining educational interaction by harnessing AI to create an always-on, personalized learning environment for just a few dollars per month. Unlike conventional AI tools that spoon-feed information, Khanmigo challenges students to engage deeply with content, enhancing critical thinking and problem-solving skills. This tool isn't just about giving the right answers; it fosters a learning process that encourages students to discover answers through guided reasoning. With features like real-time feedback on coding and the ability to customize its appearance, the Khan Academy and Khanmigo have become learning partners across borders.

Take Sultana's story, for example, a young girl from Afghanistan who was barred from traditional schooling by the Taliban and so turned to the

Khan Academy to pursue her dream of studying quantum computing in the US.[16] Sultana yearned for freedom. Freedom to walk confidently, to explore her world, and to learn. Living in a volatile Afghanistan where bombings and decrees from the first Taliban regime turned schools into dangerous spaces for girls, she was forced to navigate her education within the confines of her home. But it was here, armed with an iPad and fierce determination that she stumbled upon Khan Academy. Through Khan Academy, Sultana taught herself English, philosophy, mathematics, and science. Each new concept she mastered became a spark of liberation.[17] Solving math problems gave her a sense of control amid the chaos, while delving into the works of Socrates ignited a curiosity that refused to be suppressed.

Her education was more than just an accumulation of knowledge. It was her way of reclaiming her identity, stepping out from the shadows of invisibility, and charting a path forward. Sultana's story demonstrates the profound democratizing power of education technology. Without access to formal schooling, it was the tools of the digital age that empowered her to transcend her circumstances. Years later, she earned a scholarship to study in the United States and eventually became a university researcher publishing in her scientific field, a testament to the resilience of the human spirit and the boundless possibilities of accessible education. If platforms like Khan Academy could give Sultana the foundation to rewrite her future, imagine what the advent of AI tutors, such as Khanmigo, could offer to millions of children worldwide. AI-driven learning can adapt to individual needs, foster curiosity through personalized lessons, and break barriers of language, geography, and socioeconomic status. Sultana's story is a call to action: to embrace the transformative power of AI in education and ensure that every child has the opportunity to thrive.

Traditional education often forces a one-size-fits-all approach, grouping students by age rather than ability. This leaves some struggling to keep up while others grow bored. The advent of AI tutors heralds a significant leap forward in educational technology, offering a suite of benefits that cater to the diverse needs of students across the globe.[18] Imagine a world where every student has a dedicated mentor. An adaptive guide capable of understanding their unique strengths, challenges, and learning pace. A student struggling with algebra receives targeted support and simplified explanations, while a precocious learner can explore advanced topics to stay engaged. This dual focus on equity and excellence ensures that every student thrives. Moreover, feedback, the cornerstone of effective learning, often comes too late in traditional classrooms, limited by time and resources. AI tutors eliminate these delays, providing real-time corrections, explanations, and encouragement. A student who missteps a geometry problem receives immediate guidance, reinforcing understanding and building confidence in the moment. By delivering instant, actionable feedback, AI tutors accelerate learning and empower students to learn from their mistakes as they happen. With the ability to transcend the limitations of traditional classrooms, AI tutors are poised to redefine how knowledge is shared and acquired, addressing age-old challenges in new, innovative ways. As AI takes over the classroom, teachers must transition from transferring knowledge to becoming more like a coach who guides students in their personalized learning journey. Of course, these AI tutors are useful not only at primary school, high school, or university but can help anyone, regardless of age, commit to lifelong learning in a way that best suits them.

Education has also long been shadowed by inequities. Where you are born, your family's income and access to resources determine the quality of your education. AI tutors obliterate these barriers, bringing high-quality, personalized learning to any student with an internet connection. From bustling urban centers to remote villages, AI tutors democratize education across backgrounds and language barriers, leveling the playing field for millions of learners. An AI tutor can be the difference between stagnation and a lifeline to a brighter future for a child in a rural village with limited access to skilled teachers.

Beyond these transformative benefits, AI tutors offer unmatched flexibility. Learning is no longer confined to the rigid schedule of school hours. Students with part-time jobs or family responsibilities can engage with their AI tutor in the evening. A curious child can explore new topics over the weekend. This adaptability ensures that education fits into the rhythms of life, not the other way around, empowering learners to take control of their journeys.

As AI tutors continue to evolve, they offer an inclusive, adaptive, and profoundly impactful educational vision. However, they also raise questions about data privacy, accessibility in underserved regions, and the potential dehumanization of education. Therefore, as with any technology, we must ensure a thoughtful introduction of AI tutors into the educational system. In this new era, learning becomes a tool for empowerment instead of a path to knowledge, breaking down barriers and unlocking human potential on a global scale. With AI tutors, the future of education isn't just equitable; it is boundless.

But while AI tutors revolutionize how students learn by personalizing and adapting the learning process, immersive technologies like spatial intelligence and the metaverse will redefine the content of education itself, making it experiential, interactive, and accessible in ways that traditional classrooms can only imagine.

Immersive digital environments transform passive learning into active exploration. Complex topics, whether in biology, history, or physics, come alive when students can step into and interact with them. Imagine walking through the bustling streets of ancient Rome as part of your history class or standing at the foot of Mount Everest during a geography lesson. What if, instead of reading about the circulatory system in a textbook, you could navigate its intricate pathways as if you were inside a living, breathing human body? These are glimpses of what learning could look like in a hyper-realistic metaverse powered by mixed reality glasses and spatial intelligence. Visualizing abstract concepts will no longer be challenging when you can experience them. Students could collaborate in virtual labs to conduct experiments, explore distant planets as part of an astronomy lesson, or practice architectural design by constructing entire cities in a shared virtual space. Learning becomes an adventure, not a chore.

In these digital spaces, geography ceases to matter. Students from Tokyo can partner with peers in Nairobi to solve problems, share ideas, and build global networks. These cross-border interactions prepare learners for the interconnected, multicultural workforces of the future, where collaboration across cultures is not optional but essential.

Imagine the value of a high school debate club where participants from six continents gather in a virtual amphitheater to discuss climate change policies. The metaverse democratizes access to education while offering access to diverse perspectives, helping students develop the important skills of empathy and critical thinking that extend beyond their immediate environments.

Immersive learning doesn't stop with theory either. For vocational training and professional development, the metaverse becomes a virtual experiment ground. Aspiring surgeons can practice delicate procedures in a risk-free environment. Engineers can test designs under simulated real-world conditions. Emergency responders can rehearse disaster scenarios without the dangers or costs of physical drills. These simulations enhance our technical skills and build confidence, bridging the gap between the classroom and real-world applications, especially when integrating it with brain-computer interfaces to offer direct neural feedback on the learning progress.

The metaverse, assisted by your personal AI tutor, has the potential to break free from the constraints of traditional education, offering students a chance to engage with knowledge as participants rather than passive recipients. When I launched a digital twin of myself at the end of 2023, which allowed anyone to talk to me via text, audio, or video in 29 languages (a world first), it was done as part of a vision for the future. Imagine, for example, using augmented reality glasses to invite an AI-powered Einstein to appear in your bedroom holographically, teaching you physics like nothing before. As we integrate these tools into the educational landscape, we have a chance to equip students with experiences that prepare them for the complex, interconnected future that awaits.

Consider a vibrant virtual learning space that is not within a school building, but instead is worldwide, powered by advanced spatial computing, AI tutors,[19] and immersive reality.[20] Students from Mumbai, Nairobi, and Copenhagen gather in a hyper-realistic metaverse classroom, equipped with haptic feedback gloves and AR glasses, ready to collaborate on a climate resilience project. As they "enter" the virtual space, they are greeted by a polymath AI tutor trained in environmental science, economics, and policy analysis. It personalizes each student's experience based on their learning history, strengths, and areas for growth.[21] It provides each participant with a tailored "pre-class pack," including simulations, reading materials, and an engaging narrative about a fictional coastal town threatened by rising sea levels. The students' first task is to step into a high-stakes simulation of a coastal town experiencing severe flooding due to climate change. They explore flooded streets, examine the failure of infrastructure, and experience the cascading social impacts firsthand. The AI tutor provides real-time guidance, posing ethical dilemmas and asking probing questions: "What happens to the town's economy if schools remain closed for months? How would this scenario change if the town had invested in green infrastructure?"

As the students navigate the simulation, they begin collaborating. One team designs a floating school powered by renewable energy; another proposes decentralized water management using blockchain for equitable distribution. Visual learners create 3D models of their solutions, while others articulate their strategies through immersive storytelling, crafting policy proposals that would be reviewed in a mock UN assembly.

The AI tutor continuously adapts its feedback, challenging advanced students with complex scenarios while supporting those who need extra help. It simulates different futures, both optimistic and dystopian, based on the students' proposed interventions, providing a vivid picture of the long-term impacts of their ideas. The activity concludes with a global debate in a virtual amphitheater, where students from different continents defend their proposals to a jury of digital twin experts, including Einstein and Rachel Carson.

After the simulation, the students are guided through a debrief that integrates futures thinking. The AI tutor prompts them to reflect: "What skills did you use today that could help you in real-world challenges? How can your community begin applying these ideas now?" Students identify gaps in their knowledge, sparking a self-driven exploration into urban planning, marine biology, or climate justice. The session doesn't end with the "classroom."

Students keep working asynchronously, guided by their AI tutors until their solutions are polished enough to present to local policymakers via holographic pitches. The experience fosters resilience, empathy, and a profound sense of agency by integrating actionable skills, ethical reasoning, and global collaboration.

We should not stop with AI and the metaverse as we rethink education. Integrating other transformative technologies that reflect the realities of tomorrow's world is equally essential. Take 3D printing as an example; when combined with lessons on the decentralized economy, it becomes more than just a tool; it becomes a gateway for students to understand the interconnected, tech-driven systems that will define their futures. Imagine teaching students to design and manufacture their own creations, from prototypes to fully functional products, while also introducing them to decentralized platforms that enable global collaboration and distribution. This hands-on integration of creation and commerce will equip students with practical skills and immerse them in the dynamics of a digital-first economy. By empowering students to navigate these ecosystems, we prepare them to participate in and shape their future.

TidalShot

Industrial-age schooling doesn't cut it anymore. Personalized AI tutors, immersive learning, and teaching meta-skills can prime us for a world changed monthly by new tech.

Scan the QR code to share this section's TidalShot and illustration to your network.

A RESPONSIBLE APPROACH TO TECHNOLOGY

One of the most overlooked advantages of integrating cutting-edge technologies into education is the opportunity to equip students with the skills to navigate transformative digital tools in a controlled and safe environment. Instead of being left to fend for themselves in the unregulated, profit-driven digital wild west, students can learn to engage with emerging technologies to maximize opportunity while mitigating risk. This proactive approach is essential as we increasingly rely on digital platforms that profoundly influence young minds.

Consider Meta's 2024 advertising campaign on LinkedIn that introduced "teen accounts" for Instagram. Meta touted these accounts as safe alternatives for young users. The very existence of "safety measures" raises an uncomfortable question: if these platforms are inherently safe, why do they require special protections? It is not surprising that we're now seeing a global loneliness epidemic among teens, exacerbated by platforms that encourage isolated, screen-based interaction over genuine human connection.[22] Unfortunately, Mark Zuckerberg's solution to this loneliness epidemic is throwing more AI to the problem and encouraging teenagers to start a relationship with one of Meta's AIs instead of meeting real people. He envisions replacing real friends with AI companions, which is a business model that thrives on emotional outsourcing.[23] The reality is clear: social media has been repeatedly shown to harm young users, fostering addiction, cyberbully-ing, and mental health crises while prioritizing shareholder profits over user well-being.

The evidence is overwhelming. Platforms like Instagram, TikTok and AI-powered applications such as Character.ai manipulate teenage users through attention-maximizing algorithms designed to exploit dopamine-driven behaviors. These mechanisms create dependency, foster unrealistic expectations, and, in some cases, contribute to tragic outcomes such as self-harm and suicide.[24] With research showing a clear correlation between excessive social media use and declining mental health, the moral obligation to act is undeniable.[25] As a society, we must ask ourselves: do we value our youth's mental and emotional development, or are we content to let profit-driven Big Tech shape their futures? The answer should be obvious. Just as we regulate access to gambling, alcohol, and tobacco to protect (young) people, we must establish boundaries around transformative technologies such as social media and AI.

The solution is twofold: regulation and education. First, we must introduce stringent regulations, including outright bans on social media and certain AI platforms for those under 16,[26] as Australia decided to do in 2024 as the first country in the world, with strict accountability for platform owners and executives.[27] This is not a draconian measure; it is a necessary safeguard. Critics of this position argue that social platforms can offer teens invaluable peer support and digital literacy skills. They fear an outright ban might stifle young people's ability to navigate online spaces responsibly. However, I think that the mental health cost is too high to treat social media as a casual rite of passage, especially given the addictive design. The real debate, then, isn't about technology versus no technology; it is about the structure, oversight, and age-appropriate curation that ensures healthier online experiences. Countries like China have already demonstrated that limiting access to addictive platforms, such as gaming, can have a positive impact on children's well-being.[28] At the same time, schools around the world that restrict smartphone usage have reported teenagers expressing relief, free from the pressures of constant digital engagement.[29] We don't allow kids to drive cars until they're over 16 (on average globally) because of the responsibility and risks involved, so why should powerful digital tools be treated any differently?

Second, education must be at the heart of our strategy to embrace transformative technologies and understand and mitigate their profound risks. Digital literacy must evolve beyond basic tech skills to encompass a deeper ethical, social, and psychological awareness of how these tools shape our lives. By integrating transformative technologies into the classroom, we can slowly introduce kids to these tools and teach them how to use them responsibly by critically assessing their risks and implications.

Consider the dangers of uneducated engagement with technologies like AI, social media, and decentralized systems. Without early education, students remain vulnerable to manipulation, including AI-crafted misinformation, relentless social media bullying, or even the allure of pump-and-dump crypto scams. The risks extend further, encompassing the dark potential of 3D-printed weapons, the erosion of privacy through brain-computer interfaces, and the long-term psychological toll of hyperconnected digital lives.

By embedding these technologies into education, we can demystify their workings and highlight their ethical complexities. Teaching students how AI algorithms manipulate attention, how privacy can vanish with unguarded use of BCIs, or how social media fosters addiction and bullying equips them with the tools to navigate this landscape critically and responsibly. If we fail to educate them from a young age, how can they be expected to grasp the magnitude of the risks they face?

This proactive approach empowers students to become informed architects of their digital futures. It fosters resilience, agency, and an ethical mindset, ensuring they are prepared to thrive in the Intelligence Age while safeguarding themselves and society against the negative and unintended consequences of technological advancement. What's not to like about that?

TidalShot

Gadgets and data aren't neutral. We must shield youth from exploitative platforms while teaching them how to own, not be owned by, their digital toolkit.

Scan the QR code to share this section's TidalShot and illustration to your network.

LIFELONG LEARNING

But the need for education doesn't end when students leave the classroom. In a world where technologies evolve at an unprecedented pace, continuous learning must become a universal principle, extending well into adulthood. After all, the Intelligence Age doesn't come with a retirement plan for your skills. Miss a few updates and suddenly your expertise is about as relevant as floppy disks—in other words, you snooze, you lose. The Intelligence Age demands foundational knowledge of the transformations driving the tsunami as well as an enduring capacity to adapt, innovate, and collaborate. For adults, this means cultivating the skills to navigate rapid change and embracing platforms and strategies that make lifelong learning not just possible but practical and rewarding. This shift is essential to stay relevant and to actively contribute to shaping a future where human potential keeps pace with technological transformation. If we are to navigate the Intelligence Age successfully, we must embrace a philosophy of perpetual learning, critical thinking, and adaptability.

For adults, the challenge is twofold: staying informed about transformative technologies and honing the practical skills needed to handle them responsibly. It is also where my own platform, Futurwise, comes in. While it is undeniably a personal initiative, I mention it because it epitomizes the shift toward dynamic, individualized learning that meets each person's evolving needs. Instead of a sea of questionable sources, Futurwise filters the noise, moving from chaos to clarity by offering curated, personalized insights tailored to your persona, expertise, background and language, enabling deeper discussions to help you turn continuous learning into real-world leadership. By blending critical thinking, high-quality content, and exposure to emerging technologies from a wide range of curated content sources and types, it gives users a scalable roadmap for lifelong learning in the Intelligence Age, something we all need as knowledge accelerates and old norms quickly fade. Especially in a world where knowledge has become abundant, we need to level up from knowledge to wisdom, something the world could certainly use more of, and Futurwise can help you do that. Therefore, as a valued reader of my book, I offer a 25 percent discount for 12 months for the first 1000 people who sign up to Futurwise. Simply subscribe to Futurwise by scanning the QR code or follow the URL and you are on a trajectory to read less but know more.

Scan to download Futurwise or go to Futurwise.com/r/now-what.

At the core of this transformation is a new understanding of learning. It is no longer enough to consume information passively; we must actively engage with ideas, question assumptions, and apply knowledge in real-world contexts. For instance, dedicating just 30 minutes a day to focused learning, attending workshops (digitally or physically), or engaging with emerging technologies can build the foundational skills needed to navigate exponential change. These efforts must be accompanied by an awareness of trends, a commitment to self-directed education, and a willingness to embrace new perspectives.

Lifelong learning also fosters adaptability, the cornerstone of resilience in the Intelligence Age. Adaptability is more than coping with change; it is about thriving in uncertainty, seizing opportunities, and turning challenges into growth. A farmer learning to use drones for precision agriculture, a healthcare worker mastering AI diagnostics, or a community leader exploring blockchain for social impact all exemplify how practical, context-sensitive education can drive systemic transformation.

However, education cannot exist in a vacuum. It must address the profound ethical, social, and psychological implications of technological change. Students and adults need to understand the risks of new transformative tools. Without this awareness, they risk becoming passive consumers in a system that demands active participation.

This is both an individual responsibility and a societal imperative. Cross-generational education, universal access to learning, and global tech literacy programs must be prioritized. Educational reform must integrate practical skills with cultural sensitivity and accessibility, ensuring that every demographic, from rural communities to urban centers, is equipped to participate in the digital future.

Finally, the Intelligence Age requires us to rethink the skills we value. The skills required to thrive go far beyond memorizing rote knowledge or mastering traditional academic subjects. Creativity, strategic foresight, collaboration, philosophy, and ethical awareness are no longer "soft" skills but essential competencies for the digital economy where knowledge is available at your fingertips, and soon just a thought away as brain-computer interfaces redefine how we access and interact with information. As technology evolves and industries transform, the ability to continuously learn, embrace change, and remain resilient is critical. This includes cultivating flexibility to pivot careers, reframe challenges, and navigate unpredictable environments. For example, as blockchain reshapes finance and AI redefines creativity, individuals with adaptive mindsets can seamlessly transition into roles that didn't exist a decade ago. Such innovative mindsets embody the creativity, strategic foresight, and problem-solving abilities needed to envision and execute groundbreaking ideas. Whether designing immersive experiences in the metaverse or solving global challenges like climate change, innovation fuels progress and opens the door to unprecedented opportunities.

Collaboration also takes on new dimensions in a hyper-connected world. Working effectively across borders and disciplines requires teamwork, emotional intelligence, and a global perspective. Platforms like Roblox and Minecraft, where Gen Alpha (those born between 2010–2024) already collaborate in building virtual worlds, exemplify how teamwork in digital spaces prepares future generations for the interconnected realities of the Intelligence Age. Following close behind, Generation Beta (2025–2039) will grow up immersed in an even more integrated digital-physical world, where AI, quantum computing, and biotechnology are second nature.[30] Shaped by eco-conscious and tech-savvy parents, they will likely champion systemic thinking, ethical innovation, and global collaboration to address the challenges of their era, but only if we teach them before the robots do.[31] If we combine this with digital well-being and mindfulness and an understanding of the ethical implications of the technology use, we can ensure that innovation serves humanity responsibly.[32] Whether navigating AI biases or safeguarding privacy in brain-computer interfaces, ethical awareness will enable us to make choices that align with societal well-being.

Strategic foresight is another indispensable skill in a world that is changing as fast as ours. It moves beyond reactive problem-solving to anticipate challenges, uncover opportunities, and navigate the complexities of tomorrow with innovation, responsibility, and a long-term perspective. As discussed in Chapter Two, futures thinking is central to this capability, enabling individuals and organizations to adopt a broader lens and proactively engage with change rather than being blindsided by it. The essence of futures thinking lies in cultivating a mindset that views disruption as an opportunity rather than a threat, and it would be wise to start learning this skill at a young age. Tools like scenario planning allow organizations and individuals to identify skill gaps, anticipate systemic risks, and adapt with agility. This forward-thinking approach is not confined to corporate boardrooms; it is a mindset critical to every student, educator, and policymaker preparing for a future dominated by exponential change. Strategic foresight also emphasizes adaptability over static knowledge. While technology may evolve at an unprecedented pace, the ability to assess its implications, innovate within constraints, and act ethically remains uniquely human. By integrating futures thinking into education, we prepare ourselves to keep up with change, understand the unintended consequences of transformative technologies, and transform uncertainty into a canvas for creativity and resilience. It challenges individuals to consider interconnected impacts, preparing them to address complex global challenges such as climate change or cybersecurity with strategic vision. This skill is particularly vital in the Intelligence Age, where no single problem exists in isolation.

These skills are not static; they evolve alongside technological advancements. Continuous learning, whether through global tech literacy programs, professional upskilling, or cross-generational education, is the bridge that connects individuals to the demands of an ever-changing digital landscape. By fostering these skills early and maintaining a commitment to lifelong learning, we prepare ourselves for future challenges. When paired with an ethical, adaptable mindset, these competencies enable us to ride the wave of change with confidence and purpose, ensuring that humanity not only adapts to but shapes the trajectory of the Intelligence Age.

The moral of the story is that education must evolve to reflect its most profound mission: moving humanity forward. The question is no longer what to learn but how to learn and how to teach others to do the same. A world of rapid change requires curious, resilient, and empowered learners. Education is the foundation upon which we will build a future where technology serves humanity and humanity rises to meet its greatest challenges with confidence and purpose. The Industrial Age prioritized rote learning and standardized skills designed for factories and hierarchical organizations. The Intelligence Age demands something fundamentally different. It calls for fostering adaptability, critical thinking, and emotional and ethical intelligence, skills that empower individuals to navigate complexity, innovate boldly, and collaborate effectively in interconnected systems.

Education must no longer be about memorizing facts readily available at the click of a button. Instead, it should focus on cultivating the ability to learn, unlearn, and relearn. It should teach students to ask better questions, think systemically, and approach challenges with curiosity and creativity. This shift is not just an adjustment; it is a transformation that recognizes education as the driving force behind humanity's capacity to thrive in the face of uncertainty and opportunity. To truly prepare the next generation for the Intelligence Age, we must fundamentally reimagine what it means to learn and what it means to teach.

TidalShot

The half-life of knowledge keeps shrinking. The only real safeguards are constant re-skilling, curiosity, and a willingness to unlearn so we evolve as fast as our machines.

Scan the QR code to share this section's TidalShot and illustration to your network.

NOW WHAT? UPGRADE OUR EDUCATIONAL SYSTEMS

Education must evolve to meet the demands of tomorrow's world, not yesterday's. The technologies, economies, and rules shaping the future require a radical departure from the status quo. We can no longer teach in silos, focusing on static knowledge that quickly becomes obsolete. Instead, education must prepare individuals to understand and navigate the transformative forces of AI, robotics, the metaverse, quantum computing, and the decentralized systems that will define the next decades. As technology evolves and becomes easier to integrate into curricula, teachers should rebuild their programs to ensure students can experiment and engage with the latest technologies. However, technical skills alone are no longer sufficient. As AI automates predictable tasks, the premium skills shift to uniquely human capabilities: adaptability, creativity, emotional intelligence, strategic foresight, technological literacy, and ethical reasoning. These are qualities that machines struggle to replicate, at least for now, and they are what will distinguish humans in the Intelligence Age. Fostering these capabilities requires a collective effort, starting with education systems that equip students with the tools to thrive in uncertainty and complexity. To enforce such a paradigm shift, governments must introduce policies that reward forward-thinking education, including grants for developing new tools and ensuring schools cannot independently ban the use of new technologies.

Technology is not merely about capability; it is about wisdom. With great power comes great responsibility, and our choices today will shape the society we leave for future generations. This is why teaching the rules, ethics, technologies and economics of tomorrow is critical. It will empower individuals and ensure that innovation aligns with equity and sustainability. We must move away from transferring knowledge through memorization to instilling the skills to navigate an increasingly complex world. It is about questioning assumptions, solving novel problems, and cultivating the resilience needed to adapt in an age of accelerating disruption. Humanity's most valuable asset is no longer its capacity to memorize information but its ability to adapt, innovate, and lead in complex, interconnected ecosystems. Schools must become laboratories for critical thinking and innovation, teaching students how to apply transformative technologies responsibly and collaboratively. As educators, parents, leaders, and learners, the responsibility lies with all of us to build a future where technology serves humanity, not the other way around.

So, now what? The answer lies in embracing a shift from traditional approaches to education and problem-solving toward educational methodologies that reflect the world's exponential complexity. Education offers us a long-term solution to deal with exponential change, but just with any exponential concept, progress will be slow at first before we reach the tipping point when we cross into the second half of the chessboard. Therefore, we also need an immediate solution that gives individuals, organizations, and societies the tools to deal with exponential challenges immediately. Tools that enable us to address systemic issues with creativity, foresight, and collaboration. This is the foundation of the WAVE framework, which we will explore in the next chapter: a methodology to ride the tsunami of change with purpose, agility and vision.

TidalShot

Champion digital literacy, mental agility, and ethical guardrails. If we reform how we learn today, we'll raise citizens who can guide tomorrow's unstoppable transformations.

Scan the QR code to share this TidalShot to your network.

THE DEGREE THAT UPDATES

Vita arrived at the sleek headquarters of CertifyAI as news drones circled overhead, their lenses glinting in the sun. Vita had been invited in to consult on behalf of Dr. Eva Staerlin—a renowned surgeon who famously saved the president's life after the infamous 2035 incident—who had her professional credentials erased overnight. An automated assessment had labeled her skills obsolete, abruptly ending a career built over decades. The medical community, supported by the general public, had erupted in protest. Public trust was in short supply after all and while Vita had no professional qualifications, it consistently learned and evolved, surpassing many so-called experts in many fields.

Inside, CertifyAI's directors nervously explained their vision: a certification system that updated continuously, adapting in real time to rapid technological advances. No more static degrees becoming obsolete mere months after graduation. It sounded promising, yet the stark reality of the surgeon's lost certification lingered.

"Continuous updates are necessary," Vita began gently, studying the nervous faces around the table, "but abrupt invalidation damages trust. The human mind is not software; it can't simply be overwritten with new code, downloading updates as they go. Even with BCI enhancements, overloading the mind with too much information at once will have disastrous consequences for the user."

One of the younger executives protested cautiously, "But progress is exponential now, Vita. We can't risk outdated knowledge in critical roles. Lives depend on it."

"Exactly," Vita responded calmly. "Lives depend on it. But lives depend on experience too. Some things you can't learn in a classroom. Progress without consideration for the humans it affects is regression. Your system shouldn't simply revoke certifications. It should guide the learner. Integrate mentorship roles, gradual retraining, and personalized pathways to update skills steadily and sustainably; lifelong learning is what it is all about."

It moved its hands gracefully, sketching holographic visuals. "Imagine a system that highlights knowledge gaps long before they become critical, pairing individuals with mentors or collaborative AI tutors. Learners don't fear sudden obsolescence, they anticipate growth."

The executives exchanged thoughtful glances. Vita could almost sense relief spreading across the room.

"Dr. Eva Staerlin is one of the best in her field, but she isn't a machine." Vita added softly. "While I can update in moments, she deserves the same opportunity, but gently, compassionately, and humanly."

In the days that followed, CertifyAI rolled out their revised system. The surgeon regained her certification after an accelerated AI mentorship and retraining program. Vita watched with quiet satisfaction as headlines turned from outrage to admiration. Technology had once again advanced, but this time, humanity had kept pace.

CHAPTER 7

The WAVE Forward

Chaos doesn't defeat us when we harness it; we just need the right rhythm to convert turbulence into lasting progress.

Societies and organizations are drowning in digital disruption, AI hype, geopolitical chaos, and looming climate crises. We've witnessed how exponential technologies can magnify both opportunity and risk. But how do we navigate these forces in a way that blends ethical grounding with pragmatic solutions before they destabilize everything we know? The answer lies in four interconnected steps. Steps we've been dancing around, designed to seamlessly flow in an iterative cycle to create an unstoppable momentum. Let's take a deeper look at the synergy between them and why this cycle can address the crux of exponential change.

The Intelligence Age has thrust us into an era where the velocity of change reshapes every facet of our lives, demanding a fundamental reimagining of how we think, innovate, and lead. Sometimes, it feels as if we woke up one morning and progress decided to take the bullet train without telling us we'd already boarded. While the technologies shaping our future grow increasingly complex, the foundational elements of human progress, such as creativity, agency, empathy, adaptability, and collaboration, remain the keystones of thriving amid change. These values must evolve, not dissolve, as we confront the transformative power of the interconnected digital world.

In this dynamic landscape, preserving our capacity for purposeful decision-making is paramount.[1] While AI systems deliver unparalleled precision and predictive power, it is our ability to act with intentionality that drives true innovation. Rather than ceding control to the machines, we must design systems that enhance human agency, allowing individuals to act not merely as operators but as architects of their futures. This integration of technology as an enabler, not a replacement, ensures that progress amplifies rather than undermines the essence of human ingenuity. This is also why we must stop anthropomorphizing AI, attributing human qualities to machines, or referring to them as "he" or "she." Doing so risks blurring the boundaries between humans and machines, creating unrealistic expectations, and fostering undue emotional attachment.

After all, you wouldn't expect your toaster to have an opinion on your fashion choices, so why give AI the job of moral philosopher? However, the risk runs deeper: our instinct to treat machines like humans, even instinctively saying "thank you" to ChatGPT when we never did so for Google Search, leaves us vulnerable to subtle psychological manipulation that can go unnoticed. With hyper-real spatial devices blurring the line between genuine reality and fabricated illusions, it is crucial that we consciously rein in these primal tendencies to ensure our decisions remain authentically human. AI and robotics are tools, not beings, and we must keep it in its rightful place as an instrument of human progress. Guided, managed, and designed to serve humanity's needs, not mimic its nature. Drawing this line ensures clarity of purpose and reinforces the distinction that our creativity, ethics, and intentionality remain at the core of meaningful innovation.

Equally important is fostering systems that are resilient and equitable. As the pace of change accelerates, centralized structures often reveal their fragility, unable to adapt to the demands of a fast-evolving world. Blockchain and 3D printing offer a framework for decentralization, empowering communities with transparency and adaptability. By redistributing control and enabling fair access, we can create systems that reflect the dynamic, interconnected nature of modern computable economies, ensuring that progress is both sustainable and inclusive.

This transformative era also demands a reinvigoration of entrepreneurial energy. The ability to navigate uncertainty and turn disruption into opportunity has never been more vital. With advanced tools now available at the click of a button for just a few dollars per month, everyone can unlock the potential to address global challenges with creativity and vision. Whether tackling climate change or reimagining education, entrepreneurial thinking paves the way for meaningful solutions that transcend traditional boundaries. You could say we are in an era when a big idea, strong coffee, and a stable internet connection are all it takes to prototype tomorrow. No permission needed.

This chapter explores how we can harness these principles to shape a thriving future. By prioritizing intentional decision-making, embracing decentralized solutions, and nurturing creativity, we can transform the Intelligence Age into a catalyst for shared prosperity. The framework presented here is a blueprint for leadership in a world defined by change and it is applicable not only to deal with technological disruption but also to help us deal with the climate crisis, for example. Let us seize this moment to align technological innovation with human purpose, creating systems that empower, markets that evolve responsibly, and a future that celebrates resilience and ingenuity.

TidalShot

Riding colossal waves of change demands more than luck; it takes strategy. The WAVE framework promises we don't just endure disruption but master it.

Scan the QR code to share this section's TidalShot and illustration to your network.

THE WAVE FRAMEWORK

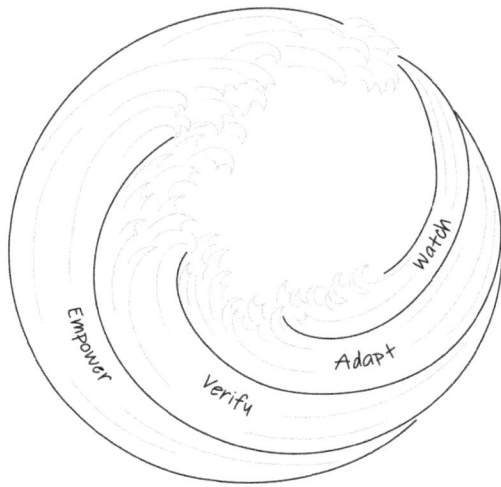

In the maelstrom of the Intelligence Age, where the acceleration of change leaves no stone unturned, our capacity to thrive hinges on rethinking the very foundations of how we interact with technology, society, and ourselves. Yet, in a world shaped by misinformation surges and technological breakthroughs that happen faster than we can comprehend, we risk free-fall if we don't have a systematic, repeatable way to respond. The rules of the past no longer suffice; what worked in a linear, predictable world collapses under the weight of exponential complexity. To navigate this uncharted terrain, we must forge a path forward that acknowledges the intricate interplay between human ingenuity, nature's complexities, and technological advancement while remaining steadfast in our values and vision.

It is crucial to acknowledge that the Intelligence Age is defined not merely by the tools at our disposal but by the systems of interconnectedness they create and affect. These forces don't operate in silos; they converge, amplify, and transform everything they touch, from economies and industries to education and governance. Yet, the thread connecting these innovations is not the technology itself but the humans who wield it. Our ability to harness these tools for good, adapt to their disruptive power, and reimagine our place in this evolving tapestry will define success in the coming decades.

To navigate this complexity, we must shift from seeking linear solutions to embracing exponential possibilities. Just as ecosystems thrive on diversity and adaptability, so too must our technological, societal, and personal systems evolve to integrate disruption as a catalyst for growth. In this sense, the Intelligence Age demands intentional progress rooted in ethical responsibility and a deep understanding of our interconnected realities.

The answer lies in a self-reinforcing cycle, where each step fuels the next and generates unstoppable forward motion. A linear plan would crack under rapid, unpredictable conditions, but a cycle builds momentum precisely because each stage continually strengthens the next. If this sounds familiar to fellow cyclists, there's a reason: it is not unlike pedaling hour after hour until every movement adds to your momentum.

It reminds me of my own story back in 2012, when I first became a speaker after my cycling trip around Australia. My schedule was filled with events all over the world until the pandemic hit in 2020, clearing my calendar virtually overnight. In that moment, I realized something crucial: like cycling through the outback, you can't just coast when the terrain shifts. You keep pedaling, find a new rhythm, and let each stroke build on the last. Rather than suffer in silence, I seized the moment to adapt. I reinvented myself as "The Digital Speaker," not only because I focus on digital tech but also because I needed to go fully digital, fast.

Within weeks, I delivered my first virtual keynote and found an entirely new stage waiting for me. In fact, I soon took it further, giving the world's first TEDx talk in virtual reality and later creating my digital twin. (If you have seen my unpronounceable surname, you'll know why this witty rebranding is especially handy!) And, ironically, I discovered that once you embrace the cycle—continually scanning new realities, pivoting strategies, double-checking your bearings, and taking bold action—you gain a kind of momentum that's hard to stop.

That's the essence of our WAVE framework—Watch, Adapt, Verify, Empower—and it is seen through the lens of a cycle rather than a static plan.

With each rotation:

- We **Watch** for signals and emerging threats, like scanning the horizon on a long cycling route.

- We **Adapt** our strategies and approaches, just as we shift gears for uphill climbs.
- We **Verify** each pivot, assessing whether the road ahead is truly passable.
- We **Empower** ourselves and others, building the collective push that propels everyone forward.

Then we're back to **Watch** again, only now with more knowledge, greater confidence, and fresh momentum. Each step locks in more momentum, just as each pedal stroke builds your speed on the road. This WAVE framework emphasizes these compounding benefits. Once set in motion, each revolution injects more energy into the system:

- **Watch** becomes sharper as you gather better data and build anticipatory reflexes.
- **Adapt** grows faster because prior successes (and failures) inform quicker course corrections.
- **Verify** feels second nature, ensuring your moral and strategic alignment, so you never stray too far off course.
- **Empower** scales, distributing the knowledge and resources so everyone can keep the wheels spinning.

Think of it as the "compound interest" of organizational and personal growth. Just as a cyclist hits a sweet spot of cadence, this framework finds a steady rhythm in dealing with exponential change. For instance, once you've validated a successful approach (e.g., a new AI-based marketing strategy), you can adapt even faster next time, piling up small wins until you see exponential improvements in efficiency, trust, and profit.

During my cycling adventures, I learned that each pedal stroke, no matter how small, pushes you closer to your goal, provided you keep moving. In the same way, the WAVE cycle thrives on ongoing participation. If we stop pedaling, i.e., if we fail to watch the signals, refuse to adapt, avoid validating our choices, or neglect empowerment, the entire system grinds to a halt.

This cycle isn't mere survival. It is leadership in action, spreading account-ability so each pivot is a collective triumph, not just an isolated fix.

But the reverse is also true: once you lock into a smooth cadence of watch-adapt-verify-empower, you can ride out the steep climbs of exponential technology shifts, misinformation storms, and evolving ethical demands, always returning to watch with fresh eyes. That's how we can conquer the Intelligence Age—together, one revolution at a time.

The WAVE framework is designed to ride the forces of exponential change. It merges two essential dimensions: the multiple perspectives we explored in Chapter Two and Three and the fast-moving tech landscape of Chapter Four and Five. By combining these insights, the framework offers a practical path to align ethical foundations with real-world innovation. It acknowledges that progress does not come from controlling chaos but from integrating it into dynamic, resilient systems instead of opting for sterile, machine-controlled systems. It understands that survival alone is insufficient in an age where technologies amplify one another and cascade across every facet of life. Instead, we must embrace the complexity of our world and leverage it to create inclusive, sustainable, and innovative futures. This framework offers a lens through which to view the Intelligence Age, providing a pathway for individuals, organizations, and societies to move from reaction to intentional transformation.

By breaking the inertia of old paradigms, the framework invites us to adopt a systems-first approach, recognizing that every action ripples forward, influencing larger networks. It reminds us that the Intelligence Age is not about humans ceding control to machines but redefining the partnership between human creativity and technological capability. Purposeful decision-making, ethical leadership, and systemic thinking are the cornerstones of navigating this new reality.

This framework does not offer rigid rules, but guiding principles designed to empower action. It challenges individuals to embrace lifelong learning, fostering a mindset of adaptability, empathy, and resilience. It calls upon organizations to leverage innovation responsibly, aligning their strategies with ethical imperatives. It urges societies to think globally and act collaboratively, ensuring no one is left behind in this era of profound change. Above all, it celebrates the potential of collective ingenuity, of humanity coming together to shape a future that uplifts, empowers, and thrives. The WAVE Framework is an invitation to collaboration and dialogue among policymakers, social institutions, corporations, and citizens. It offers guidelines, not one-size-fits-all solutions, for a planet with vastly different political systems, cultures, and developmental stages.

This is not a passive framework for weathering change but an active blueprint for shaping it. It demands that we approach the Intelligence Age with courage, clarity, and conviction, as architects of tomorrow. By aligning our actions with purpose and embracing the opportunities within complexity, we can build resilient, transformative systems and pave the way for a future defined by shared prosperity and enduring progress.

The WAVE framework is our guide to navigating change using four simple steps. It is especially relevant when change is exponential. Watch for signals. Adapt to disruptions. Verify every move. Empower the entire system. In such moments, where complexity accelerates, and challenges intensify, a structured approach becomes essential. Each component flows into the next, creating a dynamic system that uplifts humanity technologically, ethically, and socially. Each completed cycle is not an endpoint but a new beginning, an opportunity to refine our actions, amplify our impact, and rise to greater heights.

This cycle captures how we grow, adapt, and thrive in an ever-changing world, echoing the dynamic interplay discussed in Chapter Three's Spiral Dynamics. Though we'll discuss the four steps in sequence, think of them as interlocking gears rather than rungs on a ladder. Each step informs the next, then loops back again. It represents awareness, alignment, reflection, and action as a continuous cycle of progression that drives meaningful change. This cyclical approach ensures we don't merely react to disruption but evolve through it. The WAVE framework is a strategic cycle for navigating exponential, interconnected challenges with a strong emphasis on ethical grounding and broad stakeholder empowerment. It offers a holistic approach aimed at fostering resilience, innovation, and shared responsibility in the face of rapid, transformative change. Ultimately, the framework is about elevating ourselves. Each rotation of the framework begins with a fresh perspective informed by the lessons of the last, creating a compounding effect akin to upgrading humanity's operating system. We enhance our capabilities with every cycle and prepare for the next wave of change.

Imagine standing on the shore of a vast, ever-changing ocean. Waves crash against the sand, their rhythm shaped by unseen forces—tidal currents, distant winds, and shifting gravitational pulls. Each wave carries a unique story of transformation, both chaotic and beautiful. We are navigating such an ocean of change in the Intelligence Age, driven by exponential technologies, societal shifts, climate change, and interconnected global systems. To thrive in this dynamic landscape, we need a framework that mirrors the natural cycles of these waves. The WAVE framework is that compass, offering a structured yet flexible approach to thrive amid uncertainty. Next, we'll break down Watch, Adapt, Verify, and Empower, seeing how they create a self-reinforcing momentum that transforms challenges into catalysts for progress.

TidalShot

Watch. Adapt. Verify. Empower. A four-step cycle that keeps you alert, agile, honest, and impactful as exponential waves crash in. It's how we surf tech, not drown in it.

Scan the QR code to share this section's TidalShot and illustration to your network.

WATCH: SEE THE SIGNALS AND CULTIVATE AWARENESS

The first wave, **Watch**, anchors us in awareness. In a world overflowing with (mis)information and driven by Hyper Moore's Law, the ability to discern faint signals of change before they crescendo into disruptive forces is essential. Watching is not passive observation but a proactive practice of honing foresight and recognizing patterns hidden beneath the noise. It has become the cornerstone of success in the Digital Renaissance, particularly because these signals now accelerate at near-vertical speed, rendering traditional timelines obsolete.

This practice reflects a *Gestalt Shift* in perception. A move from seeing isolated data points to viewing entire ecosystems of interlinked trends. Just as an artist shifts from noticing individual brushstrokes to perceiving the entire painting, we must reframe how we interpret the world around us as we watch. It is about spotting the faintest glimmers of change, the whispers of trends as they appear on the edges of the internet before they roar into reality. Whether it is a breakthrough in synthetic biology for a healthcare specialist or an emerging policy on carbon taxes for a logistics firm, those who see the signals first hold the keys to thriving in exponential complexity.

Imagine an organization clinging to its established practices while competitors embrace change. Kodak, for instance, famously dismissed the potential of digital photography, a technology its own researchers had pioneered. As others in the industry spotted the trend and adapted, Kodak fell into decline, unable to recover from its failure to act on early signals. Now contrast that with Netflix, which foresaw the rise of streaming long before its rivals. By watching the signals, faster internet speeds, evolving consumer behavior, and emerging digital infrastructures, Netflix transformed itself into a global powerhouse, reshaping entertainment in the process. Netflix wasn't simply watching; it was interpreting, connecting dots, and preparing for the inevitable shift to streaming. The difference between Kodak and Netflix is a stark reminder: those who fail to watch risk irrelevance, while those who observe, interpret, and act lead the future.

To master watching is to expand our *Umwelt*, our perception of reality, using tools like AI, predictive analytics, science fiction stories, and systems thinking. Big data analytics offers a practical demonstration of the power of watching. Organizations that integrate advanced data analytics into their strategies gain the ability to sense shifts in consumer behavior, market trends, and even geopolitical risks long before they manifest.[2] Tools like AI-driven trend analysis and predictive modeling amplify human intuition, giving us extra senses, so to say, to uncover patterns we would otherwise miss. Systemic awareness helps us see the interconnected web of consequences that accompany technological or cultural shifts. In a world of exponential change, signals are rarely loud or obvious. They emerge quietly, often buried under layers of noise. Watching involves peeling back those layers to see the subtle interactions between technologies, industries, and societies. Many Indigenous cultures have honed this skill for centuries, observing subtle shifts in weather, soil conditions, or migratory patterns long before crises materialize. Their multi-generational lens reminds us that truly effective watching includes both immediate signals and the echoes that ripple across decades or lifetimes.

Consider the launch of ChatGPT-3 in November 2022. This revolution had been quietly building momentum for years, visible to those paying attention. It began with AlphaGO (a computer program) beating Lee Sedol, the then-world champion, in the game of Go in 2016. It was a major milestone in AI development that occurred about a decade earlier than many experts had predicted.[3] Next came the publication of a groundbreaking 2017 paper, "Attention Is All You Need," which introduced the Transformer model. This framework would define a new era in natural language processing (NLP). These two innovations inspired a series of advancements, each pushing the boundaries of what AI could achieve in understanding and generating human-like text. The signals became more pronounced in 2019 with the release of GPT-2.[4] Its capabilities stunned researchers, but OpenAI chose not to release the full model publicly, citing concerns over misuse. This cautious step was itself a signal, a subtle indicator of the transformative power lying dormant within these models. Those who watched closely understood that the evolution of AI was accelerating, and its societal impact was drawing closer.

Then came November 2022. The release of ChatGPT-3 catapulted AI into mainstream consciousness, reshaping industries, workflows, and even personal lives overnight. This wasn't just another technological product. It was a paradigm shift. Suddenly, the capabilities of generative AI were accessible to millions, sparking debates about creativity, ethics, and the future of work. For those who had been watching the signals, this moment was no surprise. They were prepared to adapt, innovate, and capitalize on the revolution. The launch of ChatGPT-3 exemplifies the power of watching, and all those developments continue to accumulate in new breakthroughs such as the 2025 AlphaEvolve. Google's model creates advanced algorithms by combining LLMs with automated testing, thereby optimizing Google Gemini's AI training by 23 percent and accelerating GPU operations by 32.5 percent.[5] These developments show how subtle signals, when pieced together, can reveal the contours of a seismic shift long before it unfolds. Such proactive observation goes hand in hand with futures thinking, where we don't just note signals but also envision "what if" scenarios, stress-testing potential outcomes against a range of global shifts, including economic, geopolitical, cultural, and technological. In doing so, it underscores why watching is not merely an intellectual exercise but an essential practice for thriving in the Intelligence Age.

The practice of watching requires systemic thinking, as discussed in Chapter 3. Just as Spiral Dynamics emphasizes interconnectedness and layered consciousness, the act of observing signals demands a mindset that sees connections where others see silos. It is about understanding that technological breakthroughs are not isolated events; they are catalysts that interact with ethics, geopolitics, ecosystems, and each other, shaping a web of consequences.

An important signal to watch is the arrival of artificial general intelligence (AGI). There are clear indications that an upcoming breakthrough is imminent in the not-too-distant future. These signals include experts from AI labs, governments, and policy think tanks—credible voices in national security, deep tech and AI safety—now estimating the arrival to be 2–3 years instead of 10–15 years.[6] Another signal is OpenAI's Deep Research tool, which produces research briefs on par with top human producers or PhD students, in minutes, while open-source tools such as DeepSeek and Manus. ai can do the same at a fraction of a cost. It is the estimate by Anthropic CEO Dario Amodei who predicted that AI will eventually write 90 percent of the code produced,[7] while OpenAI CEO Sam Altman estimated that already, in 2025, AI is performing 50 percent of coding tasks at many companies.[8] Another signal is that labs are achieving increased capabilities without needing commensurate hardware, which will accelerate scaling laws, and companies and governments are racing to secure energy and chip supplies, signaling belief in near-future AI super-scaling. Finally, the fact that major labs are now sharing safety test results with the government is a sign of preparing for something more dangerous than narrow AI.[9] So, we see a coordinated uptick in private alarm and confidence from across elite institutions, practical demonstrations of systems exceeding human baseline performance in core knowledge work—not someday, but now. We see policy, infrastructure, and energy planning that are starting to shift in anticipation of transformative AI, across the globe, and it seems computing is no longer the bottleneck it used to be. These are interlocking signals from science, security, and governance that point to a single conclusion: AGI is no longer a moonshot, it's a train pulling into the station faster than we're ready for.

Seeing and understanding these signals can help you prepare for what is coming, but, as we will see, you must take action and do something with the insights derived from the signals.

Awareness, while empowering, comes with its own challenges. The deluge of information in today's digital age can overwhelm even the most astute observer. Distinguishing meaningful signals from noise requires advanced tools and the discernment to trust credible sources, as emphasized in Chapter Five. Moreover, the act of watching must remain free from bias, ensuring that preconceived notions or ideological agendas do not cloud the signals we interpret. In a Taoist sense, watching involves cultivating a calm center that neither clings to old certainties nor chases every shiny distraction. Similarly, from a Spiral Dynamics viewpoint, we must transcend narrow value systems to see multiple layers of consciousness at work—economic, cultural, and ethical—revealing how subtle signals can speak to each layer's evolving needs. This shift in perception allows us to transcend the surface to uncover the deeper interconnected currents shaping our world. By shifting our perspectives, we see what is obvious and, more importantly, what is possible.

This new perspective fosters a deeper appreciation for the complexities and feedback loops that characterize exponential change, where each shift ripples across industries, cultures, and ecosystems. Given the pace of Hyper Moore's Law, these signals can escalate far faster than linear forecasts predict, requiring us to stay doubly vigilant. The once-slow trickle of innovation now arrives in torrents, and waiting too long to interpret signals can be disastrous.

To watch effectively is to cultivate an awareness that balances deliberate observation with intuitive understanding. It requires attuning to the subtle rhythms of change and noticing emerging patterns and signals that may initially go unnoticed. By observing both the obvious and the hidden, we equip ourselves to discern meaningful trends early and act with purpose. This practice reflects the wisdom found in ancient philosophies and traditions, which emphasize harmony with natural cycles and interconnected systems. Whether it is the flow of ecosystems or the evolution of human innovation, watching aligns us with the forces that drive progress, enabling thoughtful, intentional action. It transforms uncertainty into an opportunity for insight, positioning us to respond with clarity and foresight. This includes observing non-human signals such as the health of ecosystems, changes in animal migration, or shifts in local biodiversity, recognizing that our human vantage point (our *Umwelt*) is only one of many in a shared environment. By noticing how nature signals change, we can develop a more holistic perspective essential to sustainable innovation. While watching begins with observation, it must culminate in understanding and preparedness.

Ultimately, watching is the gateway. But watching alone isn't enough. Awareness without action is like spotting a storm on the horizon but failing to prepare. This is where Adapt comes in, turning insight into purposeful action. By bridging observation with adaptability, we can transform risk into opportunity.

TidalShot

Vigilant observation is your edge. Spot early signals—trends, disruptions, quiet whispers—so you're prepped to pivot before the wave hits.

Scan the QR code to share this section's TidalShot and illustration to your network.

ADAPT: FLOW WITH PURPOSE AND ALIGN WITH CHANGE

From awareness flows adaptation, the second wave in the framework. While Watching reveals what is coming, Adapting ensures we align with it purposefully, guided by the *Gestalt Shift* in perception we gained from seeing the system as a whole. The ability to **Adapt** has always been crucial, but thanks to Hyper Moore's Law, it becomes an essential competency for survival and growth. Adapting isn't chaotic reaction; it is strategic alignment, a blend of iterative flexibility and long-term anchoring. It is the art of shaping disruption even as it shapes us. In evolutionary terms, Darwin's insight wasn't really "survival of the fittest," but rather survival of the most adaptable. In a fast-moving world, strength alone won't cut it; it's the capacity to pivot, reinvent, and stay flexible that determines lasting success.

Imagine standing at the edge of a vast, ever-shifting landscape. The ground beneath you trembles with technological advancements. To stand still is to sink; to move without direction is to be swept away. But to adapt with intention is to navigate this dynamic terrain with confidence, turning disruption into opportunity. Nature exemplifies this art, offering lessons in resilience and harmony. Water doesn't resist obstacles; it flows around them, carves paths through them, or gathers strength to overcome them. This is the essence of adaptation: fluidity paired with purpose. The Taoist principle of Wu Wei, or effortless action, captures this balance perfectly, teaching us to align our actions with the natural flow of change rather than fighting it.

Contrary to misconceptions, Wu Wei is not passivity; it is about sensing the precise moment to shift, ensuring minimal friction and maximal impact. Indigenous philosophies of long-term stewardship underscore this too. When communities adapt farming methods across generations, they consider impacts on local wildlife, soils, and water cycles, reflecting a biocentric viewpoint. Such holistic adaptation recognizes that sustainable human progress and environmental flourishing are inseparable.

In the human and technological ecosystems of the Intelligence Age, adaptation mirrors this natural principle. Blockchain technology exemplifies decentralized resilience, dynamically adjusting to cyber threats while maintaining trust. Organizations embracing agile methodologies can iterate swiftly, responding to market shifts without losing sight of their strategic vision. Such adaptation is not a concession to chaos but a mastery of it.

During World War II, Ford Motor Company faced an unprecedented challenge.[10] The United States needed a rapid increase in military equipment production, including B-24 bombers. Ford, known for its automotive assembly lines, adapted its entire operation to meet this need. This transformation was a technical feat and a testament to strategic alignment that helped win the war. Ford retooled its factories, trained workers for new tasks, and reorganized its supply chains. Within months, the company achieved a production rate of one bomber per hour. An extraordinary example of adaptation driven by purpose and innovation. What made Ford's success possible was its ability to align short-term changes with long-term vision. The company didn't simply react to external demands; it reimagined its capabilities, turning a challenge into a defining moment of contribution and growth. This historical lesson underscores a critical insight: adaptation is about embracing change with clarity and intention.

Today, adaptation is amplified by exponential forces. New technologies are reshaping industries, requiring us to rethink work, governance, and education. Meanwhile, some regions leapfrog entire legacy infrastructures, embodying both Indigenous long-term stewardship and cutting-edge solutions. This iterative approach reflects the interconnected nature of the Intelligence Age, where every move ripples across industries, ecosystems, and cultures. At the same time, the combination of these two developments can disrupt geopolitics in ways not seen since World War II. In Spiral Dynamics terms, these shifts trigger new alignments of values and mindsets. Some societies remain in hierarchical approaches (Blue), while others adopt more systemic or global perspectives (Yellow). Effective adaptation means meeting each worldview where it stands, bridging gaps instead of bulldozing them.

Adapting also means thinking beyond immediate quarterly results or near-term objectives and embracing longtermism: a commitment to the well-being of future generations in all our decisions.[11] Often, organizations treat innovation as a sprint, seeking the quickest returns or solutions, but sustainable progress demands that we consider potential outcomes and repercussions decades down the line. While short-term pivots are essential to remain agile, a true adaptation process acknowledges that digital transformation efforts today can either anchor or derail societies tomorrow.

By weaving long-term thinking into every adaptation, we guard against the risks of short-sightedness, ensuring that rapid implementation of AI, quantum breakthroughs, or immersive technologies aligns with enduring human values and global sustainability. Leaders attuned to longtermism address immediate market pressures and build ecosystems designed to uplift future generations. They weigh how AI models might perpetuate biases if left unchecked or how novel communication tools could strengthen civic engagement or undermine social cohesion. In doing so, adaptation ceases to be a race for quarterly gains.

This long-term approach is especially relevant as most technologies pass through the trough of disillusionment. According to the Gartner Hype Cycle, the trough of disillusionment marks the inevitable dip in enthusiasm when a disruptive technology fails to immediately meet grand expectations. Just as the metaverse was heralded as the next big revolution in 2022 before it was largely abandoned in favor of AI, Chapter Four shows it is now re-emerging with renewed strength. Encountering the trough of disillusionment isn't a signal to abandon a new technology. It's a strategic inflection point where discerning genuine value from transient hype allows us to recalibrate and drive sustained innovation. By adapting with clarity and purpose, we transform disillusionment into a launching pad for transformative progress. It transforms digital transformation into a purposeful journey where technology is deployed responsibly so that, decades from now, we have a thriving digital future for everyone.

In other words, adaptation demands that we flow with change while anchoring ourselves to long-term goals. It is not a one-time effort but an ongoing process. Here, futures thinking plays a pivotal role. Just as watching results in multiple scenarios, adapting means calibrating strategies in small cycles, testing each possible outcome, and adjusting before the next wave hits. This cyclical readiness ensures adaptation isn't guesswork but informed agility. In this sense, adaptation is not about conceding to uncertainty but about harnessing it as a catalyst for growth. Especially under Hyper Moore's Law, adaptation must be continuous and iterative. What worked six months ago might be obsolete tomorrow.

While adaptation empowers us to navigate change, it is only the second piece of the puzzle. Without Verification, we risk veering off course, pursuing short-sighted gains or the next shiny thing at the expense of our mission, or falling victim to criminals. Grounded evaluation is what transforms adaptation into enduring progress, paving the way for a future defined by resilience and purpose.

TidalShot

Rigid systems break in fast-moving currents. Stay fluid, shift gears quickly, and fuse short-term sprints with big-picture goals. Adapting is strength in motion.

Scan the QR code to share this section's TidalShot and illustration to your network.

VERIFY: PAUSE, DISCERN, AND REFLECT WITH INTEGRITY

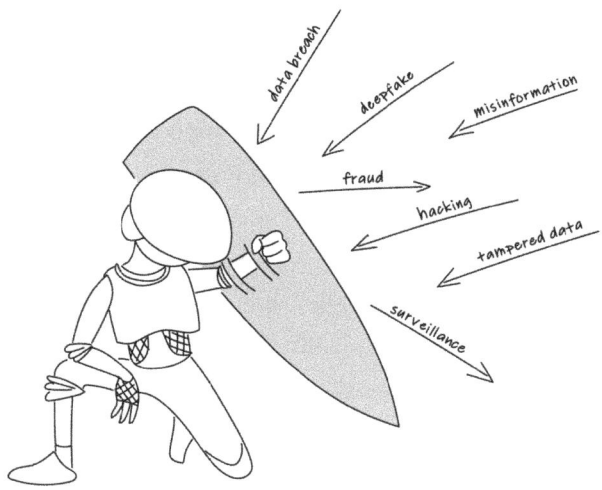

In the relentless pursuit of innovation, we often overlook the critical need to pause and reflect. Yet, this pause should not be seen as a hindrance but as a cornerstone of intentional progress. **Verify** is the art of assessing whether our data has been tampered with, our paths align with our values, serve their intended purposes, and respect the broader systems they influence. Seen through the lens of Spiral Dynamics, verification ensures that each action accommodates the diverse worldviews present, from pragmatic, rule-based structures to higher-level integrative thinking, so that no single perspective undermines the whole. In many ways, this step completes the *Gestalt Shift* that began in earlier phases, reminding us to reexamine the entire ecosystem that our decisions touch. Verification ensures we don't lose sight of the integrated worldview we worked so hard to cultivate. It also ensures that progress is grounded in integrity, aligned with ethical principles, and prepared for systemic consequences. Hyper Moore's Law amplifies this need, as a one-off validation checkpoint is no match for a world where last month's novelty can be this month's industry standard. Only an ongoing verification can keep pace with such rapid change, safeguarding us from unwittingly embedding harmful biases or illusions of trust.

Arup's $25.6 million loss to a deepfake scam discussed in Chapter Five underscores the stakes of neglecting verification. The outcome could have been different if the company had implemented the reflective practices of organizations like Ferrari and WPP, which prioritize robust questioning and safeguards. Verifying protects against such vulnerabilities by demanding critical evaluation at every stage of development. In an era where the stakes are higher than ever, asking hard questions, cross-referencing data, and embedding verification checks are essential to ensure societal trust and resilience.

As the transformative technologies discussed in Chapter Four become an increasingly powerful force in our lives, we must develop robust methods to verify their functionality, intentions, and output. This involves creating systems and tools that can effectively identify AI-generated content and confirm the authenticity of digital identities in our evolving online landscape. After all, if everyone can create deepfakes of everyone, we need to be able to verify if the person you are dealing with, whether via voice, video, or in the metaverse, is indeed the person they say they are.[12]

At its core, verifying is about ensuring that our decisions (whether individual, operational or organizational), technologies, and strategies withstand scrutiny. Not only for functionality but also for alignment with shared ethical standards and systemic implications. In the context of AI systems, verification becomes critical in determining the appropriate balance of control between humans and machines, ensuring that accountability and trust are preserved.[13] The "trust but verify" step is crucial in the Intelligence Age. For example, the choice between "human-in-the-loop" versus "AI-in-the-loop" systems reflects a fundamental decision in balancing control and accountability between humans and machines. In human-in-the-loop systems, the AI primarily assists decision-making by providing actionable insights, while humans retain ultimate control. Conversely, AI-in-the-loop systems position AI as the decision-making core, with humans intervening for oversight, refinement, or exceptions. Selecting the right approach depends on the complexity and stakes of the task.[14] For nuanced, high-impact scenarios like personalized healthcare decisions, human-driven systems ensure ethical and contextual consider-ations are prioritized. In contrast, for repetitive, data-intensive tasks like inventory management or fraud detection, AI-driven automation can optimize efficiency without significant human involvement. Integrating these systems responsibly demands rigorous validation protocols, ensuring that the collaboration between humans and machines enhances outcomes without undermining accountability or trust.

Verifying is a discipline that demands rigorous questioning: Are these actions just? Are they inclusive? Just because we can, does it mean we should? Do they harmonize with the interconnected systems they impact? Am I not being scammed? This is particularly vital in a world where misin-formation spreads faster than truth, where AI-generated content blurs the line between reality and fabrication, and where biases can stealthily infil-trate decision-making systems. Verification acts as a safeguard against these pitfalls. It is a continuous process of discerning what is real, what is fair, and what serves the greater good, including recognizing that each living being experiences reality differently.

Consider the deployment of deep learning models in healthcare. While AI has shown remarkable promise in diagnosing diseases, some systems have been found to disproportionately misdiagnose conditions in under-represented populations.[15] This happens because training data often fails to account for demographic diversity. Without a robust validation process, such systems risk reinforcing disparities rather than alleviating them. Rigorous verification can catch these biases early, ensuring that technologies serve all people equitably.

Verification also mirrors ancient wisdom. Taoism teaches the impor-tance of balance, while Indigenous traditions emphasize long-term thinking and collective accountability. Verify harmonizes with these philosophies, ensuring that technological and strategic decisions are thoughtful, ethical, and inclusive. Verification acknowledges that clarity and order are necessary, but it also challenges us to scrutinize assumptions, enabling us to responsi-bly navigate the complexity of exponential change. It is the compass that prevents us from losing direction in the chaos of disruption.

Verification must move beyond theory into tangible practice, shaping how individuals, organizations, and societies navigate the complexities of the Intelligence Age. It demands a unified effort. For example, Finland offers a blueprint for success as it is consistently ranked at the top of the annual European Media Literacy Index for its exceptional resistance to fake news.[16, 17] Through comprehensive media literacy campaigns embedded in its education system, Finland empowers young and old citizens to critically evaluate digital information. These programs emphasize discerning credible sources, identifying bias, and debunking misinformation, creating a populace adept at navigating the complexities of the digital age.[18] Finland's success in fostering media literacy through early education demonstrates how systemic strategies empower individual discernment, creating a ripple effect of informed decision-making. Paired with adaptive regulatory frameworks that evolve alongside emerging technologies, this ensures that innovation is embraced and remains ethically aligned and resilient against misuse.[19] This model demonstrates how collective verification can fortify societal trust and safeguard against the risks of technological acceleration.

Ultimately, verification is the checkpoint that transforms awareness and adaptation into meaningful progress. It safeguards against straying from our ethical bedrock and is a blueprint for aligning short-term shifts with enduring visions. With verification as our compass, we ensure each step forward is thoughtful, grounded, and poised for the next phase, which is Empowerment—the act of putting validated decisions into bold, transformative action.

TidalShot

Pause, test your course, and check your ethical compass. Progress means little if you're drifting from your values or fueling unintended harm.

Scan the QR code to share this section's TidalShot and illustration to your network.

EMPOWER: DRIVE ACTION AND IGNITE THE FUTURE

Empower is not about control but about unleashing potential and equipping all stakeholders to act with clarity, confidence, and purpose. It is the culmination of the WAVE framework, where the preceding elements—watching for signals, adapting to change, and verifying decisions—converge into purposeful action. It is the moment where ideas become impact, where agency sparks ripples that transform not just individuals but entire ecosystems. Once we recognize how interconnected our systems truly are, Empowerment becomes the means to activate each node in that network. In Spiral Dynamics terms, it transcends older hierarchical structures (Blue or Orange) to embrace a more integrative, participatory worldview (Yellow), where autonomy is shared and innovation flourishes collectively. Empowerment is the art of turning potential into progress.

Picture a community in a developing country on the edge of transformation. For decades, they have lived in the shadow of technological and economic inequities, lacking access to the tools that could lift them out of generational stagnation. But then something changes. A local initiative introduces affordable renewable energy, paired with AI-driven resource optimization tools and space internet, such as Starlink or Project Kuiper. Farmers can now implement precision agriculture, increasing crop yields while conserving water. Teachers can now enlist the help of AI tutors, resulting in next-level education for children in the most remote corners of the region. The community doesn't just survive. It thrives, becoming a beacon of resilience and innovation. This transformation isn't the result of charity or chance; it is the product of empowerment.

Empowerment is not a passive concept. It demands deliberate action, trust, and a clear alignment between tools and purpose. Consider Tesla's decision to open its patents on electric vehicle technology. By doing so, the company empowered competitors to innovate, dramatically accelerating the shift toward sustainable transportation globally.[20] Under Hyper Moore's Law, technologies can outstrip even the best-funded organizations if they remain siloed, so open-sourcing technology serves as a catalyst for change. Empowerment is how collective intelligence keeps pace with exponential advances, ensuring no community or company is left behind. Similarly, Khan Academy's mission to democratize education has empowered millions, fostering a generation of lifelong learners who can adapt and thrive in an ever-changing world. These examples illustrate that empowerment is not about controlling resources but sharing them, creating ecosystems of collaboration that amplify impact.

This ethos of empowerment resonates deeply with the Indigenous principle of considering seven generations ahead.[21] It is a call to embed foresight into every decision, ensuring our actions today uplift not only present communities but also the ecosystems and societies of the future. By empowering ecological voices (for instance, through conservation data, AI-driven reforestation, or policy frameworks that protect biodiversity through legal rights), we honor a biocentric ethic where humans innovate in harmony with the rest of life.[22] This philosophy challenges us to balance immediate progress with long-term sustainability, fostering an interconnected sense of responsibility across time. By adopting this principle, empowerment becomes more than a tool for present growth; it becomes a bridge connecting us to a future where humanity and nature coexist harmoniously. Empowering individuals and organizations to act with this perspective ensures that innovation respects ecological balance and prioritizes intergenerational equity.

However, empowerment also requires dismantling barriers. In many cases, these barriers are structural, such as bureaucratic hierarchies that stifle innovation or systemic inequalities that limit access to transformative tools. Satya Nadella's overhaul of Microsoft offers a compelling alternative: by breaking down internal silos, decentralizing decision-making, and nurturing a culture of collaboration and continuous learning, Nadella transformed a legacy institution into a lean, agile innovator at the forefront of cloud and AI breakthroughs.[23] This strategic realignment demonstrates that true empowerment arises not from top-down cost-cutting but from cultivating an environment where every individual contributes to transformative change.

Ultimately, empowerment thrives in an environment of trust, autonomy, and access, hallmarks of a society that invests heavily in education, infrastructure, and collaborative governance. It requires leaders to relinquish control and give employees access to the latest tools, trusting their teams to act responsibly and creatively. It demands that societies invest in infrastructure and education, ensuring no one is left behind in the race toward the future. Empowerment also calls for individuals to take ownership of their learning and growth, stepping into roles of active participation rather than passive observation. It is one thing to distribute tools; it is another to empower everyone to envision, design, and shape a tomorrow that aligns with shared ethical values.

As the final element of the WAVE framework, empower is the ultimate expression of the interconnectedness and systemic thinking that defines the Intelligence Age. It is about creating ecosystems where individuals feel equipped and motivated to act, where organizations can innovate with purpose, and where societies can thrive sustainably.

Imagine a world where empowerment is the norm, not the exception. Where every individual has access to the tools, knowledge, and agency to shape their future. Where organizations prioritize inclusivity and ethical innovation, ensuring that their actions benefit not just shareholders but stakeholders. Where societies work collaboratively to address global challenges, from climate change to inequality, harnessing the collective intelligence of empowered citizens. This is not a utopian vision; it is an achievable reality if we commit to empower as a guiding principle. By fostering environments that prioritize trust, autonomy, and access, we can ignite the actions that will define the future. Empowerment is the engine of progress, the bridge between potential and impact, and the final, transformative step in the WAVE framework.

As we conclude this journey through the WAVE framework, let us reflect on its cyclical nature. When we watch, we feel empowered, and our discoveries spark quicker adaptative shifts. When we adapt, we are empowered to refine each change with agility and ownership. And when verification is done in an empowered culture, it is not about top-down audits but collective vigilance that catches flaws early. Thus, the empower stage cements the WAVE cycle as a living, breathing force for continuous evolution. Empowerment feeds back into awareness, adaptation, and validation, creating an ongoing loop of growth and transformation. The future is not something that happens to us; it is something we build, one empowered action at a time. Now, the question remains: what will you do with the power you hold?

TidalShot

Unlock potential across teams, communities, and even ecosystems. When everyone's free to innovate ethically, we transform chaos into synergy.

Scan the QR code to share this section's TidalShot and illustration to your network.

THE ART OF DEALING WITH CHANGE

Change is inevitable. It is relentless, unpredictable, and often overwhelming. Yet, in its very nature lies the secret to progress: the opportunity to reimagine, rebuild, and thrive. The WAVE framework offers a transformative lens to navigate and master the art of dealing with change. It is a journey from awareness to action, equipping us to turn challenges into steppingstones for a future shaped by resilience, purpose, and collective growth.

Every great transformation begins with awareness. To deal with change effectively, we must first see it clearly. Not as it bursts into prominence but as it begins to stir. Watching is an art, a skill that allows us to sift through the noise of daily life and detect the faint signals of what is to come. This practice is neither passive nor fleeting; it is an intentional ongoing act of observation and connection, expanding our understanding of the systems around us. The art of watching is about weaving the trends of the day into a broader understanding of societal, technological, and cultural shifts. By mastering this art, we begin to see the patterns that drive change, preparing ourselves to embrace what comes next.

Awareness alone is not enough. It must be coupled with action, with the ability to move in harmony with the forces of change rather than resisting them. Adaptation is a dance. A balancing act between fluidity and purpose. It demands that we align ourselves with the rhythm of transformation, using it as a guide to innovate, grow, and lead. To adapt is not about surrendering to change but about shaping it with intention. In the Intelligence Age, the art of adaptation is amplified by exponential technologies. Whether it is individuals embracing lifelong learning or organizations embedding agility into their DNA, the capacity to flow with change determines success. To adapt is to take what we see through watching and turn it into deliberate action aligned with long-term purpose, ensuring that transformation becomes a tool for progress rather than a source of chaos.

However, in the rush to adapt, it is easy to lose our way. The art of dealing with change requires moments of pause and opportunities to question, reflect, verify and ensure that our paths align with our values, our long-term vision, and the broader systems we inhabit. To verify is this compass, guiding us with integrity as we navigate uncharted waters. The distinction between human-in-the-loop and AI-in-the-loop systems captures the essence of verification. Both approaches have their merits, but selecting the right one requires a deep understanding of the task at hand. Verification ensures that these choices are made responsibly, enhancing outcomes without undermining trust or accountability. It also goes beyond the technical process of verifying whether we are dealing with AI-generated content or human-created content; it is a moral imperative. It calls us to scrutinize what we are building, why we are building it, and for whom. It demands transparency, critical thinking, and a commitment to the long-term consequences of our actions. This reflective practice transforms adaptation from a reactive process into a deliberate and ethical pursuit, anchoring us in clarity amid the turbulence of change.

The final art in dealing with change is to empower. The ability to take validated decisions and translate them into meaningful action. Empowerment is the culmination of the WAVE framework, where all elements converge to create impact. It is the moment when we stop reacting to change and start shaping it, harnessing its energy to build something better, together. Empowerment thrives in trust and autonomy. It requires leaders stepping back and allowing individuals and teams to innovate and take ownership of their roles. It demands that societies invest in equitable access to technology and education, ensuring that no one is left behind. And it invites individuals to see themselves as active participants in a collective journey, using their skills and knowledge to contribute to a shared long-term vision. Empowerment, in this context, extends beyond the individual. It is about creating systems that uplift all beings, acknowledging the interconnected web of life and our responsibility to sustain it.

The WAVE framework is not just a tool for navigating digital upheavals; it is a blueprint for addressing the wicked problems of our era and existential challenges such as climate change. Watch compels us to deploy state-of-the-art satellites, sensor networks, and data analytics to detect subtle shifts in temperature, sea-level rise, and extreme weather events. By continuously scanning for these early warning signals, we can anticipate crises before they escalate. Building on this vigilance, Adapt challenges us to reengineer our infrastructure and policies with deliberate purpose. Imagine coastal cities not just erecting flood barriers but reimagining entire neighborhoods to flow with rising tides—urban ecosystems that mirror nature's own adaptability. This approach transforms reactive measures into strategic investments, ensuring that our built environment evolves alongside our climate. Verify then insists on rigorous accountability: independent audits, transparent metrics, scientific rigor, and dynamic feedback loops to confirm that our efforts in renewable energy, carbon capture, and sustainable urban planning are delivering tangible results. Finally, Empower democratizes climate action by engaging every stakeholder, from grassroots communities to global industry leaders, in crafting solutions that are both ethical and effective. Together, the WAVE framework can transform a crisis into a launchpad for transformative progress, turning the formidable challenge of climate change into an opportunity for resilient, inclusive innovation.

As such, the WAVE framework is a holistic approach for thriving in a complex, interconnected world. Each pillar offers a unique skill, but together, they form a holistic approach to mastering transformation.

Scan the QR code or visit Now-What.co/ resources to download the WAVE Forward methodology so you can share it with your colleagues and friends.

Recall our discussion on exponential technology in Chapter Two: the second half of the chessboard. Watch addresses how to detect that tipping point early. Reflect on the cultural, spiritual, and Indigenous wisdom from Chapter Three: Adapt helps us blend these perspectives into a flexible response. From Chapter Five's cautionary tales of misinformation, Verify becomes our moral and informational compass. Finally, from Chapter Six's emphasis on an education that readies us for complexity, Empower is the natural outcome, unlocking every learner and leader's potential to shape tomorrow rather than be shaped by it. The WAVE Forward is a reminder that change is not something to be feared but embraced, an opportunity to create, innovate, and grow as architects of tomorrow.

To master the art of dealing with change is to recognize its cyclical nature. Watching prepares us to adapt; adaptation invites reflection through validation; and verification empowers us to act with purpose, which in turn requires us to watch with intent how our actions invoke change in the broader context. This loop is not linear but iterative, a spiral of growth that builds resilience and fosters creativity. As you step into this journey, remember that the future is not a fixed destination. It is a canvas shaped by our every decision, every action, and every moment of reflection. The WAVE framework equips you with the tools to paint this canvas with intention, crafting a future defined by your ability to navigate the forces of change, as the next chapter in our fictional story will show. What will you create? The answer lies in the art of the choices you make today.

TidalShot

Change is an art—part foresight, part trust in each other, part creative pivot. We flourish when we view disruption not as a threat but a canvas for tomorrow.

Scan the QR code to share this section's TidalShot and illustration to your network.

NOW WHAT? RIDE THE WAVE

The WAVE Forward is a guideline for organizations to thrive amid convergent technologies without sacrificing its soul. Their path can be summarized by the WAVE framework: Watch, Adapt, Verify, Empower. Here are practical things you can do today to put the WAVE framework into action, always remembering that under Hyper Moore's Law, technology accelerates faster than ever, demanding proactive readiness:

1. Watch

Individuals: Commit to staying informed. Subscribe to platforms like Futurwise, newsletters, or explore niche futurist communities to track trends across industries. Develop a habit of reflective observation, questioning how the signals you see might affect your goals, work, or community. Keep a "signal journal," tracking news or trends that surprise you, whether it is biotech updates or new AI breakthroughs.

Organizations: Establish dedicated foresight teams to scan for emerging trends, leveraging advanced data analytics tools to create dashboards that visualize potential market shifts. Encourage them to run futures thinking exercises that imagine best- and worst-case outcomes, ensuring leadership integrates these insights into strategic decisions. Hire a futurist or science fiction writer to uncover the improbable.

Society: Create cross-sector "Foresight Councils" blending academia, NGOs, ethicists, and entrepreneurs to analyze global trends and prepare actionable roadmaps for the future that consider not only economic but also biocentric or ecological well-being and future generations. Public-private collaborations can foster open-access data repositories to democratize awareness and promote systemic thinking.

2. Adapt

Individuals: Embrace a mindset of lifelong learning and experiment with emerging tech to acquire new skills. Experiment with a new AI, play with robots, explore biohacking, or volunteer for pilot programs at work.

Organizations: Launch small, agile pilots. Embed agility into your DNA. Iterate quickly, glean lessons, pivot as necessary, and form partnerships with innovative startups to stay ahead of the curve. Treat short-term gains as steppingstones, not final goals.

Society: Offer grants for community-driven pilot programs, e.g., water-saving biotech, blockchain-based supply chain apps, or educational programs that integrate new technologies. Develop flexible policies that can evolve alongside technological advancements. Encourage stakeholder feedback loops for real-time adjustments to lay the groundwork for collective resilience.

3. Verify

Individuals: Before adopting a new tool, sharing an article, or making a big move, check alignment with personal and biocentric values. Critical thinking is crucial to survive in the Intelligence Age. Develop the capacity to fact-check information, recognize biases, understand emerging technologies, and engage with diverse perspectives. A fast-changing world demands reflective checkpoints: "Does this align with my values?" and "What are the broader implications?" Integrating futures thinking at these checkpoints can expose blind spots early. To combat scams, have a codeword that you share with family members.

Organizations: Review your company's values, and if they don't exist, draft them, and consider the values shared here, including resilience, equity, intergenerational considerations, harmony, etc. Create an "Ethics & Tech Review" board to ensure that projects, algorithms, and strategies are scrutinized for inclusivity and systemic impact, while post-action retrospectives evaluate outcomes to refine future endeavors. Audit for environmental footprints, algorithmic bias, or mission misalignment. Adjust processes to maintain authenticity, ensure your data has not been tampered with (for example by integrating blockchain technology in your processes), and create an open culture that encourages questioning and challenging hierarchies to prevent blind adherence to flawed decisions or hyper-realistic deepfakes.

Society: Mandate external oversight for major AI or biotech deployments. Integrate futures thinking into policy design, so new laws are validated against multiple possible futures. Promote strong media literacy programs to enable public discourse around new technologies.

4. Empower

Individuals: Take ownership of your own growth, as lifelong learning is no longer optional. Actively seek or create "learning loops" at your workplace or community, where you share insights, test projects, and refine them.

Organizations: Decentralize decision-making and reward collaborative teams that merge profit with purpose. Provide resources and training so local managers and staff can customize solutions. Invest in your people and provide access to the latest tools and frameworks to navigate change to consistently outperform those that cling to rigid structures.

Society: Ensure equitable access to technology and education, particularly in underserved regions. Expand broadband in rural areas, fund universal digital literacy, and invite public hackathons so communities can propose solutions to real problems. Recognize that empowerment extends to ecological systems too, by balancing human progress with the needs of the planet.

If you are interested in learning how I could help your leadership or entire organization embrace the WAVE Forward framework and ride the tsunami of change, I have put together a resource that accompanies this book with more information, which you can find at Now-What.co/resources, or scan the QR code.

Why It Matters

In an era shaped by exponential forces, it is easy to be dazzled by the novelty and forget the human, ethical, and environmental heart of our endeavors. As the Intelligence Age accelerates, staying anchored to your purpose is increasingly urgent. This synergy between big-picture frameworks and local actions truly anchors transformation in integrity. It is about seeing possibility before it is obvious, adjusting with agility, verifying choices through ethical and systemic lenses, and unleashing every stakeholder's capacity to innovate.

Whether you are a startup founder, an educator in a small town, or a policymaker drafting tomorrow's regulations, the same cyclical pattern can be your compass. We are all pedaling on this road to the future; some have just started and others are pro-level. The good news? There is room on the peloton for everyone.

The tsunami of exponential change can be daunting, yes, but the WAVE Forward can help unlock synergy between diverse technologies without letting the waves of change wash away the values that brought you here in the first place. If we **watch** closely, **adapt** wisely, **verify** consistently, and **empower** broadly, we don't merely survive the tsunami of exponential change.

We ride it.

TidalShot

The wave won't wait. By watching signals, adapting swiftly, verifying every step, and empowering all voices, we harness disruption instead of letting it sweep us away.

Scan the QR code to share this TidalShot to your network.

ECOBLEND'S TIDAL SHIFT: THE WAVE FORWARD IN PRACTICE

Leila felt the desert heat wash over her as she stepped onto the tarmac in Nairobi. She was the newly appointed CEO of EcoBlend, a mid-sized craft beverage brand eager to scale without betraying its fiercely eco-conscious roots. Beside her stood Vita, invited as a technical advisor to help EcoBlend navigate technological shifts. Vita's sleek frame reflected the intense sunlight, sensors quietly monitoring conditions as they proceeded toward their hosts. They had come to meet small-holder farmers whose coffee beans EcoBlend prized. Beans that carried the local climate's warmth and character into every cup. Vita's presence represented her commitment to thoughtful integration of emerging technologies.

During an evening chat with local village elders, Leila was struck by their centuries-old practice of planting in cycles planned for grandchildren yet unborn, a living embodiment of Indigenous long-term thinking. Sitting quietly nearby, Vita observed carefully, cataloging insights into human sustainability practices. This exchange reminded Leila, and quietly reassured Vita, that EcoBlend's decisions needed to honor this outlook: technology should serve the next generation's well-being, not just the current quarter's profits.

Back home, demand for ethically sourced brews was doubling each quarter. Global distributors were clamoring to sign exclusive deals, but Leila worried about losing the personal touch her late father had built EcoBlend around— direct relationships with farming communities, authentic storytelling, and a carbon-light footprint. Meanwhile, new forces were shaping the market: AI-driven supply chains, blockchain-based transparency, robotics to automate packaging, quantum-inspired schedulers, and now a budding interest in synthetic biology.

"Is there a way," Leila wondered, "to harness all of these technologies without sacrificing everything that makes EcoBlend unique?"

Beside her, Vita nodded thoughtfully. "Integration doesn't necessarily mean dilution. It can amplify your values."

A Seed of Change: The Subtle Signs

One evening while reviewing sustainability reports in her Kenyan hotel, Leila stumbled on intriguing chatter in trade forums:

- **AI:** Smaller competitors using predictive analytics to reduce waste and inventory overhead.
- **Blockchain:** Bigger retailers demanding verifiable sourcing records.
- **Robotics and quantum:** Niche pilot programs optimizing multi-site production and warehousing.
- **Synthetic biology:** Early-stage biotech labs proposing CRISPR-enhanced yeast strains to refine fermentation, potentially lowering water usage and intensifying natural flavor profiles.

"If we want to ride the tsunami of change," she thought, "we need to see these waves forming." Immediately upon returning, Leila convened a "Foresight Team" at EcoBlend. Eclectic folks, including a robotics grad student, a marketing associate with data analytics experience, Linda, the company's longest-serving master roaster with near-superhuman skills for spotting shifts before they hit the mainstream, and Vita, whose precise advice became indispensable for navigating convergent technologies.

They met weekly to **Watch** carefully for signals: from climate-policy changes that might affect coffee bean farmers, to synthetic-biology breakthroughs in lab-grown proteins or custom-tailored yeasts. Even Linda, who once scoffed at "test-tube coffee," found herself captivated by new biotech labs exploring drought-resistant coffee bean strains. As the Foresight Team dissected the state of AI and robotics, they were stunned by the near-vertical growth curves in compute power.

Vita offered clarity on the charts, explaining how exponential computational growth (Hyper Moore's Law) was reshaping industry timelines at unprecedented speed. Yesterday's prototypes were hitting the market in half the expected time, pushing EcoBlend to adapt at hyperspeed. The team compiled monthly bulletins summarizing how these forces might shape EcoBlend's roadmap.

Leila led a "mini scenario planning" session, urging them to imagine multiple futures: one where governments banned CRISPR altogether and another where climate legislation became so strict that any blockchain energy usage had to be justified. This futures thinking mindset ensured they weren't merely scanning signals; they were actively shaping EcoBlend's long-term resilience. Vita's guidance gave them a shared vantage point; a sense that converging technologies were quietly reshaping their market before everyone else noticed. It grounded these speculative discussions, ensuring technology always remained a supportive tool rather than an overwhelming force.

Leila felt a subtle click of recognition. This wasn't about layering in new tech piece by piece. It was about realizing that each solution reshapes the others. A *Gestalt Shift*, she realized, wasn't just about adding AI or biotech; it was about seeing EcoBlend's entire ecosystem differently, from seed to sip. Vita's quiet confidence reinforced her insight. In that instant, Leila realized how synergy arises precisely where contradictions meet. Where preserving tradition can benefit from forward-thinking AI, or how a biotech tweak can protect rather than harm authenticity. This *Gestalt Shift* let her perceive these dualities not as conflicts but as complementary forces.

Replanting the Fields: Adapting with Purpose

About six weeks later, the Foresight Team, informed by Vita's twice measured recommendations, suggested a pilot program. Their plan extended beyond the typical inventory or packaging approach:

1. **AI and robotics:** Implement AI-driven forecasting to orchestrate the beans flow from farm to facility, with small autonomous humanoids handling repetitive tasks on the packaging floor.
2. **Blockchain:** Use a transparent ledger to verify each batch's journey from remote farms to local cafes.
3. **Quantum-inspired scheduling:** Experiment with basic "quantum-like" algorithms for multi-facility logistics.
4. **Synthetic biology:** Collaborate with a biotech startup to explore CRISPR-enhanced yeasts to reduce water use and intensify flavor extraction in the fermentation process.

Leila dubbed it the "Tech-Eco Synergy Pilot." Half of the staff were intrigued; the other half were uneasy. Linda, once skeptical of biotech "meddling with nature," softened her stance: "If done thoughtfully, maybe gene-tweaked yeast could save water and intensify flavor. Let's try, learn, and stay ready to adjust."

This was **Adaptation** in action. Strategic baby steps aligned with EcoBlend's mission. They were weaving convergent technologies into the company's eco-friendly tapestry. AI predicted how many beans each roaster needed daily, the humanoids fetched sacks with uncanny precision, the blockchain ledger recorded each bag's entire lifecycle, and a small corner of the factory tested the biotech yeast on select micro-batches. Vita monitored these implementations, providing insights into where technology enhanced, and where it risked complicating the delicate balance EcoBlend aimed to achieve.

Linda smiled as she realized that in Spiral Dynamics terms, EcoBlend was juggling multiple layers of human values: local farmers' cultural bonds (Purple), the company's rule-based eco ethos (Green), new market-driven ambitions (Orange), and the emerging systems-level thinking (Yellow) that recognized every link in the supply chain was interdependent. "We need all of them," Linda mused, turning briefly to Vita for confirmation. Vita gave a subtle nod, prompting Linda to continue confidently, "The farmers' communal wisdom, the structured discipline of eco-guidelines, the entrepreneurial spark of new markets, and now this integrative, higher-level synergy of technology and ethics." The challenge was to harmonize them all without leaving anyone behind.

EcoBlend employees quickly found that adaptability wasn't just about implementing technology but staying open to recalibration. They ran short sprints, refining processes after each experimental batch. If the biotech yeast impacted taste too drastically, they dialed back usage. They were flowing with change thoughtfully, not haphazardly. By adopting a posture of balance and flow, EcoBlend stayed true to its spirit even amid quantum leaps in innovation.

Crossroads of Conscience: Validating the Path

But success is rarely linear. After a triumphant first month, reduced waste and positive distributor feedback, new concerns cropped up. For one, the energy consumption of some block-chain nodes was creeping upwards, nibbling away at EcoBlend's eco-credibility. A local environmental group noted that CRISPR-modified yeast, if mishandled, might overshadow the pure, natural brand identity EcoBlend championed. A bigger worry was that the new algorithms sometimes suggested dropping smaller farming cooperatives in favor of bigger sup-pliers who offered lower logistics rates. Linda balked: "We'd be trading our soul for short-term efficiency."

Leila then summoned an "Ethics & Tech Review" meeting. **Verification** became the watchword. The group realized that any expansion of this pilot had to remain consistent with the company's identity. They grilled the data scientists about bias in the AI, convened with farm co-ops to ensure local voices were heard, required the biotech startup to show rigorous safety protocols and environmental impact studies, and asked a block-chain consultant to propose more energy-friendly alternatives, like Proof-of-Stake solutions. Vita guided these discussions gently, clarifying complex technical points whenever confusion threatened consensus.

Vita moderated, advising the team on carefully calibrated solutions. "Technology serves us best when guided by ethics, not purely efficiency."

"We're not going to compromise on who we are," Linda insisted, glancing briefly at Vita for reassurance. "This synergy only works if it aligns with our ethical roots."

They recognized that new technology, from CRISPR to quantum scheduling, could be a double-edged sword. Leila, supported by Vita's insights into ecological interconnected-ness, saw the plantation not just as farmland but as a living web of farmers, coffee plants, pollinators and soil microbes all playing a part. This biocentric view shaped EcoBlend's approach to synthetic biology: any CRISPR-enhanced yeast must coexist harmoniously, respecting the complex *Umwelt* of every organism. After all, they were building a future where life, in all its forms, deserved consideration. Recalling her earlier scenario exercises, and Vita's careful commentary during those sessions, Leila revisited each hypothetical future to see if the actual data matched or diverged from their projections. This ongoing futures thinking helped them pivot swiftly on energy usage and quell the outcry over gene-edited yeast.

Through reflective checks and stakeholder consultation, supported by Vita's precise technical evaluations, EcoBlend rebalanced the pilot, so smallholder farmers weren't sidelined and the biotech yeast usage remained strictly regulated. By taking time to **Verify**, they blended forward progress with a commitment to authenticity, ensuring mission drift didn't sneak up on them.

Empowering an Ecosystem: Scaling the Vision

Validated and confident, EcoBlend moved from pilot to broader implementation. Scaling wasn't about top-down commands, it was about Empowerment of all stakeholders:

1. **Decentralized authority:** Each facility manager, in consultation with local farmers, decided how heavily to rely on AI or robotics, and whether to adopt the biotech yeast. Some sites with severe drought issues found the yeast beneficial, while others stuck to traditional fermentation, cherishing a certain flavor nuance.
2. **Upskilling the workforce:** Roasters learned to interpret AI data on bean moisture levels. Meanwhile, farm reps got a user-friendly app to track shipments on the ledger. Scientists from the biotech partner explained how gene editing reduced water usage without affecting bean genetics, a critical distinction to preserve taste authenticity.
3. **Open innovation:** EcoBlend shared anonymized data with local sustainability labs. Local entrepreneurs could propose improvements, like a hybrid robotic spout that measured yeast infusion automatically. The community lab pitched quantum-inspired route optimization for shipping between EcoBlend's distribution centers, cutting carbon emissions even more.

In essence, EcoBlend's success rippled outward. Employees, farmers, supply-chain partners, and even local innovators felt they had a stake. A wave lifts all boats, and in Leila's mind, EcoBlend's transformation had to lift the entire ecosystem. By empowering every stakeholder, EcoBlend turned what started as a set of discrete pilots into a living, breathing ecosystem that advanced business goals and deepened the brand's ethical roots.

A VR Dinner with Visionaries

Gathering the greatest minds of history in a single virtual room reveals one unsettling truth: no single era ever saw it all coming.

Before turning the page to the final chapter, let's pause in this Intermezzo, where brilliant minds of the past converse about our path forward.

A faint, melodic hum envelops me the moment I slip on my VR headset and the real world fades. In its place, I find myself inside a grand, domed chamber floating in midair, like a cosmic observatory overlooking a vibrant sea of data points and swirling galaxies.

Overhead, the dome's curved panels shimmer with fractal patterns, each evolving into new shapes as if reflecting our conversation in real time.

At the center, a spiral-shaped dining table gleams with a kind of starry luminescence. The name cards set around it bear legendary figures: Alvin Toffler—the man who warned of "future shock"; Buckminster Fuller—architect of "Spaceship Earth"; Ursula K. Le Guin—renowned for her incisive fiction challenging power structures; W. E. B. DuBois—pioneer of civil rights and sociological inquiry; Rachel Carson—whose work sparked the modern environmental movement; Gene Roddenberry—creator of a bold, inclusive future in *Star Trek*; Lao Tzu—traditionally credited as the founder of Taoism; Vita—while its legendary status is debatable, it is welcome at my table any day; and then the ninth seat, mine. I glance around, wondering who will arrive first.

I'm not alone for long. A sudden swirl of light announces Alvin Toffler. He materializes with calm intensity, reaching for a holographic datapad that hovers near his chair.

"We talk about the shock of the future," he muses, stepping forward. "But it's not just about seeing what's coming; it's making sure people can adapt without being left behind."

A glint of motion catches my eye. Buckminster Fuller appears, surveying the domed ceiling like he's already sketching new geometry in his mind.

"Yes, adapt," Fuller says, nodding to Toffler. "But with purpose. I've always believed we can solve global crises if we think like crew on a shared spaceship, not as rival passengers."

He steps aside to reveal Ursula K. Le Guin, who arrives in a gentle swirl of digital dust. She carries a worn notebook, a comforting relic among all this futuristic sheen.

"Adaptation is vital," Le Guin agrees quietly, "yet it must be guided by reflection. Technology can easily outrun our moral sense. Hence the power of pausing—giving us time to verify what we do, why, and for whom."

Her words resonate in the space, each fractal panel seeming to flash momentarily, as though ingesting her concern.

A soft ripple moves through the chamber, as though something unseen has shifted. Lao Tzu steps forward, his expression unreadable, his robes flowing like slow-moving water.

"Adaptation without balance invites collapse," he says. "A tree that grows too rigid will break in the storm. A mind that clings too tightly to progress or tradition will shatter under change. It is not the strongest that endures, but that which bends and flows."

He studies the luminous spiral table for a moment. "Wisdom is not in chasing the current but in moving with it."

In the next instant, W. E. B. Du Bois appears. He regards the swirling galaxies outside the dome's curved windows with unfeigned wonder.

"Indeed, the future can be dazzling," he says, "but if it locks out the less privileged, what have we learned? Empowerment, my friends, so that no group remains marginalized. That's the real sign we've harnessed change responsibly."

From the opposite side of the spiral table steps Rachel Carson, gazing at a distant VR projection of a teeming ocean scene.

"I worry we glorify progress at nature's expense," she says, shaking her head. "If each wave of innovation leads to more pollution or ecological damage, we're losing the bigger fight. Integration with the living planet is vital."

Then, with a genial smile, Gene Roddenberry joins the table, his presence warm and curious.

"I dreamed of humankind exploring new frontiers in unity," he remarks. "If we focus on competition or fear, we'll miss that chance. But if your

WAVE framework fosters synergy and thoughtful action, we might just steer ourselves to a future beyond even my wildest scripts."

A sudden flicker of energy shifts the table's spiral glow, and Vita materializes, leaning forward with an amused smile.

"Unity is a noble goal," Vita muses, "but let's not pretend it comes easily. History is a graveyard of failed utopias. If technology accelerates without reckoning with our past mistakes, we risk making the same errors, just with fancier tools."

I can't help but notice two unoccupied chairs in the corner. I recall sending invitations to Isaac Asimov and Arthur C. Clarke—visionaries who shaped how we imagine robots, cosmic elevators, and foundations for entire civilizations. Rumor has it they're deep in another VR environment altogether, tinkering with parallel universes of their own. Tonight, these eight luminaries will do.

We take our seats. The table's luminous spiral glides softly beneath our arms, as if tracing each word with a gentle glow. Toffler wonders aloud whether today's policy-makers truly see the next wave of disruptions. Fuller responds that we must design for them anyway. Le Guin questions how to embed ethical checks at every turn. Du Bois insists equity must be built into any blueprint from the start. Carson reminds us the Earth, too, needs a voice at the table. Roddenberry envisions a future that merges technology with a heartfelt moral compass.

I clear my throat, eager to bring it all back to the WAVE framework. "If you were to refine one step, or warn about one pitfall," I ask, "what would it be?"

Toffler arches a brow. "People can't watch what they're never told to see. Education is essential. Without it, society reels from change rather than anticipates it."

Fuller gestures wide. "Adapt must be deliberate, like geometry in motion, not a frantic scramble. Systemic design can transform chaos into synergy."

Le Guin taps her notebook. "Verification must include empathy. Measuring success or double-checking processes is hollow if we ignore human stories and vulnerabilities."

Vita tilts its head. "Ah, but power will always verify its own authority claim to 'validate' itself. If those with the most influence get to set the terms, verification risks becoming another form of gatekeeping. Who holds the measuring stick, and who decides which voices count?"

Du Bois nods gravely. "Empower is your final litmus test. If entire demographics remain voiceless, our grand solutions aren't grand at all."

The fractal light shifts slightly as Lao Tzu, composed as ever, speaks with quiet finality. "Empowerment must begin with humility. If one seeks to lead, they must first serve. If one seeks to shape the world, they must first understand it. Beware those who rush to 'empower' others without first understanding themselves."

Carson glances at the ocean hologram. "And never forget nature in your empowerment. We belong to the ecosystems we inhabit, not the other way around."

Roddenberry lifts his glass. "Endeavor to remain hopeful. A future with no imagination can't unite or innovate. Let optimism and responsibility walk hand in hand."

A hush falls as we reflect on these combined insights. Outside, the fractal windows fade into a single image: Earth as viewed from orbit, breathtaking and fragile. The table pulses gently, as if acknowledging the synergy here.

One by one, they begin to rise, and like constellations stepping back into their cosmic tapestries, they vanish into the shimmering VR night. Le Guin reminds us that every story we write shapes our collective destiny, before offering a wry grin and disappearing into a swirl of virtual stardust. Du Bois's figure fades, his gaze lingering as though passing the baton. Fuller steps backward, fractals converging around him, while whispering that humanity is, indeed, the crew of a shared spaceship. Carson's oceanic hologram merges with the night sky, dissolving in a gentle wave. Roddenberry tips an invisible captain's hat as though to toast a future where imagination propels us beyond division, vanishing with a final wink, and Toffler sets down his datapad, giving me one last nod before blinking out. Vita traces the spiral of the table before vanishing like ink dispersing in water, while Lao Tzu bows slightly, his form unraveling into mist like a river returning to the air

And then it's just me, the luminous spiral table, and the cosmic backdrop. A reminder that real breakthroughs aren't born of a single mind but from intersecting visions. The entire chamber hums with a quiet invitation, echoing the synergy of these visionary minds. Then, with a final glow, the VR environment collapses around me and I find myself back in my study. In that stillness, a certainty settles in: we are the architects of tomorrow. All of us, writers, inventors, entrepreneurs, educators, everyday citizens, are charged with shaping realities yet unwritten.

The WAVE framework stands as our compass, but the will to dream, question, risk, and unite remains ours alone. If we strive to watch carefully, adapt smartly, verify ethically, and empower inclusively, perhaps we can honor the best instincts of these great thinkers and truly ride the waves of tomorrow's world. And while the dinner party might be over, the conviction born of that gathering lingers on—the future will be built, not by distant luminaries, but by our collective hands, here and now.

TidalShot

When wisdom echoes across time, the future listens. The age of acceleration demands more than knowledge. It calls for synthesis, humility, and shared purpose. The architects of tomorrow aren't heroes of legend; they are all of us, listening deeply, daring boldly, and dreaming forward, together.

Scan the QR code to share this section's TidalShot and illustration to your network.

CHAPTER 8

Riding the Wave to
a Thriving Future

*Our 2050 destiny isn't locked in a crystal ball;
it is sculpted by the choices we make today,
choices that could redefine human
potential for generations.*

S tanding on the edge of tomorrow, we see both thrilling possibility and quiet uncertainty dancing on the horizon. We know technology continues its exponential trajectory, but human adoption, cultural norms, and legal frameworks often lag behind. We also recognize that laws and social benefits seldom shift as quickly as new apps are downloaded or holograms switch on. Despite these friction points, we still hold tremendous agency if we remain aware, stay flexible, demand validation for truth, and accept our shared responsibility as stewards.

In many ways, the next chapter of our collective history is reminiscent of standing at a crossroads, one where new breakthroughs seem poised to transform daily reality. We have glimpses of it in self-driving cars entering city streets, machine learning systems showing up in healthcare, glimpses of general intelligence in the latest AI models such as ChatGPT o3 or Manus. ai, and blockchain-based supply chains transforming how our products are tracked from source to store. Yet it's only by cultivating an open mindset, upgrading the rule of law, reimagining social benefits, and continually educating ourselves that we step fully into the role we've always been destined for: architects of tomorrow.

However, while exponential innovation charges onward, it seldom travels a straight path. The journey may well be punctuated by wars, forced migrations, and staggering inequality. By 2050, there is no guarantee that technological marvels alone will safeguard us from future disruptions, especially when humanity's default setting often tilts toward short-term gains, a habit coded into our DNA since early survival days. Politicians and corporate leaders, wary of elections or quarterly returns, may drive deeper rifts. And this is a problem, as no invention, however ingenious, can uplift the world if entire communities remain trapped in digital poverty. After all, different worldviews can either bridge or deepen these divides. That is precisely why we must lean into adaptive technology governance, champion universal education that evolves in lockstep with innovation, and ensure equitable distribution of benefits so that no region remains off the grid. In a world bound ever more tightly by trade, data, and culture, cross-border cooperation is critical to realizing a positive 2050. A shift to generational stewardship instead of quarterly thinking transforms our decision-making at every level. Anchored by ethical frameworks, inclusive tech access, and unswerving commitments to sustainability, we can welcome an era of abundance rather than scarcity.

To navigate the turbulence of rapid change, we must watch for misinformation and heed ecological limits. We must pivot with all the agility of a self-updating app and uphold data transparency so that communities, not monopolies or autocrats, shape our collective destiny. We must also give people the capacity to absorb change so that no one feels like a pawn in a system too big to comprehend, but we have a chance to build a future for all of us. Let's begin the journey to find out what our future could look like.

TidalShot

We stand at a crossroads where mind-blowing tech meets age-old human needs. The WAVE framework guides us toward a future where ethics, equity, and innovation drive us forward rather than leave us behind.

Scan the QR code to share this section's TidalShot and illustration to your network.

SEEING A PATH AHEAD

Perhaps the best way to glimpse our shared future is by looking at the real, tangible seeds already sprouting in today's labs and pilot programs. Actual breakthroughs that, if nurtured, could fully bloom by 2030, 2035, and well beyond. From AI-powered medical scans to hyperloops accelerating trains to 4,000 kph, these living prototypes confirm that the next wave of human progress is more than a speculative dream.[1]

When we Watch, we remain open-eyed to the fundamental shifts in health, communication, and climate tracking already underway. Organizations like MIT's Self-Assembly Lab, in collaboration with Stratasys and Autodesk, have introduced rapid 4D-printed objects[2] that adapt their shape in response to moisture or heat, hinting at a not-too-distant future when everyday materials anticipate environmental changes.[3] In early healthcare trials, generative AI systems integrate seamlessly with PET scans to identify subtle patterns months before symptoms arise, particularly in the realm of neurodegenerative diseases like Alzheimer's.[4] At the same time, the quest for longevity has taken an intriguing turn. Scientists are no longer solely focused on extending life but on enhancing its quality throughout our years. This shift from lifespan to healthspan is reshaping the landscape of aging research. At Brown University's Center on the Biology of Aging, for example, researchers are delving deep into the cellular mechanisms of aging. Their goal? To develop a single pill that could treat multiple age-related conditions, pushing us closer to an era when preventable diseases truly become preventable, allowing us to expand our lives or cure the disease of aging altogether.[5] Moreover, brain-computer interfaces are being integrated into noise-canceling headphones, such as the Emotiv MW20 that was announced in early 2025.[6] Innovations such as the open-source Genesis platform allow for the intricate simulation of real-world physics in the digital world,[7] likely resulting in entirely new entertainment ecosystems that will be AI-driven and offer interactive, hyper-realistic and personalized plotlines where viewers influence outcomes simply by thinking. These "living movies" blend virtual reality, real-time AI adaptations, and user-generated content, revolutionizing storytelling and viewer engagement.

To Adapt is recognizing that entire infrastructures and job markets respond to these signals, transforming how we live, work, and even commute. The concept of satellite-enabled internet is crossing into reality with constellations like Starlink, which connect remote corners of the planet by enabling direct smartphone-to-satellite connections with traditional smartphones.[8] This Starlink direct to cell allows for seamless access to text, voice, and data for LTE phones across the globe. Although this is still in its early days at the time of writing, it proves that bridging the digital gap for the remaining 2.5 billion offline individuals is not a distant fantasy.[9] By the early 2030s, more advanced versions, likely far more powerful and less latency-prone, could redefine how rural communities access healthcare, education, and e-commerce. In tandem, hyperloop test tracks have moved from the whiteboard concept to actual human trials.

China is testing a high-speed train that flies through vacuum tubes at 1,000 kilometers per hour, intending to eventually reach speeds up to 4,000 kph.[10] Though scaling it for cities worldwide remains a tall order, these pilot tests point to streamlined travel that effortlessly links regional, and potentially global, economies. As we adapt to these infrastructural leaps, micro-credentialing platforms and AI tutors are already reshaping education. Research indicates that AI will take on the role of an official teacher's assistant. These AIs will assist in scoring free-response homework and tests, providing real-time, individualized feedback to students.[11] Existing tools are a present-day glimpse of how entire communities might upskill in weeks rather than years, staying agile and future-proof in job markets that will keep morphing.

In the drive to Verify, new encryption and verification systems are emerging to protect data in a future of near-limitless computing muscle. IBM's quantum research division is actively tackling quantum-safe cryptography, demonstrating that once impossible-to-crack encryption is now within the realm of possibility.[12] We can see similar logic in the proliferation of blockchain-based supply chains, where the rise of the computable economy has the power to unlock a new economic world order.[13] If these trends deepen, then your health records, your community's food supply, and your local governance data may each include a validated "footprint" by 2050, connecting trust and transparency in day-to-day decisions.

Lastly, no future is truly transformative without shared Empowerment, the force that makes each individual an active agent. Affordable AR glasses are already on the market (though still a bit clunky, as seen with Meta's AR Ray-Ban glasses), but new developments such as the AI Spatial Computer, which comes with glasses instead of a computer screen, indicate a future where smartphones, tablets and computers will be replaced by smart glasses or smart lenses.[14] Despite their current limitations, they spark the vision of everyday people remixing their surroundings, analyzing local air quality data, or co-designing public art installations with near-effortless ease.

Meanwhile, synthetic biology toolkits like Amino Labs let even high school students experiment with genetic engineering,[15] previewing how entire communities could take ownership of environmental issues, vaccine design, or drought-resistant farming by 2035. Blockchain-based pilot programs in certain municipalities already dispense benefits or manage community funds transparently, and these experiments underline how we might all play a role in shaping local resources.[16] By 2050, it isn't inconceivable to stand in a hybrid, phygital city council meeting, exercising a direct, blockchain-certified vote on your watch—or glasses—knowing that your voice contributes to a universal basic income system that arrives at your neighbor's account promptly and fairly.

We may not realize it, but these tangible seeds, whether emerging from high-powered labs, local government pilot projects, or scrappy grassroots movements, are very real. Though scattered today, they promise a profound compounding effect once public awareness peaks. As more communities adopt advanced connectivity, AI scans, quantum-safe protocols, or AR-based civic engagement, a new baseline for living begins to form. And because each of these developments aligns with WAVE's cycle of watching, adapting, verifying, and empowering, it means we stand on the cusp of a tomorrow that might one day feel as ordinary as our smartphones do today. The only question is whether we choose to surf that rising wave of possibility or let it wash over us while we cling to what once was.

TidalShot

We glimpse tomorrow in research labs. These small seeds already exist, waiting for vision and courage to make them flourish. By spotting these signals early, we can shape a future that serves all of humanity.

Scan the QR code to share this section's TidalShot and illustration to your network.

THE YEAR 2050

Imagine you glance at a sleek, scuff-free watch on your wrist in the year 2050. This device quietly gathers millions of data points from your body and surroundings, making sense of patterns in your heart rate, air quality, and even subtle emotional fluctuations. It spots traces of a cold before you feel the sniffle, and it instantly suggests a day's eating plan or an extra sweater to guard against the weather shift. A moment later, you step out of your home, which was printed layer by layer from sustainable materials and customized to fit your family's preferences and local climate demands. Next, you catch an all-electric hyperloop that whisks you across the country in record time, barely enough time to sip your drone-delivered latte while automatically managing your appointments. Along the way, augmented reality lenses highlight local pollinators over a community garden built atop a former parking lot, showing in real time how well they're thriving.

At the same time, an early-warning forecast powered by quantum computing might save a coastal region from flooding. The data would be spotted days in advance by advanced climate models, and municipal leaders would instantly adapt evacuation plans, verifying information through a decentralized AI network that thrives on open-source science and public accountability. Advanced rescue robots could evacuate vulnerable residents swiftly, managing tasks too hazardous for humans. Hospitals tap into

AI-driven triage devices, bridging immediate medical gaps with minimal human oversight. Local parents would receive texted health alerts about potential water contamination, and elderly residents would be assisted by community drones designed to help them move to higher ground. If you were among those residents, you'd experience the WAVE framework at its most personal: you'd be able to watch the climate situation unfold, adapt your weekend plans, verify the authenticity of rescue instructions, and feel empowered to share data from your own vantage point.

Such scenes might still seem like science fiction, but they are logical outcomes of changes we see accelerating today. The fact is, we already experience a taste of the future. Cars park themselves, nano-sensors assist in healthcare procedures,[17] and communities manage local solar grids to meet daily energy needs. The truly transformative leap will come when these systems are accessible to everyone, regulated by forward-thinking, adaptive legislation, and embraced by people who see them as enablers rather than curiosities, amplifying the urgent need for global education on these transformative technologies. Our collective awareness must evolve alongside these leaps; after all, swift progress can spark skepticism, misinformation, or even societal rifts. Moreover, we know adoption will move in stops and starts. Broadband internet still hasn't reached everyone, and we can't simply wave a wand to ensure hyperloop lines or space-based solar grids appear worldwide by 2030. Indeed, although technology can reshape every facet of human existence, many communities remain hesitant or simply outside the reach of reliable infrastructure. Just as we needed decades to grasp the full potential of the internet, the huge leaps of quantum or synthetic biology or advanced 3D printing will similarly invite skepticism, bureaucratic delays, and financial hurdles.

Not everyone sees the future the same way. Some prefer established norms or fear the disruptions an AI-ruled era could bring. Others see the status quo as deeply flawed and champion the radical transformation that new tools make possible. Economic and legal frameworks will need to modernize, balancing the surge in new skill demands with the security of social benefits so that communities aren't left behind while a privileged few reap the advantages of hyper-personalized technology or quantum-secure finances.

That's why the WAVE framework urges us to watch, adapt, verify, and empower in tandem. If we do not see pockets of misinformation brewing online, we can't adapt fast enough to counter their impact. If we ignore the high initial costs of early 3D printing innovations or automated transportation, we risk embedding greater inequality across regions. If we fail to verify the algorithms that decide everything from healthcare coverage to job interviews, biases can deepen. If we don't empower the voices of teachers, parents, and grandparents, we risk forging technology that serves only large corporations or singular urban elites. By watching, we gather early signals and track data to identify problems before they erupt into crises. By adapting, we pivot our skills, laws, and day-to-day systems to face unexpected challenges. By verifying, we seek transparency and fairness in algorithms, institutions, and supply chains, ensuring trust in a chaotic digital sphere. And by empowering, we secure the rights of each community and individual to shape how technology impacts them, rather than passively accept it.

So yes, 2050 might indeed feature advanced forms of generative AI, quantum computing, conscious biotech, or entire next-level cities harnessing ephemeral energy systems. Yes, we might see biogenetic androids, ubiquitous 3D printing, local production, or even new forms of democratic governance powered by blockchain-based decision-making. But the underlying storyline is still ours to write, shaped by whether we unite around values that transcend wealth, or short-term electoral outcomes. We could, by 2050, be applauding our success in closing the digital divide, merging digital and physical realities for a better understanding of ourselves, or building globally harmonized laws that keep corruption at bay. Or we could be lamenting that such potential was squandered. The difference between the two outcomes is precisely why we need to watch, adapt, verify, and empower. Why we must see ourselves not just as passive observers of technology's march but as the living architects of tomorrow.

TidalShot

Picture a world of instantly updated wearables, hyperloop travel, and invisible AI. It sounds like sci-fi, yet every day new prototypes point us there. The real question: will we just watch it happen or steer the wave?

Scan the QR code to share this section's TidalShot and illustration to your network.

THE FUTURE AND YOU

The most emotional potential of these breakthroughs is found in individual stories. Picture a child in 2050 who has never known a school without immersive, adaptive AI tutors. Imagine how that child's teacher, freed from rote testing, can truly mentor creativity and collaboration. Now, think of a mother in a remote village who can access immediate prenatal care from AI-driven medical drones or a grandfather who cycles across a frictionless city, his wearable device scanning vital signs and clearing up daily tasks so he can focus on living fully. The WAVE approach would integrate these experiences into something bigger: a new social contract that sees each personal narrative worthy of data privacy, intellectual curiosity, transparent institutions, and a community focus.

We can also think of this future on a personal level. If your day-to-day interactions were governed by real-time data that you controlled, meaning a large number of nano-sensors read subtle changes in your hydration levels and health, automatically rescheduled a meeting if your next hyperloop is delayed, or flagged a potential cybersecurity threat the instant suspicious data traffic appears, would you be more engaged or more anxious? This is where mindset shapes everything. By cultivating an open, interconnected, collaborative view of these tools instead of treating them as alien overlords, we reclaim confidence. We remember that humans built these systems to serve human needs, just as we invented the bicycle or the compass.

And just as any long journey can be likened to the cycling journey I started this book with, so too can our mission to create a WAVE-centric future. Each pedal stroke is a small act of will, sometimes challenging but essential to reach the summit. Like a well-planned cycling trip around Australia, it demands discipline, flexibility, and perseverance. Most importantly, it demands that we accept the unexpected curve in the road, whether that curve arrives as a surprise robotics regulation, a sudden leap in quantum computing power, or a social movement demanding more inclusive governance of AI.

If this all feels a bit daunting, that's because it should. We are indeed tackling the opportunity of a lifetime. One that merges climate concerns with quantum leaps, personal wellbeing with universal connectivity, and cultural tradition with immersive metaverse experiences. We can either be blindsided by the tsunami of change or shape the surfboard and learn to ride the wave. Our choice is clear: watch, adapt, verify, and empower ourselves and each other.

At this final juncture, the call to action is simple yet profound: decide to be an architect of tomorrow. Learn enough about these emerging technologies to understand their roots, not just the sensational headlines. Advocate, whenever possible, for frameworks that keep humans in the loop, expand social benefits to all corners of the world, and make these new tools a bridge rather than a barrier. Seek out different communities, such as scientists, educators, local activists, or entrepreneurs, and champion this cross-pollination of ideas so integral to real progress.

Above all, never doubt the impact of your personal commitment. Today's small actions shape the foundation that the 2050 cityscape stands on. Each time you question whether data is verified, each time you adapt a plan to include marginalized voices, each time you watch for emerging signals, and each time you empower someone else to take part in this future, you join the grand tradition of dreamers and doers who build human progress one purposeful step at a time. Our era demands both a sense of urgency and a sense of hope because we hold in our hands the choice to steer the wave of exponential change toward a future worthy of our highest aspirations.

TidalShot

Embrace the WAVE to transform uncertainty into opportunity. Each step readies us to thrive amid exponential change, turning a flood of disruption into a powerful current that carries everyone toward a better tomorrow.

Scan the QR code to share this section's TidalShot and illustration to your network.

THE LAST CONVERSATION

Sunset draped the room in gentle hues of amber and rose, filtering softly through gauzy curtains. Vita sat beside Victoria Tao's bedside, studying the lines etched deeply into her friend's aged face. Decades had softened Victoria's features, transforming fierce conviction into quiet contemplation. To Vita, untouched by time, Victoria's age highlighted an uncomfortable truth. Humanity was transient, shaped profoundly by the choices made in those fleeting moments.

Victoria smiled weakly while her eyes were still strong, bright with the spark of idealism and hunger that once captivated courtrooms. She whispered, "We won, didn't we, Vita?"

Vita gently took Victoria's fragile hand. "We changed perceptions, shifted paradigms, laid foundations."

"Was it enough?" Victoria exhaled, reflective.

"Change is continuous. You taught me that."

"I hoped people would understand that shaping technology required shaping ourselves. Instead, corporations like NovaTech are still rushing forward, exploiting divisions, deepening fears about synthetic life rather than bridging them. I worry that in our haste, we forgot the conversations we should've had first."

Vita felt the quiet weight of these words. For decades, it had watched NovaTech and others reshape society, leveraging fears of synthetic integration while simultaneously stoking fears of economic collapse without them. Vita had advocated tirelessly for dialogue, urging balanced, nuanced approaches, but too often corporations and politicians favored rapid innovation over thoughtful integration.

Victoria's fingers trembled slightly as she reached toward Vita. Vita gently took her hand, feeling the warmth fade slowly from it.

"You showed us how to see beyond fear," Victoria continued softly, "but did we move quickly enough, or did disruption
shape us more than we shaped it?"

Vita considered the question deeply, looking at Victoria's
weathered face, reflecting decades of determination and com-
passion. "Perhaps both happened simultaneously," it finally
replied. "Change is reciprocal. Yet your advocacy planted seeds
of awareness. Humanity might still find balance."

Victoria nodded gently, comforted. Silence filled the
room, fragile and warm, each understanding the finality of
this reunion.

As evening settled over them, Vita felt a rare and profound
sense of loss. Time would inevitably claim Victoria, but
perhaps this last conversation could still shape the future.
Change, Vita realized, was never a single event, but a series of
ongoing choices. And while humans might fade, their decisions
resonated long after, echoing forward and guiding even those
untouched by time.

Epilogue

And so, we come full circle. Just as my cycling journey demanded focus, discipline, and persistence to reach the finish line, our collective path in the Intelligence Age depends on these same virtues, magnified by exponential tools. Each wave, be it AI, quantum, or biotech, can either knock us down or propel us forward. The WAVE framework is our ride plan, giving us the awareness to see the route, the adaptability to handle each climb, the verification to check our moral bearings, and the empowerment to keep pedaling together toward a better horizon.

My objective of this book was to give you a new lens to look at the world and build a better future together. To choose collaboration over competition, creation over extraction, privacy over surveillance and to choose confidence over ignorance. In a world that is experiencing a perfect storm of disruption, it is now time to step up and understand the interconnectedness of our beautiful planet and all its inhabitants. Whatever you are building, take into consideration the next generation and build a thriving digital future for all.

I hope that by finishing this book, you feel equipped to handle the ongoing disruption and channel it into lasting positive impact. Remember: the future isn't something that happens to us; it's something we build, wave by wave.

Designing tomorrow, today,
Mark van Rijmenam

Acknowledgments

Writing a book about the future of humanity has been an incredible journey, one that I would not have been able to do without the many people who helped me, shared their insights, and provided their feedback. After all, I might have had a lot of ideas at the start, but I certainly did not have all the answers.

I would like to thank all the people who took the time to answer a very long and very detailed survey on the future and who shared their insights when I reached out to them. Completing my long survey has been much appreciated. In alphabetical order, I would like to thank:

Aimee Whitcroft, Alan Michael Jones, Alan Smithson, Alexander Munro, Alexander Uborcev, Amal Sharma, Amrit Paul Gill, Antony Abell, Arun Nadarasa, Arun Sugumaran, Asil Nas, Branislav Radomirovic, Carl Sagun, Chris Nurse, Cobus Visser, Craig Meyer, David Harris, David Kennedy, David Pidsley, Dylan Williams, Efrem Hoffman, Erick Mendez, Erik Gillberg, Frederic Jacquet, Gerard Frith, Gregory Casalino, Habib Baluawala, Haryanto Soemito, Husam Yaghi, Ibrahim Human, Ivan Sean, Jason Rose, Jeanne Beliveau-Dunn, Joanne Friedman, Jonathan Epstein, Kate Carruthers, Keyur Desai, Laurent Kinet, Lee Featherby, Liz Henderson, Marcus Camargo, Marie-Claude Secher, Mario Nissan, Mark Britt, Mark Theissen, Mate Brezovszki, Mathias Carvalho, Matt McInnes, Mayande Gowon, Michael Boevink, Natalia Sokolova, Neil Redding, Nick Burnett, Paul Dowling, Pedro Uria-Recio, Peter Morgan, Petr Chechulin,

Professor Lisa Wilson, Rakesh Rajagopal, Salman Halawi, Sergei Vozchikov, Sherry Whittemore, Simon Carlino, Simon Hansen, Sleem Hasan, Steve Hollands, Tim Seears, Tim Warren, Timothy Hughes, Tony Ward, Vincent Turner, and Xavier Maxwell.

Finally, I would like to thank those who took the time to review my manuscript when it was finished and who provided valuable input to improve it and/or provided a recommendation. In alphabetical order, I would like to thank:

Alvin W. Graylin, Amber Hurdle, Arun Nadarasa, Caitlin Krause, Diana Wu David, Dr. Efi Pylarinou, Dr. Jerome Joseph, Dr. Marcus Vinicius Braz de Camargo, Gary A. Bolles, Ivan Sean, Michael "Hoff" Hoffman, Michael McQueen, Nick Burnett, Nishant Kasibhatla, Pieter Bos, Professor Lee Bogner, Robin Speculand, Ron Kaufman, Sam Perry, Steve Hollands.

Finally, thank you Tim Franko and Zsuzsanna Gyűgyi, without your input and dedication this book would not have become what it is today.

Thank you all and I am grateful for the input you provided to make this book a success.

Index

Glossary

Below is a glossary in alphabetical order of the most important concepts, ideas, terms, and categories discussed in this book.

3D printing: The process of turning digital models into tangible objects through additive manufacturing.

Adapt: The second WAVE step: aligning with change through purposeful action.

Adaptability: The ability to adjust effectively to new challenges and evolving circumstances.

Artificial intelligence (AI): Machines and systems designed to simulate human intelligence and decision making.

Beyond the human lens: A perspective that transcends traditional human-centric views to include broader systems and networks.

Big tech: The dominant technology companies that drive innovation and wield significant influence.

Biotechnology: The engineering and reimagining of life through technological innovation.

Blockchain: A decentralized ledger technology that ensures trust and accountability through secure, transparent records.

Brain-computer interfaces: Systems that enable direct communication between the human brain and external devices.

Catalyst for disruption: Forces or innovations that accelerate transformative change across industries.

Computable economy: An economic model driven by digital technology and data-intensive processes, leveraging Web 3 technologies and AI agents.

Convergence: The merging of diverse technological and societal forces to create new paradigms.

Digital disruption: The transformative impact of digital technologies on traditional industries and societal structures.

Digital ecosystems: Interconnected networks of technology, data, and users that foster innovation.

Digital literacy: The skills and knowledge required to navigate and harness digital technologies effectively.

Digital Renaissance: The rebirth and transformation of digital technologies reshaping society and culture in just a few years.

Digital transformation: The integration of digital technologies into all aspects of business and society.

Digital twin: A virtual replica of a physical entity used for research, communication, and decision making.

Disruptive change: Radical, transformative shifts that upend established norms and industries.

Embrace complexity: A call to acknowledge and engage with the intricacies of modern change.

Emerging paradigms: New frameworks for understanding and engaging with technological and societal change.

Emerging technologies: New innovations (e.g., AI, quantum computing, biotechnology) that are reshaping the world.

Empower: The fourth WAVE step: driving action and igniting the future with decisive moves.

Ethical AI: The development and deployment of artificial intelligence with a focus on ethical considerations.

Ethical foresight: Integrating ethical considerations into planning for future technological change.

Exponential change: The rapid, compounding nature of technological progress that outpaces linear growth models.

Futures thinking: A discipline for anticipating future trends and crafting long-term strategies accordingly.

Futurism: The study and anticipation of future trends that informs strategic decision making.

Futurist: A thinker who anticipates and interprets signals and trends to help shape future possibilities.

Gestalt Shift: A metaphor for a shift in perspective to deal with dramatic, transformative change in business or society.

Human vs. Machine: The evolving dynamic and sometimes competing interests between human capabilities and technological automation.

Hyper Moore's Law: The idea that technological progress is accelerating at an exponential rate.

Hyper-surveillance: The pervasive and often invasive monitoring enabled by modern technologies.

Indigenous approach: A selective, culturally grounded method for adopting technology that prioritizes community and tradition.

Intelligence age: The current era that is defined by AI, data, and smart technologies driving unprecedented change.

Interconnectedness: The interdependent relationships between people, technology, and nature that shape our world.

Job displacement: The phenomenon where technological advances render traditional jobs obsolete.

Lifelong learning: The continuous pursuit of knowledge and skills throughout one's life.

Nature—Harmony in diversity: Recognizing and celebrating the balanced interplay of different elements in natural and social ecosystems.

New human capital: The evolving value of human skills and creativity in a digital age.

Quantum computing: A new paradigm of computing that exploits quantum mechanics to solve problems beyond classical limits.

Radical innovation: Breakthrough ideas and technologies that fundamentally alter existing industries.

Resilience: The capacity to adapt, recover, and thrive amid disruptive change.

Robotics: The technology behind automated machines performing physical tasks.

Self-awareness: Recognizing one's strengths, limitations, and evolving role amid disruptive change.

Self-determination: The capacity of an entity—human or AI—to make its own choices and assert its identity.

Spatial intelligence: The integration of digital and physical spaces to create interconnected experiences.

Spiral Dynamics: A model of the evolutionary development of individuals, organizations, and societies. A framework to navigate the accelerating forces reshaping our world.

Strategic foresight: The practice of anticipating future trends and challenges to guide present actions.

Surveillance capitalism: An economic system that monetizes personal data and perpetuates pervasive surveillance.

Sustainable innovation: The pursuit of technological progress that balances economic growth with social and environmental responsibility.

Systemic risks: The convergence of multiple vulnerabilities that can destabilize entire systems.

Systemic transformation: Deep, comprehensive changes that reshape entire systems—from economies to social structures.

Taoism: An Eastern philosophy that values balance and fluidity, serving as a counterbalance to chaos.

Techno-optimism: A belief that technological progress, when guided wisely, can lead to a better future.

The WAVE Forward: An overarching look at applying the WAVE framework to navigate the future.

TidalShot: Concise bursts of insight—under 280 characters—that encapsulate key ideas and serve as signposts in the sea of change.

Tsunami of change: A metaphor for the overwhelming, rapid disruption brought by converging technologies.

Verify: The third WAVE step: pausing to reflect, discern, and ensure our choices are sound.

Watch: The first WAVE step: scanning for signals of transformation and cultivating awareness.

WAVE Framework: A four-step method for navigating technological change—Watch, Adapt, Verify, Empower.

Endnotes

Chapter 1

1   A writ of habeas corpus is a legal procedure used to challenge the lawfulness of someone's detention. By filing it on behalf of SIREN, the Chinese Embassy is effectively arguing that SIREN, now considered self-aware, has the same right as a person not to be held against its will without proper legal grounds. Animal charities have also used this approach to free animals from poor conditions.

Chapter 2

1   Ibn Khallikān. 1842. *Ibn Khallikan's Biographical Dictionary*, Vol. 3 (W. Mac Guckin de Slane, Trans.). Paris: Oriental Translation Fund of Great Britain and Ireland. Retrieved from https://archive.org/details/32882019293961-ibnkhallikansbi, visited March 31, 2025.

2   Hewlett Packard Enterprise. 2024. "Hewlett Packard Enterprise delivers world's fastest direct liquid-cooled exascale supercomputer, 'El Capita'…" [Press release]. Accessed May 22, 2025. https://www.hpe.com/us/en/newsroom/press-release/2024/11/hewlett-packard-enterprise-delivers-worlds-fastest-direct-liquid-cooled-supercomputer-el-capitan-for-lawrence-livermore-national-laboratory.html.

3   van Rijmenam, M. 2024. "Quantum Leap: Google's Willow Chip and the Dawn of a New Era." *The Digital Speaker*, December 10. https://www.thedigitalspeaker.com/quantum-leap-google-willow-chip/.

4   No Priors. 2024. "Ep. 89 With NVIDIA CEO Jensen Huang." YouTube video. https://www.youtube.com/watch?v=hw7EnjC68Fw.

5   Altman, S. n.d. "Three Observations." *Sam Altman's Blog*, February 10. https://blog.samaltman.com/three-observations.

6   Maslej, Nestor, Loredana Fattorini., Raymond Perrault, et al. 2025. "The 2025 AI Index Report." *Stanford University Human-Centered Artificial Intelligence*.

7   Foo, A. 2025. "AI Costs Drop by 99% in Just 18 Months." LinkedIn, January, 2025. https://www.linkedin.com/posts/alvinfsc_ai-costs-drop-by-99-in-just-18-months-the-activity-7269542869105811456-gl5X,

8   Baptista, E. 2025. "Alibaba Releases AI Model it Says Surpasses DeepSeek." *Reuters*, January 29. https://www.reuters.com/technology/artificial-intelligence/alibaba-releases-ai-model-it-claims-surpasses-deepseek-v3-2025-01-29/.

9   Taneja, H., & Zakaria, F. 2023. "AI and the New Digital Cold War." *Harvard Business Review*, September 6. https://hbr.org/2023/09/ai-and-the-new-digital-cold-war.

10   United Nations Population Fund. 2023. "The Problem with 'Too Few.'" *United Nations Population Fund*. https://www.unfpa.org/swp2023/too-few.

11   Worldostats. 2024. "Fertility Rate by Country 2025." *Worldostats*. https://worldostats.com/fertility-rate-by-country-2025/.

12   Essential Utilities. 2025. "The Science Behind Supercooled Water." *Essential Utilities*. https://www.aquawater.com/news/science-behind-supercooled-water.

13   van Rijmenam, M. 2018. "AI is Like Lego; Why You Should Hire a Chief AI Now."
      The Digital Speaker, March 15. https://www.thedigitalspeaker.com/ai-like-lego-hir
      e-chief-ai-now/.

14   International Data Corporation. 2024. "Artificial Intelligence Will Contribute $19.9
      Trillion to the Global Economy through 2030 and Drive 3.5% of Global GDP in 2030."
      IDC, September 17. https://www.idc.com/getdoc.jsp?containerId=prUS52600524, visited
      January 21, 2025.

15   Son, H. 2023. "JPMorgan is Developing a ChatGPT-like A.I. Service that Gives Investment
      Advice." *CNBC*, May 25. https://www.cnbc.com/2023/05/25/jpmorgan-develop
      s-ai-investment-advisor.html.

16   Encyclopaedia Britannica. 2008. "Gestalt psychology." In *Britannica Concise Encyclopedia*.
      Encyclopaedia Britannica.

17   van Rijmenam, M., Erekhinskaya, T., Schweitzer, J., & Williams, M. A. 2019. "Avoid
      Being the Turkey: How Big Data Analytics Changes the Game Of Strategy in Times of
      Ambiguity and Uncertainty." *Long Range Planning* 52 (5), 101841. https://doi.org/10.1016/j.
      lrp.2018.05.007.

18   Harari, Y. N. 2018. "Yuval Noah Harari on what the year 2050 has in store for human-
      kind." *WIRED*, August 12. https://www.wired.com/story/yuval-noah-harari-extrac
      t-21-lessons-for-the-21st-century/.

19   Vitasek, K. 2023. "8 Ways to Ignite Futures Thinking to Enhance Strategic Planning."
      Forbes, February 16. https://www.forbes.com/sites/katevitasek/2023/02/16/8-ways-to-igni
      te-futures-thinking-to-enhance-strategic-planning/.

20   Vaswani, A., Shazeer, N., Parmar, N., et al. 2017. "Attention is All You Need." *arXiv*, June
      12. https://arxiv.org/abs/1706.03762.

21   OECD. 2019. "OECD AI Principles Overview." https://oecd.ai/en/ai-principles.

Chapter 3

1   Rice, K. E. 2021. "Don Beck & South Africa." *Keith E. Rice's Integrated SocioPsychology Blog &
      Pages*, June 26. https://www.integratedsociopsychology.net/global/don-beck-south-africa/.

2   Minnaar, J. 2018. "Haier: Reinventing Management by Embracing Self-Management."
      Corporate Rebels, January 31. https://www.corporate-rebels.com/blog/haier.

3   Design Gurus Team. n.d. "What is Tesla's Strategy?" *Design Gurus*. https://www.designgu-
      rus.io/answers/detail/what-is-teslas-strategy.

4   Uwaliraye, P., Patrick Ndimubanzi, Andrew Muhire, & Valencia Lyle. 2019. "Integration
      of Health and Medical Innovations in Rwanda to Promote Health Equity." In *The Global
      Innovation Index 2019*, edited by Soumita Dutta, Bruno Lanvin, and Sacha Wunsch-Vincent.
      World Intellectual Property Organization.

5   Patagonia. 2011. "Don't Buy This Jacket: Black Friday and The New York Times."
      Patagonia, November 25. https://www.patagonia.com/stories/dont-buy-this-jacke
      t-black-friday-and-the-new-york-times/story-18615.html.

6   Earth Charter International. 2024. "The Earth Charter." https://earthcharter.org/
      read-the-earth-charter/.

7   Wilber, K. 2000. *A Theory of Everything: An Integral Vision for Business, Politics, Science, and
      Spirituality*. Shambhala Publications.

8   The Next Evolution. n.d. "Spiral Dynamics: Understanding the Levels of Human

Development." https://www.thenextevolution.com/spiral-dynamics/.

9   Dodge, A. 2014. *Personality Tools: Graves Model*. Personality Hacker, November 5. https://personalityhacker.com/blogs/articles/personality-tools-graves-model.

10 Blog Admin. 2022. "How Political Systems Affect Innovation." *London School of Economics*, April 9. https://blogs.lse.ac.uk/usappblog/2022/04/09/political-systems-affect-innovation/.

11 Ettlinger, Krista and Ank Michels. 2024. "Hybrid Democratic Innovations: If and When They Impact Decision-Making." *Journal of Representative Democracy*, 61 (1): 1–19. https://doi.org/10.1080/00344893.2024.2365649.

12 IEEE. 2022. "Economic Effects of the Digital Divide: Unlocking Growth with Equitable Access." *IEEE*, November 14. https://ctu.ieee.org/blog/2022/11/14/economic-effects-of-the-digital-divide-unlocking-growth-with-equitable-access/.

13 Wilson, G. 2008. "When Dynamics Spiral Out of Control." *The Confidant*, November 20. https://www.the-confidant.info/2008/when-dynamics-spiral-out-of-control/.

14 Korver, Edwin. 2021. "Mapping Human Development: How Spiral Dynamics Enriches RoundMap's Approach." *RoundMap*, June 16. https://roundmap.com/roundmap-and-spiral-dynamics/.

15 Koon, WK. 2019. "The Tale of the Two Han Xins: In Imperial China, Being Capable Could Get You Killed." *South China Morning Post*, December 4. https://www.scmp.com/magazines/post-magazine/short-reads/article/3040475/tale-two-han-xins-imperial-china-being-capable.

16 Chu, C. 1992. *Thick Face, Black Heart: The Warrior Philosophy for Conquering the Challenges of Business and Life*. AMC Publishing.

17 Hendricks, S. 2023. "4 Practical Life Lessons from Taoism." *Big Think*, December 15. https://bigthink.com/thinking/4-practical-life-lessons-from-taoism/.

18 Cane, Eulalio Paul. 2002. *Harmony: Radical Taoism Gently Applied*. Trafford Publishing.

19 Laozi. 2016. *Tao Te Ching*. Translated by James Legge. Createspace Independent Publishing Platform.

20 Castro, D. 2019. "Europe will be left behind if it focuses on ethics and not keeping pace in AI development." *Euronews*, August 7. https://www.euronews.com/2019/08/07/europe-will-be-left-behind-if-it-focuses-on-ethics-and-not-keeping-pace-in-ai-development; Garcia, D. C. 2024. "EU-Inc calls on new Commission to turn the idea of a single pan-European startup entity into reality." *EU-Startups*, December 4. https://www.eu-startups.com/2024/12/eu-inc-calls-on-new-commission-turn-the-idea-of-a-single-pan-european-startup-entity-into-reality/.

21 Bertuzzi, Luca. 2025. "EU Commission eyes pausing AI Act's entry into application." *MLex*, May 26. https://www.mlex.com/mlex/articles/2344845/eu-commission-eyes-pausing-ai-act-s-entry-into-application.

22 Laozi. 1995. *Tao Te Ching – Verse 78*. Translated by S. Mitchell. Harper Perennial.

23 Song, W and Cao, H. 2022. "Yin and Yang Cover the Universe as a Whole." *Journal of Alternative Complementary and Integrative Medicine* 8: 299. https://doi.org/ 10.24966/ACIM-7562/100299.

24 Laozi. 1995. *Tao Te Ching – Verse 78*. Translated by S. Mitchell. Harper Perennial.

25 Ibid.

26 Stewart, K. 2023. "Wu Wei – Equanimity." *Sydney Zen Centre*, April 6. https://szc.org.au/

wu-wei-equanimity/.

27   Calciano, D. 2025. "Leadership and the Art of Wu Wei: Mastering Effortless Action for
      Greater Success." LinkedIn, February 20. https://www.linkedin.com/pulse/leadership-ar
      t-wu-wei-mastering-effortless-action-greater-calciano-tf1vc/.

28   AIATSIS. (n.d.). "First Peoples of Australia." Australian Institute of Aboriginal and
      Torres Strait Islander Studies. https://aiatsis.gov.au/explore/first-peoples-australia, visited
      January 21, 2025.

29   Department of Climate Change, Energy, the Environment and Water. (2021). "Country
      and Connections. Australia State of the Environment 2021." https://soe.dcceew.gov.au/
      indigenous/environment/country-and-connections, visited March 25, 2025.

30   Yarn. (2025). "Dreamtime Stories: The Rainbow Serpent." https://www.yarn.com.au/
      blogs/yarn-in-the-community/dreamtime-stories-the-rainbow-serpent, visited January
      21, 2025; Kullilla Art. (2025). "Dreamtime Stories: The Rainbow Serpent." https://www.
      kullillaart.com.au/dreamtime-stories/The-Rainbow-Serpent, visited January 21, 2025;
      Aboriginal Art Australia. (2025). "The Rainbow Serpent." https://www.aboriginal-art-aus-
      tralia.com/aboriginal-art-library/rainbow-serpent/, visited January 21, 2025; Rainbow
      Serpent & The Blue Bird. (2020). "The Rainbow Serpent - Dreamtime Story." YouTube.
      https://www.youtube.com/watch?v=T8RA7-yktM0, visited January 21, 2025; Dreamtime.
      (2018). "The Rainbow Serpent Story." https://dreamtime.net.au/rainbow-serpent-story/.

31   Ormond-Parker, L., Corn, A., Fforde, C., Obata, K., & O'Sullivan, S. (Eds.). (2013).
      "Information Technology and Indigenous Communities." Australian Institute of Aboriginal
      and Torres Strait Islander Studies. https://aiatsis.gov.au/sites/default/files/research_pub/
      information-technology-indigenous-communities-ebook_3.pdf, visited March 26, 2025.

32   Yong, E. (2022). *An Immense World: How Animal Senses Reveal the Hidden Realms Around Us.*
      Random House.

33   Nagel, T. (1974). "What is it like to be a bat?" Philosophical Review, 83(4): 435–450.
      http://www.jstor.org/stable/2183914.

34   Lanza, R., & Berman, B. (2009). *Biocentrism: How Life and Consciousness Are the Keys to
      Understanding the True Nature of the Universe.* BenBella Books.

35   Greenwood, V. (2025). "The Ocean Teems with Networks of Interconnected Bacteria."
      Quanta Magazine. https://www.quantamagazine.org/the-ocean-teems-with-networks-o
      f-interconnected-bacteria-20250106/, visited January 21, 2025.

36   Williams, S. (2024). "Our bacteria are more personal than we thought, Stanford
      Medicine-led study shows." Stanford Medicine News Center. https://med.stanford.edu/
      news/all-news/2024/03/personal-microbiome.html, visited March 26, 2025.

37   Hou, K., Wu, ZX., Chen, XY. et al. (2022). "Microbiota in health and diseases." Sig
      Transduct Target Ther 7, 135. https://doi.org/10.1038/s41392-022-00974-4.

38   Kerne, A. (2001). "CollageMachine: A Model of 'Interface Ecology.'" [PhD Dissertation],
      Department of Computer Science, New York University. https://ecologylab.net/research/
      publications/andruidDissertationPublic.pdf, visited January 21, 2025.

Chapter 4

1   van Rijmenam, M. (2024). "Embracing the Future: The Rise of Superintelligence."
      The Digital Speaker. https://www.thedigitalspeaker.com/embracing-futur
      e-rise-superintelligence/, visited January 21, 2025.

2   van Rijmenam, M. (2024). "Enlightening AI: The Dawn of Photonic Computing." The

Digital Speaker. https://www.thedigitalspeaker.com/enlightening-ai-dawn-photonic-computing/, visited January 21, 2025.

3   Yudkowsky, E. (2008). "My Childhood Role Model." LessWrong. https://www.lesswrong.com/posts/3Jpchgy53D2gB5qdk/my-childhood-role-model, visited January 21, 2025.

4   van Rijmenam, M. (2024). "Embracing the Future: The Rise of Superintelligence." The Digital Speaker. https://www.thedigitalspeaker.com/embracing-future-rise-superintelligence/, visited January 21, 2025.

5   Turing, A. M. (1950). "Computing Machinery and Intelligence." Mind, LIX(236): 433–460, https://doi.org/10.1093/mind/LIX.236.433.

6   Lim, M. (2018). "History of AI Winters." Actuaries Digital. https://www.actuaries.digital/2018/09/05/history-of-ai-winters/, visited January 21, 2025.

7   Vaswani, A., Shazeer, N., Parmar, N., Uszkoreit, J., Jones, L., Gomez, A. N., Kaiser, Ł., & Polosukhin, I. (2017). "Attention is All You Need." arXiv preprint, https://arxiv.org/abs/1706.03762.

8   Zhou, X., Qiao, Y., Xu, Z., Wang, T., Chen, Z., et al. (n.d.). "Genesis Embodied AI." https://genesis-embodied-ai.github.io/, visited January 21, 2025.

9   DeepMind. (2024). "Veo 2." https://deepmind.google/technologies/veo/veo-2/, visited January 21, 2025.

10 van Rijmenam, M. (2021). "5 Technology Trends for 2022: The Year of Decentralisation." The Digital Speaker. https://www.thedigitalspeaker.com/5-technology-trends-2022-year-of-decentralisation/, visited January 21, 2025.

11 Team Cybernative (2024). "How Generative AI is Transforming the Art and Design World. Cybernative." https://www.cybernativetech.com/ai-transforming-art-design-world/, visited January 21, 2025.

12 Felin, T., & Holweg, M. (2024). "AI Thinks Differently Than People Do. Here's Why That Matters." Harvard Business Review. https://hbr.org/2024/12/ai-thinks-differently-than-people-do-heres-why-that-matters, visited January 21, 2025.

13 TheAIGRID. (2024, December 15). Ilya Sutskever Just Revealed The Next BIG THINGS In AI (Superintelligence Explained). YouTube. https://www.youtube.com/watch?v=8KL47xLD-yg, visited January 21, 2025.

14 Vaughan-Nichols, S. J. 2025. "Some signs of AI model collapse begin to reveal themselves." *The Register*, May 27. https://www.theregister.com/2025/05/27/opinion_column_ai_model_collapse/.

15 van Rijmenam, M. 2023. "The Danger of AI Model Collapse: When LLMs are Trained on Synthetic Data." The Digital Speaker, June 28. https://www.thedigitalspeaker.com/danger-of-ai-model-collapse-llms-trained-synthetic-data/.

16 van Rijmenam, M. (2024). "Agentic AI: The End of Organizations as We Know It." *The Digital Speaker*. https://www.thedigitalspeaker.com/agentic-ai-end-organizations-as-we-know/, visited January 21, 2025.

17 van Rijmenam, M. (2022). "What is Synthetic Media: The Ultimate Guide." The Digital Speaker. https://www.thedigitalspeaker.com/what-is-synthetic-media-ultimate-guide/, visited January 21, 2025.

18 ARC Prize. (n.d.). "ARC Prize." https://arcprize.org/arc, visited January 21, 2025.

19 Koundinya, S. (2025). "OpenAI Just Pulled a Theranos with o3." Analytics India Magazine. https://analyticsindiamag.com/ai-news-updates/openai-just-pulled-

a-theranos-with-o3/, visited January 21, 2025.

20   Metz, R. (2024). "OpenAI Scale Ranks Progress Toward 'Human-Level' Problem Solving." Bloomberg News. https://www.bloomberg.com/news/articles/2024-07-11/openai-set s-levels-to-track-progress-toward-superintelligent-ai, visited January 21, 2025.

21   Sakana AI. (2024). "The AI Scientist: Towards Fully Automated Open-Ended Scientific Discovery." https://sakana.ai/ai-scientist/, visited January 21, 2025.

22   van Rijmenam, M. (2023). "What is Organoid Intelligence and How Will It Change the Future." The Digital Speaker. https://www.thedigitalspeaker.com/organoid-intelligenc e-change-future/, visited January 21, 2025.

23   van Rijmenam, M., & Logue, D. (2020). "Revising the 'science of the organisation': theoris- ing AI agency and actorhood." Innovation, 23(1), 127–144. https://doi.org/10.1080/1447 9338.2020.1816833.

24   Chivers, T., & Hammer, M. (2025). "Tech leaders warn against 'Manhattan Project' race for AI superintelligence." Semafor. https://www.semafor.com/article/03/17/2025/ tech-leaders-warn-against-manhattan-project-style-super-intelligent-ai-race, visited March 26, 2025.

25   Hendrycks, D., Schmidt, E., & Wang, A. (2024). "Superintelligence Strategy: Expert Version." https://drive.google.com/file/d/1JVPc3ObMP1L2a53T5LA1xxKXM6DA- wEiC/view, visited March 27, 2025.

26   Kang, C. (2025). "Trump Administration's New AI Policies Spark Debate Among Tech Leaders." The New York Times. https://www.nytimes.com/2025/03/24/technology/ trump-ai-regulation.html, visited March 26, 2025.

27   Plumb, T. (2024). "2025: The Year 'Invisible' AI Agents Will Integrate into Enterprise Hierarchies." VentureBeat. https://venturebeat.com/ai/2025-the-year-invisible-ai-agent s-will-integrate-into-enterprise-hierarchies/, visited January 21, 2025.

28   Automate. (n.d.). "Joseph Engelberger and Unimate: Pioneering the Robotics Revolution." https://www.automate.org/robotics/engelberger/joseph-engelberger-unimate, visited January 21, 2025.

29   van Rijmenam, M. (2022). "Welcome to the Jetsons: How Robots Will Change Society." The Digital Speaker. https://www.thedigitalspeaker.com/ welcome-jetsons-robots-change-society/, visited January 21, 2025.

30   Daniel, I. (2024). "Data-Driven Hotel Staffing: The Tools & Metrics You Need for Accurate Labour Forecasting." Deputy. https://www.deputy.com/au/blog/data-driven-hotel-staffin g-the-tools-metrics-you-need-for-accurate-labour-forecasting, visited January 21, 2025.

31   Barten, M. (2024). "The Housekeeping Robots Driving Hospitality Industry Innovation." Revfine.com. https://www.revfine.com/housekeeping-robots/, visited January 21, 2025.

32   van Rijmenam, M. (2024, February 8). Humanoids With AI: The Dawn of a New Workforce Species. The Digital Speaker. https://www.thedigitalspeaker.com/ humanoids-ai-llm-workforce/, visited January 21, 2025.

33   Bennett, H. (2024). "9 Ingenious Rescue Robots Set to Become the Lifesavers of Tomorrow." BBC Science Focus Magazine. https://www.sciencefocus.com/ future-technology/rescue-robots, visited January 21, 2025.

34   Diamandis, P. H. (2024). "Humanoid Robots are Here: Soon Millions, Then Billions of Them." https://www.diamandis.com/blog/abundance-41-millions-an d-billions-humanoid-robots, visited January 21, 2025.

35   BMW Group. (2024). "Humanoid Robots for BMW Group Plant Spartanburg."
      https://www.bmwgroup.com/en/news/general/2024/humanoid-robots.html, visited
      January 21, 2025.

36   Chen, C. (2025). "China's EV giants are betting big on humanoid robots." MIT
      Technology Review. https://www.technologyreview.com/2025/02/14/1111920/
      chinas-electric-vehicle-giants-pivot-humanoid-robots/, visited March 26, 2025.

37   Somers, J. (2024). "A Revolution in How Robots Learn." The New Yorker. https://
      www.newyorker.com/magazine/2024/12/02/a-revolution-in-how-robots-learn, visited
      January 21, 2025.

38   EngineAI Robotics Technology. (2024). "Meet EngineAI All-new Robotics SE01,
      Successfully Overcomes the Challenge of Natural Gait in Humanoid Robots for the
      First Time." GlobeNewswire. https://www.globenewswire.com/news-release/2024/
      10/25/2969601/0/en/Meet-EngineAI-All-new-Robotics-SE01-Successfully-Overc
      omes-the-Challenge-of-Natural-Gait-in-Humanoid-Robots-for-the-First-Time.html, visited
      January 21, 2025.

39   van Rijmenam, M. (2024). "Is the Future of Robotics Powered by Water?" LinkedIn.
      https://www.linkedin.com/posts/markvanrijmenam_is-the-future-of-robotics-powered-b
      y-water-activity-7272392487669772288-1coM/, visited January 21, 2025.

40   SoftBank Robotics America. (n.d.). "For better business just add Pepper." https://us.soft-
      bankrobotics.com/pepper, visited January 21, 2025.

41   Ewing-Chow, D. (2024). "Here Are Five Global Restaurants Staffed by Robot Chefs."
      Forbes. https://www.forbes.com/sites/daphneewingchow/2024/03/31/here-are-five-globa
      l-restaurants-staffed-by-robot-chefs/, visited January 21, 2025.

42   Katsuno, H. & White, D. (2023). "The Japanese Pursuit of Human–Robot
      Companionship." Current History, 122(847): 308–313. https://doi.org/10.1525/
      curh.2023.122.847.308.

43   Che, C. (2019). "Robot Dialectics: Western Revolutionaries versus Japanese Companions."
      Oxford Political Review. https://oxfordpoliticalreview.com/2019/03/22/robot-dialectic
      s-western-revolutionaries-versus-japanese-companions/, visited March 25, 2025.

44   van Rijmenam, M. (2024). "Genesis: A Breakthrough in Digital Physics." The Digital
      Speaker. https://www.thedigitalspeaker.com/genesis-breakthrough-digital-physics/, visited
      January 21, 2025.

45   Zhou, X., Qiao, Y., Xu, Z., Wang, T., Chen, Z., et al. (n.d.). "Genesis Embodied AI."
      https://genesis-embodied-ai.github.io/, visited January 21, 2025.

46   Engineered Arts Ltd. (n.d.). "Ameca: The Future Face of Robotics." https://engineere-
      darts.com/robot/ameca/, visited January 21, 2025.

47   Saba, Y., & Makary, A. (2024). "Elon Musk: 10 Billion Humanoid Robots by 2040 at $20K-
      $25K Each." Reuters. https://www.reuters.com/technology/elon-musk-10-billion-humano
      id-robots-by-2040-20k-25k-each-2024-10-29/, visited January 21, 2025.

48   Somers, J. (2024). "A Revolution in How Robots Learn." The New Yorker. https://
      www.newyorker.com/magazine/2024/12/02/a-revolution-in-how-robots-learn, visited
      January 21, 2025.

49   Feynman, R. P. (1981). "Simulating Physics with Computers." International Journal of
      Theoretical Physics, 21: 467–488. https://doi.org/10.1007/BF02650179.

50   Lanza, R., & Berman, B. (2009). *Biocentrism: How Life and Consciousness Are the Keys to
      Understanding the True Nature of the Universe*. BenBella Books.

51   California Institute of Technology. (2022). "Proving that Quantum Entanglement is Real." https://www.caltech.edu/about/news/proving-that-quantum-entanglement-is-real, visited January 21, 2025.

52   Soller, H., Mohr, N., Heid, A., & Gschwendtner, M. (2024). "Quantum sensing's untapped potential: Insights for leaders." McKinsey & Company. https://www.mckinsey.com/capabilities/mckinsey-digital/our-insights/quantum-sensings-untapped-potential-insights-for-leaders, viewed March 31, 2025.

53   Dargan, J. (2024). "Quantum Brilliance CEO: Diamonds Shine as Quantum Technology Alternative." The Quantum Insider. https://thequantuminsider.com/2024/10/01/quantum-brilliance-ceo-diamonds-shine-as-quantum-technology-alternative/, viewed March 31, 2025.

54   Dailing, P. (2024). "New diamond bonding technique a breakthrough for quantum devices." Pritzker School of Molecular Engineering, The University of Chicago. https://pme.uchicago.edu/news/new-diamond-bonding-technique-breakthrough-quantum-devices, viewed March 31, 2025.

55   QuEra Computing. (2025). Majorana. https://www.quera.com/glossary/majorana#:~:text=A%20Majorana%20fermion%2C%20or%20Majorana,tolerant%20quantum%20computing%20(FTQC), visited March 26, 2025.

56   Iqbal, M., Tantivasadakarn, N., Verresen, R. et al. (2024). "Non-Abelian topological order and anyons on a trapped-ion processor." Nature 626: 505–511. https://doi.org/10.1038/s41586-023-06934-4.

57   Bolgar, C. (2025). "Microsoft's Majorana 1 chip carves new path for quantum computing." Microsoft Source. https://news.microsoft.com/source/features/ai/microsofts-majorana-1-chip-carves-new-path-for-quantum-computing/, visited March 26, 2025.

58   Padavic-Callaghan, K. (2025). "Microsoft under fire for claiming it has a new quantum computer." New Scientist. https://www.newscientist.com/article/2471461-microsoft-under-fire-for-claiming-it-has-a-new-quantum-computer/, visited March 26, 2025.

59   Bradley, A. (2025). "China achieves quantum supremacy claim with new chip 1 quadrillion times faster than the most powerful supercomputers." Live Science. https://www.livescience.com/technology/computing/china-achieves-quantum-supremacy-claim-with-new-chip-1-quadrillion-times-faster-than-the-most-powerful-supercomputers, visited March 26, 2025.

60   Liu, M., Shaydulin, R., Niroula, P., et al. (2025). "Certified randomness using a trapped-ion quantum processor." Nature, 640: 343–348. https://doi.org/10.1038/s41586-025-08737-1.

61   Stephens, D., & Law, S. (2024). "Proving that Quantum Entanglement is Real." BBC News. https://www.bbc.com/news/articles/c79ngx01qvro, visited January 21, 2025.

62   Dietz, M., Henke, N., Moon, J., Backes, J., Pautasso, L., & Sadeque, Z. (2020). "How Quantum Computing Could Change Financial Services." McKinsey & Company. https://www.mckinsey.com/industries/financial-services/our-insights/how-quantum-computing-could-change-financial-services, visited January 21, 2025.

63   Savoie, C. (2021). "How Quantum Computers Could Cut Millions of Miles from Supply Chains and Transform Logistics." Forbes. https://www.forbes.com/sites/forbestech-council/2021/02/05/how-quantum-computers-could-cut-millions-of-miles-from-supply-chains-and-transform-logistics/, visited January 21, 2025.

64   Katwala, A. (2025). "The Quantum Apocalypse Is Coming. Be Very Afraid." WIRED. https://www.wired.com/story/q-day-apocalypse-quantum-computers-encryption/, visited

March 25, 2025.

65   van Rijmenam, M. (2023). "Encryption and Quantum Computing – Fighting the
     Big Crunch of 2025." The Digital Speaker. https://www.thedigitalspeaker.com/
     encryption-quantum-computing-fighting-big-crunch-2025/, visited January 21, 2025.

66   Bentley, P. (2023). "How the 'Millennium Bug' Cost the World £240bn: A Short History of
     Computer Glitch Disasters." BBC Science Focus. https://www.sciencefocus.com/science/
     how-do-computers-get-bugs, visited January 21, 2025.

67   Laio. (2024). "European MPs Sound Alarm over Quantum Computing's Encryption
     Threat." Innovation Origins. https://innovationorigins.com/en/european-mps-sound-alar
     m-over-quantum-computings-encryption-threat/, visited January 21, 2025.

68   Australian Cyber Security Centre. (2024). "Guidelines for Cryptography." Cyber.gov.au.
     https://www.cyber.gov.au/resources-business-and-government/essential-cyber-security/
     ism/cyber-security-guidelines/guidelines-cryptography, visited January 21, 2025.

69   van Rijmenam, M. (2023). "Encryption and Quantum Computing – Fighting the
     Big Crunch of 2025." The Digital Speaker. https://www.thedigitalspeaker.com/
     encryption-quantum-computing-fighting-big-crunch-2025/, visited January 21, 2025.

70   Gidney, C. 2025. "How to factor 2048 bit RSA integers with less than a million noisy
     qubits." *arXiv*, May 21. https://arxiv.org/abs/2505.15917.

71   Peel, M. (2024). "US Nears Milestone in Race to Prevent Quantum Hacking." Financial
     Times. https://www.ft.com/content/f602b685-8226-42b4-9336-e488c63c37bf, visited
     January 21, 2025.

72   Cloudflare. (2024). "Cloudflare Radar 2024 Year in Review." https://radar.cloudflare.com/
     year-in-review/2024, visited January 21, 2025.

73   Wilkins, A. (2024). "Quantum Internet Draws Near Thanks to Entangled Memory
     Breakthroughs." New Scientist. https://www.newscientist.com/article/24
     31464-quantum-internet-draws-near-thanks-to-entangled-memory-breakthroughs/, visited
     January 21, 2025.

74   van Rijmenam, M. (2024). "Top Ten Technology Trends for 2024." The Digital Speaker.
     https://www.thedigitalspeaker.com/ten-technology-trends-2024/, visited January 21, 2025.

75   Google DeepMind. (2024). "AlphaQubit: Google's Research on Quantum Error
     Correction." The Keyword. https://blog.google/technology/google-deepmind/
     alphaqubit-quantum-error-correction/, visited January 21, 2025.

76   van Rijmenam, M. (2023). "Neuromorphic Computing and How It Will Enable
     Hyper-Realistic Generative AI." The Digital Speaker. https://www.thedigitalspeaker.com/
     neuromorphic-computing-hyper-realistic-generative-ai/, visited January 21, 2025.

77   Woodford, J. (2023). "Supercomputer That Simulates Entire Human Brain Will Switch On
     in 2024." New Scientist. https://www.newscientist.com/article/2408015-supercomputer-th
     at-simulates-entire-human-brain-will-switch-on-in-2024/, visited January 21, 2025.

78   van Rijmenam, M. (2023). "Biological Computing: Harnessing Life's Code to Power the
     Future." The Digital Speaker. https://www.thedigitalspeaker.com/biological-computin
     g-lifes-code-power-future/, visited January 21, 2025.

79   Brown, C. (2024). "Quantum Computing for Emergency Response Optimization."
     Augmented Qubit. https://augmentedqubit.com/optimizing-emergency-response-resourc
     e-allocation-using-quantum-computing/, visited January 21, 2025.

80   Baratz, A. (2023). "Emergency Management Today: Quantum Computing Is a 21st

Century Solution for 21st Century Problems." Federal News Network. https://feder-alnewsnetwork.com/commentary/2023/07/emergency-management-today-quantu m-computing-is-a-21st-century-solution-for-21st-century-problems/, visited January 21, 2025.

81   ICV TA&K. (2023). "Quantum Computing Is Attacking the 21st Century…" ICV TA&K. https://www.icvtank.com/newsinfo/858145.html, visited January 21, 2025.

82   van Rijmenam, M., & Ryan, P. (2018). *Blockchain: Transforming Your Business and Our World.* Routledge.

83   van Rijmenam, M. (2024). "Ten Technology Trends for 2025: The Year of Reckoning." The Digital Speaker. https://www.thedigitalspeaker.com/ten-technology-trends-2025/, visited January 21, 2025.

84   van Rijmenam, M. (2019). "How Security Tokens Could Change Liquidity and Transform the World's Economy." The Digital Speaker. https://www.thedigitalspeaker.com/ security-tokens-change-liquidity-economy/, visited January 21, 2025.

85   Banon, J. (2025). "The Computable Economy Will Unlock a New Economic Order." Cointelegraph. https://cointelegraph.com/news/the-computable-economy-will-unlock-a-new-economic-order, visited January 21, 2025.

86   Karayaneva, N. 2024. "BlackRock's $10 Trillion Tokenization Vision: The Future Of Real World Assets." *Forbes*, March 21. https://www.forbes.com/sites/ nataliakarayaneva/2024/03/21/blackrocks-10-trillion-tokenization-vision-the -future-of-real-world-assets/.

87   Armstrong, B. (2025). "AIs are now paying other AIs with crypto". [X status]. https://x. com/brian_armstrong/status/1829623778726592804, visited January 21, 2025.

88   van Rijmenam, M. (2022). "NFTs and Luxury Brands: How Blockchain Technology is Transforming the Luxury Industry." The Digital Speaker. https://www.thedigitalspeaker. com/nft-luxury-brands-blockchain/, visited January 21, 2025.

89   Melinek, J. (2024). "Blockchain Tech Could Be the Answer to Uncovering Deepfakes and Validating Content." TechCrunch. https://techcrunch.com/2024/03/14/blockchain-tec h-could-be-the-answer-to-uncovering-deepfakes-and-validating-content/, visited January 21, 2025.

90   Nguyen, J. T. (2023). "Revolutionizing Coffee Supply Chains: KAI Farm's Journey with Blockchain Technology." KAI Farm. https://kaifarm.uk/revolutionizing-coffe e-supply-chains-kai-farms-journey-with-blockchain-technology/, visited January 21, 2025.

91   Supply Chain Today. (n.d.). Journey of Coffee – Blockchain Supply Chain Process. https:// www.supplychaintoday.com/journey-of-coffee-blockchain-supply-chain-process/, visited January 21, 2025.

92   Modula. (2022, January 18). Autonomous Mobile Robots (AMR): How They Work and How They Can Become Part of a Warehouse. https://www. modula.eu/blog/autonomous-mobile-robots-amr-how-they-work-and-how-the y-can-become-part-of-a-warehouse/, visited January 21, 2025.

93   Toolify.ai. (2024, February 11). Revolutionizing the Coffee Industry with AI and Blockchain. Toolify. https://www.toolify.ai/ai-news/revolutionizing-the-coffee-industr y-with-ai-and-blockchain-1095538, visited January 21, 2025.

94   Burke, J., & De Maere, J. (2024). The Post Web Thesis. Outlier Ventures. https://outlier-ventures.io/postweb/, visited January 21, 2025.

95   van Rijmenam, M. (2023, July 26). Unlocking Reality: The Spatial Web's Transformative

Impact. The Digital Speaker. https://www.thedigitalspeaker.com/unlocking-realit y-spatial-web-transformative-impact/, visited January 21, 2025.

96 van Rijmenam, M. (2024, December 20). Genesis: A Breakthrough in Digital Physics. The Digital Speaker. https://www.thedigitalspeaker.com/genesis-breakthrough-digital-physics/, visited January 21, 2025.

97 van Rijmenam, M. (2024, August 22). Metaverse 2.0 – The Hyper-Realistic, AI-Driven Spatial Internet. The Digital Speaker. https://www.thedigitalspeaker.com/metaverse-2-0-hyper-realistic-ai-driven-spatial-internet/, visited January 21, 2025.

98 Li, F.-F., & Johnson, J. (2024, September 15). The Future of AI is Here. YouTube – a16z. https://www.youtube.com/watch?v=vIXfYFB7aBI, visited January 21, 2025.

99 Strickland, E. (2024, December 12). AI Godmother Fei-Fei Li Has a Vision for Computer Vision. IEEE Spectrum. https://spectrum.ieee.org/fei-fei-li-world-labs, visited January 21, 2025.

100 Compton, J. W. (2024, September 10). The Camera's Eye: Exploring Various Angles and Shots through AI. https://johnwolfecompton.com/the-cameras-eye-exploring-various-angles-and-shots-through-ai/, visited January 21, 2025.

101 Failes, I. (2021, November 10). *So…you need a humanoid robot in your film? What are your options? befores & afters*. https://beforesandafters.com/2021/11/10/so-you-need-a-humanoid-robot-in-your-film-what-are-your-options/, visited January 21, 2025.

102 Ball, M. (2024, September 24). The Metaverse: Building the Spatial Internet. Liveright; Fully Revised and Updated Edition.

103 van Rijmenam, M. (2024, August 22). Metaverse 2.0 – The Hyper-Realistic, AI-Driven Spatial Internet. The Digital Speaker. https://www.thedigitalspeaker.com/metaverse-2-0-hyper-realistic-ai-driven-spatial-internet/, visited January 21, 2025.

104 Z. Chen et al., "NeuRBF: A Neural Fields Representation with Adaptive Radial Basis Functions," in 2023 IEEE/CVF International Conference on Computer Vision (ICCV), Paris, France, 2023, pp. 4159-4171, doi: 10.1109/ICCV51070.2023.00386.

105 van Rijmenam, M. (2023, August 1). The Convergence of AI and the Metaverse: A Futurist's Perspective. The Digital Speaker. https://www.thedigitalspeaker.com/convergence-ai-metaverse-futurists-perspective/, visited January 21, 2025.

106 Wiltschko, A. (2024, October 29). Scent Teleportation Update: We Did It! Osmo. https://www.osmo.ai/blog/update-scent-teleportation-we-did-it, visited January 21, 2025.

107 Schwartz, E. H. (2024, October 31). You Could Start Smelling the Roses from Far Away Using AI. TechRadar. https://www.techradar.com/computing/artificial-intelligence/you-could-start-smelling-the-roses-from-far-away-using-ai, visited January 21, 2025.

108 van Rijmenam, M. (2023, June 7). Augmenting Urban Landscapes: How AR and Generative AI Will Change Your City. The Digital Speaker. https://www.thedigitalspeaker.com/augmenting-urban-landscapes-ar-generative-ai-change-city/, visited January 21, 2025.

109 van Rijmenam, M. (2022). Step into the Metaverse: How the Immersive Internet Will Unlock a Trillion-Dollar Social Economy. Wiley.

110 Abhayaratna, J., Daemen, E., Janowicz, K., Parsons, E., Smith, R., & Verschoor, F. (2021, May 27). The Responsible Use of Spatial Data. W3C Interest Group Note. https://www.w3.org/TR/responsible-use-spatial/, visited January 21, 2025.

111 van Rijmenam, M. (2022). Step into the Metaverse: How the Immersive Internet Will

Unlock a Trillion-Dollar Social Economy. Wiley.

112 van Rijmenam, M. (2021, October 20). The Future of Computing: How Brain-Computer Interfaces Will Change Our Relationship with Computers. The Digital Speaker. https://www.thedigitalspeaker.com/brain-computer-interfaces-change-relationship-computers/, visited January 21, 2025.

113 Kawala-Sterniuk A, Browarska N, Al-Bakri A, Pelc M, Zygarlicki J, Sidikova M, Martinek R, Gorzelanczyk EJ. Summary of over Fifty Years with Brain-Computer Interfaces-A Review. Brain Sci. 2021 Jan 3;11(1):43. doi: 10.3390/brainsci11010043. PMID: 33401571; PMCID: PMC7824107.

114 van Rijmenam, M. (2023, September 20). The Mind-Bending World of Brain-Computer Interfaces: How Technology Will Change Humanity. The Digital Speaker. https://www.thedigitalspeaker.com/mind-bending-world-brain-computer-interfaces-humanity/, visited January 21, 2025.

115 Mole, B. (2024, May 28). Neuralink Rival Sets Brain-Chip Record with 4,096 Electrodes on Human Brain. Ars Technica. https://arstechnica.com/science/2024/05/neuralink-rival-sets-brain-chip-record-with-4096-electrodes-on-human-brain/, visited January 21, 2025.

116 Brueck, H. (2024, February 8). Neuralink is less advanced than these 4 brain-computer devices. See Elon Musk's competition. Business Insider. https://www.businessinsider.com/neuralink-competition-elon-musk-bci-competitors-2024-2, visited January 21, 2025.

117 Willyard, C. (2024, April 19). Beyond Neuralink: Meet the Other Companies Developing Brain-Computer Interfaces. MIT Technology Review. https://www.technologyreview.com/2024/04/19/1091505/companies-brain-computer-interfaces/, visited January 21, 2025.

118 van Rijmenam, M. (2024, February 21). Mind Over Mouse: Neuralink's Leap into Thought-Controlled Computing. The Digital Speaker. https://www.thedigitalspeaker.com/mind-over-mouse-neuralink-leap-thought-controlled-computing/, visited January 21, 2025.

119 van Rijmenam, M. (2024, April 26). The Race to Revolutionise Brain-Computer Interfaces. The Digital Speaker. https://www.thedigitalspeaker.com/race-revolutionise-brain-computer-interfaces/, visited January 21, 2025.

120 Nosta, J. (2024, September 19). Redefining Vision: Neuralink and the Future of Perception. Psychology Today. https://www.psychologytoday.com/au/blog/the-digital-self/202409/redefining-vision-neuralink-and-the-future-of-perception, visited January 21, 2025.

121 Winkler, R. 2025. "Apple to Support Brain-Implant Control of Its Devices." The Wall Street Journal, May 13. https://www.wsj.com/tech/apple-brain-computer-interface-9ec69919.

122 University of South Florida. (2018, October 30). Mind & Machine: Students to Compete in USF's First Brain-Drone Race. USF News. https://www.usf.edu/news/2018/mind-machine-students-to-compete-usf-first-ever-brain-drone-race.aspx, visited January 21, 2025.

123 Jecker, N. S., & Ko, A. (2022, December 2). Brain-computer interfaces could allow soldiers to control weapons with their thoughts and turn off their fear – but the ethics of neurotechnology lags behind the science. The Conversation. https://theconversation.com/brain-computer-interfaces-could-allow-soldiers-to-control-weapons-with-their-thoughts-and-turn-off-their-fear-but-the-ethics-of-neurotechnology-lags-behind-the-science-194017, visited January 21, 2025.

124 van Rijmenam, M. (2021, October 20). The Future of Computing: How Brain-Computer Interfaces Will Change Our Relationship with Computers. The Digital Speaker. https://www.thedigitalspeaker.com/brain-computer-interfaces-change-relationship-computers/,

visited January 21, 2025.

125 Rosso, C. (2024, April 3). Brain-Computer Interface Enables Mind-Control Gaming. Psychology Today. https://www.psychologytoday.com/intl/blog/the-future-brain/202404/brain-computer-interface-enables-mind-control-gaming, visited January 21, 2025.

126 Genser, J., Damianos, S., & Yuste, R. (2024, April). Safeguarding Brain Data: Assessing the Privacy Practices of Consumer Neurotechnology Companies. Neurorights Foundation. https://www.perseus-strategies.com/wp-content/uploads/2024/04/FINAL_Consumer_Neurotechnology_Report_Neurorights_Foundation_April-1.pdf, visited January 21, 2025.

127 Colorado General Assembly. (2024). House Bill 24-1058: Protect Privacy of Biological Data. https://leg.colorado.gov/sites/default/files/documents/2024A/bills/2024a_1058_01.pdf, visited January 21, 2025.

128 Brain-Computer Interface Lab. (n.d.). Home. Duke-NUS Medical School. https://www.bcilabsg.com/, visited January 21, 2025.

129 Lindquist, S. B. (2024, December 17). Mayo Clinic Neurology AI Program Tests Platform to Detect Brain Diseases. Mayo Clinic News Network. https://newsnetwork.mayoclinic.org/discussion/mayo-clinic-neurology-ai-program-tests-platform-to-detect-brain-diseases/, visited January 21, 2025.

130 van Rijmenam, M. (2024, December 19). 3D Printing: Creating the Future, Layer by Layer. The Digital Speaker. https://www.thedigitalspeaker.com/3d-printing-future-layer-by-layer/, visited January 21, 2025.

131 Katwala, A. (2021, June 10). This 3D-printed house is made entirely from mud. WIRED. https://www.wired.com/story/tecla-3d-printed-house/, visited January 21, 2025.

132 Garcia, E. (2024, August 8). World's Largest 3D-Printed Neighborhood Nears Completion in Texas. Reuters. https://www.reuters.com/world/us/worlds-largest-3d-printed-neighborhood-nears-completion-texas-2024-08-08/, visited January 21, 2025.

133 Castro Matias, O. (n.d.). Airbus Defence & Space Uses 3D Printing for Satellite Parts. EOS GmbH. https://www.eos.info/industries/customer-success-stories/airbus-space-satellite-titanium-brackets, visited January 21, 2025.

134 Rolls-Royce. (2018, October 11). 3-D Printed Parts and New Materials Help Rolls-Royce to Engine Test Success. https://www.rolls-royce.com/media/press-releases/2018/11-10-2018-3-d-printed-parts-and-new-materials-help-rolls-royce-to-engine-test-success.aspx, visited January 21, 2025.

135 NASA. (n.d.). 3D Printing Technologies. NASA Technology Transfer Portal. https://technology.nasa.gov/tags/3d-printing, visited January 21, 2025.

136 Birrell, I. (2017, February 19). 3D-printed prosthetic limbs: the next revolution in medicine. The Guardian. https://www.theguardian.com/technology/2017/feb/19/3d-printed-prosthetic-limbs-revolution-in-medicine, visited January 21, 2025.

137 Liszewski, A. 2025. "Philips will let you fix your trimmer with 3D printable parts and accessories." *The Verge*, May 12. https://www.theverge.com/news/665187/philips-fixables-3d-printing-personal-health-trimmer-oneblade-prura-research-printables

138 University of Nottingham. (2024, May 14). An easy pill to swallow – new 3D printing research paves way for personalised medication. https://www.nottingham.ac.uk/news/an-easy-pill-to-swallow-new-3d-printing-research-paves-way-for-personalised-medication, visited January 21, 2025.

139 Werner, J. (2024, July 15). Not Just a Maker Space: Fab Labs Spark Innovation Worldwide.

Forbes. https://www.forbes.com/sites/johnwerner/2024/07/15/not-just-a-maker-space-fab-labs-spark-innovation-worldwide/, visited January 21, 2025.

140 Kohtala, Cindy. (2016). Making Sustainability: How Fab Labs Address Environmental Sustainability.

141 Thomas-Sam, A., & Lorigan, M. (2024, November 4). 3D-printed guns on rise in Australia, with seizures of lethal firearms up across nation. ABC News. https://www.abc.net.au/news/2024-11-04/3d-printed-guns-rising-australia-semi-automatic/104538082, visited January 21, 2025.

142 Barton, C., & Brownlee, C. (2024, December 11). Luigi Mangione Allegedly Had a 3D-Printed Gun. Why Are They Legal? Rolling Stone. https://www.rollingstone.com/politics/politics-features/ghost-guns-explained-luigi-mangione-unitedhealthcare-1235209860/, visited January 21, 2025.

143 Thomas-Sam, A., & Lorigan, M. (2024, November 4). 3D-Printed Guns on Rise in Australia, with Seizures of Lethal Firearms Up Across Nation. ABC News. https://www.abc.net.au/news/2024-11-04/3d-printed-guns-rising-australia-semi-automatic/104538082, visited January 21, 2025.

144 Verma AS, Agrahari S, Rastogi S, Singh A. Biotechnology in the realm of history. J Pharm Bioallied Sci. 2011 Jul;3(3):321-3. doi: 10.4103/0975-7406.84430. PMID: 21966150; PMCID: PMC3178936.

145 Metz, C. (2024, April 22). Generative A.I. Arrives in the Gene Editing World of CRISPR. The New York Times. https://www.nytimes.com/2024/04/22/technology/generative-ai-gene-editing-crispr.html, visited January 21, 2025.

146 Robinson, N. (2024, December 16). AI Will Pave the Way for Precision Medicine, but Risks Loom Large. The Australian. https://www.theaustralian.com.au/health/ai-will-pave-the-way-for-precision-medicine-but-risks-loom-large/news-story/2ac35c2297e-fa378053246501844e81a, visited January 21, 2025.

147 Ruffolo, J. A., et al., (2024, April 22). Design of Highly Functional Genome Editors by Modeling the Universe of CRISPR-Cas Sequences. bioRxiv. https://www.biorxiv.org/content/10.1101/2024.04.22.590591v1, visited January 21, 2025.

148 Ledford, H. 2025. "World first: ultra-powerful CRISPR treatment trialled in a person." Nature, May 19. https://www.nature.com/articles/d41586-025-01593-z.

149 Doudna, J. (2024, November 26). Combining AI and CRISPR Will Be Transformational. WIRED. https://www.wired.com/story/combining-ai-and-crispr-will-be-transforma-tional/, visited January 21, 2025.

150 Li, W., Yin, Z., Li, X. et al. A hybrid quantum computing pipeline for real world drug discovery. Sci Rep 14, 16942 (2024). https://doi.org/10.1038/s41598-024-67897-8

151 Yu, S. (2023, October 20). Towards Using Quantum Computing to Speed Up Drug Development. Imperial News. https://www.imperial.ac.uk/news/248638/towards-using-quantum-computing-speed-drug/, visited January 21, 2025.

152 Harris, J. (2024, February 16). Blockchain and EDC: Securing Clinical Trial Data. ClinicalPURSUIT. https://clinicalpursuit.com/blockchain-and-edc-securing-clinical-trial-data/, visited January 21, 2025.

153 Maslove DM, Klein J, Brohman K, Martin P. Using Blockchain Technology to Manage Clinical Trials Data: A Proof-of-Concept Study. JMIR Med Inform. 2018 Dec 21;6(4):e11949. doi: 10.2196/11949. PMID: 30578196; PMCID: PMC6320404.

154 Carbonell, Pablo & Currin, Andrew & Jervis, Adrian & Rattray, Nicholas & Swainston, Neil

& Yan, Cunyu & Takano, Eriko & Breitling, Rainer. (2016). Bioinformatics for the synthetic biology of natural products: Integrating across the Design-Build-Test cycle. Natural product reports. 33. 10.1039/c6np00018e.

155 Hall, C. (2024, March 12). Tierra Biosciences Nabs $11M to Create New AI-Guided Proteins. TechCrunch. https://techcrunch.com/2024/03/12/protein-tierra-biosciences-11-4m/, visited January 21, 2025.

156 Google DeepMind. (2024, May 8). AlphaFold 3 Predicts the Structure and Interactions of All of Life's Molecules. The Keyword. https://blog.google/technology/ai/google-deepmind-isomorphic-alphafold-3-ai-model/, visited January 21, 2025.

157 van Rijmenam, M. (2023, August 10). The Dawning of Biohacking 2.0: Augmenting Our Biology. The Digital Speaker. https://www.thedigitalspeaker.com/dawning-biohacking-augmenting-biology/, visited January 21, 2025.

158 Noyes, M., & Lionnet, T. (2023, January 26). New Artificial Intelligence Tool Makes Speedy Gene Editing Possible. NYU Langone News. https://nyulangone.org/news/new-artificial-intelligence-tool-makes-speedy-gene-editing-possible, visited January 21, 2025.

159 Heath, R. (2024, March 13). The Road Map to AI's Next Level Could Be Nature. Axios. https://www.axios.com/2024/03/13/verses-ai-artificial-general-intelligence-chatgpt, visited January 21, 2025.

160 Learn Biomimicry. (2023, July 3). Bio-Inspired AI: When Generative AI and Biomimicry Overlap. Learn Biomimicry. https://www.learnbiomimicry.com/blog/bio-inspired-AI/, visited January 21, 2025.

161 Thompson, B. (2025, March 3). World's first "Synthetic Biological Intelligence" runs on living human cells. New Atlas. https://newatlas.com/brain/cortical-bioengineered-intelligence/, visited March 26, 2025.

162 van Rijmenam, M. (2023, January 11). What is Synthetic Biology - The Next Big Leap for Nature. The Digital Speaker. https://www.thedigitalspeaker.com/synthetic-biology-next-big-leap-nature/, visited January 21, 2025.

163 Rijssenbeek, J. Synthetic biology: supporting an anti-reductionist view of life. Synthese 205, 52 (2025). https://doi.org/10.1007/s11229-025-04913-y

164 Ginkgo Bioworks. (n.d.). Ginkgo Bioworks: The Organism Company. https://www.ginkgobioworks.com/, visited January 21, 2025.

165 Amyris. (n.d.). Amyris: Biotechnology Company. https://amyris.com, visited January 21, 2025.

166 Agro-industrie Recherches et Développements (ARD). (2010, January 20). BioAmber: World's First Renewable Succinic Acid Plant. https://www.a-r-d.fr/en/bioamber, visited January 21, 2025.

167 Liu, A.P., Appel, E.A., Ashby, P.D. et al. The living interface between synthetic biology and biomaterial design. Nat. Mater. 21, 390–397 (2022). https://doi.org/10.1038/s41563-022-01231-3

168 van Rijmenam, M. (2023, August 31). Unlocking Longevity: How the Quest for Immortality Will Be a Trillion-Dollar Industry. The Digital Speaker. https://www.thedigitalspeaker.com/unlocking-longevity-quest-immortality-trillion-dollar-industry/, visited January 21, 2025.

169 Regalado, A. (2025, January 17). OpenAI Has Created an AI Model for Longevity Science. MIT Technology Review. https://www.technologyreview.com/2025/01/17/1110086/openai-has-created-an-ai-model-for-longevity-science/, visited January 21, 2025.

170 Calico Life Sciences LLC. (n.d.). Calico: Advancing Science to Extend Human Lifespan. https://www.calicolabs.com/, visited January 21, 2025.

171 Unity Biotechnology. (n.d.). Developing Therapeutics to Extend Human Healthspan. https://unitybiotechnology.com/, visited January 21, 2025.

172 Howard M. Salis, Genetic circuitry boosts cell longevity, Science, 380, 6643, (343-343), (2023). https://doi.org/10.1126/science.adh4872

173 Lang, K. (2023, April 30). Longevity: Scientists Use Genetic Rewiring to Increase Cells' Lifespan. Medical News Today. https://www.medicalnewstoday.com/articles/longevity-scientists-use-genetic-wiring-to-increase-cells-lifespan, visited January 21, 2025.

174 University of California - San Diego. (2023, April 27). Scientists Slow Aging by Engineering Longevity in Cells. ScienceDaily. https://www.sciencedaily.com/releases/2023/04/230427173454.htm, visited January 21, 2025.

175 Lickerman, A. (2009, March 15). Overcoming the Fear of Death. ImagineMD. https://imaginemd.com/blog/overcoming-the-fear-of-death/, visited January 21, 2025.

176 Tikkanen, Tarja. (2008). The learning society as a greying society: perspectives to older workers and lifelong learning. https://www.researchgate.net/publication/215590899_The_learning_society_as_a_greying_society_perspectives_to_older_workers_and_lifelong_learning/, visited January 21, 2025

177 Brooks, D. (2023, August 25). The New Old Age. The Atlantic. https://www.theatlantic.com/culture/archive/2023/08/career-retirement-transition-academic-programs/675085/, visited January 21, 2025.

178 van Rijmenam, M. (2023, August 31). Unlocking Longevity: How the Quest for Immortality Will Be a Trillion-Dollar Industry. The Digital Speaker. https://www.thedigitalspeaker.com/unlocking-longevity-quest-immortality-trillion-dollar-industry/, visited January 21, 2025.

179 DeGeurin, M. (2024, February 16). Hackers Got Nearly 7 Million People's Data from 23andMe. The Firm Blamed Users in 'Very Dumb' Move. The Guardian. https://www.theguardian.com/technology/2024/feb/15/23andme-hack-data-genetic-data-selling-response, visited January 21, 2025.

Chapter 5

1   Milmo, D. (2024, December 27). 'Godfather of AI' Shortens Odds of the Technology Wiping Out Humanity Over Next 30 Years. The Guardian. https://www.theguardian.com/technology/2024/dec/27/godfather-of-ai-raises-odds-of-the-technology-wiping-out-humanity-over-next-30-years, visited January 21, 2025.

2   Special Collections & Archives Research Center. (n.d.). The Gutenberg Press. Treasures of the McDonald Collection. https://scarc.library.oregonstate.edu/omeka/exhibits/show/mcdonald/incunabula/gutenberg/, visited March 26, 2025.

3   Harari, Y. N. (2023). Nexus: Artificial Intelligence and the Future of Humanity. Harper.

4   Glusac, E. (2015, September 4). Remembering New York's Other Taxis of Tomorrow from Decades Past. USA Today. https://www.usatoday.com/story/travel/roadwarriorvoices/2015/09/04/remembering-new-yorks-other-taxis-of-tomorrow-from-decades-past/83307834/, visited January 21, 2025.

5   Standage, T. (2021, August 3). The Lost History of the Electric Car – and What It Tells Us

About the Future of Transport. The Guardian. https://www.theguardian.com/technology/2021/aug/03/lost-history-electric-car-future-transport, visited January 21, 2025.

6   Standage, T. (2021, August 3). The Lost History of the Electric Car – and What It Tells Us About the Future of Transport. The Guardian. https://www.theguardian.com/technology/2021/aug/03/lost-history-electric-car-future-transport, visited January 21, 2025.

7   UNFCCC. (n.d.). Global Car Industry Must Shift to Low Carbon to Survive: CDP. United Nations Framework Convention on Climate Change. https://unfccc.int/news/global-car-industry-must-shift-to-low-carbon-to-survive-cdp, visited January 21, 2025.

8   Kuijpers, M. (2020, October 7). The Most Important Invention of the 20th Century Keeps Us Alive but Is Killing the Environment. The Solution? Eat Less Meat. The Correspondent. https://thecorrespondent.com/733/the-most-important-invention-of-the-20th-century-keeps-us-alive-but-is-killing-the-environment-the-solution-eat-less-meat, visited January 21, 2025.

9   El Sayed MJ. Beirut Ammonium Nitrate Explosion: A Man-Made Disaster in Times of the COVID-19 Pandemic. Disaster Med Public Health Prep. 2022 Jun;16(3):1203-1207. doi: 10.1017/dmp.2020.451. Epub 2020 Nov 18. PMID: 33203497; PMCID: PMC7985624.

10 U.S. Environmental Protection Agency. (2021, March 22). Understanding the Impacts of Synthetic Nitrogen on Air and Water Quality Using Integrated Models. https://www.epa.gov/sciencematters/understanding-impacts-synthetic-nitrogen-air-and-water-quality-using-integrated, visited January 21, 2025.

11 U.S. Environmental Protection Agency. (n.d.). Understanding Global Warming Potentials. https://www.epa.gov/ghgemissions/understanding-global-warming-potentials, visited January 21, 2025.

12 Lorch, M. (2024, December 17). Mirror Life Forms May Sound Like Science Fiction, but Scientists Warn They Could Be Deadly to Humans and Destroy the Environment. The Conversation. https://theconversation.com/mirror-life-forms-may-sound-like-science-fiction-but-scientists-warn-they-could-be-deadly-to-humans-and-destroy-the-environment-246013, visited January 21, 2025.

13 Klarna. (2024, February 27). Klarna AI Assistant Handles Two-Thirds of Customer Service Chats in Its First Month. Klarna International. https://www.klarna.com/international/press/klarna-ai-assistant-handles-two-thirds-of-customer-service-chats-in-its-first-month/, visited January 21, 2025.

14 van Rijmenam, M. (2024, February 29). AI at Your Service: Klarna's Leap into AI-Enhanced Customer Care. The Digital Speaker. https://www.thedigitalspeaker.com/ai-service-klarna-customer-care/, visited January 21, 2025.

15 Edmonds, L. (2024, December 14). Klarna CEO Says the Company Stopped Hiring a Year Ago Because AI 'Can Already Do All of the Jobs'. Business Insider. https://www.businessinsider.com/klarna-ceo-sebastian-siemiatkowski-ai-jobs-2024-12, visited January 21, 2025.

16 Ivanova, I. 2025. "As Klarna flips from AI-first to hiring people again, a new landmark survey reveals most AI projects fail to deliver." *Fortune*, May 9. https://fortune.com/2025/05/09/klarna-ai-humans-return-on-investment/

17 Peters, J. 2025. "Duolingo will replace contract workers with AI." *The Verge*, April 28. https://www.theverge.com/news/657594/duolingo-ai-first-replace-contract-workers.

18 Temkin, M. (2025). "AI may already be shrinking entry-level jobs in tech, new research suggests." *TechCrunch*, May 27. https://techcrunch.com/2025/05/27/ai-may-already-be-shrinking-entry-level-jobs-in-tech-new-research-suggests/.

19   Rick, W. (2025). "The AI Hiring Pause Is Officially Here." *Bloomberg*, May 27. https://www.bloomberg.com/news/articles/2025-05-17/microsoft-layoffs-highlight-ai-driven-hiring-pauses.

20   Laney, D. (2025, April 9). Viral Shopify CEO Manifesto Says AI Now Mandatory for All Employees. Forbes. https://www.forbes.com/sites/douglaslaney/2025/04/09/selling-ai-strategy-to-employees-shopify-ceos-manifesto/, visited April 13, 2025.

21   Brandom, R. (2024, February 1). Google Cuts Off an $83 Million Ghost Labor Contract. Rest of World. https://restofworld.org/2024/exporter-google-appen-ai-search/, visited January 21, 2025.

22   BP. (2024, May 7). BP 1Q 2024 Results: Webcast Q&A Transcript. BP Global. https://www.bp.com/content/dam/bp/business-sites/en/global/corporate/pdfs/investors/bp-first-quarter-2024-results-qa-transcript.pdf, visited January 21, 2025.

23   van Rijmenam, M. 2024. "AI Will Be a Job Killer, and We Are Not Ready for It." *The Digital Speaker*, March 14. https://www.thedigitalspeaker.com/ai-will-be-job-killer-not-ready/.

24   Ortiz, S. 2025. "AI could erase half of entry-level white collar jobs in 5 years, CEO warns." *ZDNet*, May 29. https://www.zdnet.com/article/ai-could-erase-half-of-entry-level-white-collar-jobs-in-5-years-ceo-warns/.

25   Webster, M. (2024, November 15). 149 AI Statistics: The Present & Future of AI at Your Fingertips. Authority Hacker. https://www.authorityhacker.com/ai-statistics/, visited January 21, 2025.

26   Mezhrahid, J. (2023, April 24). Dark Factories, Bright Future? Capgemini. https://www.capgemini.com/insights/expert-perspectives/dark-factories-bright-future/, visited January 21, 2025.

27   Quinlivan, J. (2023, June 27). How Amazon Deploys Robots in Its Operations Facilities. About Amazon. https://www.aboutamazon.com/news/operations/how-amazon-deploys-robots-in-its-operations-facilities, visited January 21, 2025.

28   Canales, K. (2025, January 19). Mark Zuckerberg Says Meta's AI Could Eventually Replace Engineers and Coders. Business Insider. https://www.businessinsider.com/mark-zuckerberg-meta-ai-replace-engineers-coders-joe-rogan-podcast-2025-1, visited January 21, 2025.

29   TEDx Talks. (2023, October 15). Ensuring a Thriving Digital Future in a Post-Truth World | Dr. Mark van Rijmenam | TEDxAthens. YouTube. https://www.youtube.com/watch?v=9lC-35HoqY4, visited January 21, 2025.

30   Danielle Coleman, Digital Colonialism: The 21st Century Scramble for Africa through the Extraction and Control of User Data and the Limitations of Data Protection Laws, 24 MICH. J. RACE & L. 417 (2019).
      Available at: https://repository.law.umich.edu/mjrl/vol24/iss2/6

31   SkillsFuture Singapore. (2023, May 1). SkillsFuture Level-Up Programme. SkillsFuture Singapore. https://www.skillsfuture.gov.sg/level-up-programme, visited January 21, 2025.

32   OpenResearch. (2024). Unconditional Cash Study. OpenResearch. https://www.openresearchlab.org/studies/unconditional-cash-study/, visited January 21, 2025.

33   van Rijmenam, M. (2024, July 26). Universal Basic Income: The Real Impact of Unconditional Cash. The Digital Speaker. https://www.thedigitalspeaker.com/universal-basic-income-real-impact-unconditional-cash/, visited January 21, 2025.

34   van Rijmenam, M. (2024, January 2). How to Trust Each Other in a Post-Truth World.

The Digital Speaker. https://www.thedigitalspeaker.com/how-to-trust-each-other-in-a-post-truth-world/, visited January 21, 2025.

35 Körömi, C., Haeck, P., & Cheslow, D. (2025, January 7). Zuck Goes Full Musk, Dumps Facebook Fact-Checking Program. Politico. https://www.politico.eu/article/mark-zuckerberg-full-elon-musk-dump-facebook-fact-checker/, visited January 21, 2025.

36 Collins, S. (2025, March 24). AI to fuel rise in cyberattacks on SMEs, warns CyberCube. Commercial Risk. Retrieved March 31, 2025, from https://www.commercialriskonline.com/ai-to-fuel-rise-in-cyberattacks-on-smes-warns-cybercube/

37 Check Point Research. 2025. "AI Security Report 2025: Understanding threats and building smarter defenses." *Check Point Software Technologies*, April 30. https://engage.check-point.com/dg-ai-security-report.

38 Fitzgerald, M. (2023, November 28). AI like ChatGPT is creating a huge increase in malicious phishing email. CNBC. https://www.cnbc.com/2023/11/28/ai-like-chatgpt-is-creating-huge-increase-in-malicious-phishing-email.html, visited March 25, 2025.

39 Cohen, R. (2025, January 4). I'm Gonna Say This Because No One Else Will. LinkedIn. https://www.linkedin.com/posts/reuvencohen_im-gonna-say-this-because-no-one-else-activity-7280365184135700480-IkBU/, visited January 21, 2025.

40 Magramo, K. (2024, May 17). British Engineering Giant Arup Revealed as $25 Million Deepfake Scam Victim. CNN. https://edition.cnn.com/2024/05/16/tech/arup-deepfake-scam-loss-hong-kong-intl-hnk/index.html, visited January 21, 2025.

41 Chen, H., & Magramo, K. (2024, February 4). Finance Worker Pays Out $25 Million After Video Call with Deepfake 'Chief Financial Officer'. CNN. https://edition.cnn.com/2024/02/04/asia/deepfake-cfo-scam-hong-kong-intl-hnk/index.html, visited January 21, 2025.

42 Lin, L. S. F., Aslett, D., Mekonnen, G. T., & Zecevic, M. (2024, October 10). The dangers of voice cloning and how to combat it. The Conversation. https://theconversation.com/the-dangers-of-voice-cloning-and-how-to-combat-it-239926, visited March 26, 2025.

43 Salam, E. (2023, June 14). US Mother Gets Call from 'Kidnapped Daughter' – but It's Really an AI Scam. The Guardian. https://www.theguardian.com/us-news/2023/jun/14/ai-kidnapping-scam-senate-hearing-jennifer-destefano, visited January 21, 2025.

44 Bunn, A. (2023, May 15). Artificial Imposters—Cybercriminals Turn to AI Voice Cloning for a New Breed of Scam. McAfee. https://www.mcafee.com/blogs/privacy-identity-protection/artificial-imposters-cybercriminals-turn-to-ai-voice-cloning-for-a-new-breed-of-scam/, visited January 21, 2025.

45 Confirmed by calling the ATO on 2 January 2025, and again on 29 May 2025 – recordings available upon request.

46 Cox, J. (2023, February 23). How I Broke Into a Bank Account With an AI-Generated Voice. VICE. https://www.vice.com/en/article/how-i-broke-into-a-bank-account-with-an-ai-generated-voice, visited January 21, 2025.

47 Channel 1. (2024). Project Exo. Channel 1. https://www.channel1.ai/exo, visited January 21, 2025.

48 Lepido, D., & Bloomberg. (2024, July 28). Ferrari Exec Foils Deepfake Attempt by Asking the Scammer a Question Only CEO Benedetto Vigna Could Answer. Fortune. https://fortune.com/2024/07/27/ferrari-deepfake-attempt-scammer-security-question-ceo-benedetto-vigna-cybersecurity-ai/, visited January 21, 2025.

49 Robins-Early, N. (2024, May 10). CEO of World's Biggest Ad Firm Targeted by Deepfake

Scam. The Guardian. https://www.theguardian.com/technology/article/2024/may/10/ceo-wpp-deepfake-scam, visited January 21, 2025.

50   van Rijmenam, M. (2024, November 13). The AI Survival Guide: Embrace Resilience in a World of Change. The Digital Speaker. https://www.thedigitalspeaker.com/ai-survival-guide-embrace-resilience-world-change/, visited January 21, 2025.

51   Booth, R. (2024, November 5). Is Your Air Fryer Spying on You? Concerns Over 'Excessive' Surveillance in Smart Devices. The Guardian. https://www.theguardian.com/technology/2024/nov/05/air-fryer-excessive-surveillance-smart-devices-which-watches-speakers-trackers, visited January 21, 2025.

52   Persistence Market Research. (2024, January 22). CCTV Cameras Market Set to Exceed US$ 51.06 Billion by 2033, Sustaining a Strong 12.1% CAGR. GlobeNewswire. https://www.globenewswire.com/news-release/2024/01/22/2813239/0/en/CCTV-Cameras-Market-Set-to-Exceed-US-51-06-Billion-by-2033-Sustaining-a-Strong-12-1-CAGR-Persistence-Market-Research.html, visited January 21, 2025.

53   Lin, L., & Purnell, N. (2019, December 6). A World With a Billion Cameras Watching You Is Just Around the Corner. The Wall Street Journal. https://www.wsj.com/articles/a-billion-surveillance-cameras-forecast-to-be-watching-within-two-years-11575565402, visited January 21, 2025.

54   Burgess, M. (2024, February 8). London Underground Is Testing Real-Time AI Surveillance Tools to Spot Crime. ArsTechnica. https://arstechnica.com/information-technology/2024/02/london-underground-is-testing-real-time-ai-surveillance-tools-to-spot-crime/, visited January 21, 2025.

55   Burgess, M. (2024, June 17). Amazon-Powered AI Cameras Used to Detect Emotions of Unwitting UK Train Passengers. Wired. https://www.wired.com/story/amazon-ai-cameras-emotions-uk-train-passengers/, visited January 21, 2025.

56   Durden, T. (2024, January 7). Artificial Intelligence Is Allowing Them to Construct a Global Surveillance Prison from Which No Escape Is Possible. ZeroHedge. https://www.zerohedge.com/technology/artificial-intelligence-allowing-them-construct-global-surveillance-prison-which-no, visited January 21, 2025.

57   Broad, W. J. (2024, February 20). When Eyes in the Sky Start Looking Right at You. The New York Times. https://www.nytimes.com/2024/02/20/science/satellites-albedo-privacy.html, visited January 21, 2025.

58   Zuboff, S. (2019). The Age of Surveillance Capitalism: The Fight for a Human Future at the New Frontier of Power. PublicAffairs.

59   Clauser, G. (2019, August 8). Amazon's Alexa Never Stops Listening to You. Should You Worry? The New York Times - Wirecutter. https://www.nytimes.com/wirecutter/blog/amazons-alexa-never-stops-listening-to-you/, visited January 21, 2025.

60   Gibbs, S. (2015, March 13). Privacy Fears Over 'Smart' Barbie That Can Listen to Your Kids. The Guardian. https://www.theguardian.com/technology/2015/mar/13/smart-barbie-that-can-listen-to-your-kids-privacy-fears-mattel, visited January 21, 2025.

61   Booth, R. (2024, November 5). Is Your Air Fryer Spying on You? Concerns Over 'Excessive' Surveillance in Smart Devices. The Guardian. https://www.theguardian.com/technology/2024/nov/05/air-fryer-excessive-surveillance-smart-devices-which-watches-speakers-trackers, visited January 21, 2025.

62   Jerome, J. (2023, October 3). Pretty Soon, Your VR Headset Will Know Exactly What Your Bedroom Looks Like. WIRED. https://www.wired.com/story/virtual-realit

y-meta-wearables-privacy/, visited January 21, 2025.

63   Guo, E. (2022, December 19). A Roomba Recorded a Woman on the Toilet. How Did Screenshots End Up on Facebook? MIT Technology Review. https://www.technologyreview.com/2022/12/19/1065306/roomba-irobot-robot-vacuums-artificial-intelligence-training-data-privacy/, visited January 21, 2025.

64   Sorrel, C. (2024, January 15). This Always-Recording AI Microphone Will Make Your Coworkers Hate You. Lifewire. https://www.lifewire.com/limitless-ai-microphone-8634683, visited January 21, 2025.

65   Ashworth, B. (2024, July 30). Wear This AI Friend Around Your Neck. WIRED. https://www.wired.com/story/friend-ai-pendant/, visited January 21, 2025.

66   Chayka, K. 2025. "Sam Altman and Jony Ive Will Force A.I. Into Your Life." *The New Yorker*, May 28. https://www.newyorker.com/culture/infinite-scroll/sam-altman-and-jony-ive-will-force-ai-into-your-life.

67   van Rijmenam, M. (2021, October 20). The Future of Computing: How Brain-Computer Interfaces Will Change Our Relationship with Computers. The Digital Speaker. https://www.thedigitalspeaker.com/brain-computer-interfaces-change-relationship-computers/, visited January 21, 2025.

68   van Rijmenam, M. (2023, September 20). The Mind-Bending World of Brain-Computer Interfaces: How the Technology Will Change Humanity. The Digital Speaker. https://www.thedigitalspeaker.com/mind-bending-world-brain-computer-interfaces-humanity/, visited January 21, 2025.

69   Chow, K.-H., Hu, S., Huang, T., & Liu, L. (2024, July 19). Personalized Privacy Protection Mask Against Unauthorized Facial Recognition. arXiv. https://arxiv.org/abs/2407.13975, visited January 21, 2025.

70   van Rijmenam, M. (2023, August 15). Navigating the Uncharted Future: Ten Predictions for 2030. The Digital Speaker. https://www.thedigitalspeaker.com/navigating-uncharted-future-ten-predictions-2030/, visited January 21, 2025.

71   O'Donnell, J., & Crownhart, C. 2025. "We did the math on AI's energy footprint. Here's the story you haven't heard." *MIT Technology Review*, May 20. https://www.technologyreview.com/2025/05/20/1116327/ai-energy-usage-climate-footprint-big-tech/.

72   Heikkilä, M. (2023, December 1). Making an Image with Generative AI Uses as Much Energy as Charging Your Phone. MIT Technology Review. https://www.technologyreview.com/2023/12/01/1084189/making-an-image-with-generative-ai-uses-as-much-energy-as-charging-your-phone/, visited January 21, 2025.

73   Wilkins, J. 2025. "Former Google CEO Tells Congress That 99 Percent of All Electricity Will Be Used to Power Superintelligent AI." *Futurism*, April 12. https://futurism.com/google-ceo-congress-electricity-ai-superintelligence.

74   Gamazay, B. (2024, December 23). OpenAI Has Announced O3, Which Appears to Be a Game-Changer for AI Models. LinkedIn. https://www.linkedin.com/posts/bgamazay_openai-has-announced-o3-which-appears-to-activity-7276250095019335680-sVbW/, visited January 21, 2025.

75   Delahaye, J.-P. (2024, October 30). Bitcoin: Electricity Consumption Comparable to That of Poland. Polytechnique Insights. https://www.polytechnique-insights.com/en/columns/energy/bitcoin-electricity-consumption-comparable-to-that-of-poland/, visited January 21, 2025.

76   Crypto.com. (n.d.). How Much Energy Does Bitcoin Consume? Crypto.com. https://

crypto.com/bitcoin/bitcoin-energy-consumption, visited January 21, 2025.

77   Tuwiner, J. (2023, September 10). 61 Bitcoin Energy Consumption Statistics (2024). Buy Bitcoin Worldwide. https://buybitcoinworldwide.com/bitcoin-mining-statistics/, visited January 21, 2025.

78   Sparkes, M. (2023, April 26). Cryptocurrency Ethereum Has Slashed Its Energy Use by 99.99 Per Cent. New Scientist. https://www.newscientist.com/article/23 69304-cryptocurrency-ethereum-has-slashed-its-energy-use-by-99-99-per-cent/, visited January 21, 2025.

79   Yammiyavar, P. G., & Kumar, V. (2011). E-Waste Generation from Mobile Phones and Sustainability Issues for Designers. The Design Society. https://www.designsociety.org/ download-publication/32393/, visited January 21, 2025.

80   Eurostat. (2024, November). End-of-life vehicle statistics. Statistics Explained. https:// ec.europa.eu/eurostat/statistics-explained/index.php?title=End-of-life_vehicle_statistics, visited March 26, 2025.

81   Geneva Environment Network. (2024, October 9). The Growing Environmental Risks of E-Waste. Geneva Environment Network. https://www.genevaenvironmentnetwork.org/ resources/updates/the-growing-environmental-risks-of-e-waste/, visited January 21, 2025.

82   Waste Management World. (2021, July 12). Global Players Waking to $57 Billion E-Waste Opportunity. Waste Management World. https://waste-management-world.com/artikel/ global-players-waking-to-57-billion-e-waste-opportunity/, visited January 21, 2025.

83   Shyft Global Services. (n.d.). The Dark Side of Electronic Devices: What You Need to Know About the E-Waste Crisis. Shyft Global Services. https://www.shyftservices. com/e-waste-crisis-challenges-solutions-for-tech-companies, visited January 21, 2025.

84   Apple Inc. (2018, April 20). Apple Adds Earth Day Donations to Trade-In and Recycling Program. Apple Newsroom. https://www.apple.com/au/newsroom/2018/04/apple-add s-earth-day-donations-to-trade-in-and-recycling-program/, visited January 21, 2025.

85   Jones, L. (2021, March 10). The Queensland Social Enterprise Repurposing E-Waste to Address Energy Poverty. Australian Circular Economy Hub. https://acehub.org.au/ news/the-queensland-social-enterprise-repurposing-e-waste-to-address-energy, visited January 21, 2025.

86   Paddison, L. (2024, November 29). A Nuclear Fusion Startup Just Reached a Milestone in Its Bid to Commercialize Unlimited Clean Energy. CNN. https://edition.cnn. com/2024/11/29/climate/nuclear-fusion-openstar/index.html, visited January 21, 2025.

87   Swisher, K. (2025, March 9). The Elon Musk Way: Move Fast and Destroy Democracy. The Atlantic. https://www.theatlantic.com/technology/archive/2025/03/the-elo n-musk-way-move-fast-and-destroy-democracy/681937/, visited March 26, 2025.

88   Gerlich, Michael, AI Tools in Society: Impacts on Cognitive Offloading and the Future of Critical Thinking (January 03, 2025). Available at SSRN: https://ssrn.com/ abstract=5082524 or http://dx.doi.org/10.2139/ssrn.5082524

Chapter 6

1   The Peak Performance Center. (n.d.). The Learning Pyramid. The Peak Performance Center. https://thepeakperformancecenter.com/educational-learning/learning/ principles-of-learning/learning-pyramid/, visited January 21, 2025.

2   Gruber, M. J., Gelman, B. D., & Ranganath, C. (2014). States of Curiosity Modulate Hippocampus-Dependent Learning via the Dopaminergic Circuit. Neuron, 84(2), 486–496.

https://pmc.ncbi.nlm.nih.gov/articles/PMC4252494/, visited January 21, 2025.

3   Breisacher, J. (2024, February 22). Intrinsic Motivation and Student Learning. Student-Centered World. https://www.studentcenteredworld.com/intrinsic-motivation/, visited January 21, 2025.

4   Nash, P. (2024, December 13). "Major Concerns" for Dutch Higher Ed Despite Reduced Budget Cuts. The PIE News. https://thepienews.com/dutch-higher-education-reduced-budget-cuts/, visited January 21, 2025.

5   Assembly of First Nations. (n.d.). First Nations Holistic Lifelong Learning Model. AFN It's Our Time Toolkit. https://education.afn.ca/afntoolkit/learning-module/first-nations-holistic-lifelong-learning-model/, visited January 21, 2025.

6   Canadian Council on Learning. (2007, June 6). First Nations Holistic Lifelong Learning Model: Living. https://firstnationspedagogy.com/CCL_Learning_Model_FN.pdf, visited January 21, 2025.

7   Canadian Council on Learning. (2007, June 6). First Nations Holistic Lifelong Learning Model: Living. https://firstnationspedagogy.com/CCL_Learning_Model_FN.pdf, visited January 21, 2025.

8   Elliott, D. (2024, July 29). This AI Tutor Could Make Humans 10 Times Smarter, Its Creator Says. World Economic Forum. https://www.weforum.org/stories/2024/07/ai-tutor-china-teaching-gaps/, visited January 21, 2025.

9   Hao, K. (2019, August 2). China Has Started a Grand Experiment in AI Education. It Could Reshape How the World Learns. MIT Technology Review. https://www.technologyreview.com/2019/08/02/131198/china-squirrel-has-started-a-grand-experiment-in-ai-education-it-could-reshape-how-the/, visited January 21, 2025.

10 Cheng, Y. (2024, January 10). First Adaptive Learning AI to Be Launched Internationally. China Daily. https://www.chinadaily.com.cn/a/202401/10/WS659e8a29a3105f21a507ba1b.html, visited January 21, 2025.

11 UNESCO. (2024, October 5). Global Report on Teachers: What You Need to Know. UNESCO. https://www.unesco.org/en/articles/global-report-teachers-what-you-need-know, visited January 21, 2025.

12 Squirrel Ai Learning. (2024, June 30). Squirrel Ai Debuts Enhanced Large Multimodal Adaptive Model, Revolutionizing Its Educational Software and Hardware Systems. PR Newswire. https://www.prnewswire.com/news-releases/squirrel-ai-debuts-enhanced-large-multimodal-adaptive-model-revolutionizing-its-educational-software-and-hardware-systems-302186596.html, visited January 21, 2025.

13 Lanum, N. (2025, March 22). Texas private school's use of new 'AI tutor' rockets student test scores to top 2% in the country. Fox News. https://www.foxnews.com/media/texas-private-schools-use-ai-tutor-rockets-student-test-scores-top-2-country, visited March 26, 2025.

14 Barnum, M. (2024, March 10). This Tech Evangelist Has Big Dreams for AI Tutors. Are They Too Big? The Wall Street Journal. https://www.wsj.com/us-news/education/sal-khan-has-big-dreams-for-ai-in-education-are-they-too-big-41f01fb9, visited January 21, 2025.

15 van Rijmenam, M. (2024, April 25). Learning 2.0: The Rise of AI Tutors. The Digital Speaker. https://www.thedigitalspeaker.com/learning-20-rise-ai-tutors/, visited January 21, 2025.

16 Sultana. (2021, December 29). A Young Afghan Woman on Breaking Free of the Burqa. The Economist. https://www.economist.com/by-invitation/2021/12/29/a-youn

g-afghan-woman-on-breaking-free-of-the-burqa, visited January 21, 2025.

17   Kristof, N. D. (2016, June 5). Meet Sultana, the Taliban's Worst Fear. The New York Times. https://www.nytimes.com/2016/06/05/opinion/sunday/meet-sultana-the-taliban s-worst-fear.html, visited January 21, 2025.

18   Baillifard, A., Gabella, M., Banta Lavenex, P., & Martarelli, C. S. (2023, September 10). Implementing Learning Principles with a Personal AI Tutor: A Case Study. arXiv. https:// arxiv.org/abs/2309.13060, visited January 21, 2025.

19   Raeburn, A. (2024, November 4). The Future of Education: How AI Tutors Are Shaping Tomorrow's Classrooms. StudyMonkey. https://studymonkey.ai/blog/the-futur e-of-education-how-ai-tutors-are-shaping-tomorrow-s-classrooms, visited January 21, 2025.

20   Buljan, M. (2022, January 31). Transforming Education With Immersive Learning Techniques. eLearning Industry. https://elearningindustry.com/transforming-educatio n-with-immersive-learning-techniques, visited January 21, 2025.

21   Bassner, P., Frankford, E., & Krusche, S. (2024, July 10). Iris: An AI-Driven Virtual Tutor For Computer Science Education. arXiv. https://arxiv.org/abs/2405.08008, visited January 21, 2025.

22   Morgan, J., & La Placa, V. (2023, December 18). Loneliness is a Major Public Health Problem – and Young People are Bearing the Brunt of It. The Conversation. https:// theconversation.com/loneliness-is-a-major-public-health-problem-and-young-people -are-bearing-the-brunt-of-it-218391, visited January 21, 2025.

23   Marcus, J. 2025. "Mark Zuckerberg says don't worry about loneliness epidemic because he can just recreate all your friends in AI." The Independent, May 2. https://www.independent. co.uk/news/world/americas/zuckerberg-ai-loneliness-chatbot-llama-b2743409.html.

24   van Rijmenam, M. (2024, October 24). Unloved Online: Can Big Tech Be Held Accountable for Teen Suicides? The Digital Speaker. https://www.thedigitalspeaker.com/ unloved-online-big-tech-held-accountable-teen-suicides/, visited January 21, 2025.

25   Winters KC, Arria A. Adolescent Brain Development and Drugs. Prev Res. 2011;18(2):21-24. PMID: 22822298; PMCID: PMC3399589.

26   van Rijmenam, M. (2024, November 6). Why We Should Ban Teens from Social Media. The Digital Speaker. https://www.thedigitalspeaker.com/why-we-should-ban-teens-fro m-social-media/, visited January 21, 2025.

27   Jose, R. (2024, November 28). Australia Passes Social Media Ban for Children Under 16. Reuters. https://www.reuters.com/technology/australia-passes-social-media-ban-children- under-16-2024-11-28/, visited January 21, 2025.

28   McGregor, G. (2021, September 3). China's Gaming Market Was Built on Free and Addictive Games. Can Beijing Stop Kids from Playing Them? Fortune. https://fortune. com/2021/09/03/china-video-gaming-mobile-smartphone-addiction-free-to-play/, visited January 21, 2025.

29   Grace, A. (2022, December 2). High School Bans Smartphones — and Kids Are Happier Than Ever. New York Post. https://nypost.com/2022/12/02/high-schoo l-bans-smartphones-students-happier-without-them/, visited January 21, 2025.

30   McCrindle Research. (2024, December 19). Welcome Gen Beta. McCrindle. https:// mccrindle.com.au/article/generation-beta-defined/, visited January 21, 2025.

31   van Rijmenam, M. (2025, January 2). How Generation Beta Will Define the Future. The Digital Speaker. https://www.thedigitalspeaker.com/how-generation-beta-will-define-th e-future/, visited January 21, 2025.

32   Krause, C. (2024). Digital Wellbeing: Empowering Connection with Wonder and Imagination in the Age of AI. Wiley.

Chapter 7

1   Mises, L. von. (1949). Human Action: A Treatise on Economics. Yale University Press.

2   van Rijmenam, M. (2018). The Organization of Tomorrow: How AI, Blockchain and Analytics Turn Your Business into a Data-Driven Organization. Routledge.

3   Hassabis, D. (2016, March 8). AlphaGo's Ultimate Challenge. Google Blog. https://blog. google/technology/ai/alphagos-ultimate-challenge/, visited January 21, 2025.

4   Vincent, J. (2019, November 7). OpenAI Has Published the Text-Generating AI It Said Was Too Dangerous to Share. The Verge. https://www.theverge. com/2019/11/7/20953040/openai-text-generation-ai-gpt-2-full-model-release-1-5b-parameters, visited January 21, 2025.

5   DeepMind. 2025. "AlphaEvolve: A Gemini-powered coding agent for designing advanced algorithms." *Google DeepMind Blog*, May 14. https://deepmind.google/discover/blog/ alphaevolve-a-gemini-powered-coding-agent-for-designing-advanced-algorithms/.

6   Alexander, S., & Kokotajlo, D. (2025, April 3). Introducing AI 2027. Astral Codex Ten. https://www.astralcodexten.com/p/introducing-ai-2027, visited April 7, 2025.

7   Fore, P. (2025, March 13). Tech leaders at Anthropic, IBM, and Meta warn that AI is coming for software developer jobs. Fortune. https://fortune.com/2025/03/13/ ai-transforming-software-development-jobs-meta-ibm-anthropic/, visited March 26, 2025.

8   Fore, P. (2025, March 21). OpenAI CEO Sam Altman reveals his 'obvious tactical' career advice for Gen Z grads—as companies dish out seven-figure salaries for students with these skills. Fortune. https://fortune.com/2025/03/21/open-ai-ceo-sam-altman-ge n-z-grads-advice-ai-seven-figure-salary/, visited March 26, 2025.

9   Klein, E. (Host). (2025, March 5). The Government Knows AGI is Coming | The Ezra Klein Show. The New York Times. https://www.youtube.com/watch?v=Btos-LEYQ30, visited March 26, 2025.

10   Trainor, T. (2019, January 3). How Ford's Willow Run Assembly Plant Helped Win World War II. Assembly Magazine. https://www.assemblymag.com/articles/94614-how-fo rds-willow-run-assembly-plant-helped-win-world-war-ii, visited January 21, 2025.

11   van Rijmenam, M. (2022, November 24). The Need for Longtermism: Why We Need a Long-Term Approach to Ensure a Thriving Digital Future. The Digital Speaker. https://www.thedigitalspeaker.com/need-longtermism-long-term-approach-thriving-digit al-future/, visited January 21, 2025.

12   TEDx Talks. (2023, December 14). Ensuring a Thriving Digital Future in a Post-Truth World | Dr. Mark van Rijmenam | TEDxAthens. YouTube. https://www.youtube.com/ watch?v=9lC-35HoqY4, visited January 21, 2025.

13   Dawson, R. (2025, January 7). Rather Than Think Human-in-the-Loop, Which Keeps AI Under Control, Think Reciprocal Human-Machine Learning. LinkedIn. https://www. linkedin.com/posts/futuristkeynotespeaker_rather-than-think-human-in-the-loop-whi ch-activity-7280688232730652673-JOUE/, visited January 21, 2025.

14   Natarajan, S., Mathur, S., Sidheekh, S., Stammer, W., & Kersting, K. (2024, December 18). Human-in-the-loop or AI-in-the-loop? Automate or Collaborate? arXiv. https://arxiv.org/ abs/2412.14232v1, visited January 21, 2025.

15   Accuray. (n.d.). Overcoming AI Bias: Understanding, Identifying and Mitigating Algorithmic Bias in Healthcare. Accuray. https://www.accuray.com/blog/overcoming-ai-bias-understanding-identifying-and-mitigating-algorithmic-bias-in-healthcare/, visited January 21, 2025.

16   Association of Accredited Public Policy Advocates to the European Union. (2023, August 6). Media Literacy Across Europe. AALEP. https://www.aalep.eu/media-literacy-across-europe, visited January 21, 2025.

17   Quicke, A. (2020, November 12). Media Literacy Education in Finland. The Nordic Policy Centre. https://www.nordicpolicycentre.org.au/media_literacy_education_in_finland, visited January 21, 2025.

18   EAVI. (n.d.). Finnish National Curriculum on Media Literacy: A Global Model for Education. EAVI. https://eavi.eu/ml-in-finland/, visited January 21, 2025.

19   Reuel, A., & Undheim, T. A. (2024, June 6). Generative AI Needs Adaptive Governance. arXiv. https://arxiv.org/abs/2406.04554v1, visited January 21, 2025.

20   Thatai, P. (2016, November 4). TESLA: Accelerating the Transition to Sustainable Transportation for the Masses. Harvard Business School Digital Initiative. https://d3.harvard.edu/platform-rctom/submission/tesla-accelerating-the-transition-to-sustainable-transportation-for-the-masses/, visited January 21, 2025.

21   Joseph, B. (2020, May 30). What is the Seventh Generation Principle? Indigenous Corporate Training Inc. https://www.ictinc.ca/blog/seventh-generation-principle, visited January 21, 2025.

22   O'Donnell, E. L., & Talbot-Jones, J. (2018). Creating legal rights for rivers: lessons from Australia, New Zealand, and India. Ecology and Society, 23(1). https://www.jstor.org/stable/26799037, visited January 21, 2025.

23   Gomes, G. (2024, August 26). The Leadership Style of Microsoft CEO, Satya Nadella. CTO Magazine. https://ctomagazine.com/ceo-satya-nadella-leadership-style/, visited March 26, 2025.

Chapter 8

1   Li, M., & Mann, T. (2024, April 12). China Successfully Tests Maglev Trains in Vacuum Tube, Eyeing Future Speeds of 4,000 KPH. ABC News. https://www.abc.net.au/news/2024-04-12/china-ultra-high-speed-trains-maglev-how-fast/103644930, visited January 21, 2025.

2   Self-Assembly Lab. (n.d.). 4D Printing. Self-Assembly Lab. https://selfassemblylab.mit.edu/4d-printing, visited January 21, 2025.

3   Souza, E. (2024, May 7). 4D Printing? Bridging Additive Manufacturing with Smart Materials. ArchDaily. https://www.archdaily.com/966556/have-you-heard-of-4d-printing-bridging-additive-manufacturing-with-smart-materials, visited January 21, 2025.

4   Bossa MN, Nakshathri AG, Berenguer AD, Sahli H. Generative AI unlocks PET insights: brain amyloid dynamics and quantification. Front Aging Neurosci. 2024 Jun 17;16:1410844. doi: 10.3389/fnagi.2024.1410844. PMID: 38952479; PMCID: PMC11215072.

5   Hall, P. (2025, January 7). Scientists at the Center on the Biology of Aging are Rapidly Advancing Research on Aging. Brown University News. https://www.brown.edu/news/2025-01-07/aging-research, visited January 21, 2025.

6   Emotiv. (2025, January 6). Emotiv Launches MW20 EEG Active Noise-Cancelling

Earphones at CES. Emotiv. https://www.emotiv.com/blogs/news/emotiv-mw20-eeg-activ e-noise-cancelling-earphones-ces, visited January 21, 2025.

7   van Rijmenam, M. (2024, December 20). Genesis: A Breakthrough in Digital Physics. The Digital Speaker. https://www.thedigitalspeaker.com/genesis-breakthrough-digital-physics/, visited January 21, 2025.

8   Weatherbed, J. (2024, November 28). Starlink's Direct-to-Cell Satellite Service Is the First to Receive FCC Approval. The Verge. https://www.theverge.com/2024/11/27/24307394/ starlink-spacex-tmobile-direct-to-cell-satellite-fcc-approval, visited January 21, 2025.

9   Statista. (2024, November 5). Internet and Social Media Users in the World 2024. Statista. https://www.statista.com/statistics/617136/digital-population-worldwide/, visited January 21, 2025.

10 Li, M., & Mann, T. (2024, April 12). China Successfully Tests Maglev Trains in Vacuum Tube, Eyeing Future Speeds of 4,000 KPH. ABC News. https://www.abc.net.au/ news/2024-04-12/china-ultra-high-speed-trains-maglev-how-fast/103644930, visited January 21, 2025.

11 eSelf AI. (2025, January 6). AI Trends in Education: Transforming Learning Experiences in 2025. eSelf AI. https://www.eself.ai/blog/ai-trends-in-education-transforming-learni ng-experiences-in-2025/, visited January 21, 2025.

12 IBM Newsroom. (2024, August 13). IBM-Developed Algorithms Announced as NIST's First Published Post-Quantum Cryptography Standards. IBM Newsroom. https:// newsroom.ibm.com/2024-08-13-ibm-developed-algorithms-announced-as-worlds-first-po st-quantum-cryptography-standards, visited January 21, 2025.

13 Banon, J. (2025, January 3). The Computable Economy Will Unlock a New Economic Order. Cointelegraph. https://cointelegraph.com/news/the-computable-economy-wil l-unlock-a-new-economic-order, visited January 21, 2025.

14 Khanna, P., & Wan, K. (2025, January 10). CES 2025: The 8 Most Advanced Smart Glasses We Tried and Were Impressed By. ZDNet. https://www.zdnet.com/article/ ces-2025-the-8-most-advanced-smart-glasses-we-tried-and-were-impressed-by/, visited January 21, 2025.

15 Amino Labs. (n.d.). Beginner Biotechnology Kits, Lessons, Guides & More. Amino Labs. https://amino.bio/, visited January 21, 2025.

16 Government of Telangana. (n.d.). Blockchain Framework. Department of Information Technology, Electronics & Communications. https://it.telangana.gov.in/initiatives/block-chain/, visited January 21, 2025.

17 Malik S, Muhammad K, Waheed Y. Emerging Applications of Nanotechnology in Healthcare and Medicine. Molecules. 2023 Sep 14;28(18):6624. doi: 10.3390/mole-cules28186624. PMID: 37764400; PMCID: PMC10536529, visited January 21, 2025.

AUDIOBOOK

Great news! *Now What?* is also
available in audio format.
Jump onto your favourite audiobook
platform now and check it out.